ECONOMICS
BLUE BOOK
OF THE
PEOPLE'S REPUBLIC
OF CHINA, 1999

ECONOMICS

BLUE BOOK

OF THE

PEOPLE'S REPUBLIC

OF CHINA, 1999

ANALYSIS AND FORECAST

AN AUTHORIZED TRANSLATION OF THE CHINESE ACADEMY
OF SOCIAL SCIENCES' ANNUAL ECONOMIC REPORT

EDITED BY
LIU GUOGUANG, WANG LUOLIN,
LI JINGWEN, LIU SHUCHENG,
AND WANG TONGSAN

 AN EAST GATE BOOK

Routledge
Taylor & Francis Group

LONDON AND NEW YORK

First published 1999 by M.E. Sharpe

Published 2015 by Routledge
2 Park Square, Milton Park, Abingdon, Oxon OX14 4RN
711 Third Avenue, New York, NY 10017, USA

Routledge is an imprint of the Taylor & Francis Group, an informa business

Copyright © by The University of Hong Kong, 1999
First published in Hong Kong by The University of Hong Kong
ISBN 962-8269-25-9   HK$280 (paperback)
ISBN 962-8269-26-7   HK$380 (hardback)

First published in North America by Taylor & Francis.

ISSN 1527-1595
ISBN 0-7656-0562-7

The publication of this work was made possible by a generous grant from The University of Hong Kong Foundation for Educational Development and Research

The Centre of Asian Studies is established to provide a focal point for the activities of The University of Hong Kong in the areas of East, South and Southeast Asia; research assistance to scholars in these fields and special reference to Hong Kong; and physical and administrative facilities for research, seminars and conferences dealing with both traditional and modern aspects of Asian Studies.

Economics Blue Book of the People's Republic of China, 1999

An authorised translation of the *Economics Blue Book of the People's Republic of China, 1999* edited by Liu Guoguang, Wang Luolin, Li Jingwen, Liu Shucheng and Wang Tongsan of the Chinese Academy of Social Sciences.

Translation Team: LangComp Company Ltd. (Caesar Lun, Francis Lun, et al.)
CAS Editing Team: Sun Wenbin, Michelle H.W. Fong and Geoff P. Wade
Designer of cover: Michael Lau

Caveat:

While every precaution has been taken to ensure the quality of these translations, if there is any discrepancy between the Chinese text and the translated version, the original Chinese Academy of Social Sciences publication shall be considered authoritative.

Centre of Asian Studies Occasional Papers and Monographs, No. 129.

ISBN 13: 9780765605627 (hbk)

CONTENTS

POLICY ANALYSIS

FINANCE AND FISCAL POLICIES

INDUSTRIAL SECTORS

REGIONAL DEVELOPMENT

HONG KONG ECONOMY

INTERNATIONAL BACKGROUND

Excerpts and Data

PREFACE

The encouraging response to our publication of the first English-language edition of the *PRC Economics Blue Book* in 1998 has led to a second year of cooperation between the Chinese Academy of Social Sciences and the Centre of Asian Studies of the University of Hong Kong. Further, in order to bring this work to an even broader audience, this year we will be jointly publishing the English-language Blue Book with M.E. Sharpe Inc. of the United States. It is a great pleasure to be undertaking this task with such a prominent publisher.

The economic situation in China over the last year has made it even more important that the most authoritative annual analysis and forecast of the Chinese economic situation be made available again in English. After two decades of rapid economic growth, the Chinese economy has slowed somewhat. While the Asian economic crisis has certainly had its effects on the Chinese economy, it is the domestic factors which have been attracting the attention of China's economists. Specifically, they have been looking at weak aggregate demand, the decline of personal income and the increase in unemployment as major elements in this slowdown. Diverse views on these issues from the most prominent Chinese economists are brought together within this volume. It is hoped that they will provide readers with deeper insights into the Chinese economic situation and the opinions of the economists guiding China's economic policy-making.

i

As last year, we have been following a tight schedule to ensure that the work reaches readers as quickly as possible. In this respect, we have received great assistance from M.E. Sharpe, for which we are very grateful. Readers will also notice that we have made a slight change in the English-language title of the Blue Book, with it now entitled *Economics Blue Book of the People's Republic of China, 1999: Analysis and Forecast.* Feedback from readers is always welcome and any comments on criticisms can be directed to the Blue Book Project at the Centre of Asian Studies.

Wong Siu-lun
Director and Professor
Centre of Asian Studies
University of Hong Kong

27 September 1999

FOREWORD

WANG LUOLIN

We are pleased to present to readers the 1999 *Economics Blue Book*. Like the previous seven editions of the *Blue Book*, it is based on the proceeedings of the conference "Autumn Forum on Analysis and Forecast of the Economic Situation" hosted by the Chinese Academy of Social Sciences.

The number of experts and scholars participating in this year's Forum was noticeably higher than that of previous years. Experts from the Hong Kong Special Administrative Region also participated in, and greatly enriched, the Forum. In order to present as full a range of the opinions expressed in the Forum as possible within the limited space, our editing principle has been "to allow different opinions and let one hundred flowers bloom." We have also made some changes in our editing style and welcome your opinions on this edition.

I would like to take this opportunity to touch upon some characteristics of the Forum, which I hope will benefit you in understanding this book.

China's economic situation in 1998 was a very complicated one. Domestically, we suffered from catastrophic floods. Externally, we were affected by the Asian financial crisis. From the beginning of the year, the central government implemented a series of measures to expand domestic demand and stimulate economic growth. Beginning from August, we successfully arrested the continuous declining trend in economic growth, and the economy started to recover. However, the rate and extent of the recovery are difficult to assess, as they are conditioned by a wide variety of factors. Against this background, experts presented rather divergent opinions on forecasting the economic growth rate for 1998 and 1999. Even though we were writing in the fourth quarter of 1998, experts still had difficulty in reaching a consensus on the GDP growth rate for this year. This has rarely happened before, and is the first distinctive characteristic of the Forum.

The second defining characteristic of the Forum is that, for the first time, some papers and speeches specifically focus on analysis and forecast of the world economy. This demonstrates that, after 20 years of reform and opening up, we have finally put the closed economy behind us. The extent of opening up has been enlarged substantially. Meanwhile, this factor also indicates that the emphasis of our economic forecasting has shifted from analyzing the supply-side to the demand-side.

The third characteristic is that the participants in the Forum, having observed the occurrence of many problems in the economy, reached a consensus on insufficient demand. They had not reached this consensus during the earlier Spring Forum.

The fourth characteristic is that, based on this consensus, the focus of their research has shifted to new problems. This shift can be seen from the examination at a deeper level of the causes and background of the current insufficient demand. Also, many new opinions on solving this problem were expressed in the Forum, providing an important framework for further research.

Finally, I hope that the economic problems detailed above can be examined in the light of a sober review of China's 20 years of reform and opening up. In this way, we will be able to examine short-term problems from a medium- and long-term perspective. By so doing, it is hoped that we will be able to provide sound research findings for next year's *Blue Book* and also contribute more to China's reform and economic growth for the next century.

ECONOMICS
BLUE BOOK
OF THE
PEOPLE'S REPUBLIC
OF CHINA, 1999

TWO ISSUES ON THE CURRENT MACROECONOMIC ADJUSTMENT PROGRAM

LIU GUOGUANG AND LIU SHUCHENG

Chinese Academy of Social Sciences

On the Selection of Policies and their Implementation in Expanding Domestic Demand

In the process of expanding domestic demand and initiating new economic growth, the important issue for China has been the selection and coordination of appropriate policies and instruments. From 1996, in the late phase of the successful "soft landing," the central government began to relax its policies on financing. As one of the consequences, interest rates were lowered several times. However, these policies have had no evident effect in encouraging investment and initiating new economic growth. This leads to the theoretical generalization that monetary policy has offered no cure for the problem, as many people have pointed out, and that fiscal policy should be adopted instead. In fact, to increase the strength of economic growth initiatives, the central government has implemented, for the past several months, a more aggressive fiscal policy alongside its monetarist approach. Now, a positive effect is beginning to become evident. But two questions need to be clarified. One is, how come monetary policy turned out to be ineffective? The other is, what precautions should be taken in implementing a more aggressive fiscal policy?

In analyzing why monetary policy has become ineffective, most people try to attribute this to the administrative problems brought about by the transformation of the economic institutions. Why do banks "refrain from lending", when the supply of credit is plentiful and deposits exceed loans? The answer is that the deepening financial reforms led banks to become more commercially oriented. They thus now have to consider the quality of their assets and loans. In turn, why do enterprises "refrain from borrowing" when credit supply is eased and interest rates are low? The answer lies again in the deepening of reforms. With these reforms being aimed at separating government administration from enterprise management, it is becoming more evident that enterprises are responsible for their own profits and losses. We can say that this is a sign of progress. However, since the economy is still in the process of transforming its development track, mature market mechanisms are not yet available. The mutual adaptation among different sectors has not been completed, thus they are unprepared to react to the interest rate changes. And it is not only now that we encounter this problem of "ineffectiveness" when we lower interest rates to boost the economy. In the past, when interest rates were raised to cool off the overheated economy, we also witnessed an ineffective and indifferent reaction. On the whole, this problem will be solved gradually as the reform continues to deepen, and when the market, enterprises, banks and other institutions continue to improve.

Another explanation for the ineffectiveness of a monetary policy approach comes mainly from academic circles, and recently newspaper commentaries. These commentators are inclined to think that China has fallen into a "liquidity trap," where monetary policy has become ineffective. This generalization was drawn from the American economist Krugman's analysis of the Japanese economy.

"Liquidity trap" refers to a situation which can be characterized by the following three phenomena. First, the economy is in a state of deep recession, and the nominal interest rate falls to zero or almost zero. When interest rates are that low, people prefer to hold cash rather than invest in bonds or commercial paper. Second, under such circumstances, an expansionary monetary policy has no impact on the nominal interest rates since the nominal interest rate cannot be below zero. Third, the interest rate consequently loses its leverage effect on stimulating investment and consumption. According to the classic Keynesian theory, when an economy is in a liquidity trap, monetary policy will have no effect, but a fiscal policy will be able to boost the economy. Krugman believes that the

Japanese economy has fallen into a liquidity trap, with its nominal interest rate nearly down to zero, as evidenced for example by the overnight money market rate falling to 0.37%. But Krugman disagrees with Keynesian theory. He believes that neither conventional monetary policy (i.e., short-term expansion of money supply), nor conventional fiscal policy (i.e., increasing government spending and cutting taxes), can lift the Japanese economy from its difficulties. He advocates a non-conventional monetary policy, which is to print more money to create an anticipated 4% annual inflation rate for fifteen years. That, he argues, would reduce the actual interest rate to negative in order to stimulate both investment and consumer spending. He considers this is the only way for the Japanese economy to overcome its current recession.

Krugman's article aroused interest in both Japan and in PRC academic circles, as well as in some government departments. In our current economy, "indifference" to falling interest rates is a noted phenomenon. So is our economy in a state of liquidity trap? We do not think that is the case, based on the following reasons:

(1) In a state of liquidity trap, interest rate adjustment loses its leverage effect. But ineffectiveness of interest rate leverage does not necessarily equal a state of liquidity trap. Up to now, our economy has made tremendous progress in its transformation into a market-oriented economy. Interest rate setting by market forces has already started to take shape, and the adjustment effect of interest rates on savings, investment, and consumer spending has begun to yield results. However, so far as the development of the entire financial market, and the determining factors for changes in investment and consumer spending, are concerned, the leverage effect of interest rates is not as sensitive as in a well-developed market economy. Indeed, it is still not as effective as administrative controls are under the planned economy. That is to say, under current conditions, interest rate adjustments cannot fully exercise their leverage effect, because our system has not yet completed its shift to a different economic development track. The market mechanism for interest rates to bring about a change in

investment and consumer spending has not yet taken shape.   It
is therefore groundless to say that our economy has fallen into
a liquidity trap.

(2)   Our economy is not in the same state of deep recession as
       Japan.   Since 1992, Japan has been in a state of almost zero
       economic growth.   Particularly in 1997, its GDP encountered
       the most serious contraction of negative growth (-0.7%) since
       World War II.   Although China's economic growth has
       dropped gradually since the second half of 1993, growth in
       1998 still remained at a higher level than other countries,
       especially given that the economic situation was depressed
       both at home and abroad.

(3)   Our nominal interest rate has never fallen to almost zero.   For
       example, the one-year deposit rate in our country is 4.77%.
       Admittedly, negative growth in the general price level during
       the first ten months of 1997 made the real interest rate higher
       than the nominal interest rate, which was unfavorable to the
       expansion of investment and consumer spending.   However,
       there is also the possibility of prices going up rather than down,
       which means that the nominal interest rate could be lowered.
       Of course, whether there is a need to do so depends on many
       other factors.

(4)   Consumers are presently showing little interest in spending.
       This is not because they would rather hold their cash due to the
       low nominal interest rate.   Nor is it because they would like to
       deposit their money due to the high real interest rate.   The real
       reason lies in the fall in their current and expected future
       income, as well as the rise in their current and expected future
       expenses (including the purchase of property, social welfare
       expenditures, and education expenses).

(5)   Enterprises presently lack the desire to invest.   This is not
       because the cost of borrowing is too high, but because previous
       duplicated construction and blind investment have resulted in
       excess production, while, at the same time, effective demand is

lacking. In addition, although enterprises are now aware of their risks and responsibilities, they still need an appropriate incentive system.

It follows from the above discussion that there is no reason to say that China has fallen into the same "liquidity trap" as did Japan. Therefore, the prescription of "non-conventional monetary policy" given by Krugman is obviously irrelevant for China. In other words, adopting an inflationary policy to guarantee negative or low real interest rates to lower the real cost of borrowing to stimulate investment and consumer spending simply would not work in our country under the present conditions. However, while the stimulating effect of expansionary monetary policy is constrained by some factors in China, it is still necessary to employ expansionary fiscal measures to expand domestic demand. But while undertaking expansionary fiscal measures, we cannot overlook their limitations and possible negative effects.

Fiscal policies such as tax cuts and issuing more national bonds have a much faster and more direct effect on expanding consumer spending than the traditional monetary policy of easing credit. However, the implementation of such policies has always gone hand in hand with increasing the budget deficit. Therefore, such measures can only be used under certain conditions and on a short-term basis. When there are plenty of idle resources in the economy (including capital, labor force, equipment, material resources, etc.), budget deficit as a fiscal policy can be used. For example, in the current situation, savings are greater than investments; deposits are more than loans; in terms of labor resources there are unemployed and redundant employees; plenty of production capacity lies idle or half idle; there is an excessive inventory of many products; and so on. In particular, we currently have large amounts of idle investment resources in the financial system. At such times, the treasury can borrow money from banks by issuing national bonds for infrastructure investment, and stimulate domestic demand and economic growth without any risk of inflation. But there is a limit to the amount of idle resources. As the economy expands, a bottleneck in the supply of resources will appear. If we continue an expansionary fiscal policy, serious inflation or stagflation (while economic growth stagnates, prices continue to rise) will follow. The classical Keynesian expansionary fiscal policy has brought stagflation and been discredited, as has been proven by what has happened in the western countries since World War II. Therefore, when we pursue a more active fiscal policy, we must make sure that policies are well-timed and carried out in an appropriate manner. It is unwise for us to adopt budget deficit financing as a long-term fiscal policy.

Another important factor is that the task of expanding domestic demand cannot be entrusted solely to fiscal policy. Since fiscal policies and monetary policies impose different requirements on repayment schedules, they are best implemented in different areas. Areas such as public projects and projects of no-easy-direct return favor fiscal policies and projects of direct return favor monetary policies. In the area of infrastructure, the appropriate method depends on investment returns. Some can be initiated through fiscal measures, while others can be funded by non-fiscal capital, including credits. Therefore, when we are issuing RMB100 bn worth of treasury bonds, we have to supplement this with RMB100 bn worth of loan credit. The two sums of RMB100 bn must be invested in infrastructure rather than in processing industries. This is essential in order to avoid more duplicated construction and unprofitable production capacity. On the other hand, we should not depend on fiscal measures to uplift our technological level to international standards, or to reduce unemployment by developing a large number of small and medium-size enterprises. What is needed here is stronger support in the form of credit. When we carry out expansionary fiscal policy, we must realize the need for increased credit availability rather than discard it. This is one of the restrictions on carrying out an expansionary fiscal policy.

This does not mean interest rate cuts are insignificant in increasing monetary credit supply. But to lower the interest rate is not the only monetary instrument available. Many other measures can also be used. That banks currently "refrain from lending" is only a superficial and local phenomenon. In fact, before issuing

RMB100 bn worth of treasury bonds, starting from April and May 1998, we began to witness some preliminary results from the initiating measures pervasively adopted by the central government to expand domestic demand. These results are shown in some leading indicators: for example, investment, credit, and production of some investment products are on the rise. What deserves our special attention is that, with the increase in investment, bank loans for infrastructure began to increase rapidly. And the additional investment of RMB200 bn in the second half of 1998, either in the form of RMB100 bn treasury bonds or in the form of RMB100 bn credit, was implemented in the form of bank lending and monetary instruments. Therefore, in the current period of initiating economic development, monetary policy and fiscal policy must work together. The implementation of both policies must be undertaken at the right time and in an appropriate manner. Alongside the gradual implementation of an expansionary fiscal policy, and the manifestation of the problems in structural adjustment (especially in upgrading technologies and developing small and medium-size enterprises), the role of monetary credit policy will become even more important. The authorities are getting a grip on the situation by adopting these measures. More concerted implementing efforts will depend on further clarification of the rationale behind the policies.

On Deflation and Price Policy

Is China beginning to show any sign of deflation? Raising the question could appear belated — more active fiscal policies have already been introduced specifically to solve the problem of deflation by the central government. However, it is still necessary to discuss what theoretical explanation we can provide for this problem, and what judgment we can pass on the extent of current deflation, because these will affect our selection of an appropriate price policy.

What then is deflation? Deflation is an economic process contrary to inflation.   If inflation is defined as a general and persistent rise in consumer prices, but not as a partial or short-term rise, then deflation cannot be a short-term and partial decline in prices, but must involve a general and persistent decline.   Thus how persistent is the rise or decline before it can be identified as inflation or deflation?   There does not seem to be any unified definition. We think, if a general price rise or decline lasts for more than six months, then we may conclude that inflation or deflation is already there.   In general, inflation and deflation are both monetary phenomena.   In the actual economic environment, both indicate a deviance of aggregate demand from aggregate supply, or a deviance of the actual economic growth rate from the potential economic growth rate.   When the aggregate demand persistently exceeds the aggregate supply, or the actual economic growth rate persistently exceeds the potential economic growth rate, there will appear an inflation: a continuous price rise and a devaluation.   In contrast, when the aggregate demand is persistently less than the aggregate supply, and the actual economic growth rate is persistently lower than the potential economic growth rate, then deflation appears as a continuous fall in prices and continuous rise in money worth. Inflation and deflation can be observed from both long-term and short-term angles.   In the short-term economic cycle, deflation usually occurs when an economy is in its declining cycle.   We usually observe declines in production, shrinking of markets, the falling of the profit margins of enterprises, reductions in investment in productions, increases in unemployment, drops in personal income, and so on.   Take the fall in prices in China from October 1997 as an example.   This ranged over many commodities and lasted for almost a year.   Some recessionary phenomena associated with deflation also appeared in China.   However, the degree of the price fall was not great.   The production and sales of commodities continued to grow at a pretty high rate.   On the whole, it can be concluded that China is currently in a state of slight deflation.

Of course, we should not be indifferent even to a slight deflation, since this induces a lack of public confidence in future economic development.   This, in turn, would further slow down economic growth and definitely hinder economic recovery. The policy we have applied to expand domestic demand is intended to boost people's confidence.

Considering the negative impact of the deflation on prosperity and confidence in the future, it is suggested by some commentators that a "mild inflation" policy should be adopted to keep the total price rising slightly (e.g., within 5%) in order to stimulate economic growth. This suggestion is analogous to Krugman's prescription for Japan. Regardless of its validity in Japan, we do not think it will work in China.

What policy, therefore, should we adopt concerning the overall price level? The notorious "high inflation policy" has terrible effects. Nowadays, there is hardly anyone who openly advocates this policy. But the idea of "low inflation" is still very popular. However, we believe, as a goal of price policy, that we should not encourage even a "mild" inflationary policy. We should insist on the stability of the total price. Inflation of any degree, "low" or "mild" or "appropriate," should not be accepted as a policy goal, regardless of whether it is justified in terms of its level, implementation, objective, or effect.

First of all, there is no consensus for what "low" inflation is. A few years ago, the inflation rates in Russia, Eastern Europe, and Latin America, which ranged from single to four digit percentages, were used as a reference point for China. Using these as a reference, some academics claimed that in China an inflation rate of 10% plus and up to 20% could be considered as "low" inflation and therefore merited no serious concern. However, 5% is now accepted by us as a "low" inflation rate. But our current inflation rate is minus 2% and from minus 2% to 5%, a range of 7%, which is quite large. In addition, in the global financial markets in which we now operate, the stability of a country's currency, in addition to its own domestic price stability, can be influenced by price trends of other countries. For example, until the regional financial crisis, Thailand insisted on a linked exchange rate with the U.S. dollar. From 1989 to 1996, just before the crisis, consumer price inflation in

Thailand was 5.2%, which was certainly not high. However, over the same period, inflation in the United States was only 3.6%. Using 1989 as the reference standard of 100, the cumulative consumer price index of Thailand in the past eight years was 17% higher than in the United States. But the exchange rate between the Thai Baht and the U.S. dollar stayed more or less the same during this period. Consequently, the Thai Baht was overvalued. This, in addition to the large trade deficit, left a window of opportunity for international financial speculators to attack. Therefore, it is very difficult to set a standard for a generally acceptable low standard of inflation.

Second, based on the observation of short-term economic fluctuations and the pattern of price changes, when an economy is in a downward cycle, and the actual rate of economic growth is lower than the potential one, there is unemployed capacity in the economy. When an expansionary policy is used to stimulate demand and to help the economy rise again at this time, the stimulation will not cause serious inflation. After the economy has risen, and the actual growth rate is equal to or in excess of the potential economic growth rate, prices will rise noticeably as the economy grows. At this time, what kind of policy should we use to combat the rise in prices? Should we use an inflationary policy to support price rises, or a different policy to maintain basic stability in prices? This is the time when we must maintain a close watch and adjust when the economy is growing again. We believe, during such times, that we should try to employ measures to keep prices from rising too fast, because this would have a negative impact on people's daily life. If the "inflation-suppressing" measures are appropriate and timely, then we will get a mild and slight rise in inflation. (Although zero inflation is attractive, it is very difficult to achieve in reality.) We will have the situation of "high economic growth and low inflation." This ideal situation results from suppressing inflation when the economy is on the up cycle, and not continuing inflationary stimulation. If we were to use inflationary measures when the economy is growing, even a "mild inflation" measure can boost up a high inflation. Low inflation will quickly flare up to high inflation. By its nature, "inflation" is like an opiate, to which powerful groups of a society easily get addicted.   They can very easily push "low" inflation to "high" inflation (if there is no macroeconomic adjustment program to keep inflation in check).   They will sacrifice the interests of the weak in a society.   Therefore, in the process of policy implementation, we should appropriately change from expansionary measures to preventive and suppressive measures to keep inflation in check, according to economic conditions.   We should refrain from adopting continuous inflationary measures to stimulate economic growth.

Third, the purpose of the continuous adoption of "low inflationary policy" is based on the desire to stimulate continuous economic growth.   This concerns the question of what kind of economic growth we are after.   There are two major types of economic growth.   One is the growth resulting from expansion of demand.   The other type of growth is based on improvement in supply.   Economic growth based on increasing demand is normally followed by inflation of high cost but low yield.   The Asian financial crisis clearly shows us that an economic growth based on high cost and low yield cannot be sustained.   On the other hand, economic growth based on expansion of supply generally leads to advances in technology, upgrading of industrial structure, institutional innovation, and an increase in yield.   Usually, this type of growth will not result in inflation, most probably will lead to a normal price fall.   We should not think that we can stimulate economic growth only with inflationary measures.   Under certain conditions, advances in technology, price falls, and economic growth are mutually contributive.   From the 1870s to the 1890s, a period of "great economic growth" and "great deflation" co-existed in the United States.   "Between 1870 and 1896, the wholesale prices dropped by 50%."   "From 1869 to 1898, the annual GDP growth was 4.2%, about twice as high as the potential growth rate today."   This was reported in a *Wall Street Journal* article dated August 26, 1998 entitled "Deflation is Nothing to Be Afraid of."   The article says: "Today, the expectation caused by deflation may damage old industries like automobile and aviation.   However, the same expectation will not harm any new technology industries, where the fall in price will stimulate demand and a vigorous development of technology." Now, our economic development is in the process of two fundamental changes (change in our economic institutions, and change in the form of economic growth). In our current phase of initiating economic growth and development, we must be aware that speed is not the only goal. We must also promote changes in the form, structural adjustment, and upgrade of our economy. And we must create a favorable environment for the macro economy and for long-term sustainable economic growth.

To summarize, we do not support the adoption of "mild inflationary policy" to combat deflation. We believe we should insist on a basic stability policy for the general price level. A stable price regime does not mean stagnant prices, nor does it mean "zero" inflation. It is a policy by which price fluctuation is regulated in accordance with the cyclical development of the economy, so that it will not be consistently deflationary or inflationary. On the down turn of the cycle, we should try to prevent or overcome deflation. On the up turn of the cycle, we should try to prevent or check inflation. This type of price policy will give people a sense of stability as well as confidence in the future of the economy. All this will contribute to advances in technology, suppress excessive speculation, ameliorate distorted distribution, and provide good external conditions for further structural improvement and upgrade and economic institutional reform. Basic price stability should be our main policy for the adjustment of the general price level.

ANALYSIS AND FORECAST OF CHINA'S ECONOMIC DEVELOPMENT (THE AUTUMN 1998 REPORT)[*]

ECONOMIC ANALYSIS AND FORECAST TEAM
Division of Economics, Chinese Academy of Social Sciences

Since the beginning of 1998, China's macroeconomy has maintained stable and high growth on the basis of the country's successful "soft landing" in 1996–1997. Despite the global economic turbulence, the general economic situation is in China's favor.

However, since the second half of 1997, the economy has been affected by the serious financial crisis in Asia. In the summer of 1998, China suffered from the most serious floods since 1949. The economic problems, both domestic and external, that we are now facing, are unprecedentedly complex. To manage the macroeconomy under so many adverse conditions constitutes a serious challenge. In the face of these formidable challenges, under the guidance of the 15th Party Congress, the Party Central Committee and the State Council have undertaken various macroeconomic measures to expand domestic demand and to help maintain a relatively high rate of world economic growth. Recently, the Party Central Committee decided to employ a more aggressive fiscal policy to increase investment in infrastructure; to further expand domestic demand; to expand both domestic and overseas markets; and to maintain a stable RMB exchange rate. These decisions will not only guarantee China's economic growth at an appropriately high rate in 1998–99, but will also contribute a great deal to the recovery of the global economy from the Asian financial crisis. We have every reason to believe that even under such unprecedented adverse conditions, with the correct guidance of the Party Central Committee and the State Council, we will be able to solve the existing problems in our national economy; to keep the economy growing at an appropriately

---

[*] Team directors: Liu Guoguang and Wang Luolin; executive directors: Li Jingwen, Liu Shucheng, and Wang Tongsan; authors: Wang Tongsan, Li Xiaochao, and Shen Lisheng.

fast and stable track; and to advance China's four modernizations onto a new stage of development.

This report attempts to analyze and forecast the trend and problems of China's economic development in 1998–99 by empirical analysis and model simulation.

The Forecast of Major Economic Indicators

Since the beginning of 1998, a series of events have emerged in China's domestic and external economic environment. The major manifestations are: for the very first time since the beginning of reform and opening up, through the fall of price indices, the economy shows signs of deflation. Coincidentally, extremely severe floods brought enormous damages to the Yangtse River region and the Northeast. The Asian financial crisis continued to adversely affect China. Undoubtedly these events have added to the difficulties ahead of us in our efforts to realize the economic development goals set at the beginning of this year. According to our forecast, under the current situation, our economy in 1998 will maintain its state of appropriately fast economic growth. The GDP growth will be about 8%. There will be about 3.2% value-added growth for the primary industry, about 9.3% for the secondary industry, of which about 9.3% for heavy industries and 9.7% for light industries, and about 8.3% for the tertiary industry. The GDP growth rate in 1999 will be higher than that in 1998, reaching about 8.6%. The predicted value-added growth rates for primary, secondary, and tertiary industry will be about 3.5%, 12.2%, and 8.5%, respectively.

The total fixed asset investment in 1998 will reach about RMB2,880 billion. The real and nominal growth rates will be 16.3% and 15.5%, respectively. The total fixed asset investment in 1999 will be around RMB3,330 billion. The real and nominal growth rates will be 14.6% and 15.6%, respectively.

The rate of inflation had already fallen to a very low level in 1997. We expect to see a negative growth rate in the inflation of retail prices at about -1.5%. However, with the implementation of a more aggressive fiscal policy, and the expansion of various types of demand, particularly domestic demand, we predict that the 1999 rate of growth for retail prices will return to its positive norm, but will not be very high, at about 1.7%.

The nominal and real growth rates for total retail sales are expected to be 7.3% and 9.0% in 1998 and 10.6% and 8.7% in 1999, respectively, maintaining a state of appropriately high growth rate. Personal income and expenditure will also keep on growing at a relatively stable and appropriate rate. However, the growth rate of rural income again will fall below urban income levels. Because special expansionary fiscal policies were applied in 1998, relatively large fiscal deficits will appear. In line with the changes in fiscal policies, relative changes will take place with financial and banking indices. The export growth rate has been affected by the Asian financial crisis and will be noticeably lower than in 1997, but a trade surplus will be maintained.

Forecasts for Major Economic Indicators in 1998 and 1999

	1998	1999
1. Total value and production indicators		
GDP growth rate	7.7-8.1%	8.6%
Value-added growth rate in primary industry	3.2%	3.5%
Value-added growth rate in secondary industry	9.2%	10.2%
Of which: heavy industries	9.7%	11.0%
light industries	9.3%	10.3%
Value-added growth rate in tertiary industry	8.3%	8.5%
Of which: transportation, posts, & telecommunications	10.8%	11.0%
Commercial services	8.5%	8.5%
2. Total fixed asset investment		
Total amount of investment (RMB billion)	2,880	3,330
Nominal growth rate	15.5%	15.6%
Real growth rate	16.3%	14.6%
Rate of investment	35.8%	37.9%

	1998	1999
3. Prices		
Retail price index inflation rate	-1.5%	1.7%
Consumer price index inflation rate	1.0%	2.5%
Investment price index inflation rate	-0.7%	0.9%
GDP deflator	-0.3%	0.6%
4. Personal income and consumption		
Real growth rate of average urban personal disposal income	4.9%	4.8%
Real growth rate of average rural personal income	2.2%	3.1%
Real growth rate of urban consumption	6.8%	7.6%
Real growth rate of rural consumption	5.7%	5.6%
Real growth rate of societal consumption	16.3%	15.0%
5. Consumer market		
Total retail sales (RMB billion)	2,930	3,240
Nominal growth rate	7.3%	10.6%
Real growth rate	9.0%	8.7%
6. Fiscal figures		
Fiscal revenue (RMB billion)	1,005	1,168
Growth rate	16.2%	16.2%
Fiscal expenditure (RMB billion)	1,102	1,268
Growth rate	19.3%	15.1%
Fiscal deficit (RMB billion)	97	100
7. Financial figures		
Outstanding amount of personal savings deposit (RMB billion)	5,577	6,722
Growth rate	20.4%	20.5%
New increase in loans (RMB billion)	1,446	1,500
New increase in money in circulation (RMB billion)	150	176
8. Foreign trade		
Total imports (US$ billion)	152.5	170
Growth rate	7.1%	11.5%
Total exports (US$ billion)	192.5	206
Growth rate	5.4%	7.0%

Analysis of the Macroeconomic Situation

When the world economy was suffering from the fallout of the Asian financial crisis, many countries and regions, particularly in Asia, saw their economic growth rates falling. In some cases the absolute level of the economy declined. By contrast, the Chinese economy succeeded in maintaining a stable, but high rate of growth in 1998. In the first half of 1998, the GDP growth rate reached 7%. This was a significant achievement and has received worldwide acknowledgement. This achievement shows that our capability to utilize macroeconomic measures has been greatly strengthened during the process of establishing a socialist market economy.

Currently, our major macroeconomic concern lies in the long-standing decline of the economic growth rate. According to the quarterly figures, the duration and magnitude of the decline has far exceeded our expectations. In addition, there has emerged a negative increase in price indices. Although the decline in prices has helped maintain the standard of living, it induces real bank interest rates that are too high, viewed from both an intermediate and a long-term perspective. This condition not only adds to the difficulties of financial institutions in exercising their monetary influence under the macroeconomic adjustment program, but also adversely affects enterprises' ability to initiate expanded production.

Economic theorists and practitioners are now engaged in a broad and in-depth study of the causes of the above phenomenon. Some attempt to approach the problem from the perspective of the changes in the economic system and mechanisms. Some attempt to analyze the problem from the angle of the different stages of economic cycles, and some try to understand the problem by analyzing the impact of particular events. All this will help us to work out some appropriate policies to tackle our short-term problems as well as to formulate long-term policies.

Generally speaking, there are three major direct causes for the slowdown of the economic growth. First is the inertia caused by the macroeconomic adjustment program launched since 1993 to bring the economy down to a "soft landing." The implementation of this program and its adjustment caused some necessary slowing. Second, in the process of reforming state-owned enterprises, the problems that used to be covered up are now exposed. Excess workers were laid off and the output in some enterprises was reduced as the result of the merging or bankruptcy of enterprises. In addition, difficulties in raising the price of agricultural products stood in the way of increasing the income of the rural populations. All these conditions slowed down the increase in consumer markets in both urban and rural areas. Third, the growth rate in exports declined sharply, and foreign direct investment decreased to some extent as a result of the Asian financial crisis.

All these factors make China's task of maintaining sustainable, healthy, and fast macroeconomic development extremely difficult. The unstable global economic environment caused by the Asian financial crisis brought us more externally generated difficulties. Thus, our dependence on expanding domestic demand will become stronger. Moreover, the unprecedented disaster wrought by the summer floods caused enormous economic losses. And while the reconstruction in the flooded areas, the recovery of production, and the need for restoring nationwide inventories will boost economic growth, the flooding still caused more harm than good. Even if the economy can be pulled up as a result of redressing the damage caused by these disasters, it cannot be done quickly.

In order to keep the macroeconomic growth rate at an appropriately high level, the Party Central Committee and the State Council have taken several determined measures since the beginning of 1998. To facilitate the current macroeconomic development, they have formulated and carried out additional active fiscal policies. An extra sum of RMB100 bn worth of treasury bonds was issued to the national commercial banks for increasing investment in infrastructure for the following six areas: rural irrigation, transportation networks, basic urban infrastructure, the rebuilding and upgrading of urban and rural electricity networks, the construction of direct government-owned grain storage facilities, and economical and appropriate residential housing. The formulation of these policies is of paramount importance in expanding domestic demand, stimulating economic growth, and maintaining a healthy and fast growth of the national economy. Since August, the implementation of these policies has brought about noticeable improvements. The industrial production reversed, from declining to rising. The fixed asset investment increased sharply. The decline in the growth rates of various monetary indicators was arrested, and an upturn was detected in monetary indicators. The market for consumer goods was also improved. A healthy export surplus was maintained. All the signs and indicators showed that, starting from the third quarter of 1998, the declining trend in the GDP growth rate was stopped, and a new period of economic growth is at hand.

How to Look at the 8% Economic Growth Rate

In 1995, on behalf of the National Planning Commission, we made a forecast of the most suitable average economic growth rate for the "Ninth Five-year Plan." Our forecast was 8–9%, which achieved a nationwide consensus. Under the situation of 1998, the 8% economic growth rate targeted by the Party Central Committee and the State Council is not only necessary, but fully supported by our analysis. We believe this target can be achieved.

However, with more adverse factors showing up both domestically and internationally, we need to thoroughly understand the rationale for the 8% growth target. In reality, this is not simply a rigid figure — it includes three concrete goals that must be reached. The first goal is to stop the declining trend in the economic growth as early as possible. The second goal is to guarantee the stability of the RMB exchange rate despite the fallout from the Asian financial crisis so as to assume our responsibility as a major regional economic power. The third goal is to maintain a high growth rate in order to alleviate the problem of increasing unemployment brought about in the course of the reform of state-owned enterprises. With these three goals realized, the purpose of setting an 8% growth rate will be realized.

China's economic development in 1998 received international recognition. First, the implementation of policies to stimulate and expand domestic demand, starting from the third quarter of 1998, changed the economic situation for the better and China entered a new stage of sustained growth. This followed a decline that had lasted for the past few years. Second, despite the domestic and international rumors about devaluation of the RMB, the exchange rate of the RMB has remained stable, indicating these rumors are groundless. Our foreign exchange reserve has remained steady, and a healthy trade surplus and balance of international payments was maintained. The RMB exchange rate will remain stable. Finally, with the deepening reform of state-owned enterprises, both government and enterprises spared no efforts in providing social security and redeployment for redundant workers. Meanwhile, the people's traditional preferences for career choice have undergone a dramatic change, which has enlarged employment opportunities. So far, the unemployment problem has not deteriorated. Therefore, we have every reason to believe that we have basically fulfilled the requirements to achieve our 8% macroeconomic growth target.

While we are doing our best to reach this target, we must avoid impatience, do our practical work, and respect the operation of economic laws. We should strike a balance between achieving a speedy growth rate and economic efficiency. In particular, we must abstain from speculative activity under the guise of realizing economic growth goals. What we are after is a realistic and appropriate rate of growth, not a blind growth rate. And we should definitely oppose boastful behavior and false reporting of economic growth.

The Issue of Implementing More Aggressive Fiscal Policies

The Party Central Committee and the State Council took decisive steps to create RMB100 bn worth of treasury bonds in 1998 for infrastructure investment. This strategic decision is undoubtedly correct and necessary. It provides the basis for quickly turning the declining rate of economic growth around. By stimulating domestic demand, it guarantees the growth of the economy at a stable and appropriate rate, and effectively protects the economy from the fallout of the Asian financial crisis. It further guarantees the successful completion of the Ninth Five-year Plan, and lays a firm foundation for setting the strategic goals for future development in 2010. In our 1998 Spring Report, we proposed our policy suggestion that "the government should bring itself into effective play." We stressed that "the role of the government becomes increasingly important when fiscal and monetary policies are adopted to achieve their short-term, intermediate, and long-term goals in the macroeconomic adjustment program." The Party Central Committee and the State Council have skillfully managed the macroeconomy through their fiscal policies in 1998.

It was absolutely necessary for the government to implement more aggressive fiscal policies. First, from a theoretical point of view, although both fiscal and monetary policies are important measures in the macroeconomic adjustment program, they can be differentiated in their roles in different economic environments. In general, when a macroeconomy is in a stage of expansion, the role of monetary policy will be more obvious and will have an immediate and direct impact on the rate of economic growth. However, when a macroeconomy is in a state of contraction, fiscal policy will stimulate demand in an immediate and direct way, whereas the effect of monetary policy will be slow to show up. Our economy has been adversely affected by both the Asian financial crisis and the impact of the austerity measures for soft landing during the past few years. The economy, therefore, is now in a state of relative contraction and in need of effective expansion. An expansionary fiscal policy is needed. Second, fiscal policy is more flexible and specific: concrete fiscal measures can be applied to specific situations. Currently, structural adjustment is an important part of our macroeconomic development. From the perspective of economic structural adjustment, fiscal policy is more specific than monetary policy, and hence more effective. Lastly, the actual implementation of the macroeconomic adjustment program last year showed that the decline in economic growth could not be stopped in a substantial way by relying solely on monetary policies. In the first half of 1998, although the monetary policy was becoming loose, the growth of money supply (M_2) was actually slowing down. This began speeding up only after August when forceful fiscal policies were implemented. Therefore, when monetary policy has failed to yield a desired result, it becomes necessary to reinforce the implementation of fiscal policy.

The feasibility of carrying out such an important decision depends first on our ability to manage the macroeconomy along with the establishment and refinement of a socialist market economy. Under the leadership of the Party Central Committee and the State Council, we are fully confident that we can manage every step in the entire process of the expansionary fiscal program and avoid serious mistakes. Second, our current financial situation can still withstand a certain amount of excess in treasury bonds. By international standards, China's fiscal deficit has not exceeded 2.5% of its GDP, and government debt is still under the internationally acceptable levels. Therefore, within a certain period of time, we can further increase the amount of government debt. Lastly, at present the pathway by which savings are directly channeled to investment is far from smooth. The difference between liabilities and assets of commercial banks is rather large. This offers an opportunity for the government to issue large amounts of treasury bonds to the commercial banks. However, this will not create inflationary pressure within a limited time span.

But any macroeconomic adjustment program may induce side effects with changes in time and environment. Therefore, when we adopt an expansionary fiscal policy, we must also take into consideration possible negative side-effects. We must take necessary actions to maximize the positive effects of the policy, and reduce negative effects to a minimum.

Thus, while we are carrying out various expansionary macroeconomic adjustment policies, we must be on guard against the following five possible adverse effects:

Refrain from Pursuing Speed Blindly, and Avoid Large Economic Swings

It is clear that the central and local governments share the same aim in their efforts to carry out an expansionary fiscal policy so as to stimulate economic growth. After the implementation of this fiscal policy, economic growth will be restored to a certain degree. Under such conditions, we must avoid the blind pursuit of fast economic recovery, which could ultimately result in wild swings. If the rate of growth in the fourth quarter of 1998 exceeds 10% (which could be necessary if we are to achieve our goal of 8% growth for the whole year), it may not be beneficial to sustain such a high rate into 1999. We learned our lesson from our experience in having too sharp a rise in economic growth in 1992–93. During that period, high inflation emerged after just one year of economic recovery and we then had to impose tight control and an austerity program. So, presently, we must control the degree of strength in the expansionary policy so as to extend the recovery period. By doing so, we can avoid failing by "running too fast only to fall behind," and the re-emergence of high inflation. This cautious approach is also useful in guaranteeing a proper and stable rate of economic growth, in achieving a high quality of economic growth, and in strengthening our on-going structural changes.

Avoid Blind Investment and Duplicated Construction, and Guarantee the Quality of Investment

We are currently shouldering a very complex and difficult task in undertaking a rather large-scale investment program in a relatively short time scale. This requires scientific decision making, and detailed and organized plans by various economic departments. We expect the government and the National People's Congress to closely scrutinize all projects to guard against blind investment and duplicated construction, and to use all the means available to guarantee the quality of each national investment project.

Prevent the Deterioration of Fiscal Conditions, and Actively Expand the Influence of Fiscal Policy on the Macroeconomic Adjustment Program

Since 1981, China has issued a cumulative total of more than RMB900 bn worth of treasury bonds. Up to now, the amount of outstanding government debt is about RMB600 billion. Although the level of national debt and the fiscal deficit as a percentage of our GDP is still within a relatively safe range, we must monitor two indicators: the outstanding unpaid debt and the repayment rate, which have become a very heavy financial burden. Past experience clearly shows that an expansionary fiscal policy can only function as a short-term adjustment policy. Therefore, we cannot use such a strong fiscal tool of increasing treasury bonds for a long-term purpose. It can only serve as a specific policy for a specific time and for a special purpose. In the longer term, we must carry out in-depth reform of our taxation and fiscal structures, to provide the government with increasing financial power so that we can make use of the important adjustment role of taxation in the macroeconomy.

Avoid Restoration of the Old System of Investment, and Refine the Socialist Market Economic System

There appears a distinct feature in the present process of increasing investment in infrastructure through issuing more treasury bonds. That is, the raising of capital is clearly market-oriented, but the employment of capital is clearly oriented toward the planned economy. Governments at various levels make decisive contributions to the establishment and organization of investment projects. Therefore, we must insist on the principles of the socialist market economy and consolidate recent years' achievements in reforming the investment system. We must avoid the restoration of the old system, and explore new ways through which the government can better perform its duties and through which the socialist market economy can work more efficiently.

Do Not Let the Government Fight the War Alone but Mobilize All Sectors of the Society

In the present round of promoting economic growth, the government takes more initiative than enterprises. In addition to organizing and performing its own investment task, the government — while working to expand domestic demand for stimulating a proper and fast economic growth — must actively mobilize all sectors of the society. The government should do its best to provide the enterprises with a better macroeconomic environment, to bolster their confidence and guarantee their success in making investments. Local government initiative must be also brought into play. Of the RMB100 bn treasury bonds, half has been transferred to the local governments. In fact, the central government acted on behalf of the local governments in issuing debt for special purposes.

Now, we need to pay attention to two key areas of active fiscal policy. One is that this must be a comprehensive policy, which incorporates issuing treasury bonds; investment in infrastructure; the development of financial and production sectors; as well as the overall organization of social security and fiscal management. The other is that the ultimate goal of an active fiscal policy should be an increase in consumption. Therefore, we must work out the entire process thoroughly, from issuing treasury bonds, to investment in infrastructure, and to the expansion of demand.

Policy Suggestions

In order to successfully implement an active fiscal policy; to make it effectively compatible with other macroeconomic adjustment measures to guarantee the recovery of the economic growth rate from a decline to a rise; and to realize the goal of a stable and proper economic growth rate in the long run, we made the following policy suggestions for China's economic policy in 1998–99.

The Task of Expanding Domestic Demand to Stop the Decline in Economic Growth in the Short Term Must Be Integrated With the Country's Long-term Economic Development Plan and the Long-term Structural Adjustment of the Economy

We must try to change all the macroeconomic measures from a capital-constrained system to a market-constrained system, from a supply-constrained system to a demand-constrained one. We should upgrade the quality of the economic growth to a higher stage through launching this new round of economic development.

We Must Evaluate Our Experience in Issuing Additional Treasury Bonds and Their Uses

In the subsequent macroeconomic adjustment work, we should pay attention to the active role of fiscal policy, particularly the diversity of treasury bonds in terms of their types, maturities, and functions. We hope to exercise a full-fledged stimulating effect on society to expand domestic demand and keep economic development at a stable and appropriate rate, through the limited utilization of treasury bonds.

Pay Attention to the Coordination between Fiscal Policy and Monetary Policy

In the past, in terms of fixed asset investment, local and central governments provided 3% each, foreign direct investment 12%, and bank loans covered the rest of the funds for fixed asset investment. Under the current situation, fiscal policy is obviously taking the lead in fostering fixed asset investment. However, in the long run, we must coordinate the fiscal and monetary macroeconomic policies. Both theoretical and empirical analyzes point out that without strong national finances as a foundation, it is impossible to establish a financial system capable of withstanding risk and crisis. Monetary policy must be supported by strong government financing. On the other hand, a fiscal policy can only be effective with the support of financial and monetary tools. At the same time, an expansionary fiscal policy cannot be used in an exhaustive way for a long time since it will be constrained by the increasing fiscal deficit. For regular macroeconomic adjustment, we should generally rely on monetary policy.

Other important issues in our current economic development are how to make use of the small and medium-size enterprises in economic development and structural adjustment, and how to improve our international competitiveness. To upgrade their international competitiveness, the small and medium-size enterprises need necessary equipment, technology, and capital. And their technology and equipment need improvement. None of these aims can be achieved without adequate capital. The major sources of capital should be channeled through various financial institutions such as banks. In general, a large number of public infrastructure projects can be funded by government finance. But financing for the vast majority of enterprises comes from funds other than government finance.

Try Hard to Maintain Basic Stability in Prices

Under a market economy, it is of paramount importance to maintain basic stability in prices. High inflation is detrimental to the development of the economy. However, it is also harmful for prices to stay at a stage of negative growth for a long time. Under a normal situation, the advance of production technology, the increase in production efficiency, and sometimes the fall in effective demand, will make prices fall. On the other hand, the rigidity of increases in wages, and investors' expectations of price inflation, sometimes result in a rise in prices. In the long run, price stability is most beneficial to upgrading our technology, to stimulating investment, to improving living standards, and to promoting fast quality growth of the national economy.

Currently, as funds from new treasury bonds have reached the end users, prices of some production materials have recovered and begun to rise again. This price inflation will no doubt be totally transmitted to downstream products after a while. Therefore, deflation, manifested in a fall in price indices, will not be a long-term problem for China's economy. What we should be cautious of is the likelihood of inflation. Particularly so, at the time when it is difficult to ascertain the likely outcome of the international financial crisis, and when China is more vulnerable. This requires us to take precautions against the possible re-emergence of an inflationary threat.

No Devaluation for the RMB in 1999

As evidenced in the economic development both domestically and internationally, China's decision not to devalue the RMB has turned out to be both crucial and correct. At present, the fallout of the Asian financial crisis continues to expand globally. International speculators are ready to pounce on the weakest link in the world economy to extract profit. Economies in many Asian countries and regions are falling into negative growth. Hong Kong's economy is also facing many problems. To keep a stable RMB exchange rate is of great importance in maintaining the international economic order and stability; for alleviating the impact of the Asian financial crisis on the world; and for the global economy to come out of this financial crisis. This is the consensus among many international institutions and world-renowned figures. Internally, along with the coming of a new round of investment, many product prices will rise, and maintaining the stability of the RMB exchange rate will help to avoid the return of too high an inflation rate. This is beneficial to a healthy and continually fast-growing economy. At the same time, maintaining the stability of the RMB exchange rate will maintain support for the stability of the Hong Kong dollar and economic development in that region, and help to enhance China's international reputation. This will also help us remain attractive to direct foreign investors, and thus will stimulate the economy. On the whole, maintaining RMB exchange rate stability is more beneficial than harmful to our economic development and to our international balance of payments.

Therefore, we should continue to maintain the exchange rate for the RMB unchanged, and reiterate our promise of no devaluation in 1999.

1999 is the last year in the 20th century. If we can insist on carrying out the policies laid down by the 15th Party Congress; if we can manage the direction and the strength of the macroeconomic adjustment program carefully and actively; if we can bring the initiative of all sectors of society into full play in the economic recovery process; then we can withstand any future turmoil in the international environment. If we achieve sustained and healthy development, we can usher in a new era of quality economic growth in the 21st century, with our heads high and our spirits buoyant.

A SUMMARY OF THE "1998 AUTUMN FORUM ON ANALYSIS AND FORECAST OF CHINA'S ECONOMIC SITUATION"

ZHAO JINGXING

Institute of Quantitative and Technical Economics
Chinese Academy of Social Sciences

The 1998 "Autumn Forum to Analyze and Forecast the Economic Situation" was hosted on October 8, 1998 by the "Economic Situation Analysis and Forecast" research team of the Chinese Academy of Social Sciences.[*] This was the 17th forum

---

[*] Many experts and scholars participated in this forum. They came from the following units (in no particular order): Research Office of the State Council, Development Research Centre of the State Council, Department of Investment of Macroeconomic Research, Institute of the State Development Planning Commission, the General Department of the State Development Planning Commission, Centre of Economic Information of the National Economy and the Trade Commission, Central Party School, General Planning Department of the Ministry of Finance, Policy Research Institute of the People's Bank of China, State Statistics Bureau, Institute of National System Reform and the Management under Economic Restructuring Office, General and Planning Department of State Science and Technology Commission, State Information Centre, Assessment Centre of Chinese High Technology Enterprises Development, China Securities Regulatory Commission, Resources Information Centre of the State Internal Trade Bureau, Commercial Information Centre of the State Internal Trade Bureau, Planning and Finance Department Ministry of Foreign Trade and Economic Cooperation, Development and the Research Centre of Metallurgy, China National Non-Ferrous Metals and Industry and Trade Cooperation, Ministry of Land and Natural Resources, General and Planning Department of Ministry of Labor and Social Security, Economic Planning Institute of Ministry of Railways, Analysis Research Centre of the Ministry of Machine-Building Industry, No. 710 Institute of Chinese General Company of Aeronautics Industry, Research Department of State Administration of Taxation, System Research Institution of State Commission of Science, Technology and Industry for National Defense, Economic Research Centre of Chinese Nuclear Industry, The Association of Chinese Industrial Economics, External Liaison Office of Beijing Municipal People's Government, Statistics Bureau of Beijing Municipal People's Government, Finance Bureau of Beijing Municipal People's Government, The Capital Research Insitute of Social and Economic Development, Beijing Institute of System Engineering Research, Information Centre of Shanghai Municipal People's Government, Information Centre of Tianjin Municipal People's Government, Tianjin Academy of Social Sciences, Business School of Jilin University, School of Economics and Management of Tsinghua University, Capital Economics and Trade University, Guanghua Institute of Management of Beijing University, People's University of China, Beijing Normal University, Northern Jiaotong University, Central Party Socialism Institute, Hefei Institute of Economics Technology, Development Department of the

convened by the research team since it was established in 1990.   It was attended by nearly 150 experts, scholars, and practitioners from various departments in the State Council, practical work units, research departments, and tertiary education institutions. The number of participants was the largest ever.   All the major news organizations in Beijing sent reporters to cover the forum.

Experts at the forum discussed the current economic situation and issues that needed to be addressed.   They also forecast economic developments in 1998–1999.   In particular, they discussed the problem of insufficient aggregate demand, its cause and background, and the various policy options.

For the first time, experts from the HKSAR also attended the forum.   They analyzed Hong Kong's current economic situation, and made forecasts for this year and the next.

North Star Group, Huayuan Group, National Telecommunications Development Co. Ltd., Research and Development Department of Shougang Corporation, Research Department of Chinese Agriculture Trust Company, Dingxin International Group, Shenzhen Research Institute of Comprehensive Development, Jilin Academy of Social Sciences, Henan Academy of Social Sciences, Development Centre of Hubei Provincial People's Government, Wuhan Academy of Social Sciences, Information Centre under the Planning Commission of Hebei Provincial People's Government, China National Radio Station, China Central Television, Beijing Television, *Qiushi* (Seeking Truth) Magazine Co., External Liaison Department of Xinhua News Agency, *Economic Reference Journal,* Theory Section of *People's Daily*, Economics Section of *Guangming Daily*,   Theory Section of *Beijing Daily, Chinese Financial Journal, Chinese Market Economics Journal,* Editorial Section of *China Daily*, Theory Section of *Economics Daily, Technology Daily, China Securities Journal,   China Reform Journal, Chinese Reform Magazine* Co., *China Commerce and Industry Daily, Securities Journal, Chinese Enterprise Journal, Chinese Assets News, Chinese Textiles Journal, Shenzhen Special Economic Zone Daily, Chinese Electricity Journal, Chinese and Overseas Information Weekly, Chinese Entrepreneur, Global News,* Theory Section of *People's Liberation Army News,* China News Agency, *Scientific Decision* Magazine Co., *Strategy and Management* Magazine Co., Various Related Institutes of the Chinese Academy of Social Sciences, Social Science Literature Publisher, and so on.

Current Economic Situation and Forecast for Economic Development in 1998–1999

Basic Assessment of the Current Economic Situation

Experts at the forum pointed out that both the domestic and international economic situations have become extremely complex since 1998. Domestically, China experienced the worst floods in a century. Internationally, Chinese exports were adversely affected by the Asian financial crisis. In the face of such serious problems, the central government implemented a series of measures to expand domestic demand, encourage investment, and stimulate economic growth. Consequently, in the second half of the year, the declining trend in economic growth was arrested. The economic situation recovered noticeably. However, this recovery remained hampered by a reduced level of aggregate demand. And this situation has yet to be completely reversed, as exemplified by the following:

(1) Experts pointed out that government investment in infrastructure and social welfare projects made up only a limited portion of the total fixed asset investment in the country. Thus, their short-term promotional effect on the economy was rather limited. However, when there is excess productivity in the country, the major market-driven private sector investors take a very cautious attitude in making further investments. Therefore, to a certain degree, the government is fighting the war by itself. Consequently, between January and August 1998, the fixed asset investment in state-owned units grew by 17.4% compared to the same period the previous year. In July and August in particular, growth rates stood at 22.9% and 26.9% respectively compared with the previous year. However, fixed asset investments from the non-government sectors, comprising 46% of the country's total assets, grew very slowly. The growth rate in the first half of the year was actually zero. Still, fixed asset investment for the entire year by the government sector is predicted to grow by 20%, while

the rate for the entire country will be about 15%, which is around 3% lower than the planned target.

(2) Experts believed that the two occasions when interest rates were lowered in 1998 were positive and instrumental in redistributing personal savings. In the first half of the year, personal savings grew by 0.4% compared with last year. However, because current personal income and expected future income is seen as declining, as expenses for housing, medical care, unemployment insurance, and education rise, the overall purchasing power of consumers has weakened. Between January and August 1998, the total retail sales in the country only grew by a nominal 7.3%. After adjustment for deflation, this amounts to a 10% increase compared with the same period last year, meaning the growth of total retail sales is too weak to power renewed economic growth.

(3) Total sales of production materials grew slowly, causing a sharp drop in the sector's overall growth rate. This was mainly due to the sluggish growth of domestic demand, and a sharp fall in exports. In the first half of the year, the total sales of nineteen major goods producers grew by only 0.9%. Although the growth rate started to recover in the third quarter, the aggregate number is still low. Predicted growth for the whole year is expected to be no more than 2%.

(4) Imbalance between supply and demand accelerated competition and led to the fall in prices. Between January and August, the retail price index fell by 5.5% relative to the same period last year, making this the third consecutive year of negative growth. The retail price index was also negative for most of the year, down by 2.4% between January and August compared to the same period a year earlier. It is expected that this will continue for the rest of the year, signaling mild deflation.

(5) Under the influence of these factors between January and August, total value-added industrial production grew by 7.8%

relative to the same period of last year. The growth rates for industries with different forms of ownership have all dropped to a certain degree, which is the main reason for the slowdown in the country's economic recovery.

Based on the above analysis, experts believe that realizing the 8% GDP growth target set at the beginning of the year will prove quite a difficult task.

Understanding the Economic Growth Rate in 1998

Experts agreed that the intensification of the Asian financial crisis, the sharp devaluation of the Japanese Yen, and the severe floods China was subject to were matters beyond our control. In this context, simply reaching a growth rate of 7% can be considered a significant achievement given that average GDP growth stands at only 2% in the global economy, with many countries now reporting negative growth.

They also believe that in terms of reaching the 8% growth target the question is not so much whether this can be accomplished, but whether it is really necessary. Therefore, we should consider an 8% growth target simply as part of the macroeconomic adjustment program.

First, we should clearly understand what an 8% growth rate means. GDP growth of 8% is not just a simple figure. Its real meaning is that, first, it should serve to quickly reverse the declining growth trend. Second, meeting this target helps to maintain the RMB exchange rate unchanged. Third, it helps limit increasing unemployment. So if these three goals are realized, emphasizing this growth target can be seen as valid.

We must respect objective economic laws, and not push too hard. Fixed asset investment works in its own way. The process, from preparation to completion of a project, needs scientific programming. Therefore, there must be a time lag between the investment and its effect on economic growth. If no effect on economic growth is apparent at the moment, and we jump to the conclusion that investment strength is insufficient and rush to expand the scale of investment, we will end up negatively impacting the quality of our economic growth.

We must also avoid the unnecessary economic swings caused by the blind pursuit of speed. To reach the 8% target, we will have to yield 10% GDP growth in the fourth quarter. Although this is possible, in doing so we can easily push the economy, which is just starting to recover, into an overheated one. Then, we would have to impose austerity measures to cool the economy down again, damaging economic growth in 1999 and 2000. Therefore, a prudent focus on the degree of investment expansion is key.

Forecast of Economic Development in 1998–1999

It is stressed that our economic growth rate should be mainly determined by the macroeconomic adjustment program, whether this refers to the fourth quarter of 1998 or 1999. Depending upon the different policy suggestions, the forecasts of economic development in 1998–99 are different.

Some experts predicted that China's 1998 GDP growth rate would be in the range of 7.5–8.2%. The majority estimated about 7.7%. Some experts predicted that the 1999 GDP growth rate would be about 7–9.1%, with most estimates pegged at about 8.5%. Specific predictions in terms of major economic indicators are detailed in Table 1.

How to Understand the Current Insufficient Demand?

Consensus was reached at the forum on the issue of there being insufficient effective demand. However, opinions differed in understanding the background and causes of this insufficiency as well as appropriate policy solutions. These various opinions can be summarized into two groups.

According to one group, the underlying reason for insufficient effective demand lies with the problem of the quantity and structure of product, which is caused by the mismatch of the production and demand structures. This problem has grown out of the tremendous changes, still ongoing, within the economic environment generally.

Table 1
Forecast of Major Economic Indicators in 1998 and 1999

Item	1998	1999
GDP growth rate (%)	7.5-8.2	7.0-9.1
Of which: Primary industry (%)	3.2-3.5	3.0-4.7
Secondary industry (%)	9.0-9.2	8.5-10.5
Industry (%)	9.0-9.5	9.0-10.7
Tertiary industry(%)	8.0-8.5	8.5-10.5
Scale of fixed asset investment (RMB billion)	2,875-2,987.9	3,259-3,462
Real growth rate (%)	14.5-18.1	10-20
Total retail sales (RMB billion)	2,926-2,930	3,160-3,328
Real growth rate (%)	8.7-12	8-14.1
Retail price index growth rate (%)	-3-1.2	1.7-3.1
Consumer price index growth rate (%)	0.7-1.0	2.5-4.2
Fiscal revenue (RMB billion)	944-1,005	1,035-1,168
Growth rate (%)	9.1-16.2	11.0-16.2
Fiscal expenditure (RMB billion)	1,066-1,102	1,133-1,268
Growth rate (%)	15.4-19.3	12.6-15.2
Total value imports (US$ billion)	144-152.5	150-170
Growth rate (%)	1.1-7.1	2.3-11.5
Total value exports (US$ billion)	188.1-194	184-206.5
Growth rate (%)	3-6	-5-7

Those holding this opinion believe that in China the era of shortage and quantitative expansion has already ended. The economy is entering into a new buyers' market phase, characterized by its emphasis on quality improvement. Thus, as this fundamental shift takes place, economic growth will inevitably slow down.

Within the above scenario, the demand for traditional consumer goods has already been saturated, meaning production of traditional goods is now generally in excess of demand. Consequently, to expand demand, and thereby to stimulate the economy and increase the growth rate, can only be done through an adjustment of industrial and product structures.

As far as macroeconomic policy is concerned, those sharing this view suggested that China should implement an active and stable macroeconomic policy. Setting a goal for the appropriate economic growth rate is not enough, in their view. Rather we must exert the appropriate pressure on structural adjustments as well.

The opinions held by another group likewise admitted the structural problems. However, pointing to the fact that the supply of many products is in excess, they believe that insufficient demand is the crux of the problem. And with insufficient aggregate demand, structural adjustments of industries and products lose their context, with the result that the structural adjustment process is hindered. Some experts go so far as to say that it is an economic paradox to insist on initiating and promoting new economic growth on the supply side by way of improving product structure, when aggregate demand is insufficient.

According to them, China is at the beginning of the intermediate phase of industrialization. The experience of other countries suggests that the period of high economic growth will last for quite a long time. The actuality, however, is that our GDP on a per capita basis still lags far behind those in the developed countries. Disparities between urban and rural areas, between the coastal regions and the central and western regions, are still very large. Most durable consumer goods considered to be ordinary daily necessities for urban households are taken as luxury items in rural areas. The potential demand for these products is enormous.

Even among urban residents, with their basic needs now met, traveling and living conditions still have much need for improvement. These experts believe that the potential for economic growth is the same and will remain the same for at least the next 5–10 years. Thus, maintaining the growth rate at 8–9% is quite possible. Some even say that since our GDP growth rate in recent years has remained at 9% while inflation has dropped, the potential growth rate is actually more like 10% in real terms.

This body of opinion holds that it is enough to say that because traditional consumer markets are saturated, production is in excess on the supply side. They argue that in China, weak demand is caused by insufficient consumer demand, and that this insufficient consumer demand is a result of the growth of personal income having lagged behind GDP growth for some time.

According to statistics, compared with other periods in the past, the "reform and opening up" period is one in which the rise in household income and consumer spending reaches its height. However, compared to periods since the beginning of the reforms, the growth in consumer spending and household income has lagged behind economic growth as a whole for years. Between 1986 and 1997, the average annual GDP growth rate was 9.8%, while the corresponding growth rate for consumer spending was 8.2%. Even calculated on the basis of constant prices, the final consumption rate went down from the average 65.9% during the "Sixth Five-year Plan" to 54.8% in 1997. The growth in household income during the same period also fell behind the average GDP growth rate. The average real growth in personal income was 4.2%. Based on a constant price calculation, the average household income as a percentage of the average GDP fell from 57.7% in 1985 to 45.5% in 1997.

Meanwhile, reforms in education, housing, medical care, and social welfare not only cancel out the increase in personal income, but seriously affect consumers' psychological expectations for future consumption, thus intensifying the present problem of insufficient demand.

From this analysis, another scenario results: on the one hand, our country's economic strength continues to expand. For example, our iron and steel production capacity reaches 150 million tons, but the actual yield is only 100 million tons. On the other hand, the majority of urban and rural residents still live at a very low living standard in terms of consumption. The number of impoverished in the overall population amounts to tens of millions.

To summarize what they are stressing, namely is the institutional background behind the actual situation. That is, on the one hand, our economy is highly market driven. The allocation of resources has undergone fundamental changes. On the other hand, the structure of a socialist market economy has not been completely established. Unchecked distribution hinders effective interaction between the supply and demand sides. This interferes with the beneficial spiral of production, distribution, circulation, and consumption. The change in the relationship between "consumption and accumulation" is nothing but a symptom of GDP distribution reflecting this covert conflict. Thus, prior to a viable distribution mechanism of the socialist market economy type becoming properly established, these problems can only be solved through a macroeconomic adjustment program launched by the government.

Some Suggestions on the Macroeconomic Adjustment Program

The participants of the forum believed that the trend of economic growth in 1999 would depend on the implementation and strength of the macroeconomic adjustment program. With their serious concerns about this program, they examined in detail the actual implementation of the macroeconomic adjustment program in 1998. Policy options and the coordination between fiscal and monetary measures were also discussed for 1999 and later years. They proposed many new ideas; they discussed fiscal and monetary policy as means to regulate demand, and the adaptation of both in expanding domestic demand; and they examined these issues in the context of the orientation of these fundamental policies. Since these are such important issues, the following discussions will specifically address them.

Basic Orientation of the Macroeconomic Adjustment Program and Specific Policy Suggestions

Expand Both Domestic and External Demands, but with Emphasis on the Domestic Side

As predicted by the experts, the 1999 global economy will be about the same as in 1998, maybe slightly better. It will be difficult to enhance growth in global trade, and even more uncertainties are likely to abound. Economic policy for 1999, therefore, must be made taking into full consideration these adverse conditions in terms of the world economy. The emphasis should be put on expanding domestic demand while trying by every possible means to increase exports.

Associate an Increase in Investment with an Increase in Ultimate Consumption

It was believed that increasing consumer demand was the key to overcoming the problem of insufficient effective demand. The current trend of neglecting consumer demand should be corrected and a new process promoted in which an increase in consumer demand is associated with the stimulation of investment demand. Specific policy suggestions were offered in the following areas:

(1) In the areas of reforms in housing, elderly care, medical care, and education, while expanding consumer spending, detailed plans must be made quickly, with clear aims and enough transparency to boost consumer confidence, and to stabilize their expectations for the future.

(2) Active rural market development, with specific improvements in the circulation of agricultural products. Also improvements in the rural consumer environment through infrastructure investment.

(3) The income of laid-off workers, the unemployed, and farmers should be improved by providing them with jobs rather than welfare. The unpaid salaries, retirement benefits, and medical benefits owed to teachers and other workers should also be paid, along with outstanding "white slips."

(4) When it is difficult to increase the income of employees and farmers by expanding the consumer market, we can increase our fiscal expenditures. These monies can be used to raise the income of people working in educational, medical, and governmental institutions to stimulate consumption, the market, and ultimately economic growth.

Continue to Maintain a Stable RMB–U.S. Dollar Exchange Rate

The following explanations were offered on the feasibility and the necessity of maintaining the value of RMB.

(1) In 1998, prices fell continuously, which meant that the purchasing power of the RMB rose.

(2) China has managed to maintain its trade surplus for several consecutive years. The foreign exchange reserve exceeded US$140 billion. Between January and August 1998, the growth rate of exports fell sharply, but the trade surplus remained at US$31.38 billion.

(3) For a big country like China, an export rate of 20% is not low by any standard. There is no reason for us to rely too heavily on exports to stimulate the economy. Furthermore, the short-term benefits from devaluation such as stimulating exports will

be very small. Devaluation is detrimental to the people's expectation of a stable RMB exchange rate.

(4)   Devaluation is not favorable to the stability of the Hong Kong dollar.   Experts also pointed out that keeping the RMB stable should be made conditional, and that China would benefit by requesting the cooperation of the international community in maintaining its RMB policy.

About the Price Policy

Some believed that the prices should be allowed to rise to a certain extent, which would benefit our current situation, especially in writing off the non-performing assets in the financial system. They suggested that we should allow the retail prices to rise by 4– 6% per annum.

Others argued that although we were in a state of mild deflation, we should not carry out a "mild inflationary" policy, but should insist on a policy of basic price stability.   This policy will help to stabilize people's confidence in the current economy and the future.   This is beneficial to the advances in technology, the suppression of excessive speculation, the amelioration of distorted allocation, and also provides good conditions for structural adjustment and the deepening of institutional reform of the economy.

The Choice of Policy Measures and Related Policy Suggestions

How to coordinate fiscal and monetary policies in the process of expanding domestic demand was a hot topic at the forum and diverse opinions were expressed.   On the basis of an overall analysis of the real effect of monetary policies in recent years, some suggested that, while attention should be given to the functions of monetary policies, the particular importance of an active fiscal policy in the process of expanding domestic demand should also be stressed. They also offered some systematic suggestions on how to make use of fiscal policies. Suggestions were also made on what would be the pitfalls of employing an active fiscal policy.

Assessment and Analysis of the Effect of Monetary Policies

The outcome of monetary policies up to 1996 was not so appealing even though big changes took place in the direction and strength of monetary policies. The growth rates of M_0, M_1, and M_2 in the first half of 1998 were 6.6%, 6.7%, and 14%, respectively, which were far below the targeted growth rate of monetary supply set by the Central Bank at the beginning of 1998. They actually dropped to the lowest point in the past two years. Meanwhile, the growth of loans slowed down. In the first half of the year, only 7.5% of the tasks in the new lending plan were accomplished, although in the second half of the year, the speed of lending accelerated. What was accomplished in the first half of the year made up only 1/3 of the task of the entire year.

The following explanations were offered for the "ineffectiveness of monetary policies" as described above.

First of all, with the deepened reform, the self-constraining mechanisms of banks and enterprises became effective. Therefore, we witnessed the phenomenon of banks "refraining from lending" and enterprises "refraining from borrowing."

Second, the mechanism for smoothly carrying out monetary policies was not yet in place. For example, it was very hard for monetary policies to affect all the sectors in the national economy since there was deviance between capital supply structure and capital demand structure. The problem was further aggravated by a blockage of capital circulation among financial institutions, financial markets, and between financial institutions and financial markets. The expected effects of monetary policies were thus diminished.

Third, we are not able to stimulate consumer demand, upgrade our technology, and undertake industralization through a large-scale boosting of consumer credit, because the appropriate financial instruments, financial market, and financial structure are not ready yet.

Fourth, the last several years have seen a steady drop in the money supply, but a gradual rise in the ratio between M_2 and the GDP.   This should alert policy makers to be cautious about making policies to stimulate the economy.   The decision makers should constrain the growth rate in monetary supply as a long-term policy objective.

It followed from what had been discussed above that equal attention should also be given to the special importance of fiscal policies in terms of expanding domestic demand.   The following suggestions were offered.

Suggestions of Fiscal Policies for the Expansion of Domestic Demand

(1) Expand state disposable financial resources as quickly as possible and increase the ability to expand domestic demand through fiscal means.   To achieve these objectives, we must, first of all, vigorously institutionalize off-budget income and expenditure.   We must reform the system of taxation.   The current problem of excessively dispersed distribution of fiscal resources must be changed as soon as possible.   Second, we need to gradually establish fiscal and capital raising systems which are suitable for China.   We must dissolve the conflict between the requirement for fiscal investment and the supply of capital by making institutional changes.   Third, we must improve the system of taxation and its administration.

(2) Improve and optimize the structure of fiscal expenditure and set new standards for fiscal expenditure.   The key point of this policy is to define and regulate the domain of expenditure so

that we will free the nation's finance from it functional conflict of being either "exceeding authorities" or "lacking authorities."

(3) We must implement an active, flexible, and prudent policy for national debt. To solve these presently urgent problems, we should transfer the sale of treasury bonds to financial organizations. In this way, we would enormously increase the amount of treasury bonds by many trillions of yuan. We do not even have to bother about repayment problems. A new era for national debt policy will arrive.

(4) We should seriously implement the task to reduce debts so as to encourage enterprises to invest and consumers to spend.

(5) We should fully utilize the leverage effect of fiscal policy in guiding and stimulating the expansion of demand.

Issues Related to Carrying out a More Active Fiscal Policy

The participants reached a consensus that we should implement a more active fiscal policy. However, some experts warned about the limitation of expansionary fiscal policy and its possible negative effects.

First, deficit budget financing can only be used when there are large quantities of unemployed resources and only for a short period of time. Otherwise, serious inflation and stagflation will appear.

Second, an expansionary fiscal policy should not squeeze out the demand for credit expansion.

Third, it was emphasized that China was different from Japan. We had not fallen into a "liquidity trap." Therefore, we could not utilize U.S. economist Paul Krugman's prescription for dealing with this condition. Under the current effort to stimulate economic growth, we should adopt both fiscal policy and monetary policy, and we should implement both with the right timing and in an appropriate way.

WARNING: A DEEP RECESSION COULD TRIGGER A FINANCIAL CRISIS

ZHOU TIANYONG
Economics Research Centre, the Central Party School

It should be noted that a deep recession will trigger a financial crisis in a country with a high debt ratio like China's. For enterprises with a low debt ratio, in time of economic recession when prices fall and sales shrink, the pressure on repayment of principal and interest is low. Enterprises may tide over their difficulties with their own capital and absorb the losses with their equity. That is not the case when enterprises have a high debt ratio. In our country, the debt ratio of enterprises amounts to over 85%, if we exclude the income of land sales, unrecoverable loans, non-performing assets, written-off and money-losing investments, and non-productive assets. In times of economic recession with prices dropping and sales shrinking, these enterprises will have difficulty repaying the principal and interest on time. Debt crisis will occur between enterprises and banks. Since these enterprises do not possess the rights and interests of ownership, they cannot write off their debts. The debts then will eventually become non-performing assets for banks and the financial system.

Recession starts with low prices, low growth rates, and an increase in unemployment. If recession deepens in a country with a high level of debts, then the debt crisis will become even worse. Although economic growth may further slow down and unemployment may further increase, the negative growth in prices will cause banks to accumulate more non-performing assets. The previous bad debts cannot be written off by inflationary means. The accumulation of bad debts may explode into a sudden financial crisis. At a time like that, prices will suddenly rise sharply. We hope this will not happen to China.

FORECAST

ANALYSIS OF THE CURRENT TREND IN CHINA'S ECONOMIC DEVELOPMENT: 1998–1999

LI JINGWEN AND ZHU YUNFA

Institute of Quantitative and Technical Economics
Chinese Academy of Social Sciences

The Background

In 1997, China achieved phenomenal results in her economic development.   Thanks to the successful "soft landing" in 1996, the real growth rate of China's GDP was 8.8%, nearly reaching the potential economic growth rate of 9% to 10%.   Retail prices and consumer prices rose by 0.8% and 2.8% respectively, considerably lower than the 6.1% and 8.3% inflation rates prevailing in 1996. As a result, high economic growth co-existed with low inflation.

In 1998, China's economic development faced serious challenges both domestically and externally.   First, the Southeast Asian financial crisis spread throughout most of East Asia, and thence to Latin America and finally Russia.   This constituted a great challenge to the stability of China's economic development. Second, the midstream and downstream portions of the Yangtze River and the Northeast were hit by heavy floods, which also inflicted serious damage on the economy.   Furthermore, China faced two urgent and ongoing tasks: reform and development.

The basic solution to these old and new institutional problems depends on the conscientiousness we apply in addressing them.   At the same time, our economic development has been — and remains — under pressure from insufficient domestic demand. Thus the task of reform and development has become increasingly challenging.

To cope with the situation, the central government has adopted a series of measures.   First, they have tried to stimulate economic growth through expanding domestic demand.   At the beginning of 1998, the Ministry of Finance decided to issue another RMB280 bn worth of treasury bonds for more investment in infrastructure. On March 25, the People's Bank of China lowered their deposit and lending rates for the fourth time. In 1998, the government injected another RMB250 bn of capital funds into four of the country's biggest national commercial banks, enabling them to increase credit lines. In September, the central government decided to increase the issue of treasury bonds by RMB100 bn to raise funds for infrastructure development in areas such as agriculture, forestry, irrigation, and transportation. Second, the pace of reform for the development of the socialist market economy was accelerated. This was in line with Premier Zhu's speech at the First Plenary Session of the Ninth National People's Congress. In essence, he said that before the end of this century, we must complete three major reforms: of government organizations, state-owned enterprises, and the financial system; only then would the basic system of the socialist market economy be firmly established.

Looking forward, we firmly believe that we have laid a firm foundation for the 1999 economy to foster its growth at a faster rate, and are highly optimistic that we will be able to reach the basic economic targets set at the beginning of the year, despite these unforeseen economic challenges.

Judgment and Analysis of the Trend in China's Economic Development

1998 and 1999 are the last two years in the present century. They are also the two years which form the junction of past achievements and new expectations crucial to our economic development. We have been facing the two difficult and urgent tasks of reform and development, and an ever changing international economic situation. With so many uncertainties, ascertaining whether the trend of our economic development is going up or down becomes crucial and difficult. To answer this perplexing question accurately, with regard to the validity of current economic practices, we have employed a quantitative analysis and explored two different scenarios and their feasibilities.

The Optimistic Scenario

The basic assumptions of the optimistic scenario are: despite the Southeast Asian financial crisis and its spreading adverse effects, there will be no sharp fall in foreign direct investment. Growth in international trade will be maintained to a certain degree. The government's increased commitment in budgeted fixed asset investment will achieve desirable results. So it follows that:

(1) In 1998 and 1999, the Chinese economy will continue to experience a stable growth. Real GDP growth rate is expected to be 8.1% and 9.0% respectively, without marked fluctuations. The inflation rate in terms of retail prices should be between -1% and 2%. The regional financial crises have certainly triggered a drop in foreign direct investment. Competition in the export market has intensified, and policy adjustment has slowed down. As a result, the 1998 GDP growth rate was lower than that in 1997.

In 1999, however, the policy adjustment program is expected to bear fruit. The rate of economic growth in 1999 will once again approach its potential. Real GDP growth will be slightly higher than that in 1997 and 1998.

On the whole, China's economy can be characterized as one of "relatively high growth with low inflation." There are several stimulating factors at play: First, there is the effect of a further emancipation of thought after the 15th Party Congress. The reform and opening up has entered a new climactic phase.

In particular, at the 15th Party Congress, the question of forms of ownership was raised. Accordingly, any form of ownership that fits the criteria of "three beneficiaries" can be and should be adopted for the benefit of socialism. The organization of the ownership structure, and the diversification of the state ownership structure amount to the greatest emancipation of thought since the 1980s, and Comrade Deng Xiaoping's speeches during his Southern Tour in 1992.

Second, since there is not much room for a further rise in commodity prices, and since the government has reduced interest rates, the real interest rate will stop rising and begin to fall. In addition, since January 1, 1998, the government has canceled the rigid credit quota restriction imposed on the national commercial banks, turning to a more flexible management of the asset-liability ratio. This will increase the banks' credibility. All of this shows that the government has become substantially more capable of managing the macroeconomy, therefore having a stimulating effect on the country's economic development.

Third, in 1997, the growth in money supply M_0 and M_1 was accelerated. The circulation rate of money supply was also accelerated. Moreover, the supply of capital to enterprises was abundant. As well, the speedy development of markets for stocks, bonds, and other securities has enabled enterprises to easily raise the capital necessary for development. This, in turn, has helped to ease the tension between supply and demand for capital.

There are still factors within the national economy which hinder a fundamental increase in economic growth, however: First, in the process of enterprise reform, the friction between the different systems, the alteration of the developmental tracks, and the process of the reform of the government structure have intensified the problem of unemployment. As a result, the urban unemployment rate will rise, and the transformation of excess rural labor will be slow. Second, the Southeast Asian financial crisis and the devaluation of the Southeast Asian currencies and the Japanese Yen will weaken China's competitiveness in export markets and will detract from the country's appeal as a foreign investment destination.

The multiplier effect caused by these foreign direct investment and export negatives have a direct bearing on China's slowing economic growth, and will hinder the country's economic development. Because of these two negative factors, we believe that the 1998 and 1999 growth rate will be below the country's potential of about 9.5%. Compared with 1997, and taking into consideration the stimulating and hindering factors cited above, we postulate that the hindering effects were predominant in 1998, whereas in 1999, the reverse began to be true. Moreover, the central government's ability to exercise macroeconomic control is being greatly strengthened. No large fluctuations are predicted in the macroeconomy. Therefore, China's 1998 economic growth rate will be slightly lower than that in 1997, while the 1999 growth rate will be higher than that in 1997 and 1998.

(2) The import growth rate will accelerate as the export growth rate slows. However, a trade surplus will be maintained, and the RMB exchange rate will remain stable. The trade surpluses for 1998 and 1999 are expected to be US$40 bn and US$30 billion, respectively. Taking into consideration the trade in services and the influence of international factors, the balance of payments will be maintained for the current account. The surplus in capital account will help to increase foreign exchange reserves. The major causes for the increase in import growth and the decrease in export growth are the lowering of import tariffs, the negative effect of the Southeast Asian financial crisis, and the increase in domestic demand.

(3) The growth in domestic demand, such as fixed asset investment and consumer demand, will remain stable. Because the import growth rate has increased and the export growth rate has decreased, the contribution of net exports to the increase in GDP will be 0 in 1998, and negative in 1999. Investment and consumption will be the two main driving forces for GDP growth. In 1998 and 1999, the real growth rates for fixed asset investment will be 8.5% and 12% respectively, and 8.5% and 9.5% for retail sales respectively, both higher than the

growth rate of 8.1% and 9% for GDP in the same years. However, the problem of excessive inventory will remain prominent.   It is estimated that the total value of current inventory in the country is about RMB 3,000 billion, which constitutes about 44% of GDP in 1996.   Even with a new push for economic growth, a round of the strengthening of the market mechanism and the pressure of excessive inventory will keep China's economic growth below the double digit level of 1992–95.

Looking at the majority of the fixed asset investment, we find that the most prominent changes since the 1990s are: the proportion of government-budgeted fixed asset investment has been reduced, while the proportion of foreign direct fixed asset investment has expanded.   The relative weight of government investment fell.   The share of domestic enterprise capital and the capital raised in capital markets has risen.   This amounts to more than half of the fixed asset investment in the country. As of 1998, China's economic development has entered a new and important phase.   Domestic economic development will rely increasingly on domestic demand, while investment capital will increasingly be drawn from major sources of domestic funds.   In 1998 and 1999, a key element in the optimistic scenario is the assumption that the investment cited in the national budget can successfully offset the negative effect caused by the slackening inflow of foreign investment and more intense foreign competition.   However, longer term development will depend on the establishment of a well-operated capital market and the refinement of the ownership system.

Table 1
The Proportion of the Main Types of Fixed Asset Investment

(unit: %)

	1990	1991	1992	1993	1994	1995	1996	1997
Budgeted capital	8.7	6.6	4.3	3.7	3.2	3.1	2.7	2.6
Bank loans	19.6	23.5	27.4	23.5	22.6	19.9	21.0	21.5
Foreign direct investment	6.2	5.7	5.8	7.3	10.8	11.5	12.0	12.2
Capital raised by enterprises	65.5	64.2	62.5	65.5	63.4	65.5	64.3	63.7

Source: *China Statistical Yearbook 1997.*

(4)   Depending on the growth rates in different production sectors over the next two years, the growth of agriculture and tertiary industry will accelerate.   That is mainly because the growth of the rate of investment in the early stage in basic industries (such as agriculture), and basic facilities and infrastructure (such as telecommunications) is higher.   Facing the problems of creating a new focus for growth, while developing new and better industries able to compete internationally, industrial development will slow down.

Currently, the speed of industrial growth depends on the demand both in the domestic market and the international market, the comparative advantage of China in international markets, and the speed of reforms.   From the point of view of the ownership structure, the source of Chinese economic growth will still be mainly from the non–state–owned enterprises.

Since the beginning of the reforms and opening up, China has achieved high economic growth.   The reason for this growth is that the planned economy, as represented mainly by the state-owned enterprises, only involves and employs less than 20% of the population and the labor force. As a result, the non–state-owned enterprises have grown rapidly.   In the 1990s, the disparity in growth rates between the state-owned and non–state-owned enterprises has increased.

Let us look at the industrial sector as an example: Between 1990 and 1997, the average annual growth rate of state-owned industrial enterprises was 6.8%, while the collective and other industrial enterprises managed to grow at 21.1% and 44% respectively.   In 1997, the proportion of state-owned enterprises in industry as a whole was 27.2%; collective and other enterprises made up 41.6% and 31.2% respectively, as shown in Table 2.   Now the main body of the national economy consists of the non–state-owned enterprises.   In 1998 and 1999, the state-owned enterprises will enter into a very difficult stage of reform and reorganization; China's economic growth will increasingly depend on the development of non–state enterprises.

Table 2
The Means of Ownership with Respect to Industrial Enterprises

(Unit: %)

	1990	1991	1992	1993	1994	1995	1996	1997
Growth rate: State-owned	3.0	8.6	12.4	5.7	6.5	8.2	5.1	6.4
Collective	9.0	18.4	33.3	35.0	24.9	15.2	20.9	15.2
Others	30.2	37.7	55.9	79.4	65.3	44.4	22.4	18.3
Proportion: State-owned	54.6	56.2	51.5	47.0	37.3	34.0	28.5	26.5
Collective	35.6	33.0	35.1	34.2	37.7	36.6	39.4	40.5
Others	9.8	10.8	13.4	18.8	25.0	29.4	32.1	33.0

Source: *China Statistics Abstract 1998.*

The Pessimistic Scenario

The main assumption underlying this pessimistic scenario is that the negative effects from the Southeast Asian financial crisis, among other things, will cause negative growth in foreign direct investment.   Since the growth in fiscal income is limited, and the efficacy of the government's expansion of budgeted investment in fixed assets is weak, we believe that China's economic development will display the following characteristics:

(1) The 1998 and 1999 GDP growth rates could be 6.5% and 7% respectively. In this pessimistic scenario, export demand will fall sharply due to the negative effects of the Southeast Asian financial crisis plus the friction and adjustment created by the reform of the state-owned enterprises and government structures. Foreign direct investment, as a major source of fixed asset investment, will also go into a steep decline. At the same time, the expansion of government investment in infrastructure will not be able to effectively counteract these negatives. On the whole, growth of demand for investment and for exports will fall sharply, having a "multiplier effect" on GDP growth, and ultimately setting a new benchmark for economic expansion substantially below its potential.

(2) In 1997, the actual utilization of foreign direct investment increased by 15.7% from the previous year. However, the foreign direct investment actually committed fell by 24.2% from the previous year. In addition, the adverse effects of the Southeast Asian financial crisis created a new and more cautious attitude among foreign investors. This has resulted in change in the direction of their investments and withdrawal of previous commitments. Consequently, the amount of fixed asset investment by foreign investors will decline by 10% and 5% in 1998 and 1999 respectively. In this case, even if we make the necessary policy adjustments, the growth in government-budgeted investment will not compensate for the loss of these funds. Furthermore, as the banking and financial sector has yet to be adequately developed and is in need of further adjustment, investment through bank credits will not grow fast. With respect to investment through the various non–state-owned enterprises raising capital by themselves, since they will be busy with reforming or reorganizing their stocks, their demand for fixed asset investment will in any case not be high. In fact, it is estimated that this combination of factors will lower fixed asset investment from 8.3% in 1997 to 5.5% in 1998 and 6.5% in 1999. This dropped demand and the intensive competition from foreign markets will shave GDP

growth to 6.5% and 7.0%, and consumer demand to 7% and 7.5% in 1998 and 1999 respectively.

(3)   The contraction in China's domestic market, and the intensive competition internationally, will cause the growth rate in international trade to fall sharply.   However, the trade surplus will be basically maintained.

(4)   This process of market contraction and structural adjustment will make the employment situation even worse.   The effect of the redeployment project will be adversely affected. Personal income will only show a slight increase.   Given such a scenario, the transfer of the excess rural labor force, and the redeployment of redundant urban workers, will suffer greatly. These negative events will in turn affect the economic growth and the process of reform.   A vicious cycle will thus be formed.   We must work hard to prevent this situation from taking place.

A Comparison of the Two Scenarios

The major difference between these two scenarios lies in the assumptions on budgeted fixed asset investment and foreign direct investment.   In the optimistic scenario, there is a greater increase in the budgeted fixed asset investment.   This would offset the deviation of the actual economic growth rate from the potential alternative, which is a possible result of the fall in the growth rate of foreign direct investment.   Also, foreign direct investment may not decrease and may indeed enjoy slow growth.

It follows from the above two assumptions that although the rate of economic growth will continue to go down and deviate from the potential growth rate, it will still be maintained at a relatively high speed.   For instance, in 1998 and 1999, the real growth rate of GDP will be 8.1% and 9.0% respectively, with the 1999 rate higher than the previous year.   In the pessimistic scenario, the fall in foreign direct investment will be sharper.   Although the increase in budgeted investment will accelerate, it will fail to counteract the effects of the decrease in foreign direct investment. As a result, we will experience a decline in our economy, and a great deviation from the potential economic growth rate. The real growth rates of GDP in 1998 and 1999 will be 6.5% and 7.0% respectively. The growth rate in 1999 will be lower than that in 1998. The economy will appear to be in a state of recession.

Which scenario is more likely to reflect the reality?

First, we must examine the assumptions for budgeted fixed asset investment. The government has undertaken firm measures to expand domestic demand. For example, the Finance Ministry has decided to issue another RMB280 bn worth of treasury bonds in 1998, an increase of 16.6% from last year. Most of the funds raised in this sale will be used in infrastructure construction. Then, an additional RMB100 bn of special treasury bonds will be issued for specially earmarked infrastructure projects in agriculture, forestry, irrigation, and transportation. We can predict with confidence that in 1998 and 1999, the budgeted fixed asset investment will increase at a faster rate. The assumption for the fixed asset investment in the optimistic scenario appears to be more feasible.

Let us also consider the assumptions for foreign direct investment. The basis for the pessimistic scenario is that although the actual foreign direct investment in 1997 was 15.7% higher than that in the previous year, the committed foreign direct investment fell by 24.2% from the previous year.

Under normal circumstances, the previous year's committed foreign direct investment that has not yet been realized may be realized in the following year. Therefore, in the pessimistic scenario, it is assumed that foreign direct investment will fall sharply. However, when we examine the actual situation of China's economic development in the past years, committed foreign direct investment reached a peak in 1993 at US$123.2 billion. Between 1994 and 1996, the committed foreign direct investment compared with the year before was showing a sharp decline, falling by 23.9%

in 1994, but rising by 10.1% in 1995, and falling again by 20.9% in 1996. The actual foreign direct investments made in the subsequent years all increased sharply, by 11.3%, 13.9%, and 15.7% from 1995 to 1997. This is because the percentage of the committed investment turning into actual investment rose.

Conclusively, although committed foreign direct investment fell sharply in 1997 relative to 1996, the actual amount of foreign investment in 1998 and 1999 will increase, though at a slower rate, after taking into consideration the general trend of economic development in China over the past few years. Therefore, the chance of the pessimistic scenario being accurate in terms of foreign direct investment is also slim. However, taking into consideration the effect of the Southeast Asian financial crisis, even in the optimistic scenario, what we are cautiously estimating is a slight increase of foreign direct investment.

Based on the above analysis of the assumptions of the two simulation models, the likelihood of the optimistic scenario is higher than that of the pessimistic one.

Policy Suggestions

On formulating macroeconomic policies, we should place full employment at the top of the agenda.

The employment index is easier to judge than the rate of economic growth. The rise in unemployment rates indicates that economic growth may be lower than the potential growth rate, and vice versa. From the long-term point of view, full employment is always in line with stable economic growth and stable prices. Reaching the goal of full employment will guarantee the full utilization of our manpower resources, and the maintenance of stable macroeconomic growth.

In terms of execution of the macroeconomic policies, we should attend to matching fiscal and monetary policies.

The current expansionary fiscal policy should go hand in hand with a cautious monetary policy. We should stimulate economic growth on the one hand, and suppress the upsurge in prices on the other, so as to facilitate stable development of the macroeconomy.

In the area of increasing commitment in investment, we should encourage more direct financing.

For example, we should encourage enterprises to be listed or to sell bonds in the market so as to effectively raise capital and avoid financial crisis. At the same time, this can help the development of capital markets and the reform of the enterprise system. We must prevent the emergence of new bad debts in banks, especially the national banks, which will disrupt the reform of the banking sector. We should continue to push financial reform forward, and refine our financial system, by studying and analyzing the causes of the Asian financial crisis, and in particular the lessons to be learned regarding the unsound practices of banks.

AN ANALYSIS OF THE 1998 ECONOMIC SITUATION AND PROSPECTS FOR 1999 ECONOMIC GROWTH

LI SHANTONG, HOU YONGZHI, AND ZHAI FAN
Development Research Centre
State Council

A Basic Analysis of the 1998 Economic Situation

The Chinese economy went through two stages in 1998. First was the stage of deepening deflation from January to June. In this stage, the economic growth rate continued to decline, following the consecutive declining of the previous years. Prices also showed negative growth. The GDP growth in the first quarter grew by 7.2%, compared with the same period of the previous year. The growth rates for primary, secondary, and tertiary industries were 4%, 7.8%, and by 7% respectively. Retail prices declined by 1.5% from the previous year and consumer prices rose by 0.3%. The GDP in the first half of the year rose by 7%. The growth rate of primary industry was 2.2%; while secondary and tertiary industry grew by 7.8% and 7.2% respectively. Retail prices declined by 2.1% and consumer prices declined by 0.3%.

After July 1998, the economy went into a stage of an alleviated deflation. In July, the value-added industrial production increased by 7.6%, compared with the same period of the previous year. In August, the value-added industrial production increased by 7.9%. The retail price index also rose slightly.

The economic growth in 1998 encountered unprecedented internal and external difficulties.

Starting from the second half of 1997, the Asian financial crisis, rather than being overcome, deepened. The joint intervention in the exchange rate of the Japanese currency by the United States and Japan produced only a limited effect and the Yen continued to devalue sharply. The measures employed by the Japanese

Government to lift up its economy proved ineffective and the Japanese economy proved too weak to recover. Under these circumstances, China's exports to East Asia suffered enormously, resulting in a negative growth rate.

In summer 1998, China was hit by severe floods which were rarely encountered in history. The floods caused direct economic losses of RMB166.6 billion. The floods not only caused enormous damage to people's wealth, but also lowered our productivity to a certain extent. This lowered consumer purchasing power and had a negative impact on economic growth.

It has been argued that reconstruction in the aftermath of the floods would increase demand for building materials, in turn helping to stimulate economic growth. However, this demand should not be overestimated. The demand for building materials will only increase if the government undertakes serious reconstruction.

In 1997, some signs of deflation had already begun to appear. Thus, in the second half of 1997, the government deployed some measures to boost the economy. In the first half of 1998, more active measures were undertaken to stimulate economic growth. These covered the following areas:

To increase the rates of export tax rebate. The rates of export tax rebate for five industries, textile machinery, shipping, coal, steel, and cement, were raised about 2%.

To expand investment scale and strengthen infrastructure construction. In February, 1998, the government decided to increase its investment in infrastructure to over RMB1,000 billion, among which, the investment in railways increased to RMB45 billion, and the investment in highways expanded to RMB180 billion.

To appropriately loosen fiscal policy and increase the amount of treasury bonds. The amount of treasury bonds issued in the first half of 1998 was RMB232.36 billion, up 30% on the same period the previous year.

To appropriately loosen monetary policy and lower the investment interest costs. On January 1, 1998, the Central Bank abolished its long-established quota system for credit management. On March 21, the Central Bank decided to combine the accounts of reserve requirement and excess reserves into one reserve account. In the meantime, the required ratio was lowered from the previous 13% to 8%, and the reserve ratio was lowered to 5.22%. This was lower than the 7.56% for the required ratio and 7.02% for the excess reserve ratio prevailing before the reforms and opening up. On March 25, the Central Bank slightly lowered the deposit interest rates for financial institutions, and lowered the discount rates by a much wider scale.

These measures had some effect on maintaining relatively high economic growth. However, since the seriousness of deflation was not fully realized, no strong measures were implemented. Complicated by some unexpected internal and external difficulties, the above-mentioned measures consequently failed to turn around the trend of declining growth. Therefore, since July, 1998, the central government has adopted some new measures to stimulate the economic growth:

To carry out a more active fiscal policy. To further expand investment demand, the central government decided to issue another RMB100 bn worth of long-term treasury bonds to the commercial banks. The capital raised will be used in flood control, agricultural irrigation, transportation and telecommunication, urban infrastructure, electricity transmission lines in urban and rural areas, reconstructing grain storage facilities controlled by the central government, public prosecution facilities, and soil protection and tree planting upstream on the Yangtze and Yellow Rivers.

To further reduce the rates of deposit interest and discount of financial institutions. On July 1, the Central Bank lowered the deposit interest rates of financial institutions by 0.49%, and discount rate by 1.12%.   At the same time, the Central Bank reduced the reserve requirement rate from 5.22% to 3.51%, the average reduction of base rates to financial institutions being 1.82 percentage point, while the rediscount rate was lowered from 6.03% to 4.32%.

To improve financial services.   The government encouraged the financial sector to commit more for economic development. The national commercial banks and policy-oriented banks were encouraged to increase their lending speed in projects related to infrastructure, and effective and marketable production, under the condition of guaranteeing the quality of loans.   They were also expected to improve their services to small and medium-size enterprises.   Matching with the increased RMB100 billion, the amount of credit available to banks was also increased by RMB100 billion.

To fight against smuggling and effectively protect domestic markets.

To create new employment opportunities. The government employed active measures to create new job opportunities so that 50% of the redundant and newly redundant workers could find new jobs.   It is expected that the newly employed will boost consumption.

Despite the various measures and policies undertaken by the central and the local governments to stimulate the economy, there was no obvious sign of recovery.   The causes are mainly due to the following four factors.

First, the slowdown in personal income growth during the past two years has reduced the growth in consumer spending.   Second, under the situation of weak market demand, investment from the non-state sector has declined. In the first half of 1998, investment from the non-state enterprises showed negative growth.   Since the beginning of reform, the non-state sector has been an important driving force for economic growth.   Under such a circumstance, even if investment from the public sector accelerates, the total fixed asset investment will not grow fast.   Third, the structural reform of the central government has weakened the government's ability to exercise adjustment measures through administrative procedures in the centrally planned economy.   At the same time, the investment mechanism suited for a market economy has not yet been fully established.   Fourth, the economic recovery of East Asia has continued to stall, severely affecting our growth in external demand.

No major changes were expected to take place in the global economy in 1998. China's actual rate of economic growth therefore depends on: first, the growth in consumer spending, especially rural consumers; second, the amount of investment from the non-state sector.

We admit therefore that it will be difficult to achieve the 8% growth target.   However, we hope this can still be accomplished after the implementation of various measures.

A Forecast of 1999 Economic Growth

Economic growth in 1999 will be affected by various factors:

(1)   There is uncertainty as to whether East Asia's economy will recover, and whether the crisis in East Asia and Russia will degenerate into a global economic crisis.   At the moment the economies of East Asia and Russia are in a state of profound crisis.   The G7 and East Asian countries led by Japan are implementing various measures, such as cutting taxes, reducing interest rates, and enlarging the scale of their rescue package, to save the global economy.   However, the effectiveness of this joint action has been questioned.   Judging by the performance of the stock markets after the G7 meeting on October 3, attended by their finance ministers and central-bank governors, observers are rather pessimistic about the global economy.

However, the IMF *World Economy Preview* report expresses the view that, although global economic growth in 1998 and 1999 will be lower than previously estimated, economic growth in Asia will still rebound in 1999.   The report predicts that the global economic growth rate in 1998 will be 2%, 1.1% lower than the 3.1% estimated in May 1998.   The projected 1999 world economic growth will be 2.5%, lower than the 3.7% estimated in May 1998, but still higher than the growth rate in 1998.

(2)   In the second half of 1998, China also faces internal uncertainties, such as: whether the various economic adjustment measures will be fully implemented; whether the measures will be effective; whether personal income will increase soon; and whether consumer confidence will be recovered.

If the global economy recovers from the crisis, and if the boosting measures produce the desired results, 1999 economic growth may be slightly higher than 8%.   Otherwise, it will be difficult to maintain a GDP growth of 8%.

In 1999, we should concentrate on the following key policy points:

(1)   To maintain stable fiscal and monetary policies.

(2)   If infrastructure investment in 1998 effectively stimulates the economy, then in 1999 we should concentrate our work on the on going and follow-up projects.

(3)   We should create favorable conditions to stimulate consumer spending.   We should improve the conditions of agricultural production by implementing agricultural irrigation schemes, and raise the level of outputs as well as farmers' incomes. Through developing rural enterprises, we should raise the non-agricultural income of rural citizens.   In towns, we should guarantee a   basic   standard   of   living   for   low-income

consumers, and increase the level of subsidies.   At the same time, through reforming the salary system and developing a consumer credit system, we should encourage the purchase of private housing units and establish healthy primary, secondary, and rental markets for housing.

(4)   In the area of supply, we should encourage the development of intermediary markets, which serve as the middlemen for capital markets.   The barriers against the entrance of small and medium-size enterprises should be broken down.   Favorable conditions for these enterprises to increase investment and expand production should be created.

(5)   We should apply good timing when launching new reforms. When the economy lacks the strength to grow and when price rises are slow, we should push forward reforms on price. When the economy is in a state of speedy growth, we should push forward reforms on employment.

AN ANALYSIS OF THE CURRENT ECONOMIC SITUATION AND FORECAST OF THE FUTURE TREND

HUO LILI, ET AL.

Forecast and Monitoring Office of the Synthetic Department of National Economy, State Planning Commission

In the first half of 1998, China's GDP grew by 7% from the previous year on an equivalent basis. Between January and August, the value-added industrial production increased by 7.8%; the fixed asset investment (excluding those of the collective and private enterprises) by 17.4%; exports by 5.5%; and total retail sales by 7.3%. The RMB exchange rate remained stable.

Forecast of Economic Development in 1998

Our current economic situation has demonstrated some positive impact of the expansionary policy directed to the domestic demand. The People's Bank of China has twice lowered deposit and loan interest rates. It has also announced measures to improve financial services and to support national economic development. The amount of treasury bonds issued has increased; the expenditure structure has been adjusted; and the funds for investment have been increased. All relevant departments have sped up their approval processes and initial preparatory work for infrastructure development. The investment in residential housing has increased. The organization and implementation of key projects such as railways, highways, agricultural irrigation, urban infrastructure, and housing have been strengthened.

Under the policy of increasing investment adopted in the macroeconomic program, the rate of growth in fixed asset investment rose monthly. Retail sales were basically stable despite the fact that current consumption power has weakened as a result of the expected lower increase in income and rises in long-term expenses such as housing, medical care, education, and elderly care.

However, these factors have hindered the growth of consumer sales. But with the implementation of the policy to expand domestic demand and the rebuilding effort after the catastrophic floods resulting in a higher demand for building materials and consumer goods, the market will become active again.

The government has taken measures to appropriately raise the tax rebate rate on certain products and to encourage manufacturing enterprises to export by themselves. The foreign trade enterprises and manufacturing enterprises have actively adjusted themselves to the changes in international markets and have diversified their marketing strategies. Thus exports have kept growing despite the deteriorating international environment.

Supported by higher growth in domestic demand, industrial and agricultural production has steadily increased. In agriculture, unfavorable weather conditions — especially the disastrous floods — were overcome, and good harvests resulted. With the speedy growth of demand for investment the fast-declining trend of industrial production in previous years has been gradually curbed and the sales of industrial products have rebounded each month. A sustained rise has been observed in the production of items of higher technology and items that command a real market value.

The prices of certain investment products have also started to rebound. The decline in the efficiency of enterprises has been eased. The preliminary estimate of GDP growth in 1998 will be 8% higher than that of 1997; the growth rates of primary, secondary, and tertiary industry will be 3.5%, 9%, and 8% respectively. The growth in value-added industrial production will be 9%. The growth of total fixed asset investment will be 16%, while the growth in investment, excluding that of collective and private enterprises, will be 23%. The growth in total retail sales will be 8%, or 10% in real terms after adjustment for price deflation. In terms of foreign trade, both exports and imports will grow by 3%. The trade surplus will be basically the same as in 1997. The national retail price index will fall by 2%, and the consumer price index will be about the same as in 1997.

The Environment for Economic Development
and Policy Suggestions in 1999

The major obstacles for economic development in 1999 can be analyzed from two perspectives. First, from the perspective of maintaining a high economic growth rate, the major constraining factor will still be weak demand. Meanwhile, the global economic situation is not very promising; the Asian financial crisis will still be raging; the Japanese economy will remain in the doldrums; and the financial and economic condition of Russia will continue to deteriorate. The global economic and trade development will also continue to slow down. These unfavorable factors will affect China more seriously in 1999.

The introduction of the Euro will further increase uncertainty in international markets. China's exports will face even more difficult conditions. The major driving force for economic growth will still be domestic demand. In recent years, the weakening growth in consumer demand has obviously been an increasing restraint on the sustained healthy development of the economy. It has not only directly weakened the driving force of consumer demand on economic growth, but has also reduced the multiplying effect of investment. Consumer demand is a major driving force for economic development; declining demand in turn becomes the main obstacle to the continued fast growth of the economy.

Since 1998, investment demand has obviously increased and the on-going projects will help sustain investment in 1999. Further implementation of policies and measures to accelerate infrastructure construction, improve and deepen the housing system, develop the housing estates and high-technology industry will all contribute to facilitating higher growth of investment. However, constrained by the shortage of capital and low base, the growth in investment will be lower than that in 1998. That, in turn, makes the slowdown in consumption an even more outstanding obstacle.

Second, however, is the perspective of improving the quality and efficiency of economic development in order to realize the sustained healthy growth of the future economy. From this angle, we find that the major obstacle is the conflicts in the economic structure. With the accelerating pace of economic globalization and the worldwide trend of structural economic adjustment, a key Chinese problem has become more prominent. That is the increasing lack of competitiveness of the enterprises and their products, as a result of long-term blind and duplicate construction and poor quality in both domestic and international markets.

Contributing to this problem is the failure of industrial structures to adjust to changes in market demand. As a result, China will not be able to take an active role in future international competition. The major reason for the failure of a fundamental breakthrough to this structural problem is that the macroeconomic environments and the micro mechanisms, as a complement to the adjustment structure, are incomplete and ineffective. An innovative mechanism for "the survival of the fittest" and for re-allocation of resources cannot be fully realized.

Macroeconomic policy should be directed to this major obstacle to economic development in 1999. The policy must continue to exercise appropriate adjustment and control, fine-tuning when necessary, to maintain the expansion of domestic demand, so long as a tight intermediate and long-term fiscal and monetary policy is implemented in an appropriate manner.

On the basis of continued encouragement to maintain appropriate growth in exports and investment demand, we must initiate relevant policies to boost consumption and activate stable but fast economic growth. We must utilize the favorable conditions provided by increased market constraints and worldwide economic adjustment. These conditions should be used to impose more effective measures for faster establishment of a macroeconomic environment and a microeconomic mechanism suitable for the structural adjustment.

We must endeavor to make substantial progress in speeding up the structural adjustment and bringing about the two fundamental changes. On the one hand, we must implement measures to stimulate current consumer demand. The first task is to implement further reforms in housing, elderly care, medical services, and education, expand the consumer market, and conduct in-depth research on the reform scheme and quantify its objectives with enough transparency for the people to build up their confidence. The second task is to adopt practical measures to raise the income of the urban and rural residents, especially the middle- and low-income groups and farmers, and to appropriately adjust the taxation structure in order to reduce income disparities. The third task is to extend consumer credit, improve the consumer environment, maintain market order, encourage consumers' spending, and strengthen the adjustment function of interest rate leverage on consumer demand.

On the other hand, we must bring into full play the government's role in the structural adjustment process. For this, we must first create a policy environment for structural adjustment geared to the market, with enterprises as the agent and with a focus on raising innovative ability. We must conduct research to formulate and perfect policies that will encourage enterprises to break new ground, to support the industrialization of high-tech goods, and to facilitate the technological development of private enterprises. We must also adopt measures to encourage and to reward scientific researchers, and establish a mechanism for fair competition. Furthermore, we must accelerate the establishment of social security system, eliminate workers' worries during the process of "survival of the fittest" when the enterprises go bankrupt, and accelerate the pace of reform of the state-owned enterprises. We must improve and regulate the competitive market environment, reverse the current situation of vicious competition, and form a mechanism of competition in quality rather than price war. Moreover, we must identify the major strategic adjustment for industries and work out relevant feasible measures. Everything should be based on the Chinese reality, meanwhile, we should closely monitor changes in the world's industrial structure to identify the appropriate strategy for our industrial adjustment. We should develop new high technologies to lead the transformation of the traditional industries, to encourage the development of manufacturing industries, to upgrade industries and improve the quality of their assets, and to increase the competitiveness of enterprises.

Assuming that the macroeconomic adjustment program is smoothly implemented, a preliminary estimate for 1999 is that the fixed asset investment will maintain a rather high rate of growth, approximately 13% higher than that of 1998, while the growth rate in exports could go up to about 3% compared to 1998. If the consumer and income distribution policies can effectively stimulate consumer demand, total retail sales in 1999 will increase by about 10%. The GDP growth rate will be about 7.5% higher than that in 1998. Of this, the increase in the primary industry value added, based on the average agricultural yield, will be about 4%. The increase in the secondary industry value added will be 8.5%, of which the increase in industrial production value added will be 8.5%.

In terms of the ownership structures, the productivity of the state-owned industries will gradually increase again. Other types of industries with high technology may be active foci for the new cycle of economic growth, whereas the collective economic industries, with rural enterprises as the major components, will basically maintain the current rate of growth. The increase in tertiary industry value added will be about 7.5%. The portion of finance and insurance will obviously increase. Industrialization of property, science, education, and culture will accelerate, following the further reforms of housing, education, and medical care. With the confirmation of the policy to expand domestic demand, economic growth will gradually go up again and price levels will also go up. The total retail sales in 1999 will rise by about 2%.

AN ANALYSIS AND FORECAST OF THE ECONOMIC SITUATION IN 1998–1999[*]

JIANG SHIZHANG, CHEN LEI, ET AL.

Business School, Jilin University

In 1998, our new cabinet explicitly set the goals for economic growth. And GDP growth of 8% was the major focus of China's economic effort. In 1998, both internal and external economic environments became very complex. Internally, we had to face the most catastrophic floods of the century. Externally, the Asian financial crisis adversely affected our exports. However, since the central government undertook various measures at the right time to expand domestic demand, to increase investment, and to boost economic growth, the downward drift of the economy was finally stopped and the situation was stabilized.

Analysis of the Macroeconomic Trend in 1998 and 1999

By utilizing the "Monthly Monitoring and Warning System for the Macroeconomy," which was jointly formulated by the State Information Center and our school, we have analyzed six coincident indicators reflecting different aspects of the macroeconomic situation and growth rates. The results are as follows: (Seasonal variations have been adjusted and irregular factors have been eliminated. The figures quoted are valid to August 1998.):

The growth rate of total industrial output value has been in decline since the second quarter of 1997. This decline began to level off in the second quarter of 1998. In June 1998, the growth rate stood at 9.72%, the lowest point in recent months. A small

[*]   Written by the Macroeconomic Analysis and Forecast Team. Other members of the team include: Han Dongmei, Gao Tiemei, Zhao Zhenquan, Zhang Lijin, Zhang Haizhi, Li Honggang.

recovery was recorded in July and August. Although the current growth rate is higher than the trough levels of previous economic low cycles, it is still at its lowest level since 1991.

In terms of growth rate, the variation of budgeted revenue of industrial product sales was similar to that of the total industrial production; a declining trend has leveled off since June 1998. However, negative growth was recorded every month in 1998, resulting in a growth level lower than the trough of the previous cycle, and very close to the lowest level since 1981.

Total consumer retail sales have also been in a slow decline, from 13.6% at the beginning of 1997 to 9.07% in February 1998. They began to rise again in the second quarter, and August retail sales were once again rising by a healthy 12.5%.

Since 1996, the accumulated rate of increase in (state) infrastructure investment showed a slight fluctuation at a low level. After falling for six months, this figure too began rising from May 1998 onward. Nevertheless, after seasonal adjustment, the accumulated increase from January to August was 16%, still the lowest since 1981.

M_1 growth fell sharply from 19.8% in May 1997 down to 10.3% at the end of July 1998. It recovered slightly to 10.36% at the end of August, but still showed the lowest growth rate since 1991.

In March 1998, banks' wage-equivalent cash payments — after experiencing about three and half years of decline — fell to their lowest level (near zero growth) since 1981. They subsequently started to rise again, gaining momentum in July and August.

The Coincident Diffusion Index (DI), which reflects variation trends of these six coincident indicators, remained at low levels (around zero) for nine months beginning in the second half of 1997, before re-establishing a rising trend in April 1998. By July, the DI had reached the 50% line, and in August, 83%. This provides a preliminary indication that the economic situation has been improving since July.

The Coincident Composite Index (CI), formed by the above six indicators to reflect macroeconomy (with an average value of 1987 set at 100), showed a third rapid decline in the economic downturn between April 1997 and April 1998, falling from 96.9 to 90.1, the third deep trough since 1981. Here again a positive reversal started in August, as it once again showed a modest rise to 91.6.

The Prosperity Index PCI (average value set at zero), formed by an analysis of major components, demonstrated a very similar movement to the CI. Starting in September 1997, it moved from "normal" to the "slightly cold" area, then in April sank to the lower part of this range, only to rise gradually again over the next few months.

The result is that the growth rates of the six uniform macroeconomic indicators, and the two economic prosperity variation composite indicators, although at a low level, did show signs of recovery.   This shows that although the central government's measures aimed at stimulating investment as an expedient in expanding domestic demand have not produced very obvious results, they were in fact effective, and the macroeconomy has started to once again move in the right direction.

We produced a forecast and analysis of the 1998 macroeconomic trends by virtue of yearly and quarterly simultaneous equations models: the time series VAR model; the ARMA model; plus our own macroeconomic forecast and analysis system, after taking other factors into consideration such as the increased fixed asset investment and rebuilding after the floods. The results can be seen in Table 1.

Table 1
Estimated Value of 1998 and 1999 Major
Macroeconomic Indicators

	1998		1999	
	Estimate	Growth rate %	Estimate	Growth rate %
GDP (RMB billion)	8,091.475	8.215	8,815.58	8.95
Total industrial production (RMB billion)	12,106.790	8.2	13,172.190	8.8
Total fixed asset investment (RMB billion)	2,987.930	18.1	3,379.340	13.1
Total consumer goods retail sales (RMB billion)	2,990.606	8.32	3,259.760	9.1
National commodity retail price index (%)		101.4		103.1
National fiscal revenue (RMB billion)	943.964	9.12	1,047.800	11
National fiscal expenditure (RMB billion)	1,065.603	15.4	1,199.860	12.6
Total value of imports (US$ billion)	143.663	1.1	158.890	10.6
Total value of exports (US$ billion)	193.691	3.9	206.860	6.8
Balance of deposits in national banks (RMB billion)	7,001.439	16.78	7,638.560	9.1
Balance of loans in financial institutions (RMB billion)	8,689.603	17.42	9,662.830	11.2

While compiling this forecast of annual indicators, we also employed short- and medium-term time series models to calculate an extrapolation forecast for the variation trends of the Composite Index (CI), which reflected the overall macroeconomic situation. The results are shown in Table 2:

Table 2
Forecast of Economic Condition Index

Indicators	Forecast value		
	4th quarter 1998	1st quarter 1999	2nd quarter 1999
Coincident Composite Index (CI)	94.0	96.4	97.6

The forecast result indicates that from the fourth quarter of 1998 to the second quarter of 1999, we will witness a stable economic recovery, faster in the beginning and slowing down later. In June, the CI value will reach 97.8, equivalent to the value at the end of 1995.   Starting from the fourth quarter of 1998, our macroeconomy will progress with a stable rising trend.   However, since the pace of recovery is from fast to slow, it is difficult to judge now whether this will amount to a temporary recovery or the beginning of a new round of economic growth.   As investment in 1998 began from the second half of the year, the recovery is projected to last into the first half of 1999.   Boosted by the delayed effect of the 1998 investment increase, the macroeconomy in 1999 will remain prosperous.   Based on past experience, a six-month to one-year period is required to determine whether the economic cycle has indeed reached a turning point.

Constraining Factors in Generating a New
Round of Economic Growth

Since the middle of 1993, the rate of economic growth has been declining.   In the first half of 1998, this decline dipped further, below the appropriate growth zone.   Several factors caused this:

First, low personal income caused the formation of a "buyer's market" in which consumer spending, though stable, has fallen off slightly.   Affected by the adjustment of the economic structure and the slowdown in economic growth, the increase in personal income has likewise slowed.   This has had a serious negative impact on consumer spending.   Following a more determined effort to reform housing, medical care, and employment, urban residents have expected future spending to rise, which in turn has affected the growth of demand in current spending.   Despite five reductions in interest rates, consumer desire has not really been stimulated.   At the same time, the growth in spending on food, clothing, and daily necessities has been slowing while spending on housing and transportation is staggering. This makes it difficult to generate a vibrant consumer market.

Second, there have been profound changes in the microeconomic foundation and the financial system for the economy. The financial institutions have gradually established systems for various types of risk control.   The impulse to expand credit has virtually disappeared, meaning many enterprises have been running into difficulties in raising funds.   The self-control mechanisms of the state-owned enterprises are being strengthened.   As a result, people's "investment hunger" for blind borrowing and for project registration has been alleviated.   Moreover, as there is no consumption "hot point" that can be identified in the current persistently low pace of economic development, investment initiative is also low.

Third, the strength in structural adjustment continued to increase as the industrial production growth rate fell sharply.   In terms of industry, some departments in the secondary industry are now undergoing a painful and difficult structural adjustment.   In terms of enterprises, the state-owned enterprises, and the rural enterprises that have experienced a few years of fast growth, are both faced with the problems of structural adjustment and technological upgrading.   Industry has always been the "generator" of our fast economic growth.   After entering the adjustment period, its rate of growth has obviously declined, *de facto* acting as a brake on total economic growth.

A fourth factor is the delaying effect of the "soft landing." The "soft landing" adjustment measures were primarily meant to cool down the overheated economy and to handle inflation.   After four years of hard work, from 1993 to 1996, this mission was successfully accomplished. However, the rate of economic growth has declined for four consecutive years, and evolved into a protracted trend, creating difficulties for re-stimulating economic growth once again.

Fifth is the negative effect of the Asian financial crisis. Net exports have clearly lost their power to stimulate the economy.

From the above analysis, it is clear that even though there are many factors inhibiting a new round of economic growth, the major constraining factor is still the lack of effective demand. In the current circumstances, where there are abundant resources and production capacity, the adjustment measures undertaken by the government to stimulate the economy through increased investment in infrastructure will be effective in due course.

This increased infrastructure investment has implicit limitations, however. With its tendency to circularity, its power to stimulate consumer demand is weakened. Furthermore, in the current buyers' market, consumer demand has become the key factor in stimulating economic growth. (Based on statistics in 1997, consumer spending contributed as much as 55% of GDP.) Thus, increased infrastructure investment alone cannot boost consumer demand effectively, nor can it generate growth of effective demand, let alone stimulate a new round of broad-based economic growth. This can be discerned by the CI's variation indicating fast to slow growth in the first two quarters of 1999, reflecting the general trend of the macroeconomy. Besides, up to August 1998, negative growths were still recorded in infrastructural industries, such as the total energy production, transportation capacity, and electric power generation, as compared to the same period in 1997, suggesting that economic growth has not been stimulated to expand.

Of course, the contribution of the increased infrastructure investment to the recovery of the economy cannot be denied since it has, to a certain extent, helped to turn around the vicious trend of a persistent declining economic growth since 1993, while creating the basic conditions for generating a new round of economic growth.

Policy Suggestions

Effective economic growth must start by expanding consumer spending; stimulating growth in investment; facilitating new economic growth, so that another benign cycle of macroeconomic growth can get underway. In the 1999 macroeconomic adjustment program, therefore, the following measures should be taken:

Deploying Effective Measures to Expand Consumer Demand

The consumption of all residents amounts to 80% of the demand of consumption. To expand consumer demand, therefore, we must stimulate consumer spending. Because urban and rural residents exhibit different spending patterns, we must develop separate measures to fit these patterns.

Urban residents have gone beyond the stage of the three basic needs of food, clothing, and daily necessities. Upscaling the urban spending pattern is therefore what is called for. We should, based on current conditions in China, push for the development of the estate and automobile industries as strong supports for long-term economic growth. We must also implement complementary reforms to provide related means to stimulate spending and investment for these industries, while actively developing the consumer credit system so as to make available the funds consumers need for spending. At the same time, we must actively offer purchase guidance to consumers wishing to fulfill their "dream list."

As for rural residents, concentrating on raising their basic incomes — and thereby their purchasing power — is the most important task in growing their consumer markets. Going further, in addressing the special characteristics of rural consumer spending, we should offer affordable products consistent with rural consumers' ability to pay, rather than trying to simply "move products" (from the urban market to the rural one) regardless. Through such considered expansion of the rural market, and the subsequent stimulation of consumer demand that entails, enterprise investment will also be boosted. Ultimately, this will generate a benign cycle of economic growth.

Continued Increase of Fixed Asset Investment in Infrastructure

Stimulating growth in consumer demand is the basis for sustained economic growth. However, its effect will not be marked over the short term. Yet at present, some of the effects of increased fixed asset investment in infrastructure cannot be replaced otherwise. In 1999, we should continue to invest in infrastructure construction.

Combining the Expansion of Domestic Demand and the Encouragement of Exports

In 1998, China's macroeconomic adjustment program was oriented towards "increasing investment demand to compensate for the comparative contraction in export demand," which increased the pressure on the expansion of domestic demand. Since the adverse effect of the Asian financial crisis cannot be dissolved over the short term, our exports in 1999 will still be subject to its negative influence. However, from the perspective of boosting economic growth, we must try our best to overcome the present difficulties in export markets and to relieve the pressure on expanding domestic demand.

Continued Increase of the Effort in Structural Adjustment

A buyers' market is now forming. For most major products, supply now exceeds demand or they are in balance. In some areas, there are serious problems of excess idle capacity. Therefore, for lower level and labour-intensive processing industries, and industries saddled with outdated craftsmanship and machinery, we should carry out the policy of coercive filtering out and upgrading, much as the policy of limiting production was implemented in the textile industries. Doing so will improve the overall quality of our industries.   And in 1999, with the economy starting to rebound, the price paid for this structural adjustment will not be too great.

Integration of Various Policies under the Macroeconomic Adjustment Program

Both fiscal and monetary policies are effective means to induce change within the broader context of the macroeconomic adjustment program.   However, since 1997 interest rates have been lowered five times with little effect on the macroeconomy.   This is partly due to the lower level of "marketization" of our economy.   The leverage effect of interest rates on economic adjustment is still somewhat restricted. But it is also a result of money supply not having been increased proportionately.   Consequently, in the macroeconomic adjustment program, we must integrate various policies to generate the best results possible.

In conclusion, realization of the 8% growth target in 1998 will provide the necessary conditions for a new round of economic growth.   The economic operating environment will also become more relaxed.   If the macroeconomic adjustment program offers reasonable adjustments and control, a new round of economic growth will not be far off.

TO IMPROVE THE SUPPLY-DEMAND STRUCTURE FOR STABLE GROWTH

HE LIN AND ZHOU XIAOJI

Institute No. 710, China Aerospace Industry General Corporation

Expanding Domestic Demand in the Economy Grows Gradually toward the Target in 1998

In 1998, our macroeconomy was under pressure from two sides. Domestically, our economy was in a critical stage of structural adjustment in which the reform of the economic system was strengthened, while changes in economic growth patterns accelerated. However, after the "soft landing" that was necessary after several years of implementing the macroeconomic adjustment program, adjustments to expand effective demand failed to keep pace with the economic development. Consequently, insufficient demand has become the major obstacle in economic growth. Looking at the international environment, since the onset of the Southeast Asian financial crisis in mid 1997, the malaise has spread its influence from Asia to Latin America, and from North America to Europe, affecting every corner of the globe. The pace of the world's economic growth has slowed down in the midst of the adverse situation. It was especially serious in China's neighboring countries, where their economies were obviously affected by the recession, domestic demand shrank sharply, and exchange rates plummeted. In consequence, China's exports were adversely affected, resulting in a decline in export growth.

Under such circumstances, we must take measures to stabilize exports. While maintaining the stability of the RMB exchange rate, we have implemented a new policy of free or reduced taxes for certain exported goods. We have encouraged enterprises to export, to diversify their markets, and to diversify by increasing exports to Europe and the United States, as a means of reducing the impact of declining exports on China's economy.

On the other hand, expanding domestic demand has become China's major policy approach for promoting economic growth. The government has adopted a series of fiscal and monetary policies. More treasury bonds were issued, budgeted fiscal expenditure was increased, and investment in infrastructure was reinforced. The cancellation of the quota system for national commercial bank loans and the reduction in bank reserve requirements have enabled the national banks to increase their capital supply. The reduction of interest rates in March and July 1998 encouraged investment and consumer spending and stimulated mortgage credit for personal housing. Through the completion and improvement of the financial service system for residential housing, and reform in the housing system, we have actively developed a new focal point of economic growth.

Following the implementation of these measures, growth in domestic demand in the second half of 1998 was expected to exceed the first half, and push the economic growth close to the 8% target. However, there are still some problems and conflicts which may both hinder our hitting the 8% targeted growth rate as well as improving the quality of economic growth. These are demonstrated mainly in the following areas:

Lack of Improvement in the Problem of Insufficient Demand

With respect to investment, although the state's fixed asset investment rose at a high rate, the growth of investment in the overall economy will not be that high. The government's focus of investment is in infrastructural industries and construction. The private sectors' investment demand is not as strong for two reasons. One, infrastructure investment requires a long cycle of construction, and a long period to gain returns on investment, so that stimulating private enterprise to invest is a slow process. And two, market expectations affect investors' confidence.

The current general price level is persistently low and the material market is feeble. In the first half of 1998, the commodity retail price index and materials price index dropped by 2.1% and 4.3% from 1997 respectively. The excess of supply over demand in the commodity markets will also lower the expected profits of enterprises, and increase the risks of investing in them. Private investment, which makes up 46% of the total, is growing comparatively slowly. In addition, the growth rate of foreign direct investment will definitely fall. It is therefore predicted that, although the state's fixed asset investment will possibly increase to 18%, the growth rate of total fixed asset investment will only be about 14.5%.

With respect to consumer spending, there is no clear sign of recovery in predicted consumer spending. Although banks cut their interest rates twice, the personal savings deposits still increased by 16.8% between January and August 1998. By the end of August, the money that flowed back to banks amounted to more than that in 1997 by RMB57.39 billion. The major reasons for the weakness in consumer spending are anticipated lower personal incomes, the current saturation of consumer spending, and the structural change in predicted consumer spending.

In the first half of the year, the nominal growth rate for the average urban resident's disposable income and net average rural personal income were 4.4% and -0.3% respectively, showing a noticeable decline from the previous year. The increased efforts in enterprise reform resulted in a considerable number of workers becoming unemployed or repositioned. This adds to the instability of predicted personal income, leading to the fall in consumer marginal spending. The urban consumer market is approaching saturation, and a new consumption "hot point" has not yet been established. The rural consumer market, despite its enormous potential, is still fettered by many constraints. It requires a great deal of effort to turn the potential demand into actual consumption. The absence of consumer spending and the weak market demand also lowered the multiplier effect of investment, and added to the government's difficulties in trying to stimulate economic growth through increased investment.

The Problem of Supply in Excess of Demand Is Prominent in Industrial Production. There Is No Fundamental Improvement in the Economic Efficiency of Enterprises

The pace of our industrialization has accelerated noticeably since the mid 1980s. However, due to blind investments and duplicated construction, excess production capacity was created. The third industrial census showed that the capacity utilization rate was under 60% in more than half of our industrial products. Currently, since the demand is insufficient, the problem of excess industrial production has become even more prominent. As a result, the economic efficiency of enterprises generally fell, forcing some enterprises to close down. Since 1998, the rate of increase in industrial production continued to fall, compared with that in 1997, to the lowest point since 1991. Between January and August, the industrial production value added increased by only 7.8% compared with the same period last year. The economic efficiency of industrial enterprises fell. According to the statistics provided by the departments concerned, the net losses of 40,800 state-owned enterprises reached as high as RMB6.72 billion.

The Situation in Imports and Exports Is Still Severe

For a long time, our export markets have been highly concentrated. In recent years, our exports to Asian countries and regions have amounted to 60% of our total exports, with exports to Japan, Korea, and Thailand comprising more than 30% of the total. Consequently, the Asian financial crisis has affected more than 30% of our export markets. In the first half of 1998, our exports to ASEAN, Japan, and Korea fell by 12.9%, 4.3%, and 30.2% respectively. The economies of Southeast Asian countries will be unlikely to recover quickly, their recession will remain severe, and our exports to these countries will continue to decline. Although the market diversification strategy has had some impact by increasing exports to Europe, North America, Africa, and Latin America, and some potentially new markets have been opened up, they are far from substitutes for the original export markets in the near future.

Based on the above analysis, the results of our forecast of the major 1998 indicators of economic growth are: the growth in total fixed asset investment will be 14.5%, amounting to RMB2,896.8 billion, the real growth of total retail sales will reach about 9.6%. Exports will remain severely affected. The predicted full-year export growth rate is 4–5% more than that in the same period in 1997. Moreover, constrained by weak domestic demand, imports will be weak, remaining at the same level as in 1997 or at a slight rise. The foreign trade surplus will reach over US$30 billion. The predicted GDP growth rate for the year is 7.6%, with 3.2% in primary industry, 8.7% in secondary industry, of which 8.8% is for industrial production, and 8.2% for tertiary industry.

The Transformation of the Economy Is a Primary Concern with Problems at Deeper Level

Since the 1990s, our economy has entered a new era of development. Some deeply rooted conflicts have emerged. The lack of effective macroeconomic demand constitutes the focus of all the conflicts at this stage of development.

Weak Driving Force for Economic Growth and Irrational Structure of Consumption

Fixed asset investment used to be our major means of stimulating economic growth. However, with the gradual deepening transformation toward a market economy, the constraining effect of efficiency on the increase of investment is becoming more conspicuous. When there are many bottlenecks in production, a large amount of investment will bring economic efficiency, which will in turn stimulate economic growth. The soft constraint of capital in the old system gave rise to an insatiable demand for expansion in enterprise investment. However, after the production bottlenecks have gradually been resolved and economic supply capacity has been enlarged substantially, it has become increasingly difficult to find a new "hot point" for investment. Under the new system, enterprises have to consider the issues of economic efficiency as well as the market for their products. Facing a market with inadequate demand, the desire to invest has been weakened substantially. On the other hand, blind investment and duplicated construction have been the culprit and fundamental cause of the current structural excess production capacity, under-capacity operations, and poor efficiency. Consequently, under this situation, it will be extremely difficult to stimulate economic growth in the market economy system merely by an expansionary monetary policy.

During the period of the Eighth Five-year Plan, rapidly growing export demand was the major driving force for our economic growth. The average growth rate in exports was over 30%, while the corresponding economic growth rate reached 11.6%. As we all know, the Southeast Asian financial crisis and the global economic downturn it has caused will seriously affect our exports in the next two to three years. Therefore, the effect of an increase in exports as a driving force for economic growth will be very limited. In fact, as more and more countries begin to compete on the world market, the influence of exports on economic growth will weaken. For a country with such a huge economy as China, reliance on export demand to maintain strong economic growth can be effective only for a short period of time.

Domestic demand is the source of stable economic growth for long-term development. In recent years, inadequate domestic demand has constituted the major cause for the insufficient demand. In 1997, the growth rate of consumption in urban and rural areas dropped sharply. The average growth rate during the Eighth Five-year Plan was about 9%, but only 3.2% in 1997. The drop in the growth rate of urban consumer spending was especially apparent. Since 1994, the rate of growth of urban consumer spending has persistently fallen to 2.8% in 1996, and to 1.3% in 1997. In fact, the 9% growth rate in total national consumer spending was only due to the 13.6% growth in rural consumer spending. It indicates that the urban consumer markets have become saturated. At the same time, rural consumer spending was on the rise, closely connected to the rise in rural income. It should be noted that spending on basic necessities like food and clothing still makes up around 60% of the total consumer spending of the urban and rural population, while spending on housing amounts to only 8–9% of the total urban consumer spending. Obviously, this kind of spending structure is not able to meet the need of current economic development. Therefore, consumer spending will not become the driving force for further economic growth.

The Pressure of Employment Will Last Long

The employment problem has existed for a long time in China. With the deepening of the reforms and our structural adjustment, the problem has become even more serious. Our country has a huge population and vast amount of labor resources. Every year, a fresh supply of 5–6 million people joins the workforce. For a long time, the employment pressure has taken the form of hidden unemployment. Part of the labor force was forced to remain in villages and became excess rural labor. Others were given hidden unemployment in certain enterprises. In the early years of the reform and opening up, the unemployment problem was, to a large extent, overcome by China's steady economic growth. The reforms had not touched the deep problems of the enterprises. At the same time, in the initial stage of our economic reforms, there was a "making up for the past" development in the light industry sector. Some of the industries transferred to China from developed countries belonged to the labor-intensive and low-technology industry. Thus, the employment problem was not yet that serious. Therefore, the economic development and reform mainly relied on improving capital efficiency, and reasonable allocation of resources to promote economic growth.

However, we are now forced to confront our unemployment problem. The 1997 registered unemployment rate was 3.1%, but when we include the number of people waiting to be employed, it came to 8–9%. In the next few years, the number of laid-off workers will continue to grow by 4–5 million each year. In fact, the conflict between a huge labor force supply and China's limited job opportunities will exist for a long time.

The pursuit of economic efficiency in the market economy will inevitably require the reform of the employment system. The old system of being overstaffed and low productivity must be eliminated, especially in the state-owned enterprises, which have crumbled under the heavy burden of employment and social welfare. Furthermore, as our industrial structure has developed, there appears to be an inherent problem of excess capacity. When the sunset industries are reformed, a further large number of workers will become redundant. At the same time, in line with industrial enhancements, the development of capital-intensive and high-tech industries will reduce the correlation between job opportunities and industrial development, and the need for manpower.

Finally, the growth in agricultural productivity will make the problem of excess rural labor even more serious. Following the development of the economy, telecommunications, and media technology, new concepts of life have been spreading throughout the rural villages. The redundant rural workers are longing to work in urban areas and the institutional reform gradually makes it possible. Although it has not yet become a serious threat to urban employment, rural unemployment will continue to deepen in the coming decade, while urban employment opportunities will become more scarce as employment levels approach their peak.

Solutions Are Urgently Needed for the Problem of Rural Economic Development

Under the long-term dual economic development strategy, a large pool of manpower has been accumulated in villages. However, the income and spending of the rural population is not even half of that of the urban population. In the early stage of

China's economic reforms, the fast development of the rural economy helped to lay a solid foundation for national economic development. Yet, there have not been any substantial solutions to the problems of rural economic development. Increased grain production has produced very little effect on improving the income of the rural population. Since 1997, the growth of rural income has been slow, and has seriously affected the growth in consumer demand. Undoubtedly, increasing personal income, including that of the rural population, is the ultimate goal in our economic development. With the present comparatively excess production and lack of growth stimulus, increasing rural incomes and developing the rural economy are matters of great importance for the medium- and long-term stable growth of the economy. On the one hand, rural economic development allows excess manpower to be absorbed locally. On the other hand, the increase in rural income will create an enormous market for the current comparatively saturated urban consumer production. That in turn will result in more employment opportunities, since there exists a disparity between rural and urban consumption patterns.

Therefore, after 20 years of fast growth, economic development in China has reached its turning point. The problems of low industrial levels and saturated consumer demand, low production efficiency and insufficient employment opportunities, low average production levels and excess production capacity in some areas, have compelled us to look for new concepts of economic development. To achieve this goal, our economic growth will have to go through the difficulties in raising productivity, developing high-technology industries, and improving the economic structure. This shows that economic development and the improvement of people's standard of living are mutually dependent and mutually facilitating.

Reform and Development Go Hand in Hand —
Stable Economic Growth in 1999

The goal for economic development in 1999 should be to keep on with the macroeconomic policy in expanding domestic demand, to maintain the high level of investment, and to raise the consumer demand so that a certain level of economic growth will be maintained.   At the same time, further structural reform in investment, finance, and enterprises must be carried out, direct financing must be strengthened, aggressive fiscal and monetary policies must be continued, and a favorable investment and financing environment must be created.   Systems in housing, education, medical care, and elderly insurance should be improved. More jobs should be created and the structural obstacles to sufficient demand should be gradually removed. Moreover, the structural adjustment of the economy and the upgrade of industry should be accelerated to create new stimuli for economic growth. The forecast for the 1999 major economic indicators is shown in Table 1:

Table 1
Forecast of the 1999 Major Economic Indicators

Major indicators	Scheme 1		Scheme 2		Scheme 3	
	Total value	Growth rate %	Total value	Growth rate %	Total value	Growth rate %
Total fixed asset investment (in RMB billion)	3186.53	10.0	3287.92	13.5	3331.38	15.0
Gross domestic product (in RMB billion)	9015.82	7.8	9057.64	8.3	9152.14	9.1
Primary industry (in RMB billion)	1576.02	4.2	1580.56	4.5	1586.52	4.7
Secondary industry (in RMB billion)	4435.55	9.0	4451.83	9.4	4507.43	10.5
Tertiary industry (in RMB billion)	3019.66	8.1	3025.25	8.3	3058.19	8.7
Value-added in industrial production (in RMB billion)	3836.21	9.23	3859.74	9.9	3885.4	10.7
Grain production (in 10,000 tons)	49790.1	0.8	49790.1	0.8	4979.01	0.8
Total retail sales (in RMB billion)	3267.97	10.2	3276.73	12.3	3329.25	14.1
Retail sales prices (%)		2.8		2.8		2.8
Consumer prices (%)		4.2		4.2		4.2
Average urban personal income (in RMB billion)	5788.3	5.7	5854	6.9	5913.1	8.0
Average rural personal income (in RMB billion)	2275.8	5.0	2284.5	5.4	2308.3	6.5
Urban and rural savings deposits (in RMB billion)	6264.44	15.2	6438.45	18.4	6552.64	20.5
Total imports and exports (in US$ billion)	349.53	3.68	351.6	4.3	355.92	5.6
Exports (in US$ billion)	201.04	4.8	201.81	5.2	205.26	7.0
Imports (in US$ billion)	148.48	2.3	149.79	3.2	155.17	4.5
Fiscal revenue (in RMB billion)	1132.03	13.8	1134.02	14.0	1144.93	15.1
Fiscal expenditure (in RMB billion)	1220.41	14.0	1222.55	14.2	1233.25	15.2
Narrow money supply M_1 (in RMB billion)	4387.82	11.3	4549.46	15.4	4602.68	16.8
Broad money supply M_2 (in RMB billion)	12193.18	15.02	12562.09	18.5	12699.9	19.8

Note: All the rates are nominal growth rates except for the rates for economic growth which are real growth rates.

To achieve the economic development goal, we must work harder in the following areas:

We Must Actively Implement Structural Reform. While Enhancing the Development of Enterprise Conglomerates, We Should Pay Attention to the Development Strategies for Small and Medium Enterprises and Promote Economic Growth of Industries

In order to develop industries, we must solve the problem of a backward industrial structure and low quality of production. On the one hand, we should focus on the accumulation of capital and efficiency of resources, and the development of large prestigious enterprise conglomerates that have a strong impact on the economy. We must promote their consolidation and expand their scope to a certain degree, to raise the return on capital and to promote technological and structural innovations.

On the other hand, we must pay attention to the development strategies for small- and medium-size enterprises. In a large country like ours, in addition to those large enterprise conglomerates functioning as the backbone of the economy, the contributions of small- and medium-size enterprises to economic development and providing employment cannot be ignored. At present, many small- and medium-size enterprises are facing difficulties of tight supply of capital, lagged product mix, and a lack of a favorable external environment. The government should improve enterprises' external environment, make laws and relevant regulations with respect to the development of small- and medium-size enterprises, and improve the quality of services of government departments. At the same time, the financial institutions should refine the financing system, to activate stocks and support the development of these enterprises. In the process of upgrading industrial structure, small- and medium-size enterprises should live up to the requirements of the markets and focus on diversified economic development.

Development of the Labor Market and Expansion of Employment

The basic policy as well as the long-term goal of our economic development should aim to lower the unemployment rate. Establishing a regulated labor market is an obligatory measure in guiding the labor force into employment and achieving an effective allocation of the limited employment resources. On the one hand, we must break away from the "same big public pot" system to facilitate the mobility of the labor force and to establish a competitive mechanism for jobs. On the other hand, we must really establish a social security system to provide funding as a priority for unemployment insurance, employment retraining, and redeployment subsidies.

Currently, the disparity among regions with excess labor is very distinctive. To create employment opportunities, we need the transformation and adjustment of the industrial structures on a regional basis. The government should work out strategies to support and develop new industries according to the conditions of individual regions, and encourage an appropriate inter-regional flow of the labor force.

Greater Development of Tertiary Industry, and Encouragement of Infrastructure Construction in Small- and Mid-size Towns

The development of secondary and tertiary industries depends on urban development. In general, the urban population gradually increases following the industrialization and upgrading of the economy. In fact, the development of tertiary industry is closely related to the process of urbanization. A city with a large population and a concentrated consumer group is a hotbed of tertiary industry development. In our current stage of development, a big proportion of the population is scattered in villages and small- and medium-size towns. Usually, in these small- and medium-size towns, the industrial structure is unitary with loose regional cooperation and without any economic growth point. The development of their enterprises is difficult.

By comparison, in the coastal economic development zones, small- and medium-size towns have been developing quickly thanks to the improvement in infrastructure, such as transportation and communication, and the support by big cities. The development of small- and medium-size towns plays an important part in the improvement of the demand structure, and also serves as a foothold for the gradual transfer of the rural labor force to cities.   We should eliminate the restrictions imposed by household registration in order to expand, in an orderly fashion, the scope of the townships to create new economic growth points.

Increasing Rural Infrastructure Construction as well as Promoting Rural Economic Development and Growth of Rural Income

The major challenge of our economic development is to improve our backward rural economy, and that requires the implementation of various measures.   First, we must continue to construct rural infrastructure.   In the second half of 1998, the government greatly increased investment in the electricity supply networks in the rural areas, which will provide a boost to rural production and development of consumption.   However, the scope of rural infrastructure construction covers a great number of areas and needs long-term and consistent financial support.   The agricultural irrigation system is important as the basis for the prevention of floods and natural calamities and for a bumper agricultural yield.

To improve the rural natural environment, to prevent the loss of topsoil, especially in environmentally disastrous areas, we need more large-scale education and massive tree planting and soil management.   Roads and communication construction are one of the key requirements for rural economic development.   Moreover, in order to change the conditions in which an increase in production does not lead to an increase in income, we must reform the rural industrial and agricultural structures.

The first task in expanding the rural economy is to increase agriculture's technological level.   Teams of agricultural technicians should be organized to provide effective technological services to farmers.   Ecological agriculture should be further developed to produce high value-added products.   In addition, we should not simply impose restrictions on the mobility of excess rural labor because of the rising unemployment rate in towns.   Rather, we should give our priority to offering guidance.   It should be noted that the natural flow of the rural labor force into the towns is a stimulating force for urban development.   Although rural workers compete to some extent for urban job opportunities, to a larger extent, the two work forces are complementary.

QUARTERLY ANALYSIS AND FORECAST OF THE 1998-1999 ECONOMIC SITUATION

ZHANG YANQUN

Institute of Quantitative and Technical Economics
Chinese Academy of Social Sciences

Analysis of the Economic Situation from January to August 1998

Agricultural Production

The summer of 1998 saw a large harvest because, despite the catastrophic floods that affected the Yangtze River region and the Northeast, the weather in general was normal in most parts of the country. It is estimated that this year's grain harvest will reach or slightly exceed 1997 levels.

Industrial Production

In the first and second quarters of 1998, the growth rates of industrial value-added production were 8.2% and 7.7% respectively. The growth rates for July and August were 7.6% and 7.9% respectively. These figures reflect a continuing downtrend. The major causes of this are: First, due to weak demand in domestic investment and consumption. Excess capacity has become a widespread phenomenon. Second, restricted and reduced production in some enterprises undergoing structural adjustment to reduce inventory. Third, the aftermath of the Southeast Asian financial crisis. Fourth, a reduction of the export value of industrial products. And finally the growth rate of industrial value-added fell sharply in July and August in the flooded provinces.

As industrial value-added production declined, industrial economic efficiency deteriorated as well. Between January and

June, the total profits of industrial enterprises declined by 43.2% as compared with the same period of 1997. The total losses incurred in industrial enterprises increased by 35.3% as compared with the same period in 1997. Although the sales rate for industrial products rose from 93% at the beginning of the year to 96% in June of this year, the average value of the sales rate from January to June 1998 was still below the level of the same period in 1997. With the stimulus provided by increased strength in fixed asset investment, the sales rate for industrial products in July and August continued to rise, reaching 97.6% in August, exceeding the level of the same period in 1997.

Fixed Asset Investment

Between January and June 1998, fixed asset investment by state-owned enterprises grew by 13.8%, 3.5% higher than the first quarter. In July and August, the growth rate of fixed asset investment by state-owned enterprises, compared with the same period of the previous year, increased by 22.8% and 26.9% respectively. The growth rate of fixed asset investment in agriculture, construction, transportation and telecommunications far exceeded the average 17.4% in these sectors; between January and August, they grew by 20.9%, 45.1%, and 43% respectively compared with the same period a year earlier. The growth rate in real estate investment rose remarkably, up to 16.5% in the first half of the year compared with the corresponding period the previous year. Investment in industrial raw materials continued to decline, however, down by 9% from January to August on the same annualized comparison basis.

Foreign Trade and Foreign Exchange

In the first quarter of 1998, the total value of China's exports increased by 12.8%. The growth rate of exports in the second quarter, however, fell sharply, increasing only by 3.5% as compared with last year. This was mainly due to the fact that some economies, such as Japan's and South Korea's, went into serious recession affecting on Chinese exports.   In May, a negative growth rate was recorded for the first time in twenty-two months. Signs of recovery were seen in June and July, but in August, export growth was negative again. The fallout of the Asian financial crisis mainly hit China's exports, which suffered from a demand decline in those countries experiencing recession. Between January and August of 1998, our exports to Thailand, Japan, and South Korea continued to fall, by 22.4%, 5.8%, and 32.7% respectively. As well, the recession has canceled their competitiveness through the devaluation of their various currencies. As a direct result, Chinese exports to the United States, Europe, and Africa soared by 17.4%, 23.7%, and 43% respectively from January to August.

Another reason for the decline in export growth was that export enterprises themselves undertook structural adjustments. The export competitiveness of state-owned enterprises showed a sustained decline; their growth rate of exports was below that of foreign-invested enterprises. Between January and August, export growth rates among state-owned enterprises and foreign-owned enterprises stood at 0.2% and 11.1% respectively. The proportion of exports by foreign-invested enterprises constituted 43% of the total export value.

Between January and August 1998, the trade surplus was US$314 million. At the end of August, our foreign exchange reserves were US$140 billion, an increase of US$600 million from the beginning of the year.

Employment

Compared with 1997, urban employment continued to decline. By the end of the second quarter of 1998, the number of urban employed was 2.86 million less than in the same period of 1997 and 1.02 million less than in the first quarter. The number of workers employed by state-owned enterprises was 3% less than that in the same period of 1997. Employment in government departments also started to shrink. Among all the state-owned enterprises, employment in the primary and secondary industries shrank, but increased in the tertiary industry. The proportion of employment in the tertiary industry became larger, the number of employed in tertiary industry increased from 49.8% in 1997 and of all workers in all industries to 52% this year.

Reform and Policy Adjustment

The New Financial Reform Measures

Weak domestic demand has resulted in the strengthening of the market mechanism and the establishment of a risk control system for commercial banks and investors. It has also provided a sound macroeconomic situation for the reform of financial institutions. Following the replacement of the credit quota system by a system of asset and liability management in January 1998, the Central Bank also undertook a reform of the deposit reserve requirements on March 21, 1998, by reducing its discount rates. The essence of these reforms was twofold. First, the Central Bank combined the deposit reserve account and the payable account into a new deposit reserve requirement account so that the reserve requirement actually became one of the monetary tools controlled by the Central Bank. At the same time, it also aimed to streamline the financing arrangements between the Central Bank and financial institutions, such as commercial banks. Second, interest rates on reserve requirements were reduced. In the past, the interest paid on deposit reserves and payable accounts was as high as 7.56% and 7.02% respectively, even higher than the 6.66% paid by the commercial banks on five-year deposits. The new combined reserve requirement interest rate was lowered to 5.22%, to the level of the one-year deposit rate.

The Timetable for Housing Reform Was Finalized

After a long period of discussion and consultation, the timetable for welfare reform in terms of the housing allocation system was finalized in March 1998. According to the decision of the State Council, starting from July 1, 1998, housing allocation systems will be abolished in favor of a marketized system. To encourage individuals to buy private housing, the amount of credit available for housing loans was increased in 1998. In the first half of this year, there was a noticeable increase in the pace of selling older public housing at a lower price to individuals.

Investment Increase in Infrastructure Construction

At the National People's Congress convened in March 1998, the government decided on the direction the macroeconomic adjustment program should take in order to stimulate domestic demand and increase investment in infrastructure with the long-term goal of stimulating economic growth. Investment will be concentrated on major projects in areas such as irrigation works, transportation, communications, environmental protection, municipal works, and so on. In order to achieve these goals, some earlier versions of planned targets went through substantial changes. Vice-premier Li Lanqing stated at the World Economic Forum and the Chinese Enterprises Summit Meeting in March that China would invest more in infrastructure. In the next three years, it will rise to US$750 billion. This huge amount will be raised by selling special bonds, collecting infrastructure construction levies, and bank credits, among other measures.

The Reform of the Grain Distribution System

China's grain distribution system still suffers from some serious problems left over from the old system. One of these is that the losses and unpaid debts of grain enterprises increase every year. The other is that due to the lack of supervision, grain enterprises often embezzle funds specially earmarked for grain purchases, issuing "white slips" to farmers. Grain enterprises therefore have become something of a "black hole" for government finance. A reform was mandatory.

The reform of the grain distribution system was started in May 1998. The essence of this reform was to separate government administration from that of the enterprises, as well as separating the responsibilities of the central government from those of the local governments, grain storage from grain distribution, old accounts from new ones, and improving the overall grain pricing system. Starting in May, the various related departments carried out investigations of these grain businesses to eradicate illegal practices and to rectify some of the practices of grain wholesale enterprises. After the reform of grain sales and purchases, grain prices in most of China's markets started to rise again. In thirty-five medium-size and large cities, the prices of grain products rose by more than 9%.

Cutting Interest Rates Five Times

On July 1, 1998, the Central Bank cut its interest rates for the fifth consecutive time to help lower financial institutions' deposit and lending interest rates. Also lowered were the Central Bank's reserve deposits and rediscount interest rates.

This time, the deposit rate was reduced by 0.49% and the lending rate by 1.12%. The interest paid by the Central Bank on reserve deposits shrank from 5.22% to 3.51%. The average lending rate to financial institutions was reduced from 7.43% to 5.61%.

One feature of this round of interest cuts was that the rate of reduction in intermediate and long-term deposits and lending was larger than that seen in short-term rates. The purpose was to encourage infrastructure construction and to stimulate spending on private housing. After this cut, the nominal deposit rates of the RMB were lower than those of the U.S. dollar. This triggered many black-market currency deals, such as illegal foreign exchange transactions, transfers, foreign exchange fraud, and the like.   In September, the government made a concerted effort to stamp out such deals to maintain the stability of the RMB.

In order to strengthen the supervision of financial institutions and prevent a Chinese financial crisis, the government implemented a series of new measures, showing its determination to maintain the order of the country's financial system.   On June 6, 1998, the People's Bank of China enacted "Regulations on Penalties for Responsible Officers of Financial Institutions Engaged in Illegal and Unlawful Activities." In this regulation, those financial institutions which give licenses for funds to flow directly or indirectly to stock markets or futures markets would be considered to be in violation of the law.   On July 1, 1998, the State Council promulgated another law, "Rules Concerning Illegal Financial Institutions and Illegal Financial Transactions." In addition, the Central Bank announced the closure of the Chinese New Technology Venture Investment Company and Hainan Development Bank, both of which were unable to repay maturing debts.   Hainan Development Bank became the first bank to be forced to close since 1949.

Expansionary Fiscal Policy

In the first half of 1998, the central government promulgated tax reduction policies to expand domestic demand and to stimulate exports.   Stamp duties on bond transactions, started on June 1, 1998 were reduced from 5% to 4%.   Tax rebate rates for textile machinery and shipping were raised from 9% to 17% and 19%, respectively.   In terms of the expansion of direct investment from January to May, state sector budgeted investment growth increased by 24.7%, far above the growth of budgeted lending investment of 11.4%. And the fixed asset investment growth called for in state-owned enterprises now stands at 13%.   The proportion of fiscal investment in fixed asset investment also rose.

To further stimulate economic growth, the government increased the strength of its fiscal policy and issued RMB100 bn worth of treasury bonds for infrastructure construction in the second half of the year. With this additional amount, the total funds earmarked for infrastructure investment amounted to RMB200 billion.

Quarterly Macroeconomic Forecast for the 4th Quarter in 1998 and 1999

Forecast of Major Economic Indicators

Based on current economic development, our general prediction for economic growth over the next five quarters is as follows:

(1) Pulled up by fixed asset investment, economic growth will stop declining and rise again.

(2) The annual GDP growth rate in 1998 will be 7.9%, growing by another 0.5% in 1999.

(3) Retail prices in 1998 will decline by 2.0%, returning to normal in 1999, but staying within the range of 2.0%.

(4) In 1999, global economic growth will edge marginally higher than in 1998. The growth rate in China's foreign trade will also be higher than that in 1998.

However, in the forthcoming five quarters, many uncertainties exist in terms of the country's economic development. As regards the global economy, it is still hard to predict a recovery in the countries and regions still suffering in the aftermath of the financial crisis. In China's case, domestic economic growth and fixed asset investment in state-owned enterprises have shown a noticeable rise. However, the fixed asset investment in other ownership forms as well as foreign direct investment remain at a low or negative growth level. Similarly, consumer spending growth continues at low levels. Thus, our forecast for the 4th quarter of 1998 and 1999 is made with analysis of all of these domestic and international, and favorable and unfavorable, factors. A model analysis and empirical analysis, combined with our model of macroeconomic quarterly adjustment, are also applied in the forecast. The projected major macroeconomic indicators are shown in Table 1.

Analysis of the Economic Situation in the 4th Quarter of 1998 and 1999

Economic growth rate and prices. With the effect of fast growth in fixed asset investment and rebuilding the flooded areas, economic growth in the fourth quarter of 1998 will increase noticeably compared with the first three quarters. The GDP growth rate will reach about 9.3%. The growth rate for the whole of 1998 will be around 7.9%. Since investment growth will first result in a reduction in inventory, the growth rate of industrial value-added production will increase by the end of 1998 or the beginning of 1999. By analyzing the combined effect of increases in consumer spending, fixed asset investment, and net exports, 1999 GDP growth is expected to be about 8.4%. The growth in the second half of the year will be much faster than the first, reaching a peak in the fourth quarter.

The increased demand in asset investment will push up the prices of investment products, which will in turn drive up consumer goods prices. Furthermore, because the reform of the grain distribution system requires sales at appropriate prices, food prices will also rise to a certain extent. However, on the whole, the oversupply situation of most commercial products will not change for some time. Price competition will still be the major form of competition for most enterprises. As long as fixed asset investment does not over-expand, prices in 1999 will generally be low. Retail prices for the year will only increase by about 1.7%, quarter by quarter.

Table 1
Projected Major Quarterly Economic Indicators for 1998 and 1999

Indicators	1998.1	1998.2	1998.3	1998.4	1998	1999.1	1999.2	1999.3	1999.4	1999
GDP RMB billion	1,590	1,998	1,904.8	2,611.1	8,103.9	1,701.3	2,147.8	2,038.1	2,820	8,707.2
Real GDP growth rate (%)	7.2	6.9	7.0	9.3	7.9	7.9	7.8	8.1	9.2	8.4
Primary industry growth rate (%)	4.0	1.5	2.9	3.5	3.1	3.0	3.0	3.5	3.5	3.3
Secondary industry growth rate (%)	8.0	7.5	7.7	10.1	8.5	8.7	8.6	9.1	10.8	9.4
Of which: Industrial	8.2	7.7	7.9	10.8	8.8	8.7	8.7	9.2	10.0	9.5
Building & construction	6.5	6.5	7.0	8.5	7.9	8.5	8.0	9.0	9.5	9.0
Tertiary industry growth rate (%)	8.0	7.2	8.3	8.5	8.3	8.0	7.9	8.1	8.5	8.4
Of which: Transport. Post and telecom. growth rate (%)	9.6	8.1	10.5	11.0	10.8	9.1	9.0	10.5	10.9	10.1
Commercial service growth rate (%)	7.7	7.0	7.5	7.8	7.6	7.9	7.2	7.3	7.6	7.6
Fixed asset inv. value RMB billion	283	685	617	1,415	3,000	311.3	760.3	691	1,591.9	3,354.5
Fixed asset inv. growth rate (%)	9.0	9.5	12.2	16.0	12.5	12.2	12.7	14.6	15.0	14.5
Retail sale growth rate (%)	8.5	9.9	11.5	7.8	8.7	9.1	8.2	7.5	8.8	8.6
M_0 growth rate (%)	9.9	6.6	9.6	11.6	11.6	12.5	9.6	11.6	13.5	13.5
M_1 growth rate (%)	11.8	8.7	11.8	13.3	13.3	14.8	12.2	15.0	16.2	16.2
M_2 growth rate (%)	15.4	14.0	16.0	17.0	17.0	16.2	14.3	17.3	18.0	18.0
Imports value US$ billion	30.1	35.4	35.1	44.2	144.8	31.5	37.8	37.9	48.8	156
Imports growth rate (%)	2.7	1.8	-2.5	4.5	1.8	4.8	6.8	8.0	10.5	7.8
Exports value US$ billion	40.6	47.2	49.2	53.9	190.9	42.2	50.2	52.6	58.3	203.3
Exports growth rate (%)	13.2	3.5	1.5	-2.2	4.5	4.0	6.3	7.0	8.2	6.5
Retail price growth rate (%)	-1.5	-2.5	-3.0	-2.0	-2.0	-1.5	-0.8	1.2	2.2	1.7

Note: The figures for the first three quarters in 1998 were published by the State Statistics Bureau.

Fixed asset investment. Following the implementation of increased infrastructure investment to generate domestic demand, the growth rate of fixed asset investment and the number of new projects getting underway have risen noticeably, beginning in the third quarter of 1998. The predicted growth rate in the fourth quarter of 1998 for fixed asset investment now stands at about 16%. The growth rate for the entire year will be about 13%. Because the investment in new projects will reach its peak in the new year, we are predicting that fixed asset investment growth will reach about 15% in 1999. This growth rate will be substantially higher than that seen in consumer spending, net exports, and GDP. It will also become the major driving force for economic growth.

Income and spending. After the summer floods, fourth quarter rates will rise above the levels seen in the previous three quarters due to the urgent needs for medicine and flood relief material. However, this growth in consumer spending will still be constrained by low income and consumption expectations, and a strong recovery can hardly be expected in 1999. The growth rate in total retail sales in 1999 will parallel that in 1998, with few quarterly variations. In terms of income, the growth rate of household income will still be low in the first half of 1998. Urban household disposal income will increase by 6.3% relative to the same period of 1997, but cash income for rural households will decline. In terms of income expectations, it is projected consumer spending will tend to be conservative due to the reforms in housing, medical care, employment, education, and social security. In terms of supply, the current market still lacks high technology and high quality products at prices people can afford. Consumer demand will thus be limited.

Foreign trade. From January to August 1998, export sales were essentially in decline. By geographical location, exports to Asia dropped sharply whereas exports to the United States, Europe, and Africa spiked upward. This suggests that with a stable exchange rate, China's exports have managed to maintain their competitive advantage. At the same time, export enterprises have achieved some degree of success in developing new markets.

Therefore, if 1999 world economic growth is higher than that in 1998, China's export growth should show a strong recovery. With higher growth in exports to Europe, the United States, and other countries, China's export growth in 1999 will be higher than that in 1998, the second half being stronger than the first.

As over 50% of China's exports are related to processing unfinished products, this increase in exports should enhance the growth in imports. Between January and August 1998, foreign direct contracted investment reversed a two-year downtrend and rose again. It is predicted that there will be a recovery in the import of equipment invested by foreign investors. And in general, stimulated by the growth in investment demand, import demand will trend up. Thus, the 1999 import growth rate will likely be higher than that seen in 1998, reaching about 8%. And again, the growth rate in the second half of the year will be higher than the first.

Existing Problems in the Economy and Policy Recommendations

The Continued Low Growth in Imports Will Produce Negative Effects on Our Economic Development

In the context of the fact that most neighboring countries and regions are still reeling from the recent financial crisis and showing negative growth, China is performing quite well. Between January and August 1998, the trade surplus reached US$31.4 billion, an increase of 22.7% relative to the same period in 1997. This surplus has benefited us in terms of increasing our foreign exchange reserves and strengthening our ability to pay foreign loans, thereby stabilizing our economy. However, we need to stress that the US$31.4 bn trade surplus has been achieved in a period of sustained low import growth. Between January and August, our imports, which were showing low growth even in 1997 (2.5%), grew only by 0.4% compared with the same period in 1997. The import of equipment as a form of foreign investment increased only by 3.2%.

This low import growth rate impedes our ability to fully utilize international resources and improve our industrial structures. The sustained trade surplus also increases the likelihood of international trade conflicts. Consequently, we must note this low import growth and make the appropriate corresponding policies to overcome this problem. For instance, policies to attract foreign investors to invest in China are needed to stimulate import growth at an appropriate level.

The Possible Problems Caused by More Fixed Asset Investment

The current increase in total fixed asset investment, especially for the state-owned sector, is growing sharply and is of importance in stimulating domestic demand and economic growth. Because price increases and their impacts are a long process, it will take one or two years for this current investment acceleration to push prices up, as is shown in our modeling analysis. Projects starting in 1998 will need further investment in 1999 or 2000. Therefore, while increasing the commitment in fixed asset investment, we must maintain the amount of investment and the number of new projects at a controlled level. If the growth rates of fixed asset investment for 1998 and 1999 do not exceed 15% and 17%, retail price increases will be kept manageable, that is to say below 5%.

Current total fixed asset investment leans heavily against infrastructure construction. The effectiveness of infrastructure construction can only be achieved with the support of primary and secondary industry. Investments in agriculture and in processing in the secondary industries are mostly being sourced from farmers, and small and medium-sized enterprises. In summary, while increasing investment in infrastructure construction via fiscal policy, we must implement a complementary monetary policy and the necessary reforms to encourage such investment by farmers and entrepreneurs and to provide the funds to help them reach their development and expansion goals.

CHINA'S GDP GROWTH WILL REACH 7% IN 1999

LEI GUANGXIAN, CHEN JIJUN AND MENG HONGLING
Economic Information Centre, State Economics and Trade Commission

The 1999 global economy may improve relative to 1998. At the same time, the current financial crisis may just be quietly getting worse. Certainly China's domestic demand will rely on the confidence of consumers and investors alike. And some of the country's economic problems will defy complete resolution, at least over the short term. The level of continued growth, therefore, is not expected to be spectacular. Yet with the help of adopting the right policies, we can still expect to achieve relatively high growth. Making these assumptions in applying our forecast model, we predict that China's economic performance in 1999 could be:

GDP growth of 7%. Projected GDP will reach RMB 8,490 billion, increasing 7% on a comparable basis with the previous year. The added value of primary industry will be RMB 1,450 billion, up 3%; the added value of secondary industry would be RMB 4,220 billion, up 8.5%; the realized added value of industrial production would then be RMB 3,630 billion, up 9%; and the added value from tertiary industry could be RMB 2,820 billion, up 8%.

Fixed asset investment will grow by 12%. Projected total fixed asset investment will be RMB 3,259 billion, an increase of RMB 349 bn over 1997.

Consumer spending will increase by 8%. Forecast total retail sales will reach RMB 3,160 billion, an increase of RMB 237 bn over 1998.

Foreign trade will increase 5%. Predicted total realized foreign trade will be US$356 billion, of which exports will be US$206.5 billion, up 6.4% from 1998; imports will be US$149.5 billion, up 3%. The trade surplus will be US$57 billion.

Financial situation will be stable. Projected year-end M_0 will be RMB 1,210 billion, up 8% from the 1998 year-end. M_1 will be RMB 4,290 billion, up 10%. M_2 will be RMB 11,830 billion, up 12%.

Increase in fiscal expenditures will be faster. Projected full year fiscal revenues will reach RMB 1,035 billion, up 9%. Expenditures will reach RMB 1,133 billion, up 10%.

Price levels will be close to 1998. Projected retail price index will show no increase. Consumer price index will increase about 1%.

Considering all of these factors, 7% GDP growth is more than possible for economic development in 1999. It is also reasonable. Could it go higher? The answer depends on the broad economic situation in 1999. If the global economic situation improves and domestic consumers and investors regain confidence, economic growth will be positively affected, making a higher than 7% growth rate in 1999 possible.

POLICY ANALYSIS

SEVERAL REFLECTIONS ON THE CURRENT MACROECONOMIC SITUATION AND FUTURE POLICY ORIENTATION

LI KE[1] AND YANG DAOXI[2]

[1]*Party Committee of Nanning City, Guangxi Zhuang Autonomous Region;*
[2]*Planning Commission for Guangxi Zhuang Autonomous Region*

In 1998, China's macroeconomic policy of expanding demand basically reached the expected targets. The national economy bottomed out and once again began to grow. Indeed, it was clear that an appropriately vigorous growth rate could be maintained and that the 8% economic growth target could be achieved in basic terms. It is assumed, therefore, that in 1999, the national economy will enter into a new growth stage.

Analysis of the Current Economic Situation

Since the reform and opening up, the experience of China's cyclical economic development has indicated that if economic growth is less than double digit, the adjustment takes a maximum of two years, after which the economy has been inclined to rebound quickly. Since the beginning of 1992, however, the country's economic growth rate has trended down on an annualized basis.

In 1998, the growth rate fell for the seventh consecutive year. The Southeast Asian financial crisis, which began in July 1997, reversed the favorable international economic environment in terms of our economic development. At the beginning of 1998, the central government initiated a series of expansionary and stimulating economic measures. With the negative impact of the regional financial crisis, the restraining influence of a lackluster domestic buyer's market, and the prolonging effect of policy implementation delays, however, the Chinese economy has continued to decline — and no immediate rebound is expected.

Economic growth in the second half of the year was only 6.8%, the lowest since 1992, while expansion in the first half stood at just 7%. At the same time, "deflation" appeared, causing prices to continue to fall. Retail prices, in particular, showed negative growth for eleven consecutive months. In August, the retail price inflation rate was -3.3%. Production potential remained the same, but the ongoing decline in economic growth showed that China's economy had entered a stage of great adjustment after a period of high growth.

Current macroeconomy clearly indicates a demand deficiency, particularly domestically. The priority has, therefore, been to expand domestic demand, especially investment, to compensate for the shortfall resulting from the decline in exports and to fuel steady economic growth. In fact, stimulating domestic demand has become the focus of central government economic policy, via the 1998 macroeconomic adjustment program. Aggressive measures such as lowering interest rates, decreasing the reserve requirements, and expanding fiscal and monetary programs — specifically in terms of increasing public spending — have been implemented.

The emphasis of macroeconomy has shifted from preventing "overheating" to avoiding "overcooling." Thus, "appropriate loosening" formed China's basic macroeconomic policy in 1998. The present low inflation rate has created favorable economic environment for the government's stimulation effort aimed at jump-starting the economy. Implementing relaxed monetary and fiscal policies to stimulate domestic demand is seen as the best expedient to hasten the country's necessary macroeconomic adjustment. Only with sustainable economic growth can various reforms and structural adjustment be implemented in the midst of relative social stability.

This is why we should strive for the targeted 8% growth rate, because it is indispensable if China is to ameliorate nettlesome contradictions and solve its existing problems. From our experience, we know that if GDP growth is below 7%, there will be more serious pressure for employment and redeployment, creating knock-on difficulties for the reform of state-owned enterprises and the increase of fiscal income. However, when the GDP growth rate exceeds 9%, inflationary pressures increase. Normally, GDP expansion in the 8–9% GDP range is optimum. And as the government continues to implement more active fiscal policies, it is expected that achieving this 8% target will not be problematic.

Analysis of the Macroeconomic Environment and Forecast of Economic Development in 1999

1999 is the fiftieth anniversary of the founding of the People's Republic of China and the fourth year of the "Ninth Five-year Plan." Moreover, Macau will return to the motherland this year.

1999 is also a crucial year in which to realize the great goals that inform the country's entering a new millennium. From the point of view of the macroeconomic environment, after overcoming serious natural disasters and the Asian financial crisis, China's overall economic development and macroeconomic environment is likely to become more favorable. The economic prospects most likely, in our opinion, are as follows:

In the international arena, peace and development will remain the main themes. The world is developing toward a multi-polar one.

Economic and technological cooperation worldwide is on the upswing. The globalization trend is becoming more and more prominent. The integration of the world's economy will become the main feature of global economic development. And, the pace of marketization will accelerate. As a result, more mechanisms of market economies will be evident in China.

On the domestic front, as far as supply goes, after more than twenty years of reform and economic development, the overall productivity of agriculture has increased. The "bottleneck" constraints imposed by infrastructure and basic industries limitations have clearly been relaxed. A supply market has been transformed into a buyers' market.

Based on a survey on the supply-demand equilibrium of 601 items of commodities in the domestic market, a shortage in supply was seen in 14% of the products cited in 1995, whereas in the first half of 1998, this number declined to zero. Oversupply was evident in 1/4 of the products listed, however. The inference is that shortage has disappeared from our economy, and has been replaced with relative excess. The various productive factors needed are enough to support a relatively brisk growth rate.

In terms of demand, the central government's implementation of a series of policy measures to increase input and expand domestic demand since 1998 will continue to have a substantial effect. A large portion of the new projects — including infrastructure projects — begun in 1998 will be completed in 1999. Some projects scheduled near the end of the "Ninth Five-year Plan" and the beginning of the "Tenth Five-year Plan" will start in 1999, ahead of schedule. Meanwhile, investment in 1999 will continue to increase.

The multiplier effect resulting from the active fiscal policy implemented in 1998 will become more obvious in 1999, though after a period of delay. Investment demand will increase the prices of investment products, thus stimulating consumption and investment in return.

From a macroeconomic management perspective, China's macroeconomic adjustment approach has gradually become more mature. The country has learned much from its successful experience of "soft landing" the runaway inflation problem. It is also, more recently, experienced handling recession and deflation. This underscores the fact that China's capability in macroeconomic management is improving. The macroeconomic system in place today is one in which the various disciplines, such as planning, monetary and fiscal policies, and so on, coordinate effectively. This means the power to exercise macroeconomic control has been strengthened.

In terms of resource allocation, the degree of marketization within the national economy is on the increase. The leading role of market mechanisms has gradually been established and these have started to become the main factor in resource allocation. This, in turn, has become a great engine in accelerating economic growth.

At the same time, there are unfavorable factors in 1999. The international economic environment continues to be negatively affected by the aftermath of the Asian financial crisis. This creates uncertainties about the future. Also, global productivity is in excess, while the market's overall capacity to absorb output is shrinking. Thus, competition continues to intensify. This suggests that the world economy is on the brink of macro-adjustment. Obviously, these external factors will seriously affect China's economic development, meaning specifically that the future prospects for Chinese exports must be seen as remaining unfavorable.

Domestically, the factors affecting consumer demand are still with us. Because of the acceleration of market reforms, in particular the large increase in the number of redundant workers from the state-owned enterprises, the future of health care, education, and social security reforms is unpredictable. This makes for higher risk in consumer spending. This will dampen the propensity to consume, while increasing the inclination to save.

Taken together, these factors are likely to lead to weaker consumer demand. This, in turn, will limit investment demand, reducing the room for macroeconomic maneuver. In the area of credit and monetary policy, supply leads demand in the current market. The effect of monetary restraint is relatively strong, while the marginal effect of monetary policy is becoming more feeble. Expansionary fiscal policies are expected to have only a short-term effect, as it is impossible to expand the size of the national debt and budget deficit endlessly simply in order to support an appropriate level of aggregate demand and stimulate sustainable economic growth.

Based on this analysis, we believe that in 1999, macroeconomic indicators will signal recovery. Tangentially to the economic cycle, the Chinese economy will enter a new stage of growth whilst experiencing this gradual recovery. No dramatic "leap forward" recovery — such as that seen in 1992 — can be expected, however. In 1999, preliminary estimates are calling for growth in the ideal 8–9% range at this stage of the "Ninth Five-year Plan." In short, the national economy is expected to remain in a cool phase.

Macroeconomic Policy Orientation

The direction of overall macroeconomic policy in 1999 will still be to expand domestic demand while creating an environment conducive to solving problems of aggregates as well as to facilitating the alternation of system development tracks and structural adjustment. On the whole, following these six "combinations" would be prudent:

Combining the Goals of Maintaining Necessary Economic Growth and Improving Economic Quality and Efficiency

"Development is the truth firmly established." As a developing country, nothing can be achieved without the necessary economic growth. In China's actual economic development situation, appropriately vigorous economic growth is a basic precondition to achieving social stability. Without a relative rapid growth, it is difficult for any development. Speed and efficiency are mutually dependent, however. We should not lay undue emphasis on one, such as rapid growth, at the expense of the other, longer-term efficiency.

Too high or too low an economic growth rate will bring no economic benefits. In 1999, after our national economy enters a new growth stage, we must follow the central government's "two fundamental changes" to emphasize market constraints, financial security, structural improvement, technological progress, environmental protection, and a quality improvement of our economic development. We must be determined to progress on the track of focusing on raising economic efficiency. We must expand growth while reducing inventory. We must pay attention to external expansion as well as improving the internal environment. We must emphasize both quantity and quality, while focusing on achieving as high a degree of economic efficiency as possible. As an example, we must strive to improve the efficiency of capital utilization and product quality, while lowering resource consumption and labor costs. Overall, we must raise the productivity. We must deepen the reforms, change systems, adjust and improve the economic structure, and accelerate scientific and technological progress.

Combining Expansion of Investment and Consumption

Investment demand and consumption demand are the two main factors that must be dealt with in any effort to expand aggregate domestic demand.

Investment demand acts as a short-term spur on economic growth. On the one hand, it is sensitive to government investment policy. On the other, it is a very active demand. Its multiplier effect can affect short-term economic growth very quickly and effectively. With current consumer demand seriously deficient, stimulating economic growth by increasing investment is unavoidable.

There are obvious advantages in stimulating economic growth by increasing investment demand. But once the economy bounces back, it must be accompanied by a concomitant growth in consumption. To a certain extent, investment demand is derived from consumption demand. Investment cannot be increased perpetually if it is not accompanied by consumption demand growth.

Since the "Eighth Five-year Plan," consumption demand has contributed an average 60% to total economic growth; investment, by comparison, has contributed only about 30%. It follows that a 1% growth in investment demand has much less effect than a 1% growth in consumption demand.

At the same time, the relative weight of investment in infrastructure projects as a part of the national investment total is not great. Compared with investment demand, consumption demand not only exerts more influence, but is also less subject to manipulation by the national macroeconomic adjustment policy. Consumption demand, as the final link in the chain of overall demand, will have an extremely unfavorable effect on further investment demand expansion if it is not handled adroitly.

Our current efforts to increase both investment and consumption demand are presently hampered by rather strong market constraints. The lack of a "hot point" in the country's consumer markets, and the absence of compelling investment projects are, in fact, interrelated. In 1999, therefore, we must quicken the rise in investment in aid of stimulating the recovery of consumer demand.

In particular, we should first increase investment in urban construction and accelerate the pace of construction of urban infrastructure facilities. We should stimulate the consumption demand as soon as possible by building and reconstructing any number of facilities, from urban electricity grids to roads. Second, as an expedient, we could appropriately increase the scope of government purchases. This would lower production costs and reduce cost increases caused by the number of layers of distribution. Doing this would also achieve the target of reducing inventory and stimulating production growth. Third, we should accelerate the building and reconstruction of rural electricity grids, thereby improving the rural consumption and production environment, so as to create favorable conditions for the development of China's vast rural market. At the same time, we should make the best use of the opportunities offered by the reconstruction after the floods to centralize the rebuilding of residential houses according to town planning, and accelerate the pace of urbanization in villages, enhancing the prospects for the country's long-term economic growth.

In 1999, special attention must be paid to the role played by government investment in guiding and relocating investment from society as a whole. Historical experience has shown that an expansionary fiscal policy can only be used as a short-term adjustment policy and as an emergency measure, subject to the restraints of the budget deficit; it will not serve as a long-term fundamental policy. As such, its value lies in increasing government investment as a guide and catalyst in relocating investment from the society generally, in order to gain the full advantage of the multiplier effect and the stimulus this amounts to in terms of overall demand. In this way, we will achieve steady economic growth.

Combining the Expansion of Domestic Demand and Structural Adjustment

In 1999, after the Chinese economy enters a new growth stage, the problem caused by aggregate imbalance will be resolved to a certain extent. However, the structural problems will become prominent again and will be the main obstacle to further economic growth. This problem cannot be solved through short-term measures such as stimulating demand. We must combine the goal of stimulating economic growth over the short-term through expanding domestic demand with the broader goals of economic structural adjustment and long-term development. In other words, short-term adjustment measures must be compatible with long-term development policies.

Sustained high growth can only be achieved after structural adjustments assure a marked improvement in the technological capability of industries, and, as a result of this, in their market competitiveness. Structural adjustment in 1999, therefore, must address the expansion of demand, the development of markets, technological progress, the cultivation of new economic hot points, the adjustment and improvement of industrial structures, product structures, and regional economic structures. The level of techniques used in industry generally must be raised, to assure the necessary quality improvements. Furthermore, the previous style of economic growth, which relied on "large and all inclusive" and "small and all inclusive" low-level duplicated construction with high input and wastage, must be abandoned.

First, we must accelerate the construction of industrial and other infrastructure projects. Second, we must raise the competitive edge and technological level of industries, focus on the development of equipment industries, and increase investment and the issue of capital in technological renovation. Third, we must pay particular attention to the nature of industrial competition in the 21st century and meet the challenge of the advent of the knowledge economy. We must start from a high platform to develop high technology industries such as electronic information technology; we must actively accelerate industrialization in the sense of fully absorbing high and new technologies. Fourth, new points of economic growth should be actively cultivated. Emphasis should be placed on increasing investment in housing suitable for urban economic development, while at the same time eliminating various structural and policy impediments to the growth of the housing market, so that consumption in housing can be fully stimulated.

Combining Monetary and Fiscal Policies

In 1999, fiscal policy will still be the major means of expanding domestic demand. However, without corresponding changes in money supply, and the support of monetary and fiscal tools, the "squeezing out effect" of fiscal policy will render it ineffective.

This means that the increase in government expenditures will squeeze out an equivalent amount of private and social investment, which will, in turn, eventually cancel out the increase in total demand.   On the contrary, strong government finances are the foundation for the stable operation of financial markets and the source of the basic strength needed to solve the monetary crisis. Because the ratio of fiscal resources to GDP is small, fiscal policy must be supported by monetary policies and national debt in order to stimulate economic growth. As for fiscal policy, we must lay the emphasis on establishing a healthy tax collection system, including off-budget resources and reducing the loss of fiscal income.   At the same time, the rate of fiscal collection must be raised in order to ensure the stable and efficient work of financial departments, and the need to prevent financial risks.

In the area of monetary policy, we need a healthy system for the repayment of bank loans, as well as a security system for mortgage risks to ensure a benign cycle between banks and enterprises in terms of loans.

With respect to national debt policy, we must expand the amount of bond issues as well as their diversities.   The utilization of bond procedures must be improved to maximize their effect. While treasury bonds used as a tool can lend active support to the implementation of fiscal policy, we should take a cautious attitude given the current domestic and international economic situation, and pay attention to the amount of the national debt.   While prudently increasing the issue of treasury bonds, we should also sell some state assets, as well as strengthen our effort to replace all kinds of fees by tax. Management of monopoly sales is another area that needs to be bolstered in order to enhance the country's fiscal resources, and increase support for economic growth and development, without relying too much only on issuing bonds.   At the same time, the management of foreign debts must be strengthened to reduce their risk quotient to the lowest possible level.

Combining Income and Consumption Stimulation Policies

In 1999, a key priority is maintaining steady growth in personal income, which is the foundation of a steady growth in demand. This means personal income structure must be adjusted in order to confine income disparity to a reasonable range in order to achieve the best combination of fairness and efficiency.

Experience in both the domestic and international environment shows that excessive income has a restraining effect on demand expansion because the propensity of high income people to spend is low, while their low income counterparts have little or no discretionary money at their disposal. Furthermore, attention must be paid to guiding people's expectations on income. When their income expectations drop, even if their current income remains unchanged, their inclination to consume is still affected. Therefore, stabilizing consumer expectations is the basis for consumer demand expansion as well as the major problem in the government's macroeconomic regulation. We must prudently combine the long-term effect of some reform measures with short-term policy measures. At the same time, we must place emphasis on the positive effect of a cogent consumption guide policy in order to facilitate matching and coordinating income policy and this consumption guide policy. For different income groups, different consumption policies should be used.

Combining Domestic and External Expansion

In 1999, the difficulties in expanding exports will grow. The influence from changes in the external environment will also be greater. A higher price must be paid to achieve a faster rate of growth in exports. However, it cannot be done through more export tax rebate. We must explore other potential areas through the reform process.

While refining various export policies, we must adjust export product structures, improve product quality, raise our international competitiveness, increase the export of electro-mechanical products which have high technology and added value, and increase our ability to earn foreign exchange. The market diversification strategy should be continued to fully exploit potential in the Asian market, as well as new markets in Europe, America, C.I.S., Africa, and other regions. The government should intensify its promotion and guidance, and increase its support via monetary policy, while cultivating new growth points in exports. Overseas investment, which could stimulate exports, should be encouraged to counter the negative effect of the Asian financial crisis. No effort should be spared in aid of increasing exports.

On the whole, with expanding domestic demand as the focus, the government must exercise an active adjustment and guidance function. While emphasizing the complementarity and harmonization of various macroeconomic measures, it must fully exploit the functional advantages of the market mechanism, make full use of the market economy, and offer protection for the system and its essential mechanism. All these will enable us to create a flexible, optimum macroeconomic environment to ensure China's economic growth as we enter a new millennium.

AN ANALYSIS OF 1998 NATIONAL ECONOMIC DEVELOPMENT AND PROSPECTS FOR 1999

LI XIAOCHAO
Division of General Affairs
State Statistics Bureau

In 1998, facing the unprecedented difficulties brought about by the Asian financial crisis and the catastrophic floods, the Party Central Committee and the State Council implemented active fiscal policies and flexible monetary policies to help maintain economic development in a stable fashion. After the third quarter of the year, the economy began to develop at a faster pace. It is expected that all the targets set for the current year in the macroeconomic adjustment program will be fulfilled. In 1999, with an exacting and appropriate implementation of these policies, we will be able to maintain a sustained, healthy, and quickening trend in economic development, despite present problems and difficulties.

Preliminary Analysis of National Economic Development in 1998

Compared with previous years, more economic measures were utilized in macroeconomy in 1998 to meet the intrinsic requirements of the market economy. However, while the proportion of administrative measures has dwindled noticeably, fiscal and monetary policies were used frequently. Faced with an intensifying Asian financial crisis, the Party Central Committee and the State Council made timely policy adjustments in carrying out strategic moves — aimed at expanding domestic demand and investment and encouraging exports — and to implement active fiscal and monetary policies. As an example of the fiscal policies undertaken, tax rebate rates were raised for textile machinery, iron and steel, cement, and telecommunications equipment. The implementation of these policies was instrumental in expanding domestic demand and stabilizing the economy although they created problems in balancing the budget. On the monetary side, deposit and lending interest rates were cut twice after three previous cuts in interest rates. The reserve requirement was adjusted, and the debt repurchase between commercial banks and the Central Bank was restored. All these policies have been rewarded with noticeable results.

State-Owned Enterprise Investment Grew Remarkably but the Growth of Investment from Collective and Private Enterprises Was Weak

Between January and June 1998, the total value of fixed asset investment by state-owned enterprises was RMB1,086.4 billion, 20% higher than the same period in 1997, 9.7% higher than the previous quarter, and 6.2% higher than the first half of the year. This fixed asset investment became one of the major contributions to the recovery in economic development in a broad sense. Meanwhile, these same indicators showed that the desire of collective and private enterprises to invest was weak. This was partly due to the fact that government-initiated investment was mainly in agricultural irrigation and urban infrastructure. These were not inclined to trigger any "chain reactions." The absence of investment projects with high ROI expectations was also a key factor. And the sustained decline in general price level also contributed to the lack of investment enthusiasm on the part of collective and private enterprises.

Growth of Consumer Products Total Retail Sales Remained Stable

Between January and September 1998, total retail sales of consumer products stood at RMB2,083.3 billion, 6.3% higher than the same period last year, with a stable upward trend. Since 1998, consumer demand has been stable because of the slow growth of consumer demand among both the urban and rural populations. In the case of city dwellers, because of the increase in the number of redundant workers, the growth of aggregate personal income was slow, affecting the growth of consumer spending, at least among some sectors of the population. The implementation of the housing, medical care, and social security reforms increased the expected expenditures for a large portion of the population. The growth of personal spending was weak. The disparity in income distribution was the fundamental cause restraining consumers from spending. For the rural population, the potential for increasing consumer spending was enormous. Many products in oversupply situations in the urban areas were in strong demand in the rural areas. However, because of low rural incomes, this potential demand could not be easily translated into actual demand.

External Demand Stays Weak

Between January and September, total exports amounted to US$134.1 billion, while total imports were US$98.8 billion. The surplus of exports over imports was reported as US$35.3 billion, 15.1% higher than last year, a very strong growth indicator. However, competition in international markets will intensify as Asia recovers from the ongoing financial crisis and regains its productivity. But this situation will affect export growth. It is anticipated that external demand for the entire year will reach about US$40 billion.

Trends and Forecasts for National Economic Development in 1999

It is particularly important for China to maintain stable and swift economic development in 1999, among other reasons to serve as a test of the government's ability to manage the buyers' market after its success in managing the traditional sellers' market. At the same time, economic development in 1999 will to a certain extent set the tone for how we celebrate the fiftieth anniversary of the founding of the PRC in the year of 1999.

International Environment and Domestic Environment

The International Monetary Fund estimates that the world economic growth rate in 1999 will be 2.5%, 0.5% higher than 1998. It is also anticipated that the trend in Asian economies as a whole will rebound from decline to growth. The recovery of the world economy, especially in Asian countries, will increase total world demand. However, the recovery of the Asian economy also means the intensification of competition in the world economy due to the devaluation of various currencies. In 1999, China's external demand will face an even more critical situation.

On the whole, the domestic environment remains favorable to our economic development. The political situation is stable and everyone in the country is showing an unprecedented interest in economic activities. There is an especially strong desire on the part of individuals to take part in economic development.

The Party Central Committee and the State Council have recently begun to implement active measures to accelerate the pace of reforms in agriculture and agricultural projects, reconfirming that the "Contract Responsibility System Linked to Production" will remain unchanged for thirty years. This should set people's minds at ease and reinforce the role of agriculture as the foundation of the country's economic development. The various reform measures in the areas of the housing, medical care, and social security systems are being actively and evenly implemented. Various reform measures in the grain distribution system are being carried out. The successful implementation of the macroeconomic adjustment program has provided valuable experience for the macro-management of the buyers' market and the adjustment efficiency will be raised further. Of course, we should be aware that there will be some uncertain domestic factors affecting national economic development in 1999.

The Macroeconomic Environment and the Microeconomic Foundation

There will be no fundamental changes in the buyers' market. One manifestation is that the markets for most consumer products are almost saturated. Also, the supply capacity of basic daily products such as food and apparel products is enormous at present. According to a census, the capacity utilization rate for some processing industries, like textiles and clothing, is under 60% — and worse in others. Another factor is that constrained, as it is, by the system and income, current actual demand is not strong even though the potential demand is strong. It is very difficult to transform this potential demand, which is very large in China, into actual demand, due to the restrictions imposed by the distribution system.

Both enterprises and individuals are extremely cautious about spending. This is because it is difficult for deflation — the main reason for their caution — to be eliminated altogether in 1999. Up to September 1998, the retail price index had fallen for thirteen consecutive months, while the consumer price index followed suit for six consecutive months. In September, they fell by 3.3% and 1.5%, respectively. This shows that we are in a deflationary economy.

Although deflation increases the purchasing power of investors and consumers, it also has the noticeable effect of suppressing the desire of investors to spend. Based on preliminary estimates, between January and July 1998 the marginal spending disposition of urban residents was 47.2% versus 83.5% in the same period last year. This shows that consumers are very cautious about their spending, which not only directly affects the pulling force of consumer spending on economic growth; it could also have a serious multiplier effect on fiscal policy. Because of the decline in the marginal disposition of urban residents to spend, the multiplier effect of fiscal policy will fall from 6 times to 1.9 times. No substantial changes are expected in this situation in 1999.

Long-term Trends and Short-Term Fluctuations

The long-term trend will remain in a high growth mode for a considerable period of time. This conclusion is mainly based on:

First, China's economic development has stayed at a rather low level. The average GDP per capita in 1997 is only about US$800, far below the level of the developed and developing countries. Second, the capacity utilization rate in China is low, while the potential productivity is enormous. Based on preliminary estimates, our potential economic growth rate could be as high as 8–9%, firmly within the high growth range. Third, the potential demand in the country is also enormous. Infrastructure needs improvement. The scope of consumer spending is broad, and will shortly enter into an expansion stage. We predict that in 1999, all the policy measures will show further effects. The economy will enter into a recovery period and the declining or stagnant state of the economy will come to an end.

From the above analysis, it follows that in 1999, there will be both favorable and unfavorable factors for economic development. However, on the whole, the favorable factors will outweigh the unfavorable ones. To cope with urgent problems like the low productivity and the increase in redundancies within the work force, the maintenance of high economic growth is crucial. Therefore, a range of 8–8.5% would be an ideal economic growth range for 1999. Whatever we do in our economic work, we should not miss this target.

Policy Suggestions for National Economic Development in 1999

In order to achieve this goal, we must implement the policies formulated at the Third Plenum of the 15th Party Congress and consolidate the role of agriculture in the economy as the foundation for sustained, healthy, and stable development of China's economy. We must also push forward enthusiastically and evenly all the proposed reforms in areas such as housing, medical care, and social security. We must try our best to create job opportunities for redundant workers and solve the problems of those who are under the poverty line. We must also do a good job in the following areas:

Make the Best Possible Use of the Buyers' Market Environment to Upgrade the Industrial Structure

The major characteristic of the buyers' market is oversupply. The capacity utilization rate of a large portion of Chinese industries is very low, which is conducive to upgrading the current industrial structure by means of policies. In tertiary industry, we should accelerate its development, especially in the areas of social services and medical services. In agriculture, efforts should be directed toward the production of hi-tech content and the improvement of quality. In industry, some energy-inefficient industries and industries whose products have no markets should be phased out, and replaced by concentrating on the development of high-tech enterprises. Our policies must lend support and favor this purpose so that, on the one hand, concessionary tax rates are adopted to meet the needs of upgrading the industrial structure and, on the other hand, some favorable credit policies such as lowering the interest rates must be adopted for industries with future prospects.

Prepare for Uncertainty in the International Economy, and Re-orient our Efforts Based on Domestic Demand

There are many uncertainties clouding world economic development at the present time. One is the question of whether Japan's economic rejuvenation will succeed; the other is what impact the introduction of the Euro currency will have. Even if the world economy changes for the better in 1999, the scale of change will be very small. Furthermore, the economic recovery in Asia will create strong competitive pressure for us. The focus of policy application in 1999 will, therefore, still be on the expansion of domestic demand.

The Application of Fiscal Policy Requires Close Coordination with Monetary Policy

Because our fiscal revenue is quite small, it is extremely damaging to our national finances to invoke a fiscal policy to stimulate economic growth in the long run. We need to enhance the degree of adjustment and control in our monetary policy, while releasing the pressure of adjustment and control in terms of our fiscal policy in 1999. To accomplish this, we must first solve the problem of "refraining from lending" of our commercial banks, so that the focus of their efforts will be on risk control and at the same time on their profitability. Also, we must try every means to facilitate the appropriate growth of money supply and to solve the problem of deflation more effectively.

Accelerate Income Tax Reform and Adjust the Income Distribution System

Presently, the growth in consumer spending in China is more or less stable. Other than the weakness in the growth of aggregate income and expected expenses, a major reason — often ignored — is the rise of disparity in personal income, clearly seen in the urban/rural contrast, as well as intramurally within each area separately. One of the consequences is that the rich are reluctant to spend, while the poor cannot afford to. This situation is likely to continue for some time due to the different occupational situations, education backgrounds, and knowledge structures of these different groupings. The ideal way to stimulate consumer spending, therefore, is to collect more personal income tax, and to adjust the income structure through the reform of the income tax system.

POLICY SELECTIONS FOR CHINA'S ECONOMIC DEVELOPMENT IN 1999

LI BOXI

Development Research Centre of the State Council

1999 is an important year for both China and the world. It will determine the way all countries will enter the 21st century. Since the onset of the Southeast Asian financial crisis in July 1997, many of these countries have been readjusting their economic development policies and reappraising their development strategies. China will be watching events closely.

1998 was a year when we achieved important successes. Despite the negative effect of the Southeast Asian financial crisis on the world economy, China's economic performance attracted worldwide attention and praise. In 1999, China will be concentrating on continuing all that is favorable in terms of our economic development; and this, in turn, amounts to an important stabilizing factor for the world at large. The success of China's economy in 1998 would have been impossible had the country's leadership not made the correct choices in formulating their macroeconomic policies. And it is of even greater importance that the right policies are selected to keep the development momentum going in a positive direction in 1999.

China's Choice of Economic Policies for 1999 Based on a Severe Global Economic Situation

The Southeast Asian financial crisis, which broke out in 1997, has created serious concerns, not only as regards its negative effect on the economies of Asian countries, but also because of the related negative consequences it has triggered in trade and investment. Moreover, when it spread to Japan and South Korea, people began to recognize that it had become a pan-Asian financial contagion. And when it spread to other continents, prompting among other things financial crisis in Russia, it was generally realized that Southeast Asia's economic problem had become a world problem.

The incessant fluctuations of the Japanese Yen–U.S. dollar exchange rate, wild swings in the major global stock markets, and the emergence of the bubble economy effect in the United States, combined to force us to think seriously about the global features of this crisis. International financial institutions such as the International Monetary Fund (IMF), the World Bank (WB), and the Asian Development Bank (ADB) are increasing their assistance to the countries affected by the crisis. At the same time, they lowered estimates of the world trade and economic growth rate several times in 1998, which shows that the impact of this crisis is not yet over. Even so, it has not only affected the world economy in 1997 and 1998, but will continue to do so in 1999 and 2000. Since the causes of the crisis involve not only financiàl matters but also development strategies and structural factors, it will take a long time to bring it to a close, particularly with the added factors of the complexities inherent in the world's economic relations and the changeability of the international capital market. Ultimately, resolving it will depend on the cooperative efforts taken by the countries in the world and the effectiveness of the measures chosen.

The point is that the Asian financial crisis has not changed for the better after more than a year of remedies and adjustment measures. It has even expanded to affect the currency and stock markets of other regions. No end appears to be in sight.

There are many reasons causing this situation. The most important one is that no effective remedy to cure the crisis has been found. During the last year or more, the IMF initiated the effort to lend more than US$100 bn to Indonesia, Korea, Thailand, and the Philippines. Moreover, in July 1998, they approved a US$11.2 bn loan to Russia. However, this assistance has not achieved any pronounced effect so far. Meanwhile, the maneuverable funds left to the IMF only amount to US$10 billion, and the IMF is awaiting the approval by the U.S. Congress for US$18 bn in fund support. So it seems that further international cooperation will be required to solve the problem.   All the developed countries must participate in this action. And a consensus may be reached as the situation changes.

The crash in the world's stock markets has depressed investor confidence and could easily produce a domino effect.   The speculative activities of the international hedge funds are another dangerous factor.   Even so, it is too early to conclude that the beginning of a new and major world economic recession has begun.

Economists all over the world seem to be of two minds.   One opinion holds that a global recession has already started.   The other holds that financial crisis and economic turmoil mainly rooted in psychological factors can usually be calmed.   The most direct influence on the world economic trend is the economic demand of various countries. ˙ As long as this demand remains stable, global deflation will not appear and the global economy will not sink into recession.   Further observation is necessary before a judgment can be passed on these two opinions.   However, the influence of this crisis will clearly be great, and its effects longer lasting than we have hitherto expected.

Many countries have not taken the responsible attitude toward the world economy as China has.   For the world economy in 1999, there are two different predictions being promulgated at present: one believes that recovery is underway, or at least imminent; the other holds that there will be further negative influences to deal with as a result of this crisis.   The economic policies adopted by China should be formulated sensibly in full recognition of the severity of the situation now confronting the world economy. Therefore, while exploring the international markets, the expansion of domestic demand should become the special feature of China's own economic development strategy in 1999.

Expansion of Domestic Demand in Both
Investment and Consumption

In 1998, the expansion of domestic demand was accomplished mainly through increased investment. In the long run, the rate of increase in investment should be kept within an appropriate range and a better structure. An increase of over 25% will give rise to new problems for the structural adjustment.

Stimulation of investment demand via fiscal policy can be effective. However, because the reform of the investment system is lagging behind, the government's administrative interference, departmental as well as regional vested interests, is having its own effects, meaning some projects are likely to be approved without enough reasonable justification as the scope of investment expands too quickly. Some experts estimate that the resources at the government's disposal consist of only about 22% of GDP, and resources for investment only 2–3% of GDP.

Fiscal policies, therefore, are the best guide for investment expansion. Investment expansion also requires supportive changes in credit policy and the further development of capital markets, particularly in terms of the expansion of direct financing and commercialization of commercial banks. All these have to depend on the acceleration of financial reform. If we respect the autonomy of commercial banks, we should improve the quality of the liability structure (long, medium, and short-term structures, plus the industrial structure). This can prevent, or at least minimize the financial risks. The commercial banks may take a very cautious attitude toward investing in infrastructure, given the long construction period required and the likely low return on investment. Expanding the amount of credit available to finance infrastructure development is not a very attractive proposition for commercial banks, and hence lacks domestic motivation. Meanwhile, if we attract private investment and foreign direct investment, and implement related comprehensive measures to increase the return on investment in infrastructure projects, relevant reforms are necessary. Considering that the effects of these factors are continuing to expand, there will be some restrictions on the effect of infrastructure investment.   Accelerating the pace of reforms in strengthening and expanding the investment system, guided by fiscal policies, may lead to sustainable and stable investment growth.

A country, especially a large one like ours, requires a suitable investment structure.   Likewise, banks require a good loan structure.   Infrastructure projects fall into two categories: those built essentially for public services, for the public interest, so to speak; the other with a return on investment as a prime goal.   If all infrastructure projects require fee payments, the cost of manufacturing will rise.   Currently, the traffic flow on toll roads is lower than expected because drivers prefer to take the old toll-free roads.   Therefore, we must take all the factors into consideration.

Consumer demand is the basic driving force in economic development, and the target for productivity development.   The inclination to restrict and ignore consumer demand should be corrected.   The lack of confidence in stimulating consumer demand should not be tolerated either.   The key point is to identify what stands in the way of the expansion of consumer demand.

Mr. Ding Ningning from the Development Research Centre of the State Council suggested, "The increase of investment is not the substantial solution to the problem of insufficient demand.   What matters in the current market demand is social expectations."   His view is very convincing.   Evaluation of the economic significance of any reform measures on consumption from the general public's point of view should be made before the measures are introduced. The reason the reform measures introduced in 1998 failed to achieve the desired results in stimulating the consumer market lies at least partly in the fact that people had no idea what kinds of results the measures were expected to achieve for the society.   Housing reform must be pushed forward.   Yet, when the reform measures are pushed forward, they all came out at one time.   Most salaried workers have to spend their lifetime savings and often even borrow to buy a flat.   Undoubtedly this has inhibited current consumer demand.   The reform of medical care has also been delayed.

People have no idea about how much they will have to pay, which is another factor inhibiting consumption.

In 1999, the government must "keep their promise to establish a social security system as soon as possible, so as to increase the people's confidence in their future." If the government can present a comprehensive social security reform framework, people may worry less about their future, stimulating consumption as a consequence. "To work out a price list for children's education for an ordinary family " is another thing. It will help to prevent families saving too much as a result of not knowing how much their children's education will cost in the future.

China's market has gone through the transformation from a seller's market to a buyer's market, and some products are in oversupply. Yet, on the whole, consumption levels and the quality of life remain quite low. The structural conflict between supply and demand is very obvious. Creating demand and new markets should be encouraged, and the consumption structure should be reformed to provide more choices for consumers. The transformation from suppression to encouragement of consumption should be a special feature of China's economic policy in 1999.

Appropriate Control of the Rise of the Price Index

Since 1998, prices in China's markets have been in decline. Morever, this trend has been evident for some time. Inflation, which started in 1992, hit its most serious levels at the beginning of the reforms. In order to bring it down quickly, stronger deflationary pressure was enforced. The average inflation rate indicated by the retail price index in 1993 was 21.7%; the consumer price index showed 24%. In 1996, the "soft landing" was successfully achieved. However, deflation, with its delaying effect and the 3% growth rate target in the adjustment program, has prolonged the time needed for China's economy to get out of the trough. A weak market and negative growth in the price indexes are not the objectives of the adjustment program but rather the problems of the economy.

Statistically there is a cyclical inverse relation between the inflation and unemployment rates, which is to say that when success is achieved in controlling inflation, caution should be taken as regards the rise of unemployment. If a high and stable economic growth rate is to be maintained, a high unemployment rate cannot be allowed. There is also the requirement for an appropriate rate of inflation. It is simply not true that the lower the inflation the better. An inappropriately low inflation may lead to economic recession. It is groundless to pursue a policy of pushing down prices amid price stability, unless the decline is caused by technological advances, which will bring down the cost of manufacturing production.

There are several factors causing the rise in prices. The first is the expansion of demand. In particular, reconstruction after the past year's disastrous floods will stimulate economic growth, and this will be gradually reflected in the price index. The second is that the success of the grain distribution system reform will increase grain prices. The third is that the central government is determined to stamp out smuggling activities, which will lead to a reasonable rise in market prices. The fourth is the stimulation of domestic demand, and the implementation of some public adjustment policies, which will facilitate a benign cycle, keeping prices at a reasonable level overall.

Based on analysis of the figures released by the organizations concerned, prices will probably rise in the last few months of 1998. We suggest that the target for the retail price index in the adjustment program be set at below 6%.

Maintaining a Basically Stable Exchange Rate of RMB / USD

Amid the ongoing Asian financial crisis, China has insisted on a policy of non-devaluation of the RMB. This has been a stabilizing factor for the economies of the Mainland, Hong Kong, and even the world, winning the country international approval.

The Asian financial crisis has most heavily influenced the areas of trade, the investment environment, and the expected risks. Trade is affected by the decline in both prices and income in countries suffering from the financial crisis.   International investors will re-assess their investment environment when there is a major change in the international environment.   They will alter their expectations of the countries (or regions) they have invested in. They will also show more concern about the inadequacy in China's financial system and the lack of an effective management for legal persons.   Some investors expect higher returns to compensate for what they perceive as higher investment risks, or choose projects that guarantee a more stable profit.

China has maintained, for the past few years, a trade surplus. Foreign exchange reserves stand in excess of US$140 billion.   The current account surplus will be carried forward in 1998.   The ratio of foreign debt to GDP is 16.9%.   The foreign capital cited mainly consists of foreign direct investment and long-term loans. Currency convertibility is still not in place for capital. Our success in keeping the direct impact of the Asian financial crisis outside our door does not depend on the devaluation of the RMB, which is not affected by the market; rather it will depend on the policy choices the Chinese government makes concerning the control of its own exchange. rate.

Because of the influence of factors such as the devaluation of the Japanese Yen, the RMB is devalued in the black market. Meanwhile, the U.S. dollar is in short supply, which indicates that there are some people who expect the devaluation of the RMB. This has to do with the economic situation in the country.   The RMB is not linked to the U.S. dollar.   To maintain the value of the RMB is the policy choice of prime importance in the face of the Southeast Asian financial crisis.   Maintaining the stability of the RMB exchange rate is the only way to eliminate people's expectation of an RMB devaluation.

In order to maintain the stability of currencies in Asia, the Chinese government promised not to devalue the RMB in 1998. This promise carried with it a responsibility and a certain price had to be paid. At the same time, it has helped to maintain the stable macroeconomic environment necessary for China's sustained economic growth.

Devaluation may help realize a trade surplus. However, as suggested by China's foreign trade trends in 1998, China has maintained a trade surplus thanks to the stable development of the processing trades and the measures to open markets. The problem in international trade has been created by the decline in international economic growth and world trade. It was not entirely due to prices. Crisis-hit countries devalued their currencies but their trade did not expand. Also, devaluation of the RMB will affect its attractiveness to foreign capital, and could even prompt a capital outflow. Should this occur, it will have an important impact on China's economic development. Furthermore, the most important economic benefit in exchange stability is the avoidance of credit risk. The stability of the RMB is of vital importance to the stability of the Hong Kong dollar. Non-devaluation for the RMB means that there will not be a second round of currency devaluation. It follows that in 1999 China should continue its policy of non-devaluation for the RMB.

This is not to say that we shouldn't attach certain conditions in exchange for maintaining this non-devaluation policy, however. We should request substantial international coordination. Following the devaluation of the Yen, the RMB has in fact risen against the Yen. In order to maintain global financial order — and the economic stability it underpins — it is necessary for all the major countries to make as full a commitment to the world economy as China has. Whether the crisis is slowly weakened or intensified depends entirely on the resolute coordination of efforts worldwide, specifically in aid of reforming the world's financial system. In 1999, the exchange rate policy of China should be to maintain the basic stability of the RMB, and gradually push forward the process of currency marketization.

In terms of the policy choices for our economic development, in addition to the above, we should put emphasis on:

(1) achieving effective economic growth;

(2) actively implementing the financial reforms needed to stimulate economic growth;

(3) formulating a fiscal policy which can provide stable economic growth;

(4) growing small- and medium-size enterprises for strategic purposes;

(5) attracting foreign investment whenever it is appropriate.

AN ANALYSIS OF ECONOMIC GROWTH AND PUBLIC INVESTMENT

ZHANG SHOUYI

Institute of Quantitative and Technical Economics
Chinese Academy of Social Sciences

China's economic growth in 1998 has been, to a large extent, dependent on the pulling force of public investment. We need to analyze these two economic phenomena and their relationship.

The Probability of High Economic Growth

Between 1979 and 1997, China's average annual GDP growth was 9.8%, the highest in the world. Both national strength and personal standards of living have advanced to new levels. These economic achievements have won great support from the people as well as the respect of the international community.

China has a population of 1.2 bn people. The country must maintain a high rate of economic growth in the future over the long term in order to solve the unemployment problem, and underpin the environment for reform. It must also raise the standard of living of the Chinese people while maintaining its status as an international power.

Sustaining a high growth rate is only a goal. The problem is how to make this goal a reality. Taking all the factors into consideration, however, we believe it is achieveable.

Firstly, the system provides a guarantee. Twenty years of economic reform have not only emancipated productivity and stimulated a high rate of economic growth; they have also brought about enormous changes in the economic system. The market structure has become increasingly important in the allocation of resources. From now until the year 2010, the focus will be on deepening these reforms. The relationship between the various economic sectors will be smoothed out so that necessary resources can be allocated and utilized in the best ways. This is the true pulling force of high economic growth.

Second, China is a country rich in natural resources. Although the forty-five years of industrialization have consumed many of these, those remaining can still support a long period of high growth. And if these domestic resources are not sufficient, imports can be utilized. In the past, in discussions about the ideal population size, much attention was paid to the limits of China's natural resources. But this is a one-sided view. The development of knowledge will increase, by two, ten, or fifty times, the productivity of each kind of natural resource, even in terms of some things that have not been identified as resources. While we do not agree with the idea of restricting the size of the population in proportion to our natural resources, we also do not support the view that the bigger the population the better. We would rather insist on family planning at the cost of an aging population. But from now on, when we consider population, we should also consider the investment in education as well as the availability of natural resources.

Third, we are rich in human resources. Currently, China has a labor force of 700 million, a key element in production. The question which requires in-depth research is that from 1953 until now, after forty-five years of industrialization, the pressure of creating job opportunities is still very great. In particular, there is still an enormous pool of excess rural labor. The total area of cultivated land in the country in 1997 was about 150 million hectares. The number of farm laborers was 320 million. By one person per hectare allocation, the number of excessive rural laborers was 170 million. This figure adds to the 30 million unemployed urban workers, making the total unemployment 200 million, 28.6% of the labor force. This calculation has been done on a relative basis. If China's 150 million farmers make up 21.4% of the total labor force, American farmers in 1995 would make up only 2.9% of the total of that country's labor force, 18.5% less than is the case in China.

Why is the speed of absorption of these excessive rural labor so slow in terms of China's industrialization process compared with the developed countries? There are various reasons:

(1) China is in the middle of its industrialization.   As this progresses, large quantities of excessive labor can be absorbed.

(2) The starting point of the technical level of China's industrialization is higher than was the case in western countries at the time of their industrialization. Less labor is absorbed per unit of investment.

(3) In China's industrialization, huge quantities of machinery and equipment have been imported.   These imports have facilitated China's industrialization process, and are indispensable for us to catch up with other countries. This will shorten the detour of China's industrial production, because the products imported into the country are usually finished products.   The exploration and production of raw materials and the production of semi-finished products are all done outside China.   Correspondingly, no jobs can be created inside China.   Although there are imports alongside of exports, most of the exports are agricultural by-products and handicrafts.   The detour of production is rather short.

(4) Personal income used to be low and the scope of consumption, therefore, was narrow.   Tertiary industry was not well developed.   As a result, not many people could find a job.

(5) The progress of urbanization was slow.   The economy of large cities embraced a variety of industries.   The employment of one individual requires the service of several others, who are in return in need of the service of still others. The slow progress in urbanization restricts the multiplier effect (full employment coefficient) of employment.   Excessive

labor is a pressure as well as a key factor in maintaining continued high economic growth in the future.

Fourth, we have made advances in technology. Since the beginning of the reforms and opening up, the level of our technology has advanced greatly through imports and innovation. But many problems still exist. For instance, technological imports have been abundant while technological innovations have been too few. Similarly, too much hardware has been imported, and too little software. The ratio of technology to its transformed productivity is low. When these problems are solved, substantial progress made in technological development will increasingly play a more important role in maintaining high economic growth.

Fifth, the domestic market is enormous. With 1.2 bn people, we have the largest market in the world. Personal income has increased impressively since the beginning of the reforms and opening up. However, there is a great disparity between China and the developed countries in this respect. The GDP per capita in 1995 was RMB 4,800, amounting to only US$585. Compared with US$28,000 for the United States, and US$36,000 for Japan, our GDP per capita is only 2.1% of that in the United States, and 1.6% of that in Japan. Despite this fact, there is the problem of purchasing power parity, and according to the exchange rate the figures pertaining to China have been undervalued whereas the figures pertaining to Japan have been overvalued. However, whatever standard of comparison is used, they do not contradict the conclusion that average personal income in China is still very low. The disparity among average personal incomes determines the disparity in consumption averages, as seen in Table 1.

Table 1
Average consumption in China, the United States, and Japan

Country	1980	1985	1990	1993
China (RMB)	236	437	803	2,936*
U.S. (US$)	7,500	10,896	14,595	16,429
Japan (US$)	5,336	6,549	13,620	19,574

* in 1997

Per capita consumption in Japan in 1990 at least doubled that in 1985. The effect of the high value of the Yen to the U.S. dollar was a significant factor. Per capita consumption in China in 1997 was 3.7 times that in 1990, being a period of fast growth. However, calculated with the exchange rate, it was still only US$358, 2.2% of the 1993 American level, and 1.8% of Japan's. Because of the problem of purchasing power parity, the figures are not accurate enough. However, they fully demonstrate that the potential of the domestic markets in China is huge. Along with high economic growth, personal income will increase to a high level. This means, in turn, that ultimately China will be a market for all types of products and services.

Sixth, there are international factors. From now on, China will continue with the policy of opening up in expanding foreign trade, attracting foreign capital and technology, while continuing to make use of "the advantage of developing later than others" to stimulate high economic growth.

When discussing China's high economic growth, we need to have a thorough understanding of the potential growth curve. During the eighteen years between 1978 and 1995, economic growth has been above 10% for ten years, below 10% for eight years, and averaging 9.9%. Most economists then considered the potential growth curve at about 10%, believing more than 10% would cause inflation. Based on our practical experience, this view is essentially correct. After 1995, following the changes in the economic situation, there have been changes in the potential growth curve, which might have fallen from 10% to about 8%. We are not saying that it will be absolutely impossible to have annual growth rates of 15.2% (1984) or 14.2% (1992) in the future, but they will be rare. The slowdown of the growth rate after 1995 can be understood in terms of supply and demand.

From the perspective of supply, the expansion of the economic base means a 1% growth of GDP, followed by an increase of the required absolute growth rate. If the rate of investment does not increase in tandem, the growth rate will fall. Between 1993 and 1997, the average annual rate of capital formation was as high as 39.6%. From now on, we cannot rely on such rates of increase; rather we should lower our expectation to an appropriate level. If the progress in technology cannot overcome the effect of the increase in the economic base, the growth rate will fall. Since the reform and opening up, despite the advances in science and technology, their effect and contribution to economic growth have yet to match the effect of the expansion of the economic base. Therefore, the declining trend in the growth rate is inevitable.

From the perspective of demand, China's economy is transforming from one constrained by resources to one constrained by the market, that is from a "seller's market" to a "buyer's market." In the era of the planned economy, the supply of many consumer goods was rationed. Whatever the various enterprises of that time produced, and regardless of how many items they produced, they could be sold. The size of the economy was determined by production capacity.

Today, after twenty years of reform and opening up, enormous changes have taken place. The deficiency of consumption in the planned economy era has been made up. As the consumption standard of most residents has reached the level of sufficiency, consumers are becoming increasingly choosy in the commodities they buy. Their priorities are now quality, design, type, and price instead of quantity. The demand and constraints imposed by the markets set a limit to economic growth at under 10%.

Investment in Public Sectors Is an Important
Macroeconomic Adjustment Policy

The Chinese socialist market economy is manipulated by the mutual actions of an "invisible hand" and a "visible hand." The latter is the macroeconomic adjustment program, mainly pertaining to monetary and fiscal policies.   Since 1997, the Central Bank has reduced interest rates five times.   At the end of September 1998, the one-year deposit rate was about 5%; the loan rate was above 6%. This shows that there is no "interest rate trap" in China.   There is still room for us to cut interest rates, increase investment, and stimulate economic growth.   If we divide economic structures between industrial facility and infrastructure, many production facilities at present constitute oversupply.   If we further lower the interest rate and invest the expanded capital in production facilities, this oversupply situation will get worse and economic efficiency will decline further.   This is because the effect of monetary policy tends to be general, not specific.   The investment resulting from a further lowering of the interest rates might lead to investment in long-term projects but not necessarily needed, whereas short-term needed projects may not be invested in, thus making the industrial structures more imbalanced.

In a situation where it is impossible to further use monetary policy, fiscal money with a specific feature can be used.   Since the reforms and opening up, China's infrastructure construction has gained quite an achievement.   But there is much to improve, and many problems still exist.   The catastrophic floods in 1998 offer strong proof.

In western economics textbooks, fiscal policies are usually restricted to tax increases or decreases.   This is not comprehensive. In fact, public investment is a very important macroeconomic adjustment.   In the developed countries, public investment policy is only used when the economy is in a depression.   For example, U.S. President Franklin D. Roosevelt used public investment for large-scale irrigation and highway projects to shake off the influence of the 1929–1933 economic depression.   But when the economy is in a mild recession, monetary policy is the usual tool employed to help.

Public investment is mainly used in infrastructure construction. However, up to now, there has been no precise definition of what infrastructure is. That is because there is no clear-cut distinction between infrastructure in general and infrastructure specifically for industry. Normally, railways, roads, drains, irrigation, communications facilities, wharves, airports, oil storage facilities, grain storage facilities, and so on are considered infrastructure in general. From our point of view, infrastructure in general can be defined broadly and narrowly. Those of the type listed above are infrastructure in the broad sense; but among them, railways, irrigation systems, and communications facilities can also be considered industrial infrastructure. Thus, infrastructure projects in the narrow sense are items with significant social benefits but low economic efficiency, and their construction requires fiscal expenditure.

There is another problem relating to infrastructure projects, namely "who builds them?" Based on our earlier definition of infrastructure projects, any project which generates average social capital profit (infrastructure projects in the broad sense) should be built by the private sector. When it is absolutely necessary, the government can provide suitable assistance. In the case of projects whose chances of economic efficiency are lower than the norm for industrial infrastructure (infrastructure in the narrow sense), investment should be sourced from the central and local governments. In a market economy, private, collective, and individual enterprises can collaborate in infrastructure projects.

The pulling effect on economic growth generated by public investment is closely related to an investment multiplier. For an investment multiplier to function at its best, there should be no excess production capacity. Judging from the current situation, there is plenty of excess capacity in many enterprises. As a result, the multiplier effect of the public investment made in 1998 may be less than the optimum expected of the multiplier effect. In calculating this pulling effect of public investment on economic growth, we have to consider this factor.

The experience of the developed countries shows that using deficit financing to invest in public infrastructure projects can produce positive results in the short term, but also can produce serious adverse effects in the long run.   When the government issues public debt, and expands the size of the public debt, interest rates naturally trend up.   As a result, not only is the cost of public investment increased, so is the cost of the private sector.   As the cost of production of our products increases, our products will be less competitive in international markets.   This is the major reason for the deficit in the balance of international payments.   Therefore, it is best to use a "surplus-covering–deficit" fiscal policy.   This policy will not create the above noted adverse effect on the economy.   Rather it will smooth out flucturations in the economic cycle.   This is a win-win policy.

China's Economy Is Different from Japan's

When China uses public investment to pull up economic growth, some foreign economists think that we are copying Japan, and they conclude that the results will not be good.   This view is not justifiable in our opinion.

When we visited Japan in 1997, experts from the Asian Economic Research Institute told us that in 1993, 1994, and 1995, Japan's GDP growth rates were 0.1%, 0.5%, and 0.9% respectively, which were very low.   In fact, without public investment from the government in those three years, the GDP growth would have been negative.   This shows the effect of public investment in Japan. Similarly, 1997 GDP growth stood at 0.7% on the negative side, and 1998 GDP growth is estimated to be -1.8%.   Without support from public investment, this negative growth rate would have been even greater.

There are major differences between the economic situations prevailing in China and in Japan. Japan is an economically developed country. The average personal consumption level is very high, and the domestic market is essentially saturated. When the Asian financial crisis broke out in July 1997, Japanese exports were blocked. In a situation where both the domestic and external markets were in recession, even with interest rates cut to 0.5% to stimulate investment demand and economic recovery, the result was disappointing. Japan has obviously fallen into the "interest rate trap." This problem does not exist in China.

Presently, the average production level in China is much lower than that in Japan. There is still a lot of room for economic growth in China. Compared with the situation in Japan, the structural effect of economic growth was great in China. See Table 2 for details.

The figures in Table 2 show that: First, although there are differences between China's and Japan's secondary industry, they are not big. However, there are big differences in the primary and tertiary industries. The relative weight of China's primary industry is 16.6% higher than that of Japan's. The relative weight of employment is 44% higher. By contrast, in the case of tertiary industry, China's relative weighting is 25.5% lower, and employment 34% lower. The mission of China's modernization and the focus of its economic development from now on must be to transfer manpower from primary industry to tertiary industry. Secondly, the structural effect exists in both China and Japan, but it is greater in the former than in the latter. Based on the structural effect in primary industry, which is 1, China is 165% of Japan in secondary industry, and 121% in tertiary industry. Thirdly, although the structural effect exists in Japan, the ratio of the rural labor force is already very small. In China, by contrast, the rural labor force still accounts for almost half of the country's manpower, which underscores its very high potential. It is also an important factor in maintaining the targeted high growth in the economy generally, and in terms of income and consumption.

Table 2
Production and Employment Structure of China and Japan

Unit %

Indicator	Primary industry	Secondary industry	Tertiary industry
China (1997)			
Production output value	18.7	49.2	32.1
Employment	49.9	23.7	26.4
Japan (1993)			
Production output value	2.1	40.7	57.6
Employment	5.9	33.7	60.4
China			
Relative labor	0.37	2.08	1.22
Productivity			
Primary industry as 1	1	5.54	3.24
Japan			
Relative labor	0.36	1.19	0.95
Productivity			
Primary industry as 1	1	3.35	2.68

Note: Relative labor productivity = production output value proportion/employment proportion.

See Table 3 for the consumption structures of the population in China and Japan.

Table 3
Consumption Structures of the Population in China and Japan

Unit: %

Country	Food	Clothing	Housing	Home appliances	Education	Medical and health care	Transportation and communication	Others
Japan (1992)	20.1	6.2	20.2	6.1	10.3	11.0	9.8	16.3
China (1996) Urban	48.6	13.5	7.7	7.6	9.6	3.7	5.1	4.2
Rural	56.3	7.2	13.9	5.4	8.4	3.7	5.0	2.1

In 1997 Engel's coefficient of China's urban population was 28.5% higher than that of Japan; the rural population was 36.2% higher. At the same time, expenditures in housing, cultural activity and education, medical care, transportation, and communications were higher than those in Japan. This comparison shows a clear direction for China's future economic development and industrial structure adjustment.

ANALYZING ECONOMIC SITUATIONS IN 1998–1999 AND CONTEMPLATING POLICIES

CHENG JIANLIN

Economic Forecasting Department, State Information Centre

1998: The Preliminary Success of the Macroeconomic Adjustment Program and 8% GDP Growth Rate Were Expected

Entering into 1998, the effects of the Asian financial crisis on China's economy have proven to be increasingly severe. After the "soft landing," China faced a new and equally serious problem: insufficient effective demand. In order to prevent a sharp decline in growth, the Party Central Committee and State Council made timely adjustments and implemented a series of economic measures to stimulate domestic demand and increase investment. From the second quarter of 1998 onward, the country's economy has leveled off and become stable. Indeed, in the third quarter, the economic growth rate noticeably rebounded. The economic pattern and trend for the entire year is expected to be "first low then high" growth.

Between January and August 1998, according to major macroeconomic indicators: accumulated state fixed asset investment growth stood at 17.4%, with 16.1%, 22.9%, and 26.9% increments recorded in June, July, and August respectively. The effects of the government's increased infrastructure investment had begun to show. Consumer demand in 1998 was affected partly by the slow growth seen in personal incomes, and partly by the reforms in housing and social security. These factors have increased uncertainties among consumers, and consequently consumer spending has proven unstable.

In the first half of 1998, growth in consumer demand was slow. Between January and June 1998, growth of total retail sales was only 6.8%. In July and August, consumer demand had noticeably recovered, showing 8.1% and 9.3% increases respectively.   With the help of an effective market diversification strategy, we did well with exports in the first half of 1998. Between January and June, these grew by 7.6%, lending strong support to renewed economic growth.   However, in the second half, buffeted more seriously by the Asian financial crisis, the export situation became severe.   In August, export growth was negative for the second time since May 1998, at 2.9%.   The accumulated export growth rate between January and August was 5.5%, 18% lower than the previous year.   The slowdown in foreign trade suggested that a greater increase in domestic demand was needed to maintain stable economic growth in 1998.

From the perspective of demand, it is expected that state fixed asset investment will maintain the vigorous growth seen from June through August over the coming months.   State fixed asset investment in 1998 as a whole will grow by more than 20%.   Due to the weakness in investment growth in the non-state sectors, however, the predicted total 1998 fixed asset investment growth for the entire economy will be slower paced, at about 15%.

Consumer demand in July and August 1998 will reverse the decline seen earlier in the year.   At the same time, the July and August demand increase was, in part, due to the effect of flood relief. In other words, these items should not be taken as constant factors. Otherwise, consumer spending remained unchanged, mostly because the other conditions affecting it did likewise. The tendency to save grew stronger. Consequently, the expected growth in consumer demand for the entire year will be slightly lower than in 1997, with a nominal growth of 8%, or real growth of 9.6%.

In terms of contributing to the country's economic growth, both total fixed asset investment and retail sales are important factors. However, fixed asset investment does not mean the formation of capital, while total retail sales are only a part of the final consumption status quo. The real growth in fixed asset investment and retail sales, therefore, is expected to reach about 15% and 9.6% respectively.   The amount of inventory in 1998 may be reduced.   It is also indicated that the consumption on services may continue to grow, although slowly.

From the perspective of capital formation and final consumer demand, capital formation is expected to grow by about 10% more than last year, while final consumer demand will grow by less than 8%. If the export of goods and services does not decline further in the last few months of the year, the 1998 economic growth target of 8% will be met, though this will require some hard work.

1999: Confidence Will Be Restored in the Microeconomic Mainstream and Economic Growth Is Expected to Be Slightly Higher than that in 1998

The prediction of the trend of 1999 economic development is mainly made based on the following three aspects: first, changes in the world economic environment, or the possible deterioration of the external factors; second, the macroeconomic adjustment programs of 1999, in particular the direction of the fiscal and monetary policies; third, the microeconomic foundation of the macroeconomy, combined with domestic enterprises, family investments, and changes in spending behavior.

Looking at the World Economic Environment, the External Situation May Not Deteriorate Further and Our Exports May Improve, but at a Slow Growth Rate

The global economy was affected by the Asian financial crisis in 1998.   Consequently, some Asian, Eastern European, and Latin American countries experienced negative economic growth.   The American economy also started to slow down while the Japanese economy deteriorated.   However, according to the IMF forecast for the 1998–1999 global economy, the 1999 economic growth rate will be slightly higher than that in 1998.   The growth rate of the global economy in 1998 was 2%, while in 1999 it is expected to be 2.5%. This indicates that the external conditions should not worsen in

1999, although the impact of the financial crisis cannot be quickly shaken off.

In 1999, Government Policy Is Likely to Maintain the Continuity of the Macroeconomic Adjustment Program. Both Fiscal and Monetary Policies Will Show Appropriate Flexibility and Aggressiveness

Externally, the Asian economy will take a long time to recover. And domestically the behavior of our microeconomic mainstream will respond to the changed economic situation.   Both the external and domestic factors will postpone the recovery of our domestic consumption.   Therefore, in order to stimulate demand to make up for the medium-term slowdown caused by the decline in growth in 1997–98, and to regain the confidence of the consumers, our macroeconomic   adjustment   program   will   embrace   further stimulating measures and policies.

The basic goals of the macroeconomic adjustment program are: to maintain relatively stable economic growth, to continue to expand domestic demand, and to overcome deflation. At the same time we must stimulate aggregate growth; arrange the framework for advancing the industrial structure so that aggregates improvement and structural adjustment can be carried out together; and properly manage the reform of the state-owned enterprises and increase job opportunities to maintain social stability.   In policy measures, on the one hand, the fiscal policy will play an important role in performing the task to stimulate the economic recovery.   On the other hand, the monetary policy will closely monitor the money supply indicators and will be coordinated with the fiscal policy in a flexible and active way to promote stable economic growth.

In the Light of the Trend of Enterprise and Family Investment, and Changes in Consumption Behavior, Investment by the Non-state Sectors in 1999 Will Increase and the Growth in Consumer Spending Will Remain Stable

In 1998, changes were evident in our microeconomic foundation. These were that the investment by enterprises and families, and consumption patterns, manifested weak motivation in investment and caution in consumer spending.

Whether or not we are able to change the weak incentives to invest and the high propensity for savings will have a direct affect on whether or not the recovery of domestic demand by the government's expanded investment in infrastructure in the second half of 1998 can be realized and sustained, so that the economy can enter into a benign cycle. The weak strength of investment by enterprises is attributed to direct and indirect causes. The direct cause is that total price level is still experiencing negative growth, which will reduce the expected return on investment. Therefore, the government insists on implementing policies to stimulate domestic demand (both in the aggregates and in the structure). When the total demand gradually increases, the 1999 price level will rise from the current negative growth to a normal positive growth, and the expected return on investment will be improved. The indirect cause is that the supply and demand structures of capital do not quite match in the existing financial structure. The development of a direct capital fund-raising market has been slow. Meanwhile, there are barriers for the non-state sector to enter into infrastructure investment. All of these problems must be quickly resolved.

Our economy is going through a period of intensive reform and adjustment. On the one hand, many reform measures such as those in social security are quite intensive. On the other hand, the growth of urban personal income is slowing down, and the consumer credit system has not yet been established. Consequently, the demand for housing and cars by urban consumers is limited and a large portion of consumer demand will be deferred.

In terms of rural consumer demand, there is an enormous potential demand for "food, clothing, daily commodities, housing, and transportation." However, the potential for value-added agricultural production is limited, and prices for agricultural products cannot be sharply raised. Therefore, based on the current production patterns, it is impossible to substantially raise rural personal incomes, and it is difficult to convert this potential demand into actual demand.

In short, the world economic environment in 1999 will not deteriorate further. While the macroeconomic adjustment program will continue to maintain its appropriate expansion, confidence in the microeconomic mainstream will recover to a certain degree. Consumer demand will grow steadily. Investment demand will continue to recover. 1999 economic growth will be the same or slightly higher than that of 1998, reaching the rate of 8–8.5%.

Enhancing the Effectiveness of the Macroeconomic Adjustment Program and Maintaining a Sustained, Healthy, and Fast Rate of Economic Growth

In 1999, while actively implementing China's fiscal and monetary policies, we will have to deepen the reform of the economic system. By transforming the system, we hope to ensure the implementation of government policies, and to maintain a sustained, healthy, and fast economic growth.

Adjust the Current Dual Financial Systems; Quickly Improve the Capital Market for Small- and Medium-size Enterprises so as to Fully Utilize the Economic Stimulating Force of these Enterprises and their Ability to Absorb More Labor

Of all the difficulties encountered by small- and medium-size enterprises, the topmost one is the shortage of capital, which forms a sharp contrast with the inability to effectively utilize the resources of the national commercial banks.

The main reasons for the dislocation between the supply of capital and the demand for capital are fourfold. First, in our financial system, for a long time the client base for the national commercial banks has always been the medium-size and large state-owned enterprises. The client base for shareholding banks and private banks is the non-state small- and medium-size enterprises. However, in terms of capital supply and branch networks, the latter institutions cannot compare with the state ones. Second, given that the market risk is great in the increasingly competitive environment, it is difficult for small- and medium-size enterprises to secure adequate guarantees. Third, the national commercial banks at the grass-root levels have been either shut down or merged, and their authorization for credit approval has been taken away. This measure makes it even more difficult for small- and medium-size enterprises to secure credit. Four, the financing channel for small- and medium-size enterprises is unitary, mainly through indirect fund-raising methods.

To solve the problem of shortage of capital for small- and medium-size enterprises, we should concentrate our work in the following areas in 1999:

(1) Through legislation, we should abolish the discriminatory policies toward small- and medium-size enterprises, especially those in the private sector.

(2) We should establish specialized financial institutions to serve small- and medium-size enterprises, including policy banks funded by the government, local share-holding banks funded by private organizations, and cooperative trusts funded by small- and medium-size enterprises by means of membership.

(3) We should establish a credit insurance fund and a credit guarantee association for small- and medium-size enterprises.

(4) While the above conditions are lacking, the national commercial banks should actively establish appropriate credit policies and streamline their approval procedures. This would

enable them to serve the small- and medium-size enterprises by allowing them to borrow quickly and to tap market potentiality for a better fiscal situation.

(5)   We should establish a direct channel to raise capital, allowing small but hi-tech intensive enterprises with high market potential to enter stock markets to raise capital.   We should at least begin pilot work on this in 1999.

Open Infrastructure Investment Projects to Private Enterprises so as to Stimulate the Development of Infrastructure and Private Investment

Under the current situation, the desire of enterprises to invest is generally low. The opening of infrastructure projects to private enterprises will not only avoid the concentration of debts to the national banks and the government, but will also promote private investment.   Recently, in some regions, private enterprises have already started to invest in infrastructure projects like highways, and bridges or have purchased the operating rights of toll bridges and roads.

Through the sale of operating rights, the government can recoup its investment at once, and use this capital to invest in new infrastructure projects on the one hand, and cut operating costs on the other.   The result has been satisfactory.   Based on this experience, we should encourage the development of infrastructure projects by the private BOT method, which will have some positive effect on the development of private enterprises and the maintenance of stable economic growth.   We suggest that people from the related government departments conduct some specific research on this issue.   And we also suggest publishing a catalogue of infrastructure projects in which private enterprises can invest, to encourage the appropriate private enterprises.

Reform the Current Consumption System; Actively Develop the Consumer Credit System; Convert Potential Demand into Effective Demand to Stimulate Stable Economic Growth

The level of development of our consumer credit lags far behind the credit development at the production level. On the one hand, we have excess supply of private housing, and excess production capacity in cars and electronic products — even though the potential demand is enormous. On the other hand, there is serious dislocation between production and consumer demand which hinders the economic cycle, the investment by enterprises, the standard of living, and economic development.

At this current stage, the consumption of the urban population is being upgraded to the demand level where housing and automobiles become the major purchasing items. However, the consumers have difficulties in making a lump sum payment; we need to actively develop consumer credit for housing and cars so that people who can afford payment can pay by installment. This will result in turning potential demand into actual demand so that the difficult situation of being driven along a unitary track of investment can be overcome. We can then advance on a set of dual tracks propelled by investment and consumption to stimulate a long-term and stable economic growth.

Currently, the key to establishing a consumer credit structure lies in establishing a personal credit approval, guarantee, and mortgage system. The approval process has to be simplified as much as possible. The qualifications for credit approval can be by possessing either a certain amount of deposit, or long-term stable income, or by assets, both in terms of property or securities.

AN ANALYSIS OF THE ECONOMY AND ITS INVESTMENT ENVIRONMENT AND POLICY PROPOSALS

ZHANG HANYA AND WANG XIN, ET AL.[*]

Institute of Investment, State Planning Commission

The Economic Situation since 1998

Slowdown of Economic Growth

In the first half of 1998, the total GDP was RMB3,473.1 billion, 2.5% lower than the same period of the previous year, and 1% below the target for the entire year. The growth rates in July and August were also around 7%, which created certain difficulties in China's efforts to meet the 1998 growth target. The main cause for the slowdown in economic growth was that there was a monthly decline in the growth of industrial production. From January to July 1998, the total national industrial value-added production increased by 7.8% on a comparable basis, but the rate of increase was down 3.2% from the same period of the previous year. It was only in August that industrial value-added production recovered, up 7.9% from the same period of the previous year.

A Stable Growth in Consumer Spending

In the first seven months in 1998, sales in the domestic market were stagnant. Some improvement was seen in August, and total retail sales for the first eight months reached RMB1,858 billion, 7.3% higher than 1997, an increase of 10% after the adjustment was made with the price deflator.

---

[*] Other authors include Zhang Changchun and Liu Lifeng.

Fixed Asset Investment Increased Monthly

Because the government implemented a series of policies and measures to encourage investment, there was a monthly increase in fixed asset investment. (See Table 1.)

Table 1
The Growth of State-owned Enterprises Fixed Asset Investment in January to July 1998

	January, February	March	April	May	June	July	August
Current investment (RMB bn)	65.4	96.4	109.5	129.2	182.2	153.4	158.1
Increase from the same period of the previous year (%)	10.2	10.4	15.3	13.8	16.1	22.9	26.9
Accumulated investment (RMB bn)	65.4	161.8	271.3	400.6	582.8	736.2	894.3
Increase from the same period of the previous year (%)	10.2	10.3	12.2	12.7	13.8	15.6	17.4

In the first eight months of the year, state-owned enterprises yielded RMB894.31 bn of fixed asset investment, an increase of 17.4% on an equivalent basis, and higher by 6.6% than the same period of the last year. Of this figure, RMB513.81 bn was from infrastructure investment, which is an increase of 17.7%; RMB176.8 bn was from renewal and reconstruction investment, an increase of 17.4%; RMB157.29 bn was from real estate investment, an increase of 16.9%; and RMB46.41 bn was from other investments, an increase of 15.9%.

However, the growth rate for total fixed asset investment was lower than the same period of last year. Based on an estimate by the State Statistical Bureau, the fixed asset investment by collective and private enterprises may be negative or zero growth at best. In that case, the estimated growth rate for total fixed asset investment for the first half of the year will not exceed 9%. After adjustments for price declines, the growth in investment will not exceed 11%, 2.5% lower than last year. The slow increase in investment should induce a recovery in demand for personal housing spending, as well as for building materials and steel. But for the moment, there is no evidence of a pulling effect on investment on the demand for production materials.

The Disparity between Supply and Demand Is Great

In the first seven months of 1998, there was no sign of any encouraging outlook of growth in consumer or production materials demand. Based on a data analysis of the departments in charge of materials on 19 key products, the growth in total demand in the first half of the year was only 0.86%. When most industries could not utilize their full capacity, supply exceeded demand by 2.16 percentage points. For most products, the growth in production resources was faster than the growth in demand. A nationwide survey by the concerned departments for 601 items of commodity showed that 446, or 74.2%, were in equilibrium between supply and demand, while for 155 items, or 25.8%, supply exceeded demand. The oversupply intensified competition and pushed prices down.

Export Growth Experiences More Difficulty

The East Asian countries are in recession generally and the negative effect on China's exports is being felt. Between January and August, the total value of exports and imports grew by 3.3% on an equivalent basis, of which exports were US$118.7 billion, an increase of 5.5%. But exports were still lower by 18.6% than for the same period last year.

Financial Support for the Economy and Investment Increased Slightly

By the end of August 1998, the balance of loans made by financial institutions in the country grew by 16.4% on an equivalent basis. Medium and long-term loans were on an increasing trend from February. The accumulated amount of loans was RMB42.7 billion, RMB31.6 bn more than last year. The loans for fixed asset investment reached RMB201.5 billion, higher by 15.4% than last year.

Investment Structure Continued to Improve

State-owned enterprises maintained a high investment growth rate in the first eight months of 1998 in sectors including: agriculture, forestry, animal husbandry, fishery, and irrigation industry, with a 20.9% increase; machinery industry 24.4%; construction industry 45.1%; transportation, post and telecommunication industries 43.0% (of which post and telecommunication industries constituted 68.4%); real estate and public services industries 21.0%; education, health, and broadcast service industries 26.4%; technology and technical services industries 20.9%. Most of the industries with a fast growth rate are those encouraged by the government.

In terms of geographical locations, investment in the West took the leading position, with a growth rate of 29.7%, 12.3% higher than the national average, and 13.3% higher than the 16.4% in the East, and 20.5% higher than the 9.2% of the Central region.

Analysis of the Investment Situation in 1998

Observing the general trend of the economy in the first eight months, it follows that the following factors will have a great influence on the development of the economy and investment.

The New Fiscal and Financial Policies Will Be Favorable to Stimulating the Growth in Investment and the Economy

In order to guarantee the 8% economic growth rate, the government introduced a series of fiscal and financial measures to encourage investment from the beginning of the year. The major fiscal measures were: the exemption of import duties for machinery as fixed asset investment and value-added taxes on imports; the exemption of the income tax for share transfers of shareholding companies and issues of bonus shares, to create favorable conditions for enterprises in direct fund raising.

The major financial measure was the abolition of the quota system for fixed asset investment loans made by national commercial banks. A new system of asset and liability ratio management and credit risk management was instituted. The payable accounts of the national commercial banks were transferred into the deposit reserve requirement account, and the reserve requirement ratio was lowered. After three-time interest rate reductions for deposits and loans by financial institutions last year, interest rates were cut twice to reduce the interest burden on investors. The provisions for non-performing loans were increased. Special treasury bonds were issued to increase the paid capital of the national commercial banks to increase their monetary power. The implementation of these measures undoubtedly changed in favor of the expectations of investors and built up their confidence, stimulating investment and economic growth.

There Was Still Conflict between Market Effect and Government Intervention

In the current economic stimulation process, in order to guarantee meeting the macroeconomic target, the government increased investment. The major focus of investment to increase domestic demand was in infrastructure projects and public services; these yield high social benefit but offer low economic benefit in the short term. However, these investments made up only a limited portion of the total investment in the country and their stimulating effect on the economy in the short term was also limited. In the current economy, there exists a large amount of idle production capacity. The market's self-adjustment effect forces the non-state sectors to take a cautious attitude toward investment. There was a degree of conflict between the government's intervention in the economy and the market's self-adjustment mechanism. The latter limited the effect of the government's macroeconomic adjustment program to a degree, and created additional difficulties for economic stimulation.

The Pulling Effect of Investment on the Economy Has a Time Lag Its Effect

Fixed asset investment has its own rhythms. The increase in this investment does have an important pulling effect on economic development. However, investment projects, from construction assessment to actual completion, require a strict, scientific process to achieve the desired results. The large sums of capital required for project construction generally create a materials demand after the completion of the initial plan. That is to say, it normally takes at least six months for a project to go through the initial stage of project investigation to the investment of large sums of capital before it enters the stage where these funds begin to circulate. It may take a year or even longer for a large-scale project.

The Flood Relief Effort and Rebuilding Tasks Will Help to Stimulate Economic Growth

The 1998 floods caused economic losses of more than RMB160 billion. However, a large portion of these losses were in stored capacity assets. The negative effect on economic growth from the floods was less severe, and was estimated to be no more than 0.5%. The flood relief effort and the reconstruction tasks after the floods will bring about a more stimulating effect on economic growth than the negative effect from the floods. The estimated economic growth rate from the flood relief effort is about 1%. After deducting the losses suffered from the floods, we can say that the floods have some positive effect on the economy, accelerating economic growth by 0.5%.

The Influence of the East Asian Financial Crisis Is Still Strong

The intervention by international organizations and big countries like the United States may stop the continuation of Asia's financial crisis. But the influence of the crisis will probably be more obvious in the second half of the year. First, our export growth will continue to decline, to below 3% for the year. Second, the growth in foreign direct investment continues to decline. The actual amount of foreign direct investment will be lower than last year.

Analysis and Forecast of the Economic and Investment Situations in 1999

The economic environment and situations we will face in 1999 will be better than in 1998 as manifested in the following:

(1) The positive effect of all the macroeconomic policies and reform measures introduced in 1998 by the government will gradually begin showing up in the next year. These policies and measures will therefore create a loose policy environment for 1999 economic growth and investment growth.

(2) Although the adjustment of our industrial and product structures will last for a rather long time, the adjustment in recent years has already resulted in either the transfer or withdrawal of capital, material, and manpower resources from the declining industries and loss-making enterprises. Destructive competition will decrease to a certain extent in 1999. This development is beneficial to the development of new industries with competitive vitality.

(3)   The large-scale investment in infrastructure construction which began in 1998 will continue to drive the next year's growth in investment demand. The completion of a large number of projects in 1998 and 1999 will show their effect in providing hardware support for the development of other industries.

(4)   Following the opening up of the administrative monopoly enterprises and the improvement of the competitive environment for enterprises under different forms of ownership, many more profit growing points will be formed in 1999. More investment, development, and profit opportunities will be created.

(5)   The financial system is progressing in the direction of "fair, just, open, and high efficiency." The repurchase of national debt and the further development of the national debt futures market will greatly increase the ratio between capital market fund raising and direct fund raising.

(6)   The East Asian financial crisis will be eased gradually after the hard work put in by the East Asian countries and international financial institutions. A new picture will emerge in Asian economic development, which is crucial to the recovery of our exports to the East Asian countries.

On the whole, because of the investment-stimulating policies and measures implemented in 1998, the scale and scope of the construction in progress in 1999 will expand substantially. The total growth in investment will reach about 20%, and will stimulate consumer spending by more than 12%. After the easing off of the East Asian financial crisis, our exports in 1999 will show a degree of growth from the lower base of this year. All these factors should ensure that the GDP growth is increased by 8–9% in 1999.

Suggestions for Fiscal and Monetary Policies in the Second Half of 1998 and 1999

Implement a Tax Stimulation Policy on Investment

The effect of the fiscal policy should be directed to the entire national economy and not just to the public sectors. Funding through issuing treasury bonds is generally appropriate for infrastructure projects with low economic, but high social benefit. This is a typical government function. The tax stimulation policy on investment can generate investor interest, and stimulate investment growth in other industries, especially in manufacturing.

This policy can also be used to attract investors to invest in infrastructure projects. The tax stimulus for investment can be achieved through reduction or exemption of investment taxes, the concession or deduction for profit taxes, investment credit, or accelerated depreciation, among others. The government can rearrange a time schedule for tax concessions (like the deferral of the tax concession period to later years) to avoid the negative effect of reduced fiscal revenue in that year. However, the stimulating effect of investment can still be realized in that year.

Expand Fiscal Interest Subsidies

Currently in the country, the scope of using budget funds to provide fiscal interest subsidies for fixed asset investment projects is rather limited. Therefore, we may transfer a portion of the budgeted funding from direct investment to create a specific project fiscal interest subsidy in order to stimulate the expansion of the scope of the entire investment. Obviously, if the expansion of the fiscal interest subsidy is only a change in the form of the fiscal expenditure, it will have no negative effect on the fiscal balance.

Reduction or Exemption of Land Use Fees

This policy has already been employed. However, we should make the policy more transparent and more standardized. Given the present situation, we can apply it more in land-sensitive projects like agriculture, irrigation, and transportation.

Raise Capital through the Sale of State Assets

A large portion of China's state assets are owned by the state-owned enterprises. The government can sell part of the shares (so long as it still holds a majority of the shares.) of the profitable state-owned enterprises to raise funds. Then, these raised funds can be used in infrastructure construction to reorganize state assets. Using this method of asset transformation, the government does not lose the holding status in the enterprises, and neither does it affect the normal running of the enterprises, which means it will not produce a negative influence on them. On the contrary, this transformation in the ownership structure of enterprises will facilitate the change in the management structure as well as the development of a capital market.

Expand the Scope of Issuing Public Enterprise Bonds

Because of the budget law and guarantee law, local governments cannot issue local government bonds, nor can they provide guarantees for bonds issued by the enterprises. As a substitute, we can consider expanding the issuing scope for public enterprise bonds, and provide tax concessions on the interest. At the same time, on the premises of strengthening local governments' responsibility, we could make amendments to these laws to allow local governments to establish capital channels for infrastructure construction.

Implement the Constraints on the Benefits from Banks Operation

Currently, there are loud calls for China to use commercial bank lending to support investment expansion. However, we must be very cautious. Undoubtedly, the phenomenon of "refraining from lending" should be changed. But, this change should be the result of further improvement within the banks' internal mechanisms and financial management systems, not that of administrative changes in regulations. We should establish the following principle: between economic growth and the improvement of the financial mechanism, we would rather bear the short-term pain of slowing down economic growth than go back on the road of financial reform, even for a short while. In this context, the monetary policy should always be "rather tight" since this is the market economy's intrinsic requirement.

Remove Financial Discrimination

It is necessary to implement measures to remove the *de facto* financial discrimination. The commercial banks should use their own judgment to appreciate the enterprises' credit position and the economic benefit of credit before determining whether to grant credit facilities to enterprises. This measure will encourage and stimulate investment of the non-state economy and different types of small enterprises, and will also improve the operating condition of banks, as an important stimulator in the expansion of investment and increase in employment in the country.

Weaken the Capital System for Construction Projects

As banks start to operate independently on commercial principles and strengthen responsibility constraints, the historical mission of the capital system for construction projects is not only almost over in a certain sense, but will also bring about a negative effect because of the shortcomings in the original system (for example, the capital requirement for some industries is too high and too inflexible).   Therefore, from the angle of bank operations, we can consider weakening this system, and give the banks freedom to operate efficiently to make sure that good projects are not hindered because of lack of capital.

Suggestions on the Key Projects for Investment in 1999

Construction of Primary and Secondary School Facilities

Education is an important part of our future development. Although the country spends large sums of money in constructing school facilities, there is still a wide gap between the reality and actual demand.   The shortage of capital adversely influences our education system. In particular, in primary and secondary schools in some rural areas, education facilities are woefully inadequate, which directly affects the quality of education provided to pupils at their schooling age.

Currently, some local government investments are mostly directed to well-developed university campuses.   By contrast, the sum available for much-needed investment in rural primary and secondary schools is very limited.   Many areas rely on the Hope Project donations to build schools. In fact, the capital needed for building primary and secondary school facilities is not large — the money spent on a single well-equipped university could solve the problem of tens or hundreds of primary and secondary schools.

The Transformation of the Findings of Scientific Research

Every year in China there are many scientific achievements. Patent applications amount to over 100,000 every year (114,000 for 1997).   Approved patents by the patent offices amount to about 50,000 (51,000 for 1997).   In addition, in the enterprises, scientific research organizations, universities, and colleges, there are many scientific research achievements which have not been registered for patents.

Transforming the results of scientific research into productivity will be a very important aid to our country in improving production facilities, improving the product structure and quality, and catching up with or pushing ahead of the advanced technological level of the rest of the world. In particular, at the present stage, since there is no hot point of growth, the transformation of scientific research into productivity is of even greater importance. To transfer scientific findings into improving the productivity of enterprises would require more investment, of which a large portion would need to come from venture capital investment. Enterprises would not wish to take the risk; the government should provide this type of investment instead.

Environmental Protection and Facility Manufacturing

In the current market, the supply and demand relationship is at ease and there is no production pressure on enterprises. We should take this opportunity to clean up the pollution by the enterprises and their facilities, which would not then affect the basic running of the enterprises. But at the same time, because the enterprises are not operating at full capacity, operating funds are tight. The local and central governments can provide assistance to investment to a certain degree. We can start by choosing some industries with serious environmental pollution problems like petrochemicals, fertilizers, paper making, and cement as key points for clean up. Investment in environmental facilities and production enterprises is also very important to ensure that we have a coordinated environmental development. This industry will have a bright future. The government should encourage its development.

Equipment Industry

In recent years, because of the government's negligence in the development of the processing industry, the development of our equipment industry has not kept pace with economic development. Although the electro-mechanical industry is deemed to be one of our pillar industries, the current state of its development is still far from being of pillar industry standard. The level of the equipment industry directly reflects the economic strength of the country. Without a strong equipment industry, we would be under the control of others. The state of our equipment industry lags far behind that of the developed countries, which will place us in a disadvantageous state in international competition both economically and politically.

At present, we should not neglect those rather backward electro-mechanical industries and let them drift by themselves in the free market. Rather, we should provide appropriate support and investment for technological advance and replacement of facilities, on the basis of varying need as well as the country's development strategy. At the same time, we have to set requirements on the percentage of homemade products to prevent the import of equipment and machinery which is already available domestically. We can thus provide a market and source of funds for domestic enterprises.

Promote Technical Innovations in All Industries and Enterprises, and Upgrade Their Products

In the current market, most products are in a state of oversupply or supply-demand equilibrium. Technical innovation and product upgrading are effective tools for enterprises to win in the competitive market. Therefore, we encourage those enterprises with better financial conditions to look further ahead, not to be content with the current situation but to look forward to the international market and upgrade their products through technical innovation. For enterprises in economic bad shape, technical innovation and product upgrades are a life-saving cure. However, they often lack the funds to invest in technical innovation. The local governments and the central government should lend appropriate support in technological innovations to those loss-making but big enterprises which cannot be forced to go bankrupt.

AN ANALYSIS OF THE CURRENT MACROECONOMIC SITUATION AND POLICY OPTIONS

LIU NANCHANG AND LI KEMING

Division at Large, State Economic and Trade Commission

Our Economy is Entering into a Period of Stable Growth and Accelerated Adjustment of the Economic Structures

There Has Been a Big Change in the Framework for Our Economic Development

In the light of our domestic economy, with fast development and structural changes in the system as seen in the twenty years of reform and opening up, the developmental phase characterized by a shortage economy and quantity-driven development has come to an end. The national economy is in the process of transition into a new era of development characterized by the buyer's market and quality-driven development. On the whole, we have bid farewell to the shortage economy, except for some rare cases where imports are the main sources for crucial equipment of technological content and high in added value. The economy shows a relatively low level of oversupply.

Under such circumstances, in order to maintain a fast, healthy, and sustainable economic growth, the form of economic growth must go through a fundamental change. We must depart from our old ways of overcoming the shortage economy by applying quantity raising as a main tool and adopting a quick expansion with emphasis on speed only. And we must advance to a new system which aims at solving structural conflicts, raising the quality of the entire economy, and pursuing effectiveness with speed. Conventional wisdom tells us that during the period of transition, it is inevitable for the economic growth rate to fall for a certain period of time, since the supply of traditional industries is in excess, demand is insufficient, the relative weight of new industries is low, and the stimulating power is inadequate.

Facing these domestic and international changes, although an expansionary policy to maintain an appropriate rate of economic growth is needed, we should not aim at too high an economic growth target. What we should do is to draw lessons from those countries which have been seriously affected by the financial crisis and which are forced to undertake drastic measures in their economic policies. After the "soft landing," we should take the opportunity to maintain stable economic development for our country. We should anticipate and keep up with the global technological revolution and the era of the knowledge economy, by taking the initiative to reform our economic structure so that we can actively participate in this new international cooperation and division of labor. We must strive to command more markets for our development in this ever more competitive international environment.

Two Main Obstacles to Our Fast Sustained Economic Development

One of the obstacles is that the failure to upgrade consumption is weakening its function as a driving force for economic growth.

The effective expansion and stable recovery of our aggregate demand depend crucially on a fast and steady recovery of consumer demand. Since 1998, the government has introduced a series of measures to stimulate consumer spending. Entering into the third quarter of 1998, some results were achieved but with little effect. This ineffectiveness is in part attributed to the decline in the economic growth rate, the increase in unemployment, the general fall of expected household income, and the rise of expected expenses for social security, education, and housing. Consequently, the desire to save increased, while the desire to spend weakened. The crux of the matter is the income accumulation effect and the gap in income scale.

In real life, there is a simultaneous growth relationship between the income level and the leading consumer products. With the rise in personal income, and propelled by the actual and potential purchasing power, new leading consumer products at a higher price will emerge. The emergence of these products is often in a leap forward style, as it is often referred to as "a hundred RMB item, or a thousand RMB item, or a ten thousand RMB item, or a hundred thousand RMB item."

At present, the market for leading consumer products in the range of one thousand to ten thousand RMB is saturated for the urban and rural consumers. The leading consumer products in the range of ten to one hundred thousand RMB (such as cars and private houses) are lying there, waiting for the majority of consumers to save enough to consume them. During a period like this, the growth in consumer demand is normally slow, the traditional consumer products are in oversupply, and the rate of economic growth is also stable. In particular, the recent numbers of laid-off and unemployed workers have increased, and the growth rates of current personal income and expected income have been falling continuously. Thus, the waiting period for high consumption to occur has been prolonged. Therefore, we can hardly expect the urban consumers to leap forward from consumer products worth several thousand RMB to a new scale of products like those worth ten to under one hundred thousand RMB in a short period of time. It will take some time before cars and private housing become the first choice in their purchasing choices, which will in turn contribute to a fast growth rate.

In terms of rural consumer demand, enterprises in the rural areas have recently entered into a period of retrenchment. Their competitiveness and growth rates have fallen. The employment and income for rural workers have also fallen. In addition, affected by the increase in redundant urban employees, the income of rural employees in non-agricultural jobs has seen a decline. At the same time, farmers' incomes remain at the previous level and are difficult to increase quickly. Under such a situation, we will have to wait longer for the rural consumers to be able to afford to buy household appliances, thus generating a new consumption spree.

The other obstacle is that the production capacity of traditional industries is in excess and their ability to generate a driving force for industrial and economic growth is lower.

Our traditional labor-intensive industries like textiles, coal, metallurgy, construction materials, and light industry used to make an important contribution to the development of our industry and economy. They were the main driving forces for our high rate of economic growth in the years since the beginning of reform and opening up. However, in recent years, with changes in international demands and intensifying competition, the problems of product structure, enterprise organizational structure, technology structure, ill-arranged regional structure of planning, particularly the problem of excess productivity in these industries are becoming more serious. The technological content of their products and their potential for upgradability are low. They lack market competitiveness and their effects on increasing industrial and economic development continue to decline. These traditional industries have entered into a stage of retrenchment in general. But, it will take quite a long time to upgrade them and to form new areas of economic growth for them.

In terms of supply and demand, the two obstacles detailed above are in fact two sides of one problem. The current excess capacity in traditional industries is a low level of structural-caused capacity against the background of the market experiencing difficulties in elevating consumption and more restrictions on demand. It is not excess in supply. The oversupplied products are mainly those consumer products whose markets are basically saturated, such as general consumer products and low quality products. And the production capacity of products with high technological element and high added value is rather limited, and their supply has to rely on imports. In particular, little effort has been put into developing products which will meet the needs of urban and rural consumers at their income levels.

Therefore, we must turn to structural adjustment to expand the domestic demand, to stimulate the economy and its growth. We should learn from the successful experience of the western countries in their structural adjustment, and should concentrate our efforts on transforming our traditional industries in response to the international pressure and the opportunity brought on by the Asian financial crisis.   In accordance with the requirements of the market economy and our economic development, we should take active measures to adjust the industrial structure and gradually the entire system of China's economy.   Only in this way, will we improve and elevate the industrial structure so as to lay the foundation for effective economic growth and for upgrading our economy to a new stage of sustained development.

Structural Adjustment Will Be the Major Task for Our Economic Work in the Next Few Years, and the Pace of Optimizing the Structure and Elevating Industry Should Be Accelerated

Based on the above analysis, we should insist on the principle of "growth at an appropriate pace" for our economic work in 1999 and the following years.   While increasing efforts in structural adjustment, we shall insist on and utilize well the active macroeconomic policy so as to increase investment, stabilize consumption, encourage exports, control imports, maintain stable growth, and raise the quality of economic operations.

Implement an Active and Stable Macroeconomic Policy.   While Insisting on Appropriate Economic Growth, Apply Appropriate Pressure and Incentives for Structural Adjustment

We should subsequently implement another series of complementary measures so that the policy implemented in 1998 can more effectively stimulate growth in consumer spending.   The first measure is to strive harder for the innovation of the electricity grid so as to improve the conditions of consumption.   The second measure is to offer more financial assistance to the laid-off and unemployed workers, the low-income strata, and the flood victims, meanwhile to strengthen the reform of social security and to guarantee the stability of consumer demand of impoverished people. The third measure is to accelerate the development of a sound consumer credit system as a fiscal policy, using credit facilities to meet the shortfalls of personal income, and to provide financial support for people with high incomes to spend on cars and private housing. By doing so, we will be able to increase the economic growth as well as the growth of the emerging industries. At the same time, we should also properly control the timing and ordering of these reform measures so as to stabilize personal income and expected consumer spending.

In particular, we must properly control the degree of expansion in actual operations. As mentioned before, because the difficulties we have encountered are long-term ones, we cannot and should not realize a high rate of growth in the intermediate stage of development. Therefore, the expansion must be done in a prudent way preventing the occurrence of impetuosity and excessive speed. The macroeconomic policy must serve the needs of the structural adjustment, the government's industrial policy, and the long-term development plan. We must remind ourselves of the domestic and international changes in terms of economic development, and not pursue blindly a high growth rate. Neither should we start a new round of duplicate construction. We must also work hard to form a policy mechanism ready for changes. The current situation of the excess supply over demand in the buyer's market should be maintained so that it can provide appropriate pressure and incentive for structural adjustments and production upgrades.

Further Deepen the Reform. Eradicate Structural Shortcomings Caused by Institutional Arrangements. Lay a Foundation for Structural Adjustments and Production Upgrades

First, we can make use of the capital market to accelerate the pace of restructuring state assets and the strategic restructuring of the state economy.   We suggest selecting some profitable industries and selling part of their assets or shares in the overseas capital markets.   The profit generated can be used to support the reform of traditional industries and production upgrades.

Second, we should further our efforts on merging and bankrupting some enterprises to accelerate the pace of their restructuring.   We can adopt the restructuring experiences of the oil and petrochemical industries.   With the government playing a leading role and with the market backing this up, we can rely on assets as the bridge to accomplish more in the merging and bankruptcy of enterprises.   Through the formation of large-scale holding companies, we can overcome the problems of having too many small, scattered, messy, and uneconomical enterprises in some industries.

Third, we should accelerate the reform of the social welfare system, and establish a sound social security system to solve the problem of large-scale unemployment as traditional industries are forced to reduce excess production capacity.   The social security system will provide basic livelihood for the unemployed and redeployment opportunities to maintain social stability and to provide guarantees for a smooth operation of the structural adjustment.

Fourth, we should also accelerate the pace of the reform in the fund-raising system and further improve the macroeconomic adjustment program so as to change the extensive style of planning-oriented investment in economic growth.   Also, the role of government must be reformed so as to separate its own administration from the management of enterprises.   By so doing, we will be able to establish a structure of investment which will meet the requirements of a socialist market economy.   The mechanisms of risk management and responsibility are to be established to prevent the problem of duplicate construction and the problem of pursuing "large and all inclusive" and "small and all inclusive" from happening again.

Fifth, we must continue the reform of the state-owned enterprises on a large scale. By way of deepening and speeding up the pilot reform in the modern enterprise system and publicizing their experiences, we will accelerate the change in their operating mechanisms so that they will be able to take an active role in changing their organizational structure, technological structure, product structure, and market structure to meet the demands of the market and to increase their competitiveness in both domestic and international markets.

The Major Policy Tools for Structural Adjustment and the Focus of Our Efforts

The major task of the current structural adjustment is to concentrate our efforts on solving the problem of low level production and excess production capacity. We must be firm in closing down industries with backward technology, production techniques, and facilities. Production capacities of the traditional industries need to be reduced. At the same time, more effort must be put on the upgrading and improvement of the technology of these industries, and on the development of new industries.

The basic idea and principle of needed structural adjustment can be summarized as follows: insisting on controlling the total quantity; eliminating the backward to maintain the total balance; insisting on the balance of the adjustment of increased capacity and the restructuring of the stored capacity; insisting on progress through technological advance for the improvement in production and enterprise upgrading; insisting on "Three Reforms and One Strengthening" for the improvement of quality of enterprises and industries; insisting on "Reform the Large Enterprises and Let Go of the Small Ones" to realize a balanced development of large, medium-, and small-size enterprises; insisting on regulating bankruptcy to encourage merging; insisting on reducing staff and increasing profits; and carrying out the redeployment project. We should also combine our three-year plan of reforming large and medium-size state-owned enterprises with the structural adjustment process.

Structural adjustment affects every aspects of the economy. Our agricultural economic base needs to be strengthened. The agriculture structure needs to be improved. Agriculture with high yields needs to be developed. Tertiary industry must be developed to increase its relative weight in the economy. In particular, the development of the service sector should be given priority, which is closely linked to the daily life of the people and to the improvement of consumption quality.

Industrial structural adjustment means the elimination of backward facilities and excess production capacity, for a balanced aggregate supply and demand, and the upgrade of structure. We should concentrate our efforts on restructuring the traditional industries one by one. We must strengthen the implementation of production policies, the planning of industrial development, and the management of enterprises, adjusting and restructuring the traditional industries within a few years' time.

Product structure also needs adjustment to guide enterprises to meet the challenges from the market, to eradicate backward production techniques, and to develop new products. On the basis of satisfying the needs of the domestic market, we should enlarge our international market share.

Enterprise organizational structure also needs to be adjusted in the process of reforming enterprises. The measures of bankruptcy, merging, and reorganization will be employed by way of "Reform the Large Enterprises and Let Go of the Small Ones." Then, large holding companies will be big and strong, and small enterprises will be small but with specialities. We should create a situation in which large, medium, and small-size enterprises can coordinate for development.

In terms of the adjustment of technological structure, research in the basic sciences should be stressed. We should concentrate on those domains which will be of significance to our economic development and enhance the ability to transform research findings into productivity as soon as possible. Also, we should actively introduce advanced technologies and techniques, eliminate those backward technologies, and encourage technological innovation to form our own intellectual properties and high technology.

In order to fully implement the adjustment policies, we must seriously follow the guidelines of the 15th Party Congress and concentrate our work in the five following areas:

Fully Utilize the Measures of Industrial Policy and Planning to Make Annual Mid-term and Long-term Plans of Structural Adjustment and Industrial Development

One way to do this is to work out a plan to reduce the total capacity. The plan should also include the goal, tasks, key aspects, schedule, and required policies. We will try to fulfill the initial adjustment needed in the textile and coal industries within one or two years. The other option is to accelerate the development of industries with high growth potential or with the driving force of economic growth such as electronics, and the petrochemical and pharmaceutical industries. Related support in terms of fiscal and financial measures should be provided to meet the above aims.

Continue to Deepen the Reform of Enterprises so as to Achieve New Progress

We can accelerate the pace of reorganizing and merging enterprises. For those large enterprises undergoing reorganization, we should further improve their structure. Based on our experience in the reorganization and merger of the oil and petrochemical industries, we will accelerate the reorganization of building materials, non-ferrous metals, tobacco, defense, metallurgy, and textiles industries, in connection with technical innovations. Mergers should be carried out within leading enterprises. In addition, for small and medium-size enterprises, we will pay attention to two aspects.

(1)   We will close down the small coal mines, small cement factories, small flat-glass factories, and small electric furnace factories.   And,

(2)   we will support the reform and development of small and medium-size enterprises, making them the new areas of economic growth.

Spare No Effort in Promoting Technological Advancement and Filtering out Backward Facilities

The first measure we should apply is to fully utilize excess capacity and inadequate demand to enforce closing down or renovating fixed assets and upgrading industrial facilities.   The second is to spend strenuous efforts to build technology centers for enterprises and to exploit the potential of our researchers at scientific research institutes.   The third way is to increase the investment in technology, to accelerate the reform of the traditional industries, and to upgrade these industries.   The fourth way is to transfer the advanced and upgraded technologies to the western part of China.   The fifth is to encourage enterprises to increase their investment in technologies and to employ advanced and applied technologies, and to get rid of energy-inefficient and polluting facilities.

While Ensuring an Appropriate Economic Growth, Lay Emphasis on Optimizing the Economic Structure, Increasing Efficiency, and Building New Economic Operating Mechanisms

The main idea is to optimize quantity growth to activate stored capacity, find new ways to solve previous unresolved problems, and regulate economic operations in order to increase efficiency.   We need to improve the capital allocation system so that efficiently functioning enterprises are able to get their required capital. The flow of capital should also be improved. The key point here lies in the improvement of the credit system. Unjustified use of capital should be stopped. The work on stopping losses and increasing profits should be continued. The crucial point here is the coordination of structural adjustment with asset reorganization. Through bankruptcy, leasing, mergers, trustees, and other methods of operation, we will raise the productivity of assets to obtain the goal of low input and high output. Also, we should gradually establish and expand the government's role in purchasing. By putting those important government construction projects out to competitive bidding, we carry out full-scale government purchase at a nationwide level so as to increase the government's ability in exercising macroeconomic control and in supporting leading state-owned enterprises.

Adapt Our Work on the Demand Changes of the International Markets. Work Hard in Market Expansion, Market Protection, and Market Planning

We should first of all continue to make efforts to develop new markets. The emphasis of domestic market development is on the rural areas. Second, we need to exercise appropriate protection for the domestic market. Due to the deepening of the financial crisis, competition has intensified in both domestic and international markets. Thus, we must insist on combating smuggling in 1999. And we should employ anti-dumping measures, which are widely used internationally, to achieve a balance between exports and imports for the protection of our domestic market. Third, relying on market regulations and orders, we must hit out at the feigned and poor-quality goods and take measures to stop malpractices, and to prevent dumping, regional trade barriers, and improper competition.

ON THE ISSUE OF "ENSURING 8% GDP GROWTH"

LI YIYUAN AND HUA RUXING
School of Economics and Management, Tsinghua University

For us, the issue of "ensuring 8% growth" is not whether we are able to fulfill it, but whether we need it, and whether it is good for our economy.

To our knowledge, despite the unexpected Asian financial crisis and the catastrophic floods, we did not adjust the original GDP growth target at all at either the local or the central governments. All provinces and big cities had targeted growth rates exceeding 8%. The lowest is Heilongjiang province, which set its growth target at 8.5%. If just for the sake of keeping the original targets, and all human, material, and financial resources were employed in maintaining the economic growth rate of 1998, then the 8% GDP growth target is not impossible for us.

The real question is, considering our economic stability, and the future of the reform and development, after such serious unexpected events, is it the best way to insist on keeping the original target? How much is the opportunity cost for doing this? Will a single-minded "ensuring the 8%" only achieve things in the short term?

We believe that the government will re-assess the 8% target realistically and try to realize it only on the basis of overall social development. However, if we only achieve a 7% GDP growth rate due to factors beyond our control, it is already a miracle because the global economic growth rate is only 2%, and some of our neighboring countries even record negative growth rates. Based on our estimation, China's nominal GDP growth for 1998 will be 7.5%. If we take into consideration the decline of the price index, the real GDP growth rate will be 8.2%.

We do not overly worry about whether we can reach the 8% GDP growth rate in 1998. What we really worry about is whether we can maintain the trend of high economic growth and the development of the society after 1999. Because of the unpredictable nature of the international environment, we should be prepared for a variety of situations, to fight for the best, and to face the worst.

What is crucial is how to handle the proper relationships amongst stability, reform, and development, and how to work out a long-term overall plan.   What we want is the right policy to tap the potential demand, not one or two percentage points of growth rate that may last for one or two years.

A FORECAST OF THE 1999 EMPLOYMENT SITUATION AND POLICY SUGGESTIONS

YANG YIYONG AND LI JIANLI

Institute of Macroeconomic Research
State Planning Commission

The Supply and Demand of the Labor Force

The Supply of the Labor Force in 1999

(1) The natural growth of the labor force. According to a survey of the rural and urban area labor forces, the net increase of the economically active population in 1999 will be down by 1.88 million on that in 1998. This will therefore ease the pressure of the natural increase in the labor force. Based on a rough estimate, if the labor employment rate remains at 85%, then there will be 9.14 million new entrants in need of jobs in the labor market. About 2.63 million of them will be in the urban areas.

(2) Farmers changing into non-farm workers. Based on our previous experience, there are about 3 million such changeovers each year under the traditional definition of "farmers changing into non-farm workers." Due to the implementation of the new policy on household registration management, such cases may increase. However, this increase, according to our estimates, will be limited in 1999.

(3) New laid-off workers from the state-owned enterprises and repositioned civil servants from government sectors. In 1999, the number of newly laid-off workers from the state-owned enterprises is estimated to be about 3 million, almost the same as that in 1998.

In 1999, the reform of government organizations and institutional units at local levels will commence. The impact of this reform, i.e., the repositioning of their staff, will be greater than that in 1998 at the central government level. Based on our preliminary estimates, the local government organizations will have to reposition 4 million staff within three years.

If we also include the organizations under the administration of the Party committees, the National People's Congress, and the Chinese People's Political Consultative Conference, then the figure for repositioned staff for the next three years will be 5 million. In this case, if 1999 will see one-third of these people being relocated in terms of their specific work and work units, then 1.67 million employees from government organizations will be repositioned.

The total number of those employed in institutions, which include those of science, education, culture and art, and health, has reached about 26.5 million. If these institutions need to cut 15% of their employment, then the total number of repositioned staff within the next three years in these institutions will amount to 4 million. And 1999 will see about 1.33 million staff being repositioned.

(4) The registered unemployed in 1998 and the accumulated laid-off workers who wish to be employed. According to the estimate made by the Ministry of Labor and Social Security, the number of registered unemployed will reach 6.1 million by the end of 1998, an increase of 320,000 people from the end of 1997. The year-end registered unemployment rate will be 3.2%, 0.1% up from the end of 1997. By the end of 1998, those laid-off workers who are still unemployed will reach 6 million, with an increase of 1.5 million people from the 4.5 million laid-off workers at the end of 1997.

To summarize these various figures, the newly increased employment pressure in 1998 in the urban areas was: 4.5 million laid-off workers, 5.78 million registered unemployed, 3 million newly laid-off workers of enterprises, 3.22 million net increase labor supply in urban areas, 2 million repositioned staff from government departments, 3 million farmers changing to non-farm workers, making up a total of 19.52 million. The employment pressure in 1999 will be: 6 million laid-off workers, 6.1 million registered unemployed, 3 million newly laid-off workers in enterprises, 2.74 million new increased labor supply in urban areas, 3 million repositioned staff from labor supply institutional units, 3 million farmers changing into non-farm workers, making up a total of 23.84 million.

Thus, the pressure of creating job opportunities in 1999 will be higher than in 1998. China will have to find 4.32 million more job positions in 1999 than in 1998, an increase of 22.13%.

The Demand for a Labor Force

Employment, as one of the inductive variables in the macroeconomy, is influenced by many factors. There are two major elements that will affect labor force demand.

One is the employment elasticity coefficient. In 1998, we predict that the elasticity coefficient will probably rise to about 0.134, and that tertiary industry and small- and medium-size enterprises will develop further, with a rise in their elasticity coefficient to 0.144, or 0.01% above the 1998 level. This can be attributed to the strong impact of the development of tertiary industry and small- and medium-size enterprises. The increase in the elasticity coefficient means that there will be an increase in the number of employed per percentage point in the rise of the GDP.

The other major factor is the rate of economic growth. Presently, there are different opinions concerning the economic growth rate in 1999. We made our forecast of the employment situation based on the assumption of a 7–8% growth rate in 1999.

Using the total employment of 703.46 million in 1998 as a base, and applying 0.144 for the employment elasticity coefficient, we predict the employment situation to be as follows. With a 6% growth rate in 1999, the newly created employment in the urban and rural areas is 6.08 million, of which 4.86 million are in the urban areas (a 1% increase in GDP creates 810,000 new jobs).

With a 7% growth rate in 1999, the newly created employment in the urban and rural areas will reach 7.09 million, of which 5.47 million are in the urban areas.

With an 8% growth rate in 1999, the newly created employment in the urban and rural areas will reach 8.10 million, of which 6.48 million will be in the urban areas. With the 6.48 million new jobs created by an 8% GDP growth in 1999, then we will have about 16.2 million urban unemployed. If we deduct the figure of 6.5 million registered unemployed (the registered unemployment rate will be controlled at below 4%), the figure of 600,000 newly laid-off workers (20% of the total number of laid-off workers, who will not find jobs anymore), and the figure of 1.5 million of repositioned staff from government organizations (who may go to training and need not find jobs in 1999), there remain 7.66 million people whose unemployment problem needs to be solved in 1999.

The Key Conflicts Occurring in Employment in 1999

The Economic Growth Rate Is Low and the Supply of Labor Remains High

The increase in employment is basically determined by China's economic growth. In 1999, affected by many factors,

China's GDP growth rate will not be very high, which restricts the increase in job opportunities.

Unemployment Is More Serious in Some Especially Difficult Regions

Due to some unsolved problems within Chinese economic and social institutions, the unemployment situation will be more serious in the Northeast, Northwest, and Southwest than elsewhere in the country. The common characteristic of the above regions is that the weight of the state-owned enterprises is relatively higher. The state-owned enterprises there suffer from heavy losses, and are difficult to restructure. In addition, the traditional mentality of maintaining employment still predominates. Consequently, the number of laid-off workers will be larger and the redeployment scheme becomes even more difficult.

Some Policy-related Problems in Terms of Solving Unemployment

(1) On the policy of "Reform the Large Enterprises and Let Go the Small Ones." In carrying out this policy, it often results in the situation that "those reformed big enterprises cannot survive," and "those freed small enterprises die out." By nature, small enterprises should have greater ability to absorb labor. However, when we let go the small enterprises, the number of laid-off workers increases at a faster rate. At the same time, the usual practice to "reform the big enterprises" is to "cut staff to increase profits." Therefore, large enterprises continue to lay off workers. In reality, this policy results in two sources of unemployment, subsequently increasing the pressure to create jobs.

(2) Reducing staff to increase profits. The policy of "reducing staff to increase profits" is one of the ways to restructure the state-owned enterprises. But some managers have applied

the policy in a literal way, believing that benefits would increase just by cutting employees (and naturally this does reduce expenses to some extent).   However, this has resulted in a large increase in redundancy, while the enterprises remained unprofitable. Further staff cuts were implemented in order to increase profits.   This in turn creates a vicious cycle and creates even more unemployment.

(3)   Establish redeployment centers within enterprises. One of the important preconditions for reforming the state-owned enterprises is to push their labor force to enter the job markets. However, China's policy requires that redeployment centers should be established within all enterprises, which no doubt will have a beneficial effect on social stability.

But, the burden of these enterprises is still there. The problem of excessive manpower is still unsolved and makes reforming the enterprises and establishing a modern enterprise system more difficult.   To say the least, it will be much harder to meet the targets of cutting the losses of the large and medium-size enterprises in three years, or to quickly make employment subject to the market.

(4)   One-third of the laid-off subsidy by the enterprises.   After being given "Notice," some enterprises believed that it would be difficult for them to survive for three years, since they already had difficulties in paying wages. However, workers in these enterprises are willing to take redundancy payments, because they have difficulties in receiving their salaries even when they work, but as laid-off workers, they receive some subsidy. However, this has triggered an increase in redundancies. Some enterprises simply increased the numbers of those laid-off, as they were willing to pay their 1/3 share of the laid-off subsidy, in order to get the 2/3 payment from the government.

(5)   Contract system for the entire labor force.   Based on a survey, by the end of 1997 there were about 107,201 million urban

employees who have signed contracts with their enterprises, comprising 97.4% of the total urban workers. Most of the state-owned enterprises have adopted the labor contract system. However, in the survey, we found that in many state-owned enterprises, the labor contract system was only a formality. Some enterprises have contracts for 20 to 30 years, which are equivalent to lifetime employment. Many five-year contracts signed in 1987 have expired, and some 10-year contracts have expired. But many enterprises registered these workers as laid-off and collected redundancy benefits in their name. Furthermore, enterprises went to redeployment centers for help. This is extremely unreasonable. The policy should be made clear in order to eliminate any possibility of abusing government policy.

(6) Local governments should provide the guarantee of a minimum standard of living in their regions.

The earlier the establishment of a minimum standard of living, the better the social environment for laid-off workers, who can then rely less on their enterprises. Currently, people have gradually accepted the direction of the reform. However, there is a strong imbalance among different regions in terms of economic development. There is also a wide disparity in terms of the number of laid-off workers. Under the current policy, local problems have to be managed by local financial resources. The result of this policy is that "the region that should be protected does not have enough resources to protect anything, whereas the region that does not need protection enjoys plenty of financial resources."

The labor market will be difficult to operate if the urban minimum standard of living system cannot provide protection for those who need it.

(7) Early retirement. Currently, some regions adopt an early retirement method to artificially create employment positions. The biggest problem with this method is that it shifts the

potential danger to a future pension system. Another widely existing problem is that the retired are still working. In the context of the society as a whole, the actual effect of this early retirement method is minimal. In addition, this method disrupts the implementation of labor-related regulations.

Reflections on 1999 Employment Policy

Insist on Implementing the Various Reform Measures

The above detailed analysis shows that the main difficulty in 1999 urban employment is that of the increased numbers of laid-off workers from enterprises and repositioned staff from government sectors and institutions. This is the price we have to pay for economic structural adjustment and the reform of the economic system. Even though there will be a lot of difficulties ahead, we must insist on maintaining the direction of the reform.

Currently, China's registered unemployment rate is only 3.2% (1998 year-end estimate). If we add the unemployed laid-off workers, the unemployment rate would rise to 4%. In addition, among the laid-off workers, 50–70% of them belong to the category of hidden unemployed. Therefore, the current unemployment and redundancy problems can still be tolerated socially. The laid-off workers from enterprises and the repositioned staff from the government sectors are the last important factor to enter into the labor market. We have now almost achieved an established labor market. But we have paid a high price for it. The implementation of various reform measures is the key to maintaining high economic growth as we enter the 21st century. Therefore, we must remain determined in pursuing this goal.

Give Special Concern for the Regions in Most Difficulties

In some especially difficult regions, the problem of obsolete industries is extremely serious and the burden is very heavy. It is impossible for them to overcome these difficulties by themselves. The central government must, to a certain extent, support these regions in their structural transformation and employment expansion. In practical terms, infrastructure construction projects should favor the large cities in the Northeast, Northwest, and Southwest. In addition, the central government should also give priority to upgrading production efficiency in these cities.

Spare No Efforts in Developing Tertiary Industry and Expanding Community Services

At present, the development of Chinese tertiary industry is still backward, particularly for community services, which can provide many employment positions. We therefore should spend great efforts to develop community services, which will be an important measure in raising urban employment in 1999, and in solving the problem of the laid-off workers. The major obstacle dragging down the development of the tertiary industry and community services is the slow process of urbanization, which fails to provide the demand and conditions for the development of community services. It is therefore mandatory to accelerate the pace of urbanization.

While the Economy Is Developing, We Must Take Care of the Expansion of Employment

In the process of developing high-yield agriculture and upgrading China's traditional industries, we must consider their impact on employment. And we must take enterprise size into consideration. The top priority for large enterprises should be placed on upgrading their technology. For medium- and small-size enterprises, priority should be given to their ability to absorb labor.

In the process of industrial development, emphasis should be given to the principle of job creation, which we must adopt as a long-term principle.

Gradually Separating the Redeployment Centers from Enterprises

The establishment of redeployment centers and their function are the two important components of the current reform. We should establish different kinds of redeployment centers, depending on their enterprises' ability. The centers should be established according to specific conditions of the particular industry or region in question. In practical terms, the greatest difficulty faced by redeployment centers is the lack of funding resources. Some of the redeployment centers set up by enterprises are nothing but empty shells and cannot function in any way. We should take note of this situation. The government should provide the necessary conditions for establishing redeployment centers that can serve social needs.

Handle Labor Relationships According to Laws and Regulations

With the development of various forms of ownership, in particular the development of the joint-stock system, the stock cooperative system, and the private economy, labor relationships have become multi-dimensional and more complicated. Also, following the implementation of enterprises' acquisition, bankruptcy, restructuring, and the execution of "Reform the Large Enterprises and Let Go the Small Ones," labor relationships will encounter more changes, dismissals and contract terminations, which may result in a sporadic increase of collective industrial disputes.

The state-owned enterprises must regulate labor relations. With the development of the non-state sectors of the economy, the problems related to labor relations become increasingly more complicated and subsequently the requirement for regulating labor relations will be higher.   Therefore, it is necessary to build up a mechanism to regulate this "tripartite" relationship.   In the face of new changes in labor relations, policies, measures, methods, and channels handling labor relations must all be improved.   In particular, we must spend our efforts in supervising and monitoring labor-related issues, to actually protect the legal rights of labor and the enterprises.   We must ensure that laws are obeyed and unlawful activities are prosecuted.

GREAT ADJUSTMENT: THE INEVITABLE CHOICE FOR CHINA'S ECONOMIC DEVELOPMENT

ZHANG SHUGUANG AND ZHANG PING
Economics Institute
Chinese Academy of Social Sciences

The global economy is undergoing great adjustment, as is China's. This is the unavoidable challenge of our time. Therefore, what really matters is not whether we can achieve the targeted growth rate in 1998, but how we improve the quality and efficiency of China's economic growth. With this understanding in mind, we should concentrate on handling this great economic adjustment, rather than focusing our efforts on ensuring the 8% growth rate. Success in taking this approach will generate at least 10 years of high growth rates.

China's Economy Enters into an Adjustment Period after High-speed Growth

After the success of the "soft landing," China's economy should have rebounded. The government has implemented a series of expansion-oriented policies and stimulation measures. But these have not achieved much: the economy has continued to decelerate, and future expectations have turned gloomy. Indicators that growth will soon resume seem feeble. Therefore, this kind of situation cannot be explained satisfactorily by short-term economic fluctuations.

Some long-term factors are becoming increasingly important. Although the potential for economic growth may not have changed, continuous economic decline and the negative growth in prices indicate that changes have occurred in the economic environment; this will result in further changes in the ways to achieve high growth in the 1990s. In short, after the high growth years, the economy has entered into a period of great adjustment.

The Two Major Factors that Supported the High Growth Rate in the 1990s

One was the extraordinary speed of investment, which generated high economic growth by breaking through infrastructure bottlenecks in energy, transportation, and other sectors. It also engendered hugely excessive production capacity. The idle production capacity in industries like processing machinery and household appliances was as high as 40–50%. Another cost of this high growth was high inflation and economic "bubbles." When inflation fell, the "bubbles" became bad debts. This kind of input-driven economic growth lacked technological innovation and depended on short-lived quantity expansion. A great adjustment was, therefore, inevitable and necessary.

Export-led growth was the other major factor in the high growth rate of the 1990s. This was especially true after 1992, when the pace of reform accelerated and openness was expanded. Exports increased sharply while the overall structure of exports changed. The development model and economic structure of China's southern and southeastern coastal regions underwent a fundamental transformation and formed the basic export-oriented model. At the same time, unprecedented levels of direct foreign investment poured in, providing the driving force for the new growth dynamic. The expansion of openness and the development of an export-oriented economy allowed China to utilize this foreign investment to accelerate her development. But the large-scale export-oriented transformation also made the Chinese economy susceptible to attacks from abroad.

Institutional Change for High Growth Rate and Some Other Changes

The high growth rate of the 1990s was achieved within this accelerated reform aimed at moving China toward a market-oriented economy. The main structure of the economy was adjusted. The non-state economy became the main force in national economic development. The corporatization of the state owned enterprises laid an institutional foundation for their overall reform. The reform of the land-use system changed the situation in terms of using land; from without compensation to with compensation, and from a low price level to a high one. It also became one of the primary driving forces fueling fast economic growth. The reform of the capital market, especially the development of non-bank financial institutions, initiated a breakthrough for investment. The widespread development of the special development zones also accelerated the pace of the development of the export-oriented economy. The progress and widening of the reforms provided thrust for accelerated economic growth. But they also altered the institutional base of the country's economic operations. Thus, a series of new problems emerged.

First, the prime factor restricting China's economic growth has changed, from restriction of the bottlenecks under the planned economy, to freeing demand under the market economy. Economic cycles, by their nature, are more influenced by commercial factors than planned-economic factors. The key issue in macroeconomic control is changing from preventing "overheating" to preventing "overcooling." Although the influence of the government in directing the economy is still enormous, we should not overlook the possibility of "overheating."

Second, under the present circumstance of intensified competition, credit constraints, "hands on" constraints on enterprise budgets, and excessive production capacity, a great number of workers have been, or will be, made redundant and unemployed. When enterprises make huge losses, the losses create a high debt ratio, which often results in non-performing loans for banks. This concentrates the risks for the state, especially in a systematic sense. Diffusing these risks, therefore, has become an urgent task.

Furthermore, the reforms have progressed from the stage of adjusting the productive capacity into the area of stored capacity. The multinational corporations in China have forced this adjustment on China's state-owned enterprises. Hereto, however, breakthroughs in the reform of state-owned enterprises are giving rise to many other complex problems. The inherent limitations of the non-state sector, which now is a major economic engine, are gradually being exposed. Only if these limitations are improved will the non-state sector be able to form new focal points for economic growth.

The International Environment for High Growth and Its Changes

First, China's fast economic growth was realized within an international environment itself undergoing epic change. By fully utilizing the opportunity provided by the end of the Cold War, China was able to accomplish its developmental transformation from an inward-looking economy to an export-oriented one. Following the footsteps of the Asian "four little dragons" (or "four little tigers"), vast areas of the southern and southeast coastal parts of the country became essentially export economies. The Asian financial crisis was caused, to a certain extent, by the over expansion of this new export-driven development model. China avoided this crisis successfully, however, and strengthened its awareness of risks inherent in making these changes too broadly and too fast. It also began to understand what effective precautions could be taken. Nevertheless, the crisis has changed the global economic order, making China's ongoing development more difficult. Chinese exports have been directly affected as well.

Second, in revealing the shortcomings of the export-driven development model, the crisis has cast doubt on the validity of high economic growth driven by high input. It also has challenged the development model of government-led growth. If, in the development of export-driven and high-input economic growth, governments have played an important role as organizers or coordinators, then after the failure of the development model, the role of governments needs to be redefined. This is an issue worth our attention. China is now in the process of marketization. The role and function of the government are also undergoing changes and adjustments.   There is no precedent for this.   And it is not an easy task.

Furthermore, the Asian financial crisis has created a situation in which one problem follows another.   The global economy could yet fall into a depression.   And unlike the situation in the 1930s, the world's economy is now integrated; and because of this, no country is immune should such a crisis occur.   Only the degree of damage would vary from country to country.   In this scenario, combining the long cycle of technological innovation, the fusion of the global medium-term cycle, and the short-term economic cycle of China, giving serious consideration to how we should face and handle this situation has become an important issue.

The Nature and Characteristics of China's Great Adjustment

First, in terms of timing, an economic adjustment can take place before or after a crisis.   But if it occurs after the fact, the adjustment will be mandatory.   The great adjustment that China is undertaking now is not of the post-crisis sort.   Rather it is occurring after 20 years of high economic growth, sometimes described as "the Chinese miracle." This adjustment has been implemented proactively, and in fact some of its aspects are more of a pre-adjustment.

Since China is a huge country with enormous market opportunities, the present excessive capacity is not due to a limited domestic market, but rather to the underdevelopment of this domestic market, especially the rural market.   Also China is a developing country, meaning it has the advantage of late development.   The reforms in China have not yet been completed, so there is still a great deal of room for institutional innovation. Consequently, the so-called pre-adjustment means: (a) economic adjustment that has come earlier than usual in the general process of economic development; and (b) an adjustment that is, by nature, preventative and protective; making hay while the sun shines, so to speak.

Second, in the case of an economic crisis inducing a depression and chaos, any adjustment then is normally in aid of recovery. In China's case, since the pre-adjustment is being carried out at a time of slow economic growth, the initiative of the adjustment is firmly within our control.

Third, in terms of orientation, since China is undergoing a dual process of adjustment — a systemic transformation and a development model transformation — this macro-adjustment is multi-dimensional. Unlike developed countries, China's market system is still rudimentary, and needs further reform. At the same time, China is still in the midst of modernizing its two economies, urban and rural, while confronting the issues of urbanization and industrialization. Unlike most developing countries, China not only has to alter its development track from a planned economy to a market economy; it also has to change from export-driven development to domestic-demand–driven development in regards to production. China cannot emulate small countries lacking our problem of regional disparities. Furthermore, the country's enormous population and manpower resources constitute another unique problem, making adjustment just that much more complicated and difficult.

Fourth, while a core element of this macro-adjustment is industrial adjustment (including industrial organization and industrial structure), it is much more than this in terms of its scope. Because Chinese society is undergoing tremendous change, China's economic adjustment must also encompass significant adjustment of the regulations which govern its economy. In fact, this may be the key to the success of any macro-adjustment. Such regulatory adjustments would include adjusting the regulations for government conduct as well as market regulations. These two areas are closely interconnected. One cannot exist without the other. In the process of establishing regulations and order, the government plays a vital role. The misconduct of some officials has often resulted in compelling enterprises to react in a way deviating from government policy. Consequently, the adjustment of the regulations governing their conduct is most important. The scale of this adjustment is broad. For instance, economic growth is the result of innovation and interaction regulated by the market. The government, therefore, should not make economic growth the target of its administration. But the government should announce its forecast of future economic growth as a guide to help enterprises plan and subsequently execute those plans.

The Direction and Content of China's Great Adjustment

Initiate Domestic Demand and Resist External Attacks

Initiating domestic demand is the major goal of this great adjustment, especially with the enormous changes that have taken place in international markets. China's prosperity, from the beginning of the reforms until today, is a result of an export-driven economy replacing an import-substitution domestic demand economy. This shift upgraded the country's economy to a whole new level. With this achievement, if we can once again transform, this time into a domestic-demand–driven economy by exploring the potential of our domestic demand, we can take our economic development a significant step further. In the process of expanding investment demand, the major goal is to greatly develop telecommunications, roads, railways, urban facilities, environmental technologies, flood protection schemes, and the like.

However, there are limitations. A major measure in initiating domestic demand is stabilizing consumer expectations while broadening the demand factor. This is important because consumer demand is the genuine and consistent force pulling economic growth upward. It is necessary, therefore, to appropriately integrate the long-term effect of the reform measures with short-term policy. It is also hoped that the redeployment project will alleviate the problem of unemployment so as to diffuse one of the key negative factors in boosting consumption. Housing consumption and investment are another long-term strategy needed to boost consumption. An important initiative here is to open a second-hand market, thereby lowering housing costs to an appropriate level. The development of consumer credit is also crucial in expanding consumer demand (including credit for emergencies, daily goods, and durable goods as well as for the financing of houses and cars). At present, production credit is way ahead of consumer credit. Yet with capital supply now relatively ample, developing consumer credit could prove a timely innovation.

Accelerate the Reorganization of Industry and Adjust the Industrial Structure

This is the main theme of China's great economic adjustment. If past adjustments were mainly attributable to the termination or transformation of enterprises under government control, today's major enabler is the market mechanism. We should emphasize the pivotal effect of capital, and the reorganization effect of the capital market. We should also emphasize the role played by intermediary services so that all players in the market effectively participate in the reorganization of national industry. Industry reorganization includes not only the reorganization of large multinational enterprises, but also the division of labor in small and medium-size enterprises. We should not cast any doubt on the necessity and strategic importance of large enterprises just because large Korean enterprises have gotten into trouble. At the same time, we should not overlook the development of small and medium-sized enterprises.

Reorganizing large enterprises should not simply be considered something to be carried out by the government. Rather, any such restructuring should go through the market. Similarly, the development of small and medium-size enterprises should not simply depend on deregulation. Various types of service agencies should be established to facilitate small and medium-size enterprises to improve their ability to innovate and to improve their organizational structure. The ways and means of industrial structure adjustment are varied. The key is to raise the enterprises' ability to expand substantially and to fine-tune domestic market segmentation. If these abilities can be improved, the reorganization will be successful. Whatever the adjustments, however, we must insist on the basic principle of optimizing the price of essential elements. We should not weaken the budget constraints and create new distortions, otherwise all the previous achievements will fall flat.

Accelerate the Pace of Urbanization and Encourage the Formation of a Unified Market

The development of the rural areas has always been the key issue for China's development. Since the beginning of the reforms, non-farm development in the rural areas has made great progress. However, the level of urbanization lags far behind, ensuring long-term underdevelopment of tertiary industry and the excessive growth of heavy industry. This can also be attributed to currently insufficient effective demand. At the same time, the income disparity between the urban areas and their rural counterparts has become noticeably wider. The 1995 ratio was 2.47: 1, which was 10% higher than that recorded in 1978. National disposable income expressed in the Gini coefficient was as high as 0.445, 7% higher than in 1988 and the highest in Asia. Urbanization will increase the income level of farmers, which in turn will increase demand. The demand so created will rely on traditional industries. So, the acceleration of urbanization is both an important step for China's industrialization and modernization and a key factor in initiating domestic demand. In fact, the hope of China's economic development is focused here.

The crux of the delay in urbanization is the discriminatory arrangements for the development of the urban areas and the rural areas in terms of institutional arrangements and policy design. Therefore, a process of urbanization is a process of making new institutional arrangements and adjusting previous policies. In terms of urbanization, we must borrow from the experience of other countries, but we should rely more on our own innovations. Trying to force through only one model is not the best policy. We should follow the natural evolution with some suitable and effective guidance from the government.   It may not be the best choice but it is one with more benefits than harm.

Actively Develop a Capital Market and Strenuously Resolve National Risks

Currently all the risks of the country are expressed as national risks.   In this great adjustment, one of the important tasks is to diffuse the existing risks, to prevent the appearance of new risks, especially risks of the system.   The major method to reduce national risks is to lower the government's shares and to open a direct fund-raising market.   However, the function of a capital market is mainly to disperse future risks.   The solution for existing risks mainly relies on the gradual establishment of a sound deposit insurance system and a real name system.   From then on, all the national commercial banks would be covered by the insurance. Interest rates of other financial institutions can fluctuate, but the government will not insure them.   The government will certainly not insure illegal fund raising and, in fact, will punish it.   The goal of developing a capital market is to serve the needs of state-owned enterprise reform.   The government must implement strict controls, like the allocation of listing quotas based on sectors and regions, and its decision to close some regional stock markets.   It should be stressed that if the government uses market forces to achieve non-market goals, serious problems may arise unexpectedly.

On the whole, our great adjustment just discussed, to a certain extent, coincides with the current economic expansion policy. However, the way of understanding our problems is obviously different.   Furthermore, we should be careful when we employ anti-cyclic fiscal and monetary policies.   We believe that under the current situation it is the best time to change our approach to understand the problems and their related policies.   Therefore, we offer the following three suggestions:

(1)   The government should not use the economic growth target as part of its administration, but should forecast the expected

growth rate and make relevant indicators available to the public.

(2) The government should not insist on the claim of not devaluating the RMB in absolute terms, but rather announce conditions for not devaluing the RMB. These conditions should be made in consideration of the exchange rates of the Japanese Yen, American interest rates, and the situation of the Hong Kong dollar.

(3) We should not just focus on a high growth rate for one or two years but should integrate short-term growth with long-term development.

NO DECLINE IN CHINA'S "NATURAL GROWTH RATE"

ZUO DAPEI

Economics Institute
Chinese Academy of Social Sciences

Since the 1980s, our national annual rate of increase of potential production (Natural Growth Rate) has been about 9%. Even though since 1995, the economic growth rate has been noticeably lower than that of previous years, many factors indicate that the natural growth rate has not fallen.   In fact, it may have risen.   The reason for this argument is that the reform of the state-owned enterprises has created a large number of redundant workers, thus increasing the efficiency of the entire economy. Evidence for the rise in the natural growth rate was the continued fall in inflation between 1995–1997, while economic growth still remained at about 9%.

The Chinese economy as a whole has developed an adaptable expectation for the inflation rate in recent years.   Under such an expectation, the noticeable fall in the inflation rate reveals that the economy is operating below its potential production level (Natural Growth Rate). Consequently, beginning at the end of 1995, the rapid decline of our inflation rate means that our economy is below the potential production level.   When the actual growth rate was still about 9% in 1996 and 1997, if we were to utilize the potential production level, the actual growth rate should have been over 10%.   The reason that it did not reach 10% in 1996–1997 was because of the constraints of aggregate demand, which were due to our determination to further bring down the inflation rate to additionally lower people's inflationary expectations, and to lay a solid foundation for future healthy economic growth.   In 1998, inflation all but disappeared.   The general price level for various price indicators showed negative growth.   Under these circumstances, there is absolutely no need to further suppress demand, and we should expand aggregate demand appropriately to generate economic growth and reach China's potential production output level.

ANALYSIS OF AND POLICY SELECTION FOR CHINA'S 1998–1999 ECONOMIC GROWTH

HE XIAOMING AND CHANG JIAN

Economic System and Management Research Institute
State Commission for Restructuring Economy

The economic growth China achieved in 1998 was accomplished during a time in which the Southeast Asian financial crisis was spreading to all Asian countries and some Eastern European and North American countries as well. This financial crisis has caused global repercussions.

With a new political reshuffling the Chinese central government has announced its prime economic target of ensuring a growth rate of 8%. Local governments and large state-owned enterprises have joined the government in trying to achieve this goal by introducing their own plans. However, three months of catastrophic floods in the north and south wreaked havoc on the country. Since the implementation of the "appropriately tight" macroeconomic austerity program, of 1997, GDP growth has fallen to 8.8%, its lowest point, while the inflation rate has sunk to near zero. As a consequence, the economic situation in 1998 and related macroeconomic policy have aroused great concern.

1998 Economic Growth and the Characteristics
of the Adjustment Policy

1998 Economic Growth Situation

Economic Growth Has Continuously Wound Down Amid Changes in the Macroeconomic Environment

Since the successful "soft landing" in 1996, the macroeconomy has been in a state of sustained slow growth. In terms of general price levels, retail prices fell for 10 consecutive months from October 1997. Beginning in April 1998, consumer prices have likewise fallen continuously, compared to the same period of the previous year. In terms of market supply and demand, the majority of consumer products and production resources have been in equilibrium or oversupply since 1997.

In the meantime, bottleneck constraints on production, imposed by transportation, energy, and electricity, have been greatly eased. It follows from this that product inventory remains high and actual product sales rates have fallen sharply. Economic efficiency has also continued to decline. Meanwhile, consumer, investment and export demand are insufficient to generate a new round of high national economic growth.

All of these factors underscore the fact that the era of an economy characterized by shortages and quantitative expansion has come to an end. We are entering a new developmental stage, one which will require structural improvements, and a total quality upgrade.

With Its Huge Size and Potential, the Chinese Market Retains the Possibility of Further Development

The end of the shortage economy and quantitative expansion does not herald the final formation of a buyer's market in China. Neither does it mean the emergence of a situation of general excess in terms of output and production capacity nationwide, such as that seen in the developed countries. In fact, in China, markets and room for economic development always exist at two different levels.

At one level, there is room for economic development represented by the state-owned enterprises and the market led by consumers in large and medium-size cities. At another level, there is the economic development opportunity represented by the agricultural economy and rural industries and the market led by the consumers within these vast rural areas and the small towns found there.

In this new developmental phase, the reality China faces can be summarized as follows: on the one hand, there is an urgent need in these rural areas to develop rural markets and to foster new economic growth points. Also, an industrial chain is expected to grow out of these new growth points. On the other hand, urban markets are in urgent need of adjustment which, it is hoped, will enhance their potential for new growth. As the new development mode advances, the highest potential is in the structural adjustment of urban markets and the improvement of economic quality. The potential of rural markets mainly lies in the latent demand for basic consumer goods and commodities. This will last at least 20 years, over which period stable and continued economic growth is surely possible, for all that the growth rate achieved may not reach double digits.

This potential for economic development will remain just that, while the old development cycle transforms into its likely replacement. This means that the current economic growth remains in the trough of the previous cycle, which is simultaneously the starting point of a new cycle. The 7% growth rate seen as the last result of this old cycle has resulted from applying an appropriately tight macroeconomic program. The delayed effect of this cycle was expected to end in the first half of 1998. Beginning in the second half of 1998, economic growth started to rise slowly as the new macroeconomic adjustment measures took effect.

Structural adjustment and market development as basic priorities have been agreed upon by most government departments and enterprises. The consensus is that after implementing these measures, economic growth will resume. In the first half of 1999 (or no later than the second half), expectations are that GDP growth in excess of 8% will signal that the new cycle cited above has begun. Given these changes in the domestic market and the effect of the international financial crisis, we expect that growth will reach 7–8% over this period. In other words, the new economic cycle is starting in an environment of structural adjustment and various other qualitative changes in the national economy. In this context, 8% GDP growth can be considered high.

The Characteristics of Current Policy

Macroeconomic Policy Has Changed from Appropriate Tightness to Appropriate Expansion

The intent of this policy shift is to reverse the current declining growth trend while easing the "knock on" effects of the Southeast Asian financial crisis.

First, the People's Bank of China has employed the appropriate monetary tools to implement a series of measures to stimulate domestic demand and encourage the commercial banks to increase credit.

Specifically, these measures entail: the Central Bank resuming its purchase of bonds from the state commercial banks to increase liquidity; reform of the deposit reserve system to lower the requirements, thereby increasing the balance of financial institutions and their ability to provide credit. In March and July 1998, deposit and loan interest rates were cut twice. The formula for calculating discount and rediscount rates was also changed. Lending policy on fixed asset investment has been relaxed to support infrastructure construction as well.

In the first nine months of 1998, the accumulative increase in loans of financial institutions was RMB 761.2 billion, RMB 125.5 bn more than over the same period last year. The 1998 total planned national lending target was RMB 900 billion. All banks have been asked to accelerate lending in order to hit this target. If the funds allocated are insufficient, further support can be requested from the Central Bank. As noted, the number and frequency of monetary measures introduced by the Central Bank since the first half of 1998 are unprecedented.

Second, fiscal policy was fully utilized in the macroeconomic adjustment program.

(1) Fiscal expenditures in terms of infrastructure investment were increased. Beyond direct funding, increases in other fiscal measures have also been adopted as part of the broad fiscal support aimed at enhancing economic growth. This can be seen in the adjustment of the fiscal budget, the expansion of budget deficits, and the increases in treasury bonds. Based on an initial estimate, the demand growth that will be generated from treasury bond inputs could boost economic growth by as much as 2%. In retrospect, it is clear that, to a large extent, these measures helped to ensure achievement of the 8% overall growth target.

(2) Fiscal taxation measures have been implemented to boost exports. On the one hand, the processing of export tax rebates was accelerated and the scope of tax "exemption, offset, and rebate" was gradually expanded. On the other hand, tax rebate rates were raised for five industries, including steel, cement, shipbuilding, coal, and textiles.

(3) Special treasury bonds totaling RMB 270 bn were issued to increase the capital base of China's state commercial banks to enhance their lending capacity, and consequently their capability to help support the smooth implementation of these monetary policy measures.

Third, new infrastructure investment was increased in order to improve the environment for economic growth. The original target allocation for highway construction, for instance, was RMB 120 billion. By March, this had increased to RMB 160 billion. In the second half of 1998, it increased again to RMB180 billion, a 50% rise over the amount originally allotted.

Electricity bonds targeted to raise RMB 2.907 bn earmarked for investment in 19 electricity infrastructure projects were also issued. And in 1998, investment in the first phase of the resettlement program stood at RMB 41.904 billion. The State Development and Planning Commission listed 117 key construction projects, 84 of which were focused on developing electricity, transportation, irrigation, and coal industry. Over the next five years, the government plans to invest RMB 250 bn in railroad construction. In 1998, the government increased its railroad construction allocation to RMB 120 billion. The original budget for postal and telecommunications service enhancement was RMB130 bn; this has subsequently been increased to RMB150 bn. Similarly, the government also plans to invest over RMB120 bn to raise the rate of waste treatment and transformation from the current 7% and 6% to about 20%. And in July, the State Development Bank of China decided to lend RMB 50 bn over the next three years for the construction of a rural electricity grid. The funds to be injected into this project in 1998 were estimated at some RMB 20 billion.

Various Reform Measures Are Progressively Being Implemented, Amounting to an Unprecedented Effort in this Regard

In 1998, the new Cabinet, immediately after its formation, announced eight reform tasks under an umbrella program entitled "Three Implementations and Five Reforms": implementation of the reform of state-owned enterprises, implementation of financial reform, and implementation of government structural reform, along with reforms of the food distribution system, investment and financing system, housing system, medical care system, and fiscal and taxation system.

These reforms were immediately introduced and carried out in 1998, and more so, a timetable and targets for these reforms were also set. Among them, the goal cited for large and medium-size state-owned enterprises is to convert them from loss- to profit-making within three years; 512 large key enterprises are expected to become profitable next year, or face closure.

Housing system reform got fully under way in the second half of 1998. The distribution of welfare housing has stopped. Provinces and cities have begun reforming their housing allocation procedures.

In 1998, the reform of government departments at the central government level reached its final stages. Government departments have been reorganized: all job positions were classified, and new job descriptions, functions, and schedules fixed. The new departments have started to work based on these new classifications. Between 1999–2000, the reposition of personnel in the central government will be completed.

At the same time, reforms have begun in local governments meaning those below the provincial administrative level.

In terms of reforming the food distribution system, the principles of the reform have been announced: grain purchases will be open, grain sales will be dictated by market prices, and capital for grain-oriented purposes will be administered through separate accounts.   If these reforms can be implemented smoothly in 1998, the macroeconomic environment will be improved.

From the above, we can see that the central government has implemented many macroeconomic policies and reform measures to ensure that the 8% economic growth target will be realized. This has taken an enormous effort.   However, actually achieving 8% growth has proven very difficult. As noted above, the reason is that 1998 marked a turning point as the economic cycle moved into a new stage. That is to say, after 20 years of rapid economic growth, China is entering a new era of development. And if the country cannot adjust to the requirements of this new reality, and make the timely policy and target adjustments required, the national economy will again enter a vicious cycle characterized by "hot-expansion and cold-contraction."   Thus, we must consider the problems confronting economic growth in 1998 soberly, so as to find a realistic development course.

Some Considerations on 1998 Economic Growth

On the Growth Rate

After several years of high economic growth, China has entered into a period of slow but stable economic growth, characterized by predominant production capacity excess in most sectors, many unemployed social resources, and a marked drop in consumer demand.   All of these should be considered normal.

The 7% growth rate in the first half of the year was essentially the delayed effect of the appropriately tight macroeconomic program.   After policy adjustment, it will rise again.   However, targets should be kept realistic. In particular, the local governments at different administrative levels should not aim to increase inputs in every year without considering local realities; nor should they treat the growth target as a political task.

That is because the background of our macroeconomic situation is very different than it was ten years ago. At present, China's basic market potential is already much reduced; and its new market potential has yet to be developed. Increased investment in infrastructure and high technology for industry will require considerable time to transform the new economic growth points into consumer demand. Consequently, it does not matter whether the growth rate is 7% or 8%: the hard fact that the 1998 economy is an economy in transition cannot be changed. Many structural problems at the present cannot be overcome fundamentally. We must, therefore, adopt the right attitude toward economic growth, and spend more of our effort raising the quality of the national economy. And to achieve solid long-term development, we must tackle and overcome the structural problem of the stored resources.

On Deflation

Deflation, like inflation several years ago, is a very hot topic today. The difference is that when people talk about inflation they are referring to something that actually has happened, whereas deflation is creating anxiety and fear ahead of the fact. Beyond marked and continuing price declines, deflation amounts to an ongoing decrease in consumer demand and a general recession in economic life. We cannot yet say categorically that deflation has appeared in China, necessitating our trying to implement inflationary measures again.

Rather, we should consider that the situation in the first half of 1998 is a result of the delayed effect of the anti-inflationary macroeconomic austerity program. That is to say, after the "soft landing" for the national economy was achieved in 1996–1997, we should have adjusted this policy — meant for an inflationary period — and not have insisted on appropriate tightness; in other words, appropriate tightness became excessive tightness.

In addition, the Southeast Asian financial crisis and other international conditions deteriorated. Under these circumstances, we could not simply switch to a policy of arbitrarily generated inflation. An appropriate expansionary policy is necessary. But over the long term, whether a macroeconomic adjustment program is expansionary or contractionary, it remains artificial and not natural. In a market economy, we must respect the market's fundamental effect on resource allocation. What we can do is to expand the channels for direct fund raising and enable enterprises to become investors.

On Not Devaluing the RMB

Like the issue of the rate of economic growth, we should not consider the issue of devaluing, or not devaluing, the RMB in its absolute sense. In particular, under a market economy, we must work according to market mechanisms. Variations in exchange rates should be decided by the supply-and-demand relationship. It is reasonable for China to announce that it will not devalue the RMB to increase consumer confidence in the market, to stabilize the financial markets, and to stop the negative chain reaction caused by the Southeast Asian financial crisis.

However, we cannot ignore the fact that the stability or even appreciation of the RMB has forced us into a position whereby, if we are to achieve economic growth, our only possible way to do so is by expanding domestic demand. This, in turn, means we will have to increase our deficit to ensure investment demand. This measure can, over the short term, stimulate economic growth while overcoming some other problems. But, we must ask ourselves whether we can afford to do this, bearing in mind the heavy burden of debt repayment, and whether we can effectively prevent duplicate construction and an overheated economy happening again. More importantly, doing so puts us at odds in terms of the macroeconomy of the market economy we have already established.

The 1999 Economic Growth Situation and Policy Options

A Slight Rise in Growth

Because many macroeconomic measures aimed at expanding domestic demand were introduced in 1998, the effects should show in the first half of 1999 and afterward.   Therefore, the 1999 growth rate will be higher than that of 1998, although the increase will not be great.   When investment demand changes to consumer demand, growth will accelerate.

Economic growth in 2000 is likely to reach 8.5%.   This is to say that after 1998, when the new economic cycle gains momentum, the growth rate should be in the range of 8–8.5%.   A higher rate is unlikely.

During this transitional period, in order to move quickly into the new developmental stage, other than maintaining the appropriate rate of growth, we should emphasize structural adjustment, and adopt policies appropriate to achieving this goal. This, in turn, means we must first understand the fundamental characteristics of this new stage.

First, market demand will become the major restricting factor. Second, the foundation of this new stage is an increase in economic efficiency and technical innovation.   Third, the main supports will be new economic growth points and newly-developed markets. Fourth, the main engines will be the rapid development of the non-state sector, and medium and small enterprises.

Policy Choices Should Be Made in the Context of a Short- and Long-term Plan

In stimulating economic growth, policy normally consists of mostly short-term adjustments supplemented by an improved macroeconomic environment, along with some long-term policies. When economic growth enters a new period, ushering in a new development paradigm, government policy choices should be based on the interaction of short- and long-term plans.

First, short-term adjustment policies should be mainly of the monetary sort, with the appropriate assistance of fiscal policy. Traditional monetary policies, like interest, exchange, and reserve requirement rate adjustments, and the use of rediscounts, open market intervention, bond repurchases, and so on, should be initiated in coordination with the effective development of a consumer credit system to deal with the current problem of weak demand. This measure will have a much more direct effect in generating consumer demand than investment credit policy.

Second, long-term policies should be mainly focused on the improvement of industrial policy and economic institutions. Industrial policy is the key to overall structural adjustment, and therefore broad structural improvements. In particular, to increase the strength of industrial structure adjustments in sectors like the coal and textiles industries is a mandatory administrative priority. This task may take some time. But, over the longer term, it will ultimately succeed in stimulating economic growth.

What is urgently needed for institutional reform is to expand the channels for direct fund raising while providing support for medium and small-size enterprises. Such comprehensive institutional reform will contribute greatly to the effective implementation of the government's economic policy.

THE CHOICES OF OBJECTIVES OF MACRO-ECONOMIC COORDINATION AND CONTROL AND POLICY MANIPULATION UNDER THE NEW ECONOMIC BACKGROUND

CHEN DONGQI
Graduate School
Chinese Academy of Social Sciences

The New Economic Background: Characteristics and Causes for Insufficient Effective Demand

After 20 years of reform and development, the phenomenon of insufficient effective demand as described by Keynes in 1936 in his work, *The General Theory of Employment, Interest and Money,* is finally showing up. China's insufficient effective demand is a structural one. What, then, is structural insufficient effective demand?

From the perspective of industrial structure, excessive supply or insufficient demand is mainly a phenomenon manifested in industrial goods. When public goods are in shortage for a long period of time, the chief goal of government management is not to stimulate demand, but to increase supply.

From the angle of consumption structure, insufficient demand is manifested in food, clothing, and household durable goods, while the supply of housing and transportation is relatively insufficient. In the first half of 1998, a survey by relevant institutions arrived at the conclusion that the supply for most products was in excess or in equilibrium with the demand.

Naturally, at a time of slow economic development, insufficient effective demand also appears in those industries or products that are subject to short supply. Housing is an example. Currently the average area of housing is 8.8 and 22.5 m^2 for each urban or rural resident respectively, 145% and 178% higher than the 3.6 and 8.1 m^2 in 1978.

However, the absolute level is still rather low by world standards.   The potential demand for housing from urban and rural residents will remain enormous for a long time.   However, due to the demand pressure which has existed for a long time, we cannot eliminate the possibility of a short-term insufficient effective demand.

In 1997, the accumulated inventory of private housing increased by 25.4% from that of 1996. In the first seven months of 1998, residential housing investment increased by 22.2%. The area of housing completed has increased by 15.1%.   The area of housing sold has increased by 55.3%.   However, there is still over 70 million m^2 of unsold residential housing across the country. The cause of insufficient demand mainly lies in the fact that the prices are too high. In 1997 when the economy slid, total prices rose only by 0.8%, but the price for housing rose by 8.1%.   In the first half of 1998 during the economic downturn, general price levels fell by 3%, but the price for housing went up more than 3%.   Clearly, the high price of housing inhibits market demand.

The major problem of China's economic development is insufficient demand for general industrial products.   There are several reasons for oversupply and insufficient demand of general industrial products.

First, there is a mismatch between production and consumption and between supply and demand. The problem lies in the structure.   The rises in personal income and consumption level have given rise to a quick change in the structure of consumer demand and a constant change in consumers' preferences. However, many enterprises, particularly the state-owned ones, still operate in the pattern that "supply automatically breeds demand" within the planned economy, where the product structure cannot tailor itself to consumer demand. The result is that there is no market for finished goods, which are left idle in the warehouses.

Second, as the economy declines, unemployment increases. The growth of the average disposable income slows down, affecting demand. From 1995 to 1997, the average income growth rates of urban and rural residents fell from 22.5% and 29.4% to 6.6% and 8.5% respectively. From January to August 1998, the growth of average urban personal income was only 6%; the growth of rural personal income was 2% in the first quarter, and −0.7% in the second quarter.

Third, marginal consumption tends to fall. This increases the preference for holding cash and restricts consumer demand. The reasons for the fall in marginal monetary consumption disposition are: as employment has become market-oriented, and the problem of unemployment has come out in the open, people worry about their jobs and a decrease in future income. Moreover, they are concerned about their old age and children's college education fees. All these account for the declining tendency in marginal consumption.

Fourth, the prices of high-level consumer products are too high, which affects the expansion of consumption in the process of structural adjustment. The high-level consumer products we refer to are mainly consumer products in housing, transportation, and cultural activity. After the basic needs of clothing and food have been satisfied, people look for a higher quality of life with an emphasis on a higher level consumption of housing and means of transportation. However, in relation to the average personal income level, the current prices are still too high, particularly the prices for residential housing. As a result, there is insufficient demand for housing.

Fifth, deflation, which appeared during this economic trough, depressed consumption. In recent years, total retail prices have continued to fall. On a monthly basis, inflation reached zero in September 1997, and stayed within the negative value range up to August 1998. Moreover, the negative growth rate is on the rise almost every month (see Table 1).

Table 1
Inflation Rates of Retail Prices since September 1997

Unit: %

Month	1998				1997							
	9	10	11	12	1	2	3	4	5	6	7	8
Inflation rate	0.0	-0.4	-0.8	-1.2	-1.5	-1.9	-1.2	-2.1	-2.7	-3.0	-3.2	-3.3

The result shows that total retail sales grew slowly and consumer demand slowed down.

Sixth, as well as the slowdown in consumer demand, capital formation also cooled down. The reasons are:

(1) Expectations of the return on investment fell. The original opportunities for huge profits were missing, and the time when "profit guaranteed by investment" was once a fact has become a fiction.

(2) The budget constraints on public enterprises, especially the state-owned enterprises, changed from loose to strict, and the debt became corporatized. The original hunger for investment generally disappeared, and the degree of expansion of institutional investment fell.

(3) The quota system for credit was abolished, and the freedom of credit increased; thus, the proportion of black market credit and total credit declined. In addition, the competition among commercial banks has intensified. The increase in the supply of credit has been faster than the demand. With all these factors, the total actual investment demand, compared to the supply of investment item facilities, has become inadequate.

Target Setting in Recent Macroeconomic Development

The Speed of Economic Growth

Up to now, the government and the media are still insisting on a "guarantee for an 8% growth target." I believe, from the perspective of the government, there is a good reason for them to insist on the 8%, because it is an indication of confidence. At this difficult time, when we have experienced flood disasters, declining exports, and continued crisis in neighboring countries, if the government changes its target, it will shake people's confidence in the government's policy to maintain stable economic growth. People might then expect more difficulties in the next stage of economic development.

From a research perspective, is it still possible to realize 8% growth in 1998? I think it is a difficult task and the actual growth rate will probably be about 7.5%.

From simple calculation, to reach 8% growth for the whole year, we will have to obtain 9% growth in the second half, 2% faster than the first half, which seems almost impossible. Reviewing the growth variations in the five indicators of industry, agriculture, exports, retailing, and investment confirms that the possibility of reaching 9% growth in the second half is not great.

First, looking from the angle of supply (production method), growth in industry in the first half of the year was 7.8%, rising to 7.9% in August. However, the strength of the recovery was weak. The growth of agriculture in 1998 showed a "stable or slight decline." The growth of the tertiary industry was "accelerating slightly." Growth in industry must reach about 10% in order to guarantee the 8% GDP growth rate. But that sector's growth in July and August was less than 8%. Even if the growth in industry exceeds 10% in the last four months, the GDP growth rate in the second half can only reach about 9.5% (see Table 2).

Table 2
Monthly Variations in the Growth of Industry in 1998

Unit: %

Month	1	2	3	4	5	6	1st half	7	8	Whole year
Growth in industry	1.8	5.1	9.0	7.2	8.0	7.8	7.8	7.6	7.9	≈9.5

Then, from the angle of demand (expenditure method), the growth of exports in 1997 was 20.8%. Between January and August 1998, it was only 5.5%. The growth rate in August was -2.9%; and in the final four months of the year, a low or even negative rate was expected. The full year estimate is under 5%, a shrinkage of nearly 16% from that in 1997. The current contribution of exports to the national economic growth is about 20%. In this situation, the exports affect the total economic growth by about 3%. That is to say, when the growth rates of consumption and investment demand remain unchanged, GDP growth will fall to 5.8%. In this way, to realize a growth rate of above 5.8% will require the expansion of domestic demand.

Among domestic demands, consumption is noticeably the weakest. The growth of market sales is slow, and the desire to purchase is the lowest in the 20 years since the reform. In the first half of 1998, the growth in total retail sales was 6.8%. A recovery was witnessed in July and August when growth reached 8–9%. Driven by a series of measures to stimulate consumption, the growth in retail sales in the next four months should exceed 10%. However, there have been no fundamental changes in the people's deflationary expectations. When the growth of monetary income is restricted, the process of accelerating consumption demand will be slow.

What remains as a possible source of demand expansion is investment. The situation for investment demand in 1998 was more optimistic than in 1997. After bottoming out at 10.3% in the first quarter, the growth of total fixed assets investment in the second quarter was 13.8%, and it reached 22.8% and 26.9% respectively in July and August.

It may reach a growth rate of 20% for the whole year, doubling that of 1997 (see Table 3 below). However, because the delaying effect of the economic recovery generated by the recovery of investment generally lasts six months, economic recovery will not be realized until the end of the third quarter when the stimulus of the growth in investment demand starts to take effect.

In addition, the focus of the accelerated investment will not be on general industrial products, nor duplicating construction, but rather mainly on public products such as infrastructure projects of transportation, irrigation and environmental protection, and public service facilities. The multiplier effect on the growth value of these public products and their ability to absorb employment are not as obvious as industrial products. Consequently, even after several months of growth in investment, the recovery of GDP growth will not be fast. It will be quite difficult for accelerated investment growth to make up for the shortfall in the export growth in 1998. It is therefore possible that the actual GDP growth rate will be about 0.5% lower than the target rate.

Table 3
Monthly Variations in the Growth of Fixed Assets Investment

Unit: %

Month	1	2	3	4	5	6	7	8	1-8	Whole year
Growth of investment	10.1	10.2	10.3	12.2	12.7	13.8	22.8	26.9	17.4	20.0

What should be emphasized is that two problems will arise if we interpret the 8% target as a political mission. One is that various local governments will revert to the road of the "Great Leap Forward." In order to achieve this goal, they will falsify the actual figures by reporting a fast growth rate, which will affect the quality of economic growth.

The other is that various local governments will blindly approve proposals just to create new projects at low levels and will license duplicate construction. This will affect the transformation of the modes of growth as well as the structural adjustment, and will ruin the good results that have been achieved in the five years of the macroeconomic adjustment program. Viewed from a government policy perspective, the principle of "progress with stability" in economic growth should still be strictly followed into the future, and then a gradual economic growth on the basis of improving the quality of growth and structural adjustment will be realized.

How high should we set the target for economic growth in 1999? In terms of the factors such as the inertia of the cyclical trend, and the internal and external environmental changes, in the following five years, the appropriate range of economic growth should be set between 7% and 11%, so far as the policy goes. If 7.5% can be reached in 1998, it is close to the bottom of policy preferences. In 1999, we may work out a plan for above 7.5%. I suggest we set the target at 8 to 8.5%. In this way, the rate of growth will remain stable, while giving people a high expectation.

On Variations in Currency Value

In terms of the variations in currency value, there are presently two different schools of thought. One believes in depreciation to soften the upward pressure on the RMB from currencies of neighboring countries, so that the goal of stimulating growth and stabilizing exports can be achieved. The other insists on retaining the current RMB value, allowing the RMB to appreciate when other currencies depreciate, on the grounds that the RMB is entering a phase of automatic appreciation. We believe that implementation of the policy to regulate the value of the RMB depends on the economic situation. Among it, the four most important ones are: changes in prices, export growth, trade balance, and foreign exchange reserves.

From a theoretical perspective, a sustaining fall in general price level or even a deflation indicate a rise in the purchasing power of the domestic currency. In this case, usually no depreciation is necessary. If deflation turns into inflation, and the inflation rate is far above the one-year deposit rate, we should then consider depreciating the currency value.

In terms of trade balance, despite a slowdown in export growth, an even faster decline in the import growth rate has been experienced, resulting in a rapid increase in the trade surplus. Between January and August 1998, the trade surplus reached US$31.38 billion, with a monthly average of about US$4 billion. Following the recent temporary embargo on the import of oil and diesel, in the following few months, the growth of imports will still decline. Under such circumstances, it is not reasonable to depreciate the RMB.

In terms of the foreign exchange reserves, the current amount is over US$141 billion, way above reasonable international standards, which should meet the demand of four months of imports. At present, four months of imports require only US$44 billion. There is therefore no reason to depreciate the RMB significantly. That the Japanese Yen used to be depreciated substantially even when its reserves were sufficient seems to be a counter-proof for our theory. However, we note that the lack of domestic demand in Japan is obviously more serious than that in China.

In recent years, to stimulate external demand, foreign investment, and economic recovery, the countries in Southeast Asia, East Asia, and Japan depreciated their currencies. As a result, their financial assets shrank by 60% to 80% and their GDPs shrank by about 50% (in U.S. dollar terms). However, their actions led to a shrinkage in foreign investment, and their economies sank further into recession.

In early September 1998, the Malaysian Ringgit was depreciated by more than 40%, but the amount of foreign investment remaining in the country was only 10% of the level before the crisis, and the economic growth for 1998 will be -2%. Indonesia's economic growth rate in 1998 is estimated to be -10%, Thailand -4%, and South Korea -6%.

Japan will record a further decline in its growth, with -0.5% expected, after 1997's economic growth rate of -0.7%. The growth rate in the Philippines will fall from 5.7% in 1997 to 2% in 1998. We can see that depreciation of currency value to stimulate exports and economic growth is not very effective. For a large country like ours, with an enormous population, high employment pressure, many areas still below the poverty line, great potential of rural markets, incomplete upgrades of urban and rural consumption structures, and an incomplete industrialization process, external demand is important but domestic demand is even more important. In particular, when China's reliance on foreign trade reaches 30%, and that on exports reaches 20%, it may be unwise to depend too much on foreign trade and exports to stimulate economic growth.

We believe that there is no urgency to depreciate the RMB when there has not been any noticeable change in our current economic situation. From a strategic point of view, China has promised "to maintain the value of the RMB." We should not change what has been said. Moreover, with many Asian currencies depreciated, the depreciation of the RMB would worsen the Asian financial crisis. And this would not be favorable to China itself, including the Mainland, Hong Kong, and Taiwan. Again, there is still room to use administrative measures to increase exports, such as loosening the administrative restrictions on international trade and adjusting the restrictive policies on exports/imports. In addition, even if we were to depreciate the RMB, we should do it only once our neighboring countries are experiencing economic recovery and prosperity.

How Should the Government Execute the Macroeconomic Policy?

In order to stimulate economic recovery when export growth is in decline and the value of the RMB remains unchanged, the government should concentrate on strengthening the efforts of the macroeconomic adjustment program in "stimulating domestic demand." In the circumstances when enterprise production falls, deflation increases, the export growth rate declines, and the consumer market is weak, the government should increase its fiscal expenditures. The government can appropriately expand the budget deficit to raise fiscal resources to cover the shortage of investment in public projects, especially in infrastructure construction, so as to generate a reasonable growth in total investment demand. Now, reviewing the policy implementation since July and August, we find that there is a clear tendency of "appropriate loosening" in place.

— Special treasury bonds worth RMB270 bn have been raised to inject capital into the four major state banks: Industrial and Commercial Bank of China, Agricultural Bank of China, Bank of China, and People's Construction Bank of China.

— There was an increase of RMB100 bn of treasury bonds for investment in infrastructure projects and suitable housing projects.

— There is an increase of investment in road construction from RMB120 bn to RMB180 billion.

— There is an increase of investment in irrigation construction and public infrastructure projects, such as environmental protection, communication, and welfare facilities.

— Banks have been requested to increase loans.

— There is sudden rise in M_0 from 6.6% at the end of June to above 10%.

— A series of measures to reduce enterprise taxes have been implemented.

— There was an increase in the fiscal deficit from RMB45 bn at the beginning of the year to RMB96 billion.

The implementation of these policy measures is necessary and mandatory for the economy to rise from the trough. We cannot understand why the Ministry of Finance and the research departments of the Central Bank are reluctant to exercise the policy of "appropriate loosening" and are still maintaining the policy of "appropriate tightness." If this is the case, is it true that China will never carry out the "loosening" policy? From a dynamic point of view, economic adjustment should be sometimes tight and sometimes loose, sometimes tense and sometimes relaxed, with appropriate tightness and looseness, and flexible expansion and contraction.

There is no consensus on when the next step of loosening should take place. Some are in favor of further cutting the interest rates. We believe that even if we are to cut the interest rates again, the range should not be too great; otherwise, the nominal interest rates will be too low, and the room for the general price level to recover will be too small, producing unfavorable effects on economic growth. In this economic recovery, we can consider leaving 6% to 8% room for the general price level to rise again. In other words, the inflation rate of 6% to 8% is acceptable when the economy prospers again. In addition, the current deposit rate is already lower than the U.S. dollar deposit rate or its equivalent. Any further cut in interest rates will force people to change their holdings of RMB to foreign currencies, which would be unfavorable to the RMB.

For the next step, monetary policy can be applied in the following areas:

(1) On the basis of maintaining stable growth in cash supply, we can accelerate the transformation of savings into investment

and consumer spending by renovating the financial system instead of cutting interest rates.

(2)   We can accelerate the marketization of interest rates by transferring the decision-making rights on deposit and loan interest rates from the Central Bank to the commercial banks, allowing them to implement a floating interest rate system. The Central Bank can adjust the basic interest rates on one hand and set the upper and lower limits for deposit and loan rates for commercial banks on the other.

(3)   Open market operations should be encouraged to raise the frequency of short-term capital fund market adjustment, so that the stable growth of money supply will be guaranteed.

(4)   Money supply can be increased appropriately to change people's expectation of price levels.

Fiscal policies in 1999 can play a bigger role in the expansion of debt. Treasury bonds worth about RMB380 bn have been issued in 1998. Based on this, it will be acceptable to issue treasury bonds of RMB450 bn in 1999. Of this amount, RMB50 bn can be used as social security bonds.

In addition, we can increase the day-to-day fiscal expenditure appropriately, mainly for the salaries of staff in institutions. With the salary increase, we can stimulate consumer spending. In the area of taxation, there is not much room for tax cuts. However, we can accelerate the unification of the tax systems and carry out the reform of "a single taxation system." In the next step, the implementation of the fiscal and monetary policies can be combined with the reform of their systems.

AN ANALYSIS OF THE CURRENT INSUFFICIENT CONSUMPTION DEMAND AND POLICY SUGGESTIONS

ZHAO JINGXING

Institute of Quantitative and Technical Economics
Chinese Academy of Social Sciences

Since the "Seventh Five-year Plan," China's rate of consumption (the proportion of final consumption in GDP) has been in continual decline. However, this trend has generally been masked by changing price levels, and has therefore tended to go unnoticed. At the same time, average family income has fallen seriously behind GDP growth over this period, though this too has been masked by price change factors. If we put aside the influence of these price changes, we can easily deduce the real cause of the current insufficient demand. We thus reach a new understanding of all the important economic relations by analyzing constant prices in the country's economy since the beginning of the reform and opening up.

The Slow Growth of Consumer Spending Is the Basic Cause for the Current Insufficient Demand

Since 1986, our rate of consumption has fallen sharply. On the basis of constant prices, compared with the average rate recorded during the "Sixth Five-year Plan," it dipped to 11.1% in 1997, an appalling rate of decline. See Table 1 for details.

The basic cause for this is that consumption demand growth has long lagged behind GDP growth. Between 1986 and 1997, average GDP growth was pegged as high as 9.8%, while the average annual growth of final consumption stood at only 8.2%, or 1.6% less. Table 2 compares the growth of GDP and final consumption since the "Sixth Five-year Plan."

Table 1

Unit: %

Year	Consumption Rate at Constant Prices
1981-1985	65.9
1986-1990	61.1
1991	61.3
1992	61.3
1993	59.0
1994	56.5
1995	55.9
1991-1995	58.8
1996	56.1
1997	54.8

Note: Based on relevant data in *China Statistics Abstract 1998* and *Historical Materials of the National Accounting of the Gross Domestic Product (Abstract)*. The same applies for the following table.

Table 2

Unit: %

Year	GDP	Final Consumption	Consumer Spending	Gov't Spending
1981-1985	10.7	11.0	10.9	11.6
1986-1990	7.9	5.9	5.7	6.9
1991-1995	12.0	10.4	10.2	11.3
1996	9.6	10.0	10.2	9.5
1997	8.8	6.3		
1986-1997	9.8	8.2		

This perennial disparity problem between GDP and final consumption demand growth has inevitably given rise to insufficient domestic demand since growth in investment demand is derived from growth in consumer demand. What, then, are the root causes of the current consumption demand deficiency?

The Main Cause for Insufficient Consumption Demand Is Low Average Family Income

First, we must acknowledge that, compared with most other periods in Chinese history, the period after the reform and opening up achieved one of the highest rates of personal spending and income increases ever. Taking another perspective, however, it is clear that just as the growth of consumer spending fell behind that of GDP growth during this period, so growth in personal income fell behind GDP growth. This is the root cause of the present lack of consumer demand, and even total demand.

In the early and mid 1980s, personal incomes were excessive. "Salaries eating up profits" was the popular phrase of the day. As a result of the market reform process, however, this phenomenon has been corrected. As a consequence, since the "Seventh Five-year Plan," average family income growth has fallen behind GDP growth. Between 1986 and 1996, the annual average family income growth rate was only 6.3% after price adjustments.

Even after taking into consideration 1.2% population growth, total family income growth was no more than 7.5%. Between 1986 and 1996, the real annual average salary of workers grew at the even lower rate of 4.2%. Since average annual family income growth was substantially lower than GDP growth, the proportion of average personal income to average GDP at constant prices fell from 57.7% in 1985 to 45.5% in 1997. Table 3 shows the proportions of average personal income to average GDP, and average consumption to average GDP.

Table 3

Unit: %

Year	Average Personal Income /Average GDP	Average Consumption /Average GDP
1985	57.7	50.1
1986-1990	51.1	48.3
1991-1996	47.1	44.3
1996	46.2	41.9
1997	45.5	40.2

The personal income in Table 3 has not been adjusted for the additional expenses occasioned by the reforms in medical care, education, and housing. If we deduct the effect of these factors, the proportion of average family income to average GDP since the "Eighth Five-year Plan" will be lower than 45%, about the same as the proportion of average consumption to average GDP. In Table 3, the proportion of average personal income to average GDP, and those of average consumption to average GDP, show a similar trend and have very close mathematical values. This relationship shows clearly that low family income is the basic cause for insufficient consumption demand.

Policy Suggestions

Based on the above analysis, we believe that China should not simply expand the amount of fixed asset investment to expand domestic demand; instead, we should, while maintaining an appropriate rate of increase for fixed asset investment, greatly increase family incomes in order to enhance consumption demand.

The reasons are: first, our current scale of fixed asset investment is already quite large. Since 1992, the percentage of fixed asset investment as a component of GDP has continued to rise, reaching 34.4% in 1996 (see Table 4 for details). Second, because a full-scale oversupply situation has developed in the country's commodity markets, actually inhibiting further investment expansion, to try and force this expansion further may well incite blind investment and/or duplicate construction. If we only increase infrastructure project investment, for instance, it will still be difficult to achieve the goal of generating long-term economic growth. Third, because of the lack of stimulus on the demand side, it is difficult to adroitly direct the present effort in product structure adjustment. Whereas, increasing consumption demand will be beneficial to both utilizing idle production capacity and stimulating product structure adjustment.

Table 4

Unit: %

Year	Fixed Asset Investment Formation	Inventory and Net Exports
1981- 1985	28.1	6.0
1986-1990	28.3	10.6
1991	26.6	12.1
1992	28.8	9.9
1993	31.7	9.3
1994	33.1	10.4
1995	34.0	10.1
1991-1995	30.8	10.6
1996	34.4	9.5

The questions are: what is the most viable way to increase personal incomes, and how can we make use of this increase to more effectively stimulate economic growth?

Both historical experience and theoretical analysis prove that up until now, in all different models of the market economy, there lacks an economic mechanism to guarantee that labor income will automatically grow with GDP growth. Even in developed market economies, the increase of workers' wages is achieved through non-economic mechanisms such as union negotiations and strikes.

Therefore, finding an effective solution to the need to raise family incomes remains a key unsolved problem.

Judging by the requirements of our present macroeconomic adjustment program, one possible way is to first promote a substantial increase in the salaries of those staff who work in the areas of education, science, arts, health, and government. In focusing on this portion of the population, the hope would be to expand demand, activate the market, stimulate private investment, expand employment, and stimulate economic growth. On the foundation of economic growth, using these people as an "active ingredient," we may well be able to ultimately encourage enterprises to increase remuneration to workers, which in turn will help to raise the income level of other people.

The reasons are as follows:

Rural residents. In 1997, the average net production income of the farmers had increased by RMB1,620 from 1985. Of this amount, the real income generated from primary industry growth was only about RMB190, and from inflation of farm product prices, RMB790. The remaining RMB640 was from the growth in non-agricultural industry. In recent years, agricultural production has also been affected by the problem of insufficient market demand; prices have not risen but fallen. It has now become impractical to increase farmers' incomes by increasing the prices of agricultural products. At the same time, the development of non-agricultural industry has similarly been hindered by insufficient demand. If the market environment is not changed, this industry can hardly be expected to serve as an effective expedient in increasing farmer incomes.

Urban residents. Following the deepening of the reform of economic system in urban areas, almost all enterprises have now become market-driven. The government can no longer, as under the previous planned economic system, increase workers' salaries through administrative order. If the current situation of weak demand and difficult operating conditions continues, it will be impossible to expect enterprises to increase staff salaries.

Income disparity.   The income of those who work in the areas of education, science, arts, health, and government is obviously too low. This has prompted many problems, such as corruption.   The income of these people should be raised.   Doing so will not only increase consumer spending, expand demand, stimulate investment, increase employment, activate the market, and generate economic growth; it will also facilitate the establishment of a clean and hardworking government and the implementation of the policy of building up the country through science and education.   In short, it is a policy with many benefits.

Increasing the salaries of the above-mentioned staff is not only necessary but also feasible.   As the great majority of such people are civil servants, the government has the authority — and obligation — to increase their income at appropriate times.   This can be accomplished through planned increases in fiscal expenditure. Doing so is in line with the direction of the current expansionary fiscal policy.   In addition, under the current economic situation, this measure is even more reasonable; its likelihood of exerting a stimulating effect on the economy in general is obvious. It is likely to facilitate more active markets, drive a more rapid rate of economic expansion, and yield more tax income for the government. This, in turn, means that eventually there will be no additional fiscal burden for the government to bear.

The above measures can be implemented at the same time as other policy improvements, such as housing reform.   At the same time, such moves will increase the effectiveness of disciplinary action within these related economic sectors. With meaningful salary increases, prosecution of illegal and unlawful behavior on the part of staff is likely to become *de rigueur.*   The incentives, in this regard, are obvious; and the result would amount to real progress in terms of creating the necessary social environment for economic growth.

ANALYSIS AND FORECAST OF CHINA'S MACROECONOMIC SITUATION *

ZHENG CHAOYU

Institute of Economics
People's University of China

China's current economic cycle started to expand in 1991 and reached its peak in 1994; then it entered a contraction stage. In 1998, China's macroeconomic operation showed a decline in economic growth, deflation caused by unemployment, and other recessionary phenomena. The trough of the economic cycle will be formed in 1998. Starting in 1999, the economy will enter a expansionary stage of the next cycle.

In the first half of 1998, the GDP growth was 7.0%, while the retail price index fell by 2.1%. Most economic development indicators showed a sharp decline from the same period last year. Starting from the second half, investment demand and consumer demand started to gradually increase. A series of adjustment measures aiming at expanding domestic demand began to show their initial effect. Under the strong pulling force of domestic demand, the industrial production growth rate started to recover in August. Both retail and consumer prices were still low in August, but the decline was slowing down. In fact, prices, after several months of decline, rose again compared with the previous months.

It was possible that this continuing deflationary trend would be reversed in September. But the persistently weak economic conditions will not end in the third quarter and the recovery of the economy will be delayed till the fourth quarter. In 1998, the growth rate of the total retail price index is expected to be below -1%. Therefore, the 8% growth target, set at the beginning of the year, looks unattainable.

---

* This paper was prepared by the Macroeconomic Analysis and Forecast Research Team, People's University of China. The discussants for this paper were Hu Naiwu, Yang Zhi, Huang Taiyan, Yang Ruilong, Zhang Ming, and Zhu Nansong.

The forecast results of China's 1998–1999 macroeconomic situation are given in Table 1. The major assumptions for the 1999 forecast are based on:

(1) that the 1999 fiscal policy continues to be an expansionary one, as in 1998;
(2) that the exchange rate of the RMB versus the U.S. dollar is 8.5:1.

Table 1

Forecast indicators	1998	1999
1. GDP growth rate %	7.75	9.6
Of which: increase in primary industry	3.3	4.1
increase in secondary industry	9.5	11.8
increase in tertiary industry	7.7	9.2
2 Total value of fixed asset investment (RMB billion)	2,922	3,521
Total value of retail sales (RMB billion)	2,907	3,328
3. Exports (US$ billion)	194	211
Imports (US$ billion)	153	175
4. Narrow money supply M_1 growth rate (%)	12.4	18.6
Broad money supply M_2 growth rate (%)	15.8	22.5
5. Retail price index growth rate (%)	-1.2	2.1
Consumer price index growth rate (%)	0.7	3.9

Is it a Question of Economic Structure or Insufficient Effective Demand?

Mainstream Macroeconomic Theory and the Principle of Appropriately Tight Management of Demand

The cyclical recession of China's economy was more prominent in the second half of 1997. The judgment by the policy makers and mainstream macroeconomic theorists was that it is a problem of long-term economic structure, not a problem of cyclical insufficient effective demand. They insisted on appropriately tight fiscal and monetary policies, failing to understand that applying a demand suppression policy in the final stage of an economic contraction cycle was a mistake. The policies initiated for expanding demand after the Asian financial crisis were also problematic ones, since they tried to subsidize for the weak demand of net exports on the one hand, and in the meantime to set a long-term policy target of easing effective demand restrictions on China's economic growth, on the other hand.

The viewpoint against the mainstream economic theories argued for appropriate tightness. This means that the stable management of demand should be applied as the policy candidate for an intermediate stage or the stage of economic transfer through the entire economic cycle. Addressing the macroeconomic situation of enterprises running with under capacity, increased unemployment, and the oversupply of most products, the mainstream economic theorists believed that the policy of suppressing demand only served to reveal the problems in the existing economic structure. In addition, under the pressure of market competition, the economic structure was forced to undergo an even adjustment, thus softening the structural imbalance of the economy instead of overloading it. Consequently, it was necessary to ease efforts to suppress demand. However, the orientation of the overall macroeconomic policy should still be toward tightness in order to make use of a relaxed macroeconomic environment for adjusting the economic structure.

Another Approach to Analyze China's Macroeconomy

Empirically speaking, the structural problems in China's economic system is complex and is subject to the following categorization: the long-term structural problems whose solution depends on economic development and reform of the economic system in connection with our special economic development stage; the short-term structural problems whose solution depends on the adjustment in the macroeconomic policy in connection with short-term macroeconomic trends.

The following three structural factors in fact form the background for the slowdown and stagnant economic growth since 1997. First, the economic development since 1979 created the so-called Chinese miracle, and successfully narrowed the disparity between China and developed countries. At the same time, China has been gradually losing its late-starter advantage. At the end of this century and the beginning of the next century, China's economic development will enter the adjustment era from the high growth stage into a new stage of an appropriate degree of growth. Second, the reform of state-owned enterprises has not yet achieved real progress. The problems of low efficiency in supply and bad debts, which will harm the financial system, are becoming increasingly serious. They not only affect the leading role of the state economy, and the leading position of public ownership, but also become the major institutional obstacle in the way of China's sustained economic development. Third, the Chinese economy has made a historic turn from being a shortage economy to a relative oversupply economy. A limited buyer's market has been established. Effective demand has started to restrict the utilization rate of potential aggregate supply and its long-term growth.

Therefore, when aggregate demand increases, the structural hindrance of potential aggregate supply will decrease. Subsequently, the economic structure will be improved along with economic expansion. When aggregate demand decreases, the structural hindrance of aggregate supply increases, and economic structure deteriorates when the economy contracts.

The transformation of the economic cycle from expansion to contraction is triggered by the negative social welfare effect of inflation (similar to the view of the mainstream theorists), but not because the economic growth has reached its technical upper limit of aggregate supply (different from the mainstream opinion). At the peak of the economic cycle, there is still the ability to supply resources to support continuing economic expansion. The identical trends of aggregate demand and inflation are only possible against the historical background of diffusion of personal income, and where the collective expenditure is financed by the levy of an inflation tax. If we can establish a regulated mechanism for savings-investment, it is very possible to increase the utilization rate of production capacity by increasing aggregate demand, with prices remaining stable.

The mainstream opinion is self-fulfilling. If we emphasize the problems of economic structure and suppress aggregate demand, we will definitely exacerbate the economic structural problems, thus justifying the mainstream opinion and lending sufficient confirmation for the implementation of a demand suppression policy. It is precisely this mainstream opinion in China's macroeconomic management that inappropriately emphasizes and directs attention to the economic structural problem. Insisting on a medium-term policy of appropriate tightness and rejecting adjustment of the orientation of counter cycle policy create a short-term structural problem, worsen the economic structure, lower the total utilization rate of production capacity and employment level, and finally cause an unnatural decline in economic growth, deflation, and recession.

Critique and Opinion of China's 1998 Macroeconomic Policy

The Contraction Effect of an Unbalanced Exchange Rate Policy

The negative effects of the Asian financial crisis on China's exports were twofold: the replacement effect and the income effect. On the one hand, the RMB's passive revaluation lowered the competitiveness of China's export products. On the other hand, the recession in Asia and other related countries reduced their imports of Chinese goods.

The nominal RMB exchange rate has been stable after the reform of combining the two tracks in 1994. Because our major trading partners devalued their currencies substantially in 1998, while since 1994 China has experienced high inflation, the external exchange rate for the RMB in 1998 was too high.   Under the current system of foreign exchange, the People's Bank of China is responsible for buying the balance remaining at specialized foreign exchange banks after the sale and purchase at the published exchange rate, in order to clear out the foreign exchange in the nation's exchange markets.   The amount of foreign reserve, therefore, has a direct relationship with the proportion of foreign exchange used at the People's Bank of China, as part of the assets of the Central Bank.   The decline in 1998 exports and the subsequent decline (relative) in the trade surplus reduced the domestic money supply following the decrease in currency issued.   The contraction effects of overestimating the unbalanced exchange rate policy include at least:

(1)   decline in export demand;
(2)   decline in domestic money supply;
(3)   corresponding domestic deflation.

The RMB has already achieved free convertibility in international current account settlements.   The promise not to devalue the RMB helped to stabilize the expected nominal RMB exchange rate in the short term and prevented attacks from international speculative funds.   However, this policy also hampered the channel of adjusting the nominal exchange rate for the balanced modification of the RMB exchange rate.   The actual depreciation of the RMB through the balanced modification of the RMB exchange rate was realized through domestic deflation.

Possible Forms of Balanced Adjustment of the RMB Exchange Rate

The unbalanced intervention against the requirement of balancing the RMB exchange rate could not eliminate the intrinsic inclination for RMB devaluation.   Objectively speaking, it nurtured the outflow of international capital for potential speculative profit. Then international speculative capital flowed out to the profiteers because of the expected support for devaluation of the RMB.   This process exacerbated the pressure for RMB devaluation in both domestic and international exchange markets. Through the intervention in exchange markets on net sales, the Central Bank tried to counter-attack the money supply contraction effect caused by the fall of the foreign exchange funds of the People's Bank of China. The hedging effect was limited. On this occasion, the mismatch between the goals of a stable balanced domestic economy and the goals of external balance are manifested as a conflict between the monetary policy and the exchange rate policy.

If emphasis is placed on the domestic balance goals for economic stability and an expansionary monetary policy is to be adopted to expand effective demand, then it is necessary to carry out hedging operations to increase the domestic money supply. In this way, the deflationary trend in domestic prices would be stopped. The balanced adjustment of an overvalued RMB cannot be realized through de facto devaluation by domestic deflation. If the emphasis is placed on the external balance goals for economic stability to devalue the RMB in order to fix its nominal exchange rate, then we must abandon the hedging operation and allow the balance of international trade accounts to reduce the domestic money supply through the reduction in basic money supply. Domestic deflation would eventually occur and the monetary policy would be contractionary, but not expansionary; in fact, as a cyclical operation to suppress the increase in effective demand.

The decision makers feared that the free fluctuation of the RMB would cause a large-scale devaluation in the short term. It was necessary to consider the seriousness of the imbalance of the RMB, and be cautious about the negative impact of large-scale devaluation on domestic production and international trade. Yet, continually delaying to implement the balanced adjustment process of the RMB exchange rate will only increase its degree of imbalance, and leave it facing virulent attacks from international speculators.

If we chose to devalue the RMB gradually and lower the nominal RMB exchange rate in small steps, the international speculators' profits would be directly built on the immediate devaluation of the RMB. The realization of speculative profits would attract cashing in further international funds. It would be highly probable that a serial devaluation of the RMB would bring it down to below the balanced level, causing so-called overshooting, a strong fluctuating movement. Because of the high liquidity of the international financial markets, an abrupt balanced adjustment of the exchange rate is better than the gradual one. For the same reason, the possible attack by international speculative funds on the international payment balance would inevitably cause, by itself, the unbalanced trend of exchange rate policy. That in turn would form external constraints on China's exchange rate policy under the condition of opening up.

The Orientation of Expansionary Fiscal and Monetary Policies and Their Implementation

Since the beginning of 1998, the monetary policy has showed a totally relaxed orientation. Various measures were implemented, such as lowering the reserve requirements, canceling the credit quota system, and lowering deposit and lending interest rates. At the same time, investment in infrastructure projects was increased. Financial support was increased for exports and for small- and medium-size enterprises and the private sector. The actual expansionary effect of the monetary policy was not so obvious. The turnover of money supply structure was apparently low. The contraction effect of unbalanced exchange rate policy suppressed the increase in basic money supply. The multiplying effect of increased money supply from the increase in the currency base was canceled out by the lowering of the monetary multiplier. The fall in the turnover rate of money supply further canceled the stimulating effect of increase in money supply and expansion of demand.

The impotence of the expansionary monetary policy is not only due to: 1) policy hindrance, 2) partial externalization of the domestic money supply under the nearly fixed exchange rate for U.S. dollars, and 3) the sustained high real interest rate because of deflation, but also due to the inadequacy in the transmission mechanism of monetary policy. That is, the relaxed money supply could only improve the fund-raising condition for enterprise production and investment, and personal spending. However, it could not directly improve the expected personal income and the coordination of product distribution of enterprises. This is particularly so in an economic recession when the expectation for economic prosperity is generally pessimistic.

Given the policy effect and technical factors of the taxation system, the leverage of taxation would lack the operating space for corresponding adjustment. An expansionary fiscal policy can only lean on increasing expenditures for fiscal investment. The demand expansionary policy led by the fiscal policy should mainly function as signaling information to raise the expected economic coordination of the non-state sectors, instead of only functioning to achieve the multiplying effect of fiscal expenditure and also the input of fiscal investment projects to produce related increased effective demand. The amount of fiscal expenditure should be fixed by guaranteeing the utility efficiency of fiscal funds and based on the actual requirement of counter-cycle adjustment. In addition, the timing of investment should be adjusted suitably to avoid the accumulative peak of investment in times of prosperity.

New increases in fiscal expenditure lean toward infrastructure investment, taking care of both the short-term target of stabilizing the economy and the long-term target of economic development. New increases in fiscal expenditure are also in accordance with the strategic adjustment of the state economy transforming into departments of public goods. In the cycle of economic slowdown, deflation, and economic recession, the loose monetary policy goes along with the relaxed fiscal policy, and investment in infrastructure coordinates with investment in direct production. The fiscal investment expenditure funded by debt financing does not have the squeezing-out effect as postulated in theory.

THE ASSESSMENT AND SELECTION OF CHINA'S CURRENT MACROECONOMIC POLICY

LIU XIANFA, ET AL.*
Research Centre of Macroeconomics
Shenzhen Institute of Integrated Development and Research

The Macroeconomic Adjustment Policy since 1998

Beginning with the central government's Document No. 3, which was decreed in early 1998, there have been enormous changes in the orientation of macroeconomic policy. Based on its understanding of the current economic situation, the government recognized the problem of insufficient domestic demand. Therefore, in terms of policy, there has been a change from braking the speed of growth to maintaining the speed; from controlling inflation to stimulating employment; from controlling demand to jump-starting demand, while the 8% growth target was made one of the goals. In terms of policy measures, the initial decision was made on the combination of appropriate expansion of monetary policy and investment policy.

With the changed orientation of the macroeconomic adjustment program, the first adjustments were to monetary policy. To deal with the deflationary phenomenon from the second half of 1997, the Central Bank lowered the nominal interest rate to maintain the policy of neutral interest rates, and at the same time, loosened the base money supply.

Meanwhile, the government also applied a semi-fiscal investment policy and introduced a series of measures such as investment projects in railroad, highway, private housing, agricultural irrigation, and urban construction, as well as 117 key national projects. The size of the planned investment increased

---

* Research team director: Li Luoli; members: Tang Jie, Liu Xianfa, Guo Wanda, Liu Zhanjun, Yuan Yuan.

from RMB2,800 bn at the beginning of the year to RMB3,000 bn at the end of the year. The growth rate of fixed asset investment was adjusted from 10% at the beginning of the year to 18% at the end.

Judging by the prevailing economic conditions during the first half of 1998, this investment program was basically a successful one. However, the implementation of the monetary policy was not as successful as expected. First, the growth rate of the money supply at three different levels continued to decline for 13 months. Second, the growth rate of lending was low. Third, price levels continued to languish. China's inflation rate has shown a continued declining trend since the peak of the reform period in October 1994. In October 1997, the inflation rate sank below zero to negative growth, and continued to fall. The continuing decline in inflation caused a rise in the real interest rate, and caused actual deflation. Meanwhile, the expected profit growth rate of enterprises also declined, and consequently suppressed the investment demand of enterprises, which in turn worsened the deflationary situation in a vicious cycle.

Therefore, in the first half of the year, we experienced difficulties with the money supply, which was the cause of deflation. Without strong monetary policy support, it became more difficult for investment policy to have an effect.

Under such circumstances, in the second half of 1998, in order to increase the stimulus to the economy, the government launched a combination of monetary, investment, and fiscal policies, creating a situation of "three chariots racing together." It broke through the proposed target of eliminating the deficit and realizing the balanced budget set in the Ninth Five-year Plan. A series of economic stimuli and expansionary fiscal policies were introduced. In terms of fiscal expenditure policy, more treasury bonds were issued. The original planned issue of treasury bonds was RMB264.4 billion. In August, the Ministry of Finance announced an increase of RMB100 bn in long-term bonds for specific investment in nationally budgeted infrastructure construction, increasing the government's expenditure in this area. In 1998, the government increased fixed asset investment and infrastructure by RMB100 bn in order to stimulate economic growth.   This meant that RMB100 bn had to be funded by treasury bonds and RMB100 bn by bank loans.

In matters of taxation policy, first, the export tax rebate rates for selected industries were raised.   The export tax rebate rate for textiles was raised from 9% to 11%, while those for shipbuilding, steel, cement, and coal were raised to 14%, 11%, 11%, and 9%, respectively.   Second, the import tariffs and value-added import taxes were exempted for investment projects encouraged by the government.   Third, the value-added tax for small enterprises was lowered from 6% to 4%.   Fourth, the proposed target for increased tax collection was lowered from RMB100 bn to RMB80 billion.

The Effect of Fiscal Measures to Stimulate the Economy

Implementing the Fiscal Expenditure Policy to Stimulate the Economy Can Also Effectively Initiate the Operation of the Monetary Issuing Mechanism and Fully Achieve the Intended Effects of Monetary Policy

The expansion of fiscal expenditure can get the system in gear for basic money supply and credit expansion in the following ways. First, the government issues bonds, which will enable the Central Bank to stimulate the money supply system for lending.   Second, the treasury bonds are supplementary capital for banks.   When banks increase their holdings of treasury bonds, their asset structure will be improved and their credit line enlarged.   Doing this will also facilitate the control of the Central Bank over money supply through an open market operation. When it deems necessary, the Central Bank can repurchase treasury bonds in the open market, and hence   increase   the   money   supply.   Finally,   government expenditure can stimulate investment projects effectively, actively provide guidance for enterprise investments, and further create investment demand through the multiplying effect of fiscal expenditure. In turn, this will stimulate banks to lend more to enterprises.

The Other Advantage of Employing Fiscal Policy under the Current Economic Situation Is That the Expansion of Government Expenditure Will Not "Squeeze Out" Enterprises from their Short-term Investment. The Effect of Fiscal Policy Can Be Brought into Full Play

The impact of employing fiscal policy, i.e., increasing government expenditure for the increase of aggregate demand, normally results in the shortage of capital, less opportunity for enterprise investment, or inflation. Given the current macroeconomic situation in China, we do not think this will happen to our economy. Therefore, by issuing more treasury bonds and increasing the deficit, we will overcome the problem of a lack of fiscal capital. We also hope this will overcome the problem of "over-saving," changing the tendency of saving to that of investing.

In addition, the inflation rate signaled a monthly decline to −3.2% in July 1998. Currently, a certain degree of inflation is necessary for economic health and to prevent deflation. On the whole, the current macroeconomic condition is very favorable for China to employ a fiscal policy.

Expanding Government Expenditure Is Beneficial to Utilizing the Excess Production Capacity and Stored Inventory, Overcoming the Bottleneck of Market Demand, and Expanding the Market Demand

Relative excess productivity has been a major problem affecting China's economy in recent years. The current estimated rate of productivity utilization is less than 70%. Observing the composition of the government fiscal expenditures, the government investments include: agricultural irrigation, urban environmental protection, municipal construction, state grain storage facilities, improvement and construction of the rural electricity grid, and private housing. The industries related to these government investments include steel, cement, and machinery. These industries are the largest in terms of scale of production and are also traditionally the most powerful, with major excess capacity problems. The government investments in these areas will utilize these industries' excess capacity, and digest their stored inventory.

Meanwhile, most of the products and services provided in these areas belong to the category of so-called "public goods," which for a long time have been under-invested. Some areas, like the urban and rural electricity grid and private housing, have been so inadequately invested that they have become bottlenecks in the expansion of market demand. Government investments in these areas will help some industries like household appliances, construction, and decoration materials to expand their market demand, and will also make possible the transfer of demand from urban to rural areas, and from high income strata to low income strata.

Reconstruction after the Flood Will Provide the Geographic Locations for Increasing Investment Demand

The catastrophic floods in July and August 1998 exerted a certain degree of negative influence on the economy. However, the reconstruction after the floods had a positive influence on economic recovery. The stimulating effect on investment and demand was obvious. For the short term, this reconstruction will help to stimulate demand, investment, and the consumer market and will reduce the heavily accumulated inventory of production resources and consumer products. It will also contribute to the suppression of the possible emergence of deflation.

However, the flood relief and reconstruction measures are only short-term tasks. For the medium and long term, the government must lay out an integrated plan and invest large sums in flood prevention and improvement of the ecology of the Yangtze River

Valley so as to fundamentally solve the problem. The government has decided to increase the investment in flood control construction substantially, from RMB17 bn at the beginning of the year to RMB35.8 bn at the end of the year. This will accelerate the process of integration and modernization of the economy of the middle and lower reaches of the Yangtze River so that this region will become a new source of growth for China.

Under the Current System of Macroeconomic Decision Making, Fiscal Measures Will Provide the Quickest and Most Effective Stimulus to the Economy

In developed market economies, there are usually three problems when using fiscal measures to stimulate economic growth. The first one is the delay in the decision-making process. The second one is the difficulty in matching government policy and monetary policy. Within our current decision-structure for macroeconomic policies, these problems basically do not exist. The third one is the lack of a cooperation mechanism between fiscal policy and commercial banks. In China, commercial banks, in particular the national commercial banks, cooperate very closely with government institutions. On the whole, under China's current decision-making system, the fiscal measures to jump-start the economy can meet with quick reaction and provide effective results.

The logic of our current fiscal policy runs as follows: by employing a fiscal policy as a start, the government will increase its expenditures in the hope of raising the demand for investments, thus increasing enterprise investment demand as well as expanding the scope for demand. By so doing, it is hoped that eventually the fiscal policy will stimulate consumer demand. Meanwhile, it is hoped that the strong impact of fiscal policy will expand the banks' credit lines. The fiscal policy in turn will activate the mechanism for the Central Bank to increase the base money supply, and for the banking system to create a monetary mechanism. At present, the government employs a combination of fiscal policy, monetary policy, and investment policy to stimulate the economy. The current policies are strong enough, and all the measures that can help to manage the total demand have been utilized.

The Problems Faced by Implementing Fiscal Policy

The Pulling Force of Government Investment on Enterprise Investment Demand

Three important aspects may restrict the enterprise investment demand. The first is the speed of attracting foreign investment. Since the 1990s, foreign direct investment has been the major pulling force of investment by enterprises. The introduction of foreign direct investment accelerated the adjustment and upgrade of our industrial structure. The second restriction comes from our investment and fund-raising system. For a long time, the small- and medium-size enterprises in China have had difficulties gaining access to the existing main channels of capital markets, namely, bank loans and bonds and shares issues. They have been relying on private funding, which is outside the mainstream and limited in size, and is becoming even more restricted under the supervision and management of the government. Consequently, to a very large extent, this suppresses the investment demand of enterprises. The third restriction is institutional innovation. Under the current system of principal-agency relationships, the owners cannot build an effective incentive mechanism to satisfy the interests of both the managers and the long-term interests of the enterprises. In practice, most of the enterprises aim at short-term gains for maximal profit. The absence of an incentive system for enterprises conditions their investment demand and dynamism.

Effectiveness and Profitability of the Government-invested Projects

The main reasons for the poor return on the government-invested projects are: first, the allocation of resources is not effective. The allocation of resources to these projects mainly flows through administrative methods. The budget constraint is "soft" so that it inevitably leads to low effectiveness. This has been proven to be true by both Chinese and other countries' experience. Second, the areas in which the government invests are often of low economic benefit. Looking at the current breakdown of government investment, the major areas are "public products" such as irrigation, ecology-concerned construction, environment protection, urban infrastructure projects, and state grain depots. But it is difficult for these projects to produce an immediate economic impact. Their main contributions are social and long-term benefits. The financing channel of government investment is mainly through issuing bonds. And bond operations require projects with a high return on investment to guarantee repayment of the interest and principal. If we cannot identify new sources of income, such as taxation, these low profit and low effective projects will not only have difficulties in repaying to investors, but will also have difficulties in simply maintaining their routine operations.

The Capability of State Finance

Expanding fiscal expenditure requires definite support from the state. Since the beginning of the reforms and opening up, the country's income structure has undergone enormous changes. The most important change is the increased weakness of the government's ability to command social resources. The financial strength of the governments at different levels, especially the central government, has declined as well. Although the current national debt shows that the size of the national debt and fiscal deficit are still below the alarming line of international standards, we must realize that we have accumulated an enormous amount of hidden debts in the process of changing the track of economic development in China.

The largest amount of hidden debt in China is the long-term accumulated bad debts of banks. Based on an estimate, in terms of the state-owned assets, there are about RMB 1,500 bn of "bad debts" which cannot be settled, which represents about 25% of total state assets and about 20% of the banks' loan portfolios. Enterprises and banks simply cannot digest these "bad debts" domestically. Besides, we also need capital to subsidize the 50 million laid-off workers of the state-owned enterprises, to pay for the retirement fees for 30 million employees, and so on. It is estimated that RMB5,000 bn will be required for the reform of state-owned enterprises. This enormous expense is actually also one of China's hidden debts, but must eventually be paid. To sum up, based on the current financial strength and debt burden of the country, we cannot afford to maintain large-scale expenditures on public projects.

The analysis above shows that the government has already employed all measures available to increase aggregate macroeconomic demand. A macroeconomic policy to stimulate the economy has been implemented. We have to adopt certain measures in order to enter into a new economic growth cycle, that is, not just a short-term economic recovery. We should concentrate our policy on solving problems of medium and long-term growth and development in the Chinese economy, in addition to continuing to improve the management of demand. We will have to establish new mechanisms and sources for economic growth, so that China's economic growth will be built on a base of high quality and efficiency.

Policy Suggestions

Adjust the Structure of Income and Expenditure and Improve the Taxation System

For long-term considerations, an active adjustment of income and expenditure structure, and the improvement of taxation, will have profound effects on aggregate demand and long-term aggregate supply.

(1) For declining industries and developing industries, tax reductions or exemptions could be granted. This would act as a major tool in overcoming structural unemployment and forming a new economic growth point.

(2) An effective policy is needed to stimulate exports, to support the technical innovation of export enterprises, to increase the rebate rate of export taxes, and to accelerate the rebate process.

(3) Under the current conditions, we can systemically streamline various administrative fees and regulate taxation.

Improve the Money Supply System and Maintain a Stable Monetary Policy

When China's monetary authorities implement further economy-stimulating policies, they should be extremely cautious. First, the growth rate of the short-term money supply is low, but continues to exceed the GDP growth rate. After the completion of China's monetarization, the difference between the growth of broad money supply M_2 and the GDP growth rate will be manifested as a pressure for inflation. In 1998, although the growth in money supply was lower than the average level since 1993, the M_2 growth rate was still above the GDP growth rate. This further shows that limiting the growth rate of the money supply should be a long-term monetary policy goal.

Exchange Stored Capacity for Circulation Capacity so as to Accelerate the Reform of State-owned Enterprises

The smooth implementation of state-owned enterprise reform is a key factor in improving the economic efficiency of China's economy. There are three major problems we have to overcome. One is that we need to clarify the direction of the reform of state-owned enterprises. We believe that the direction of reform should see the government withdraw from competitive industries. The withdrawal should not be guided by size, but by the nature of the industry or enterprise. The other is that there must be a clear definition of "withdrawal." The government withdrawal from competitive industries should finally be realized by selling the state-owned assets for cash, and exchanging stored capacity for circulation capacity, not just the withdrawal from the management of the enterprises. The third problem is that the state-owned assets should be valued at market prices. The valuation method should not rely on replacement value but on net income. When a state-owned enterprise is operating at a loss or without yielding any profit, and the factory and machinery as well as the production techniques are almost obsolete, the capital value at the market is close to zero.

Accelerate the Development of Small and Medium Cities to Accelerate the Process of Urbanization in China

We should take the opportunity provided by the rebuilding of the flooded areas in the middle and lower regions of the Yangtze River to build a cluster of satellite towns based on the consolidation of natural villages and the utilization of the existing industrial transportation base. Through the process of accelerating urbanization, we can raise the level of commercialization of villages, change the traditional style of living in villages, and realize the transformation from rural to urban consumption levels. We can thus create new openings for economic growth to advance into a new developmental stage.

Increase the Degree of Opening to the Outside. Use Regional Opening to the Outside to Stimulate the Country's Openness

Based on the experience of Shanghai's Pudong area, we should fully implement an opening policy to a larger degree in those already opened areas, like the cities of Dalian, Tianjin, Wuhan, and Chongqing. This means that the opening up of capital and labor markets should be in conformity with the operation and regulations of internationally accepted practice for totally open markets.

Through institutional innovation and structural transformation, we can cultivate new economic growth points and focus on these open development areas, and gradually expand to the entire country. At the same time, we should also allow Pudong of Shanghai and the Shenzhen Special Economic Zone, which have a better opening foundation and more flexible systems, to implement the free trade zone policy. Through the opening in these regions, we can encourage the opening up of the entire country.

Industrial Structural Adjustment and Regional Structural Adjustment

A combination of a developed market system and a clearer structural industrial adjustment can, in the short term, accelerate the adjustment process of China's industrial structure. Shenzhen offers an excellent example of how institutional changes can stimulate economic growth. Shenzhen has always maintained an economic growth rate above the country's average by one to several times. The major reason for this is due to its high level of development of a market system, the allocation of market resources, and its integration with a clear industrial structural adjustment.

Under the market mechanism, the growing new economic focus in the coastal regions should be on the replacement of the imports of materials and spare parts by export-oriented industries. A clear industrial structure and regional structural adjustment will not only recover the competitiveness of the coastal regions but will also stimulate the growth of the central regions. Since 1992, the growth rates of the five central provinces of Hunan, Hubei, Jiangxi, Anhui, and Henan were close to or exceeded the average east coast levels. If — in the current process of increased investment — we can improve the transportation links among the five provinces and the coastal regions, and draw on the potential of the improving telecommunications system, we can elevate the five provinces into the new high growth regions in China.

The Establishment of a Sound Social Security System Is the Basic Condition for Maintaining Macroeconomic Stability

During the process of our 20 years of reform, state-owned enterprises have borne the burden of social security. This often results in their having difficulties in operating the enterprises and in making any profit. This may also partly explain the high level of non-performing assets of state commercial banks, whose clients are mainly state-owned enterprises.

With current high unemployment, we should quickly establish a sound unemployment protection system and job retraining program. This should be the main policy goal of the government at present. Although the establishment of a sound unemployment protection system requires a long time and a great deal of effort, it is still possible to establish a rudimentary social security system in a short period of time, which could help to relieve the difficulties encountered by the unemployed. The most important step to do this is to reform the fiscal system with a strategic plan. In a nutshell, we should make the central government the main supporter for the welfare system to serve the entire country and provide a basic living for the unemployed.

FINANCE AND FISCAL POLICIES

FISCAL POLICY ORIENTATION AND OPTIONS FOR THE EXPANSION OF DOMESTIC DEMAND

LIU RONGCANG AND LI YANG

Institute of Finance and Trade Economics
Chinese Academy of Social Sciences

After China's success in engineering an economic "soft landing," there have been some distinct changes in the country's macroeconomic situation. The most important change is the shift from a seller's market to a buyer's market. Both theoretical analysis and actual practice have shown that the degree of commitment to a market economy in China is quite high. The method of allocating resources has also undergone fundamental changes. The most important problem — at the present and for the foreseeable future — is insufficient demand.

Given the unpredictability of the external trading environment and intensifying international competition, the key and the necessary means for achieving the 8% growth target in 1998, and for maintaining a sustained vigorous economic growth rate, lies in expanding domestic demand appropriately; and in specifically within that process, adjusting, guiding, and stimulating the country's current and potential demand. Fiscal and monetary policies are now seen as the main tools to use in managing this demand, making them the focus of domestic and international attention.

Policy Orientation for Expanding Domestic Demand

Based on the recent situation in China, we believe that the orientation of fiscal and monetary policies should take different factors into "consideration" or "combine them."

In Identifying Key Policy Areas, We Should Combine Investment Increases with the Ultimate Stimulation and Expansion of Consumption Demand

In the traditional planned economy, essentially an economy of shortages, meaning a seller's market, we used to place the emphasis on investment and production in order to stimulate the economy; i.e., bolstering the supply side since a supply deficit constituted the major problem. In a market economy, meaning a buyer's market, this emphasis is reversed. Stimulating consumer demand is crucial since effective demand is the key to economic development. Stimulation of investment and production creates demand, but only of an intermediary type. How much effect it has on economic growth, and an increase in economic efficiency, all depends on aggregate demand levels.

In Weighing Our Policy Strength, We Should Combine Appropriate Quantity Expansion with Optimum Structural Adjustments

The crux of the current problem is not simply an economic crisis caused by excess production. It is also not a result of the lack of aggregate demand alone. Rather it is rooted in transitional difficulties, themselves stemming from changes in the country's development track, along with institutional and structural obstacles. Because the economic system has not been completely transformed, structural conflicts stand out. In such circumstances, if we emphasize and then only partially implement a broad expansionary policy, we could trigger a new round of inflation and jeopardize the needed structural adjustments.

In Determining Our Policy Direction, We Should Combine Support for the State-owned Sector with Encouragement for the Development of the Private Sector

The private sector nowadays plays an increasingly important role in expanding domestic demand, and ultimately economic growth. Its far-reaching effects on the economy can also be seen in tax and employment increases. And its potential impact on further development is nothing short of profound.

In practice, of course, the private sector is also subject to many problems in terms of financing and taxation. There is an urgent need for government policy to address these problems.

In Terms of Policy Effects, We Should Combine the Current Effects of Domestic Demand Expansion with the Effects of Long-term Policy

If insufficient demand is the most important factor limiting China's sustained economic development, to solve the problem we cannot just consider short-term effects and those likely to unfold over the long term. To decide policy orientation, and to analyze and estimate the long-term effects, we must take the current and future factors into consideration as well.

Policy Focal Points Regarding Recent Domestic Demand Expansion

Theoretical analyses and international experience show that although fiscal and monetary policies are important in the management of demand, the implementation focus of the two policies are different, depending on differing stages of economic development and different market conditions. In our case at present, while we stress the function of monetary policy, we must also consider and actively utilize fiscal policy, particularly in the specific effect it has in expanding domestic demand.

First, theoretically, when an economy is in a period of acceleration or expansion, the effect of a loose or tight monetary policy on the economy is most pronounced. In fact, it can directly influence the rate of economic growth. Correspondingly, when the economy is in a period of relative contraction or recovery, expansionary monetary policy has little effect on economic recovery because of its delay in taking effect and the lengthy time it takes for policy intermediary transmission. By contrast, adjustments and changes in taxation policy, and expanding fiscal expenditures, have a direct expansionary effect on investment and consumer demand. And the impact on the economy is immediate. This is the underlying reason why fiscal policy adjustment is popularly applied in market economies.

Second, applying monetary policy as a means of expanding domestic demand has encountered obstacles and has been less effective in terms of the Chinese economy over the last several years. Since 1997, we have experienced a unanimous call for the country's financial institutions to play a more active role, to increase the money supply to be more precise — a natural reaction to an economic decline. The problem is that in a modern banking system, the main money supply originates from various types of deposits which are generated by bank credits.

So if there is no growth of bank credit, talk of increasing the money supply is meaningless. In recent years, commercial banks have exhibited a reluctance to lend because they, as the main credit release agents, are overburdened with excessive low quality assets at a time when there is no apparent improvement in enterprise profitability. And market demand is so sluggish that enterprises are cautious about expanding.

A more serious concern is that, even if the Central Bank wishes to implement looser monetary policies and measures, there is still no way to know for certain what kind of impact this would have on the economy.

With a smooth policy transmission system, there are two basic ways to monitor the effects of monetary policy. One is quantitative. When money supply (M_1) increases (decreases), do price levels rise (fall)? Do production output and employment increase (decrease)? Does the speed of currency circulation change? Beginning in the first quarter of 1996, money supply (M_1) has been rising. Price levels, somehow, have been falling. Quantity increases have likewise been slow and employment poor.

Taken together, these indicators suggest that, with regard to money supply, the turnover speed of currency circulation is falling at a faster rate.

"Price" is the other way to analyze this situation. When market interest rates fall (or rise), will business interest costs decrease (or increase)? Will capital asset prices rise (or fall)? And will the actual investment rate rise (or fall)? Obviously, the four interest rate cuts since 1994 have had little noticeable effect on business transaction costs; but capital asset prices have continued to drop. And the actual rate of investment fell further. All these results have shown that, since 1996, even after China made an even more pronounced effort in terms of monetary policy and made further adjustments, monetary policy change alone did not deliver the desired result.

There are also further complexities within this problem. Since 1996, the adjustments implemented in our monetary policy *per se* (for example, abolishing credit quotas, lowering interest rates and the deposit reserve ratio, lengthening loan terms, and implementing credit guidance principles, to name a few) were basically regular operations within the current monetary policy framework. In a national economy with a relatively smooth monetary policy transmission system, these measures should have proved sufficient. However, in China, the status of such a smooth transmission system is questionable. Therefore, in researching an effective monetary policy in China, we need to propose a new approach for overcoming financial structural problems.

To effectively address China's financial structure from the perspective of a monetary policy transmission system, two issues need to be considered.

One is whether the capital supply structure matches the demand structure. The fact is supply and demand structures have been mismatched ever since the reforms began. In terms of finance, a dual structure exists, namely the planned mainstream and market driven, non-mainstream financial systems. The mainstream financial system commands the overwhelming majority of the credit supply. Its clients are mainly the state economy and various large enterprises. The non-mainstream system services mainly the non-state sector of the economy plus, small- and medium-size enterprises. The amount of credit it commands is very small, and the legality of its existence has always been in question. This mismatch between the official and actual economic structures has resulted in a serious dislocation between the total capital supply and the corresponding total capital demand structures.

Meanwhile, obstacles exist with regard to the flow of capital within financial institutions, within financial markets, and between financial institutions and financial markets. Given this asymmetry within the financial structure, the effects of monetary policy can be difficult to transmit smoothly to the various sectors of the national economy. In the process of transmission, such policy changes can easily be twisted and weakened, meaning any positive effects can be greatly reduced.

On the relationship between finance and economic growth, there are also some problems that require attention. For example, stimulating consumer loans for private housing, durable goods, and cars should be the main task and priority for the financial industry if we wish to stimulate consumer spending in these new economic conditions. However, the likelihood of developing large-scale consumer credit is very low given our current financial and market structure. Furthermore, because the development of trust relationships is being seriously impaired, the possibility of granting this type of loan, with its typically long repayment schedule and consequent high risk, is very remote.

Under the current conditions prevailing in China, the financial industry should play an important role in supporting mergers and acquisitions and the development of hi-tech enterprises in order to stimulate economic growth. In the case of the first, we have already realized that, in a market economy, an enterprise itself is a commodity. Supporting the sale and purchase of this kind of commodity is equivalent to supporting mergers and acquisitions, which is one of the main functions of the financial industry. Furthermore, with regard to economic growth patterns, the extensive model of growth keeps getting transformed into the intensive model. The priority is to support the development of highly efficient enterprises, while abandoning inefficient enterprises.

Concerning the second aspect, i.e., developing hi-tech industry, China must transform the potential of high technology into actual high productivity. This transformation process will require large-scale financial support crucial to upgrading our industrial structure as a whole; this is essential if we are to improve the quality of our national economic growth. Such support would also effectively enrich the technological component of our financial assets and the potential growth of financial capital. The problem is that with our current financial structure, financial tools, financial markets, and, to a certain extent, financial policy, the requirements for developing this high-tech industry are not being served.

Fiscal Policy Options for Expanding Domestic Demand

From now on, in order to maintain an appropriate rate of growth in investment and consumption, we should enhance our ability to control and adjust the function of our fiscal policy in this context, and emphasize solving the following urgent problems while implementing the related fiscal measures.

Increase Government-disposed Financial Resources and Our Financial Ability to Expand Domestic Demand

Based on the current economic situation, we offer the following three macro-measures to achieve the above detailed goal.

(1) Change the current — and abnormal — situation of too widely dispersed distribution of government financial resources as quickly as possible, and increase the amount of disposable finance.

Since the beginning of the reform and opening up, our financial resources have been used to support, disproportionately, local governments, enterprises, and residents.   This has not only resulted in a dispersed and chaotic distribution of the country's financial resources. It has also obstructed, time and again, the government's efforts in raising the "Two Weights" because of the lack of human resources and financial resources at its command.

The most obvious problem is that the dispersion of funds is too diverse.   Off-budget finances have grown vast, especially in terms of the various types of fees and funds, which squeeze and, in effect, expropriate the tax base.   Facts and data show that in many enterprises "fees" now exceed taxes. In some regions, the situation has become so aberrant that the size and growth of fee income greatly exceeds that of taxes. With tax revenues "falling behind," non-taxation income has become a serious threat to the normal growth of fiscal revenues and, therefore, the meaningful improvement of our financial situation.   It also seriously erodes the consumption and investment demand of farmers, as well as rural and other enterprises.   Obviously, if we incorporate off-budget finances into our budget, we will be able to increase the government's disposable financial resources and, thus, increase our expenditures.   In the short term, this may not produce noticeable results in increasing income and reducing expenditures.   However, in the long run, by so doing, we will be able to maintain the integrity of our budget and to more effectively utilize our limited financial resources in order to alleviate the deficit problem.

(2) We should gradually establish an investment and fund-raising system that suits China's needs so as to overcome the inherent institutional conflict between investment supply and demand. This is also an important expedient in increasing the government's disposable financial resources.

We should actively seek to establish an investment and fund-raising system that suits China's economic situation. This includes actively developing fiscal investment sources to increase the government's infrastructure development expenditures to alleviate chronic industrial bottlenecks. By establishing a sound financial investment and fund-raising system, we will overcome the shortage of fiscal funds for construction and strengthen the government's control over macroeconomic adjustment.

(3) Further improve the taxation structure and vigorously improve the management of tax collection.

The main source of fiscal revenue is taxation. Therefore, we must continue to improve the taxation system and fully explore tax collection potential. This is an important step in increasing the country's financial strength. The large-scale increase in taxes over the last four years signaled a breakthrough and progress in the reform of China's taxation system. However, there is still great potential for further adjustment and improvements in terms of sources and rates of taxation (for example, personal income tax, and consumption and resource taxes). As well, new categories of taxes need to be levied, such as property, estate, gift, and corporation taxes. Increased effectiveness through strengthening tax collection is also expected to produce beneficial results. If we consider the tax burden of our current system, compared with both the developed and most developing countries, our tax rate is low.

This suggests the potential is there to substantially increase total tax revenues.

Adjust and Improve the Fiscal Expenditure System and Encourage Innovation in the Expenditure Structure

There are three important tasks in adjusting and improving the fiscal expenditure structure: adjusting the framework, identifying the key issues, and encouraging institutional innovation.

Adjusting the framework means establishing a new framework and guidelines regarding the parameters of expenditures strictly based on the fiscal powers of the different administrative levels. In particular, we must cease intervening in the operation and output of business enterprises. In this new mode, we must avoid the mistakes made in previous ones in which the authorities dominated. The important point, first, is to complement the reform of government structures by regulating the various administrative fees which have grown excessively in recent years. Second, we should gradually reduce the huge operating deficits and price subsidies to enterprises to complement the reform of state-owned enterprises and the improvement in the supply-demand relationship of agricultural products. Third, the government should immediately withdraw related expenditures on competitive processing industries and general commercial services. Through the means of "suppressing, reducing, and withdrawing," we can set free the country's fiscal functions from its problems of "overtaking" and "lacking function."

By emphasizing the key issues, we can focus our fiscal expenditures on a prioritized basis in accord with affordability. Experience over many years suggests that we should not apply the so-called method of "spraying pepper on the surface"; this only lends itself to the creation of many subsequent loopholes which will need further passive repair via fiscal arrangements at a later date. Similarly, we should not encourage moonlighting activities in government departments and other work units as a means to bridge the expenditure gap. This has created chaos in terms of financial order and distribution.

By institutional innovation, we mean through reinforcing expenditure efficiency, we should actively push for government purchase systems. The expansion of fiscal expenditure should reach a point where it genuinely stimulates effective demand. In the meantime, we should strengthen the leading role of government expenditure and its enabling power vis-à-vis structural expansion.

Seriously Implement the Tax Reduction Policy and Promote an Increase in Consumption and Enterprise and Consumer Investment

This means that we should create the favorable conditions needed for the expansion of rural markets and the capital resources needed for investment and technological upgrades. This means reducing all types of heavy non-tax burdens on farmers and rural enterprises as well as other types of enterprises.

In particular, all types of fees and levies on real estate development must be regulated if we wish to make real estate development and residential housing a viable new growth area. Such fees and levies drive property costs too high, contributing to vacancy rate increases every year.

Actively Implement a Flexible and Cautious Policy to Deal with the National Debt

If we wish to increase fiscal strength as a means of stimulating the economy, increased taxation is not viable since it is merely a tight financing policy. Reducing expenditures is a useful reform measure, however, at least to some extent. But it too is a contraction measure in ultimate terms, and is therefore not plausible at the present.

This leaves increasing treasury bonds as a financial expedient. There are many practical problems standing in the way of doing this though.   The crux of these is that the debt burden in fiscal expenditures is too high, which saddles the central government with a heavy interest and principal repayment load.

When our future targets are at cross purposes, we must take care to prioritize them on an urgency and importance basis.   An increase in treasury bonds is inevitable.   Therefore, a key mission is to develop the treasury bond market.

There is still a lot of work to be done in building and developing the treasury bond market.   Some is fundamental.   At the moment, however, the most urgent issue is the need for a breakthrough in terms of bondholders.   In short, this means that financial institutions should be the major holders of treasury bonds. Commercial banks, other financial institutions, and the Central Bank should play important roles in China's treasury bond market.

The necessity for financial institutions to participate in the treasury bond market can be summarized from three perspectives. The first is that of the commercial banks. In a market economy banks become increasingly prudent. This provides a good basis for both enterprises and individuals to invest their welfare funds in the form of treasury bonds through commercial banks.

From the point of view of the Central Bank, if we want to increase the role of the Central Bank as an open market expediter of monetary policy, an active, liquid, and large-scale treasury bond market is absolutely necessary.

Similarly, from a national finance point of view, be it the cost of fund raising, or the speed of entry into the treasury, or providing a principal debt instrument for financial institutions, or even the reduction of social impact, treasury bonds are clearly the best choice.

On the question of whether financial institutions should purchase and hold treasury bonds, there is little controversy. It is widely agreed that we should carry out liability management effectively in an unstable economy and financial environment. And financial institutions should hold a certain amount of treasury bonds, which would amount to a "secondary reserve" beyond their required reserves.

In a market economy, various types of treasury bonds customarily make up 10% of the total assets commercial banks carry. Correspondingly, financial institutions also serve as bond holders and normally account for a significant part of the treasury bonds. After the growth of financial institution assets, the outstanding balance of treasury bonds held as financial institution assets continues to increase. If we open the gate to allow financial institutions to hold treasury bonds, a very large and stable market for treasury bonds will develop naturally. If we use 10% as a simple ratio for estimate purposes, the size of the treasury bond market in China could be as large as RMB 700 billion.

If financial institutions hold large quantities of treasury bonds, and the Central Bank employs an open market operational mode (mainly for the purchase and sale of treasury bonds) to adjust the basic money supply, the question of the Central Bank's holding of treasury bonds will automatically be raised.

First, we should realize that central banks in most countries are not allowed to provide direct overdraft loans to the government. However, the Central Bank's purchase of treasury bonds as a means of enhancing the basic money supply clearly could provide the financial wherewithal to overcome the government's deficit. The problem is that the Central Bank is not directly but indirectly raising funds from the treasury bond market. Precisely because of this layer of insulation, the Central Bank could fulfill its mandate to stabilize prices for the country while, to a certain extent, providing financial support for the government.

In conditions of no change in the amount of money supply, the Central Bank could also, to a degree, use treasury bonds to substitute for other types of assets. So the question is not entirely whether or not the Central Bank enhances the basic money supply through the sale and purchase of treasury bonds, but whether or not the operation of controlling the basic money supply matches the requirements of economic development. Under such a premise, the Central Bank's purchase, sale, and holding of treasury bonds is non-inflationary.

In the same way, because the money supply keeps growing, consideration does not have to be given to repaying the principal on treasury bonds held by the Central Bank (only on rolling it over). In this sense the treasury bond market would serve as a reservoir capable of holding several thousand bn RMB in China at a rough estimate.

Finally, we should note that encouraging the financial system to purchase and hold treasury bonds is definitely not the only solution to the problem of fiscal fund raising. Under a developed treasury bond market, on the one hand, the implementation of monetary policy would need the assistance of additional market measures and a more effective transmission mechanism. On the other hand, our fiscal and monetary policies will need a more market-oriented communication channel and complementary mechanism. This is a very important area in terms of establishing a viable macroeconomic control system.

Actively Utilize the Leverage Effect of Fiscal Policy in Expanding Domestic Demand

(1) We should use fiscal measures to achieve the above target, for example, the flexible use of a fiscal subsidy for certain social groups. By making the social welfare of urban employees a key focal point, through guaranteeing a minimum standard of living for the low-income group, we can meet their basic needs

and also prevent a large-scale shrinkage of purchasing power in the society in order to maintain social stability.

(2) Some economic measures, such as the fiscal interest subsidy, fiscal investment, and fiscal guarantee, should also be applied to encourage people to participate in investment and infrastructure construction, high-tech industries, real estate development, and so on. By doing so, we can achieve the result implied in the phrase "using four ounces to move one ton." When social investment sources and bank lending resources are more plentiful, we should consider using a limited amount of funds from national fiscal resources to apply to this leverage and initiating function. Doing so will produce much better results than direct total fiscal investment.

(3) We should selectively employ measures such as accelerated depreciation, investment credit, and tax measures to achieve the necessary structural adjustment, as well as to upgrade industry, encourage exports, and so on.

CONTINUE TO PROPERLY IMPLEMENT THE MACROECONOMIC PROGRAM TO STIMULATE ECONOMIC RECOVERY

WANG YIDA

General Department
Ministry of Finance

As the central government has gradually adopted a series of measures to expand domestic demand and stimulate economic growth, the effects of these measures are beginning to become apparent. This has caused the current economic situation to show some positive changes. A moderate recovery is expected. We must therefore continue our effort to guide consumer spending and maintain this trend of economic recovery while encouraging the appropriate investment increase to produce a multiplier effect.

Analysis of the Macroeconomic Environment

Although the series of policy measures implemented by the central government to stimulate demand achieved a certain degree of success in producing signs of recovery in August, the difficulty is much greater this time compared with our previous "immediate start upon stimulation" program of economic stimulation. The time needed for economic recovery will be longer. Clearly, the current economic situation indicates that the situation that produced the high growth of the early 1990s has since undergone tremendous change.

Our Economic Growth Is Gradually Transforming the Former Shortage Economy, with Its Emphasis on Quantitative Growth, into a Subsequent Stage of Structural and Overall Quality Improvement. The Market's Constraining Mechanism Is Obviously Consolidating

Based on a statistical analysis of market supply and demand among 610 major products in the second half of 1998, conducted by the Commercial Information Centre of the Ministry of Internal Trade, 66.1% of these products have attained a balance in supply and demand, while about 33.1% are oversupplied, 8% higher than in the first half of the year. Basically, no products are in short supply.

This demonstrates that our economy has bid farewell to the shortage economy, and has gradually changed into a buyer's market for major production materials and consumer products. In other words, we have progressed from a supply-constrained economy into a demand-constrained economy. As market competition intensifies, most manufacturers are now facing the constraints of market demand. For various reasons, the current innovative capability of these enterprises is not adequate, and the product structures have proved unable to make the necessary timely adjustments to meet the challenges of market demand. As a result, China's potential productivity has not been fully utilized and effective supply is not fully realized.

In this period of economic fluctuations, a demand-limited economy faces more obstacles in recovering from the trough and the time required will be longer than was the case in the previous period of a supply-constrained economy. Apparently this is also the case in western countries as they struggle to recover from varying degrees of economic recession.

Investor Behavior Undergoes Change. Risk Limitation Is Now a Big Concern in Investment

Local governments have gradually changed from their previous fixation on "blind borrowing" for processing projects to their present focus on economic profitability and locating viable financial sources. This means that investment is now concentrated in the primary and tertiary industries, with their capability to increase local fiscal revenues. Enterprises have also changed their emphasis from starting new projects whenever funds were available, to capitalizing on the returns possible in their invested projects.

Based on a survey completed by the related government departments charged with monitoring investment attitudes among some 5,000 industrial enterprises, the intervention of government in enterprise investment has fallen to a very low level. This shows a marked difference from the prevailing situation several years ago. Satisfying market demand and adapting to market competition have become the main driving forces in increasing investment.

Banks have also changed, from the reckless lending which characterized their past to a more prudent risk management approach today. On the one hand, since banks are affected by their non-performing loans, they have been restrained from lending to a certain degree. On the other hand, as the structures for project evaluation and research (and intermediary agents for assessment) are not yet firmly established and the market is subject to various uncertainties, banks are taking a more responsible attitude to lending.

These behavioral changes on the part of investors are favorable to China's long-term economic development and structural adjustment. However, they also have an impact on the current growth of investment. Consequently, in the short term, it is necessary to stimulate domestic demand while attracting investment from other resources through increasing the government's appropriate investment effort.

As Our Economic Dependence on Foreign Trade Has Increased, Fluctuations in Foreign Trade and Policy Changes in Neighboring Countries Have Become an Important Factor Affecting Our Economic Growth

In 1997, the contribution of our net exports to economic growth reached 19.2%, 10% higher than the average level established since the beginning of the reform and opening up. It shows that the influence of exports in relation to our economic growth has increased annually.

Ever since the financial crisis, conditions have been extremely unfavorable for our exports as well as for our success in being able to utilize foreign investment. Our total export growth rate has been declining on a monthly basis. From January to August 1998, it stood at only a 5.5% increase, 1.4% off compared to the period between January to July in 1998, and 18.6% lower than January to August in 1997.

In recent years, our exports to Asia have made up 60% of our total exports. Of these, Hong Kong's share amounted to 24%, Japan 17%, Asian countries 7%, and South Korea 5%. Exports to the United States constituted 18% of the total.

Affected by the Southeast Asian financial crisis, these countries and regions have seen their economic growth rates dip, one by one. This means their ability to pay has likewise decreased and their import demand levels have shriveled. This has inevitably affected our exports. And the future outlook is still not optimistic.

In addition, the financial crisis has affected investor strength in Southeast Asia. The weakness of their capital markets has added to China's difficulties in attracting foreign investment and foreign capital. Based on our survey, many foreign investors from various regions have terminated their joint venture contracts and some have even withdrawn their capital since 1998. It is estimated that the actual use of foreign investment for 1998 will decline.

Preliminary Forecast of the 1999 Economic Development Trend

From a demand perspective, factors affecting economic growth can be analyzed from three points of view: consumer spending, investment demand, and net exports.

Consumer Spending

In recent years, consumer spending has remained more or less stable. Between 1993 and 1997, total retail sales grew by 13.4%, 7.2%, 10.1%, 10.5%, and 12.2% respectively on a yearly basis, amounting to a declining trend in terms of contributing to economic growth. However, taking a long-term perspective, consumer spending is still an engine of economic growth. It is estimated that between 1979 and 1997, consumer spending's contribution to overall growth was about 63%. Before 1993, it was about 65%. During the five years between 1993 and 1997, it was about 57%. This clearly indicates the important part played by consumer spending.

In 1999, there will still be some factors which will be conducive to increasing   consumer spending. First, the full-scale reform in housing was implemented in 1998, which has transformed and will continue to transform some savings into consumer spending. Based on related department estimates, 40% of current personal savings are disposable, among which about 10% can be changed to direct spending. Second, interest rate cuts in 1998 will register in increased consumer spending in 1999. Third, in 1998, in order to stimulate economic growth, the government issued RMB100 bn worth of treasury bonds, while the commercial banks increased RMB100 bn of complementary loans for infrastructure construction. A large portion of these funds will be turned into consumption in 1999. Fourth, the current work underway to increase electricity supply and the construction of electricity grids in rural areas will likewise stimulate the demand for home electrical appliances for rural consumers, which, in turn, will stimulate growth in consumer spending.

Of course, there are still some factors limiting consumer spending growth. As an example, it is almost impossible to reverse the declining growth of urban income. The structural adjustment of industries and the deepened reform of the state-owned enterprises will give rise to more redundant workers. Affected by agricultural production constraints and product prices, it is also impossible for farmers' incomes to show a marked increase. Moreover, as the reforms of retirement arrangements and medical care are implemented, the personal propensity to save will increase. There is also a time-lag effect as a result of the effort to reform the housing system, although this effect is not expected to be significant in 1999.

On the whole, if we can arrange some complementary measures and utilize the conditions favorable to the growth in consumer spending, that growth will be higher this year than last.

Investment

In recent years, in the process of implementing the macroeconomic adjustment program, the struggle against inflation was successful as a result of suppressing investment. This led to a steady but declining investment growth trend. In 1998, in order to stimulate domestic demand and economic growth, the government increased its investment. The estimated growth rate of fixed asset investment for the year is 15% or higher. This is of vital importance for 1998 economic growth.

In 1999, there will be new factors favorable to the growth in investment. First, the flood damages in some parts of the country in 1998 are close to RMB 200 billion. The reconstruction after the floods requires huge amounts of investment. Second, the measures implemented in 1998 to stimulate domestic demand, like the lowering of interest rates and increased investment in infrastructure construction, will create a certain pulling effect on the increase of investment in 1999. On the whole, investment will be of great importance for its contribution to economic growth. However, its pulling effect and contribution to economic growth will be slightly lower than that in 1998.

Net Exports

Judging by the current situation, the Southeast Asian financial crisis will mainly affect our exports in the second half of 1998 and in 1999. Based on our survey, the fulfillment rate of export orders in many areas in 1998 will decline. The orders received by enterprises will be reduced, and some enterprises will fail to secure new orders in trade fairs. Under this influence, our short-term export outlook is poor.

Of course, we should also note that because our macroeconomy is stable, some European and American countries will consider our investment environment favorably and will invest. In addition, finance is generally tight in Southeast Asian countries; they will reduce imports of high priced western goods and look for cheaper products. This creates opportunities for our products.

In addition, the RMB was not devalued and the government implemented concessionary policies to encourage the development of domestic investment projects, as well as tax exemptions for foreign investor equipment and machinery imports and import replacements for value-added tax. As a result, imports will increase to a certain degree in 1999. Based on the above analysis, 1999 will see a slow rate of growth in both imports and exports. The growth in imports will be slightly higher than in 1998. Thus, the contribution of net exports to economic growth can be reduced to zero or even to a negative figure. Our preliminary estimate for the GDP growth rate of 1999 is between 8–8.5%.

Continue to Expand Domestic Demand
to Stimulate Economic Growth

There are fundamental changes in our macroeconomic environment in the current economic cycle. The transmission mechanism of the economic cycle has undergone substantial changes and is showing the feature of a fluctuating market economy. In 1998, in order to ensure economic growth, the government tried to jump-start it by stimulating investment demand. The focus of investment was in infrastructure projects like transportation, agricultural irrigation, telecommunications, reconstruction of urban and rural electricity grids, and urban infrastructure facilities.

These measures are of great importance for expanding domestic demand, creating employment opportunities, and stimulating economic growth. Noticeable results have been achieved. However, we should be aware that the effectiveness of solely relying on investment is becoming increasingly limited. In particular, our country is currently in the process of altering its developmental track. The macroeconomic environment and the supporting conditions for economic growth have undergone tremendous changes.

Under the current buyer's market, eventually economic growth will have to depend on the stimulation of consumer demand. Therefore, we believe the focus of macroeconomic control in the next stage of the economic cycle should be on the generation of effective demand. As we try to generate the investment multiplier effect, we should concentrate on effectively guiding consumer spending, increasing consumer demand, strengthening economic recovery, and consequently stimulating a stable economic growth pattern.

First, the reform of social security should be accelerated to improve the system and ease people's worries over the expected increase in expenses. We should complete the reform of the social security system as soon as possible. We should offer basic protection for medical care, old age pensions, and unemployment subsidies, so as to reduce people's psychological burden and to turn part of their personal savings into current spending.

Second, we should raise wages to increase spending ability, particularly those of the lower income groups. While we are providing minimum wages for urban employers, we should also arrange a scheme where, instead of paying subsidies, we try to create more job opportunities. We should encourage redundant workers to go into business with support from the government. Through industry development and the creation of new employment opportunities, we must strive to increase the income of the redundant and unemployed workers and raise their purchasing power.

Third, we need to actively improve the supply structure and commercial services and develop the consumer market in the rural areas. Enterprises must raise their ability to create demand quickly and produce consumer products that meet farmers' requirements, especially for consumer durables. This can facilitate the advancement of the rural consumer spending structure to fill the enormous gap between urban and rural consumer spending.

At the same time, great improvement is needed in the commercial system to create a smooth channel for services, to organize the delivery of consumer products to rural areas effectively, and to solve farmers' buying difficulties.

Fourth, we should implement a consumer credit policy to stimulate expansion of effective demand. The experiences of other countries show that the implementation of installment consumer credit can stimulate consumer spending. It is also favorable to the maintenance of a basic balance between supply and demand.

Currently, a buyer's market is taking shape in our country. The supply of credit is sufficient. The basic conditions for a consumer credit market are already in place. While we are expanding consumer credit for private housing, we should also carry it over to a variety of home durables so as to expand effective demand.

THE DIRECTION OF CHINA'S MONETARY POLICY IN 1998–1999

QIN WANSHUN, JIN YUNHUI, AND LIU MINGZHI
Guanghua School of Management
Beijing University

In 1998, in order to complement the government's macroeconomic policy to expand domestic demand, the People's Bank of China carried out a rather active monetary policy. Since we can only expect an initial recovery of the economy in 1999, and the external demand situation does not merit optimism, China's macroeconomic policy including monetary policy should still concentrate on the expansion of domestic demand.

Analysis of the 1998 Monetary Policy

Implementation of the 1998 Monetary Policy Was Active

In 1998, the Central Bank implemented a series of active monetary policies with expansionary characteristics, such as canceling the quota control of commercial bank loans, decreasing the bank reserve ratio, twice lowering the deposit and loan interest rates for financial institutions, encouraging loans to private enterprises by the national commercial banks, granting credits to small- and medium-size enterprises and loans for personal housing.

Interest Adjustment Showed Its Effect on Stimulating the Domestic Demand

It is very difficult to observe the actual macroeconomic effect of the interest rate adjustment since interest rate policy is only part of monetary policy. It is not feasible to differentiate the interest rate effect from other effects of a monetary policy. However, the direct effect of the interest rate adjustment is that the interest rate burden on state-owned enterprises is reduced.   Interest rate policy covers every aspect of society and influences directly personal decisions on savings and spending.   Looking at the index of the increase in the personal savings of the urban and rural residents, the new increase in 1997 and 1998 in savings deposits was close to zero. This showed that after the lowering of interest rates, personal savings as a percentage of personal income have fallen, whereas the percentage of consumption and other types of savings have increased.   The lowering of interest rates has achieved the goal of diversifying savings and stimulating consumption.   The final consumption rates in 1996 and 1997 were 60.5% and 59.9%, slightly higher than the 58.2% and 59% in 1994 and 1995. Between January and August 1998, total retail sales increased by 7.3% from the same period in 1997.   The final consumption rate in 1998 is estimated to reach about 60%.   The Central Bank's policy is of positive importance in consuming inventory and lifting the economy up from the trough.

The Central Bank's interest rate policy is the major policy factor affecting the financial market.   These interest rate adjustments have displayed a noticeable effect on the monetary market.   The most obvious result was the trend of low monetary interest as represented by the rate of interest in inter-bank market lending.   However, the lowering of the interest rate caused a magnifying effect on the volume of transactions in the inter-bank market.   This showed that in China the monetary markets, including the inter-bank market, are not mature enough.   Those interest rate cuts have had only a limited effect on the capital market. There was only a temporary resurgence in the secondary market and the action failed to stimulate investment through any surge in the stock market.   The response of the capital market to interest rate policy was less than ideal, demonstrating the immaturity of China's capital market.

The above facts show that the transmission mechanism by which interest rate policy is transferred through the financial markets is still imperfect.   Other than the behavior of banks, the effect of changes in interest rates is basically limited to the direct influence on the public's decisions about investment and consumption.   China still lacks the market conditions for a monetary policy to be able to indirectly adjust the market.   This analysis also shows that at the same time China's monetary policy should focus on quantitative adjustment.

The Planned Target Set in the Monetary Policy Can Basically Be Achieved

Considering all the factors, we can basically meet the 8% growth target.   At the end of June 1998, retail prices rose at -2.6% and zero growth is expected for the entire year.   There should not be any problem in realizing the price increase of below 3%.

In order to ensure the realization of the ultimate goal of the monetary policy, the People's Bank of China has set some interim targets, including the money supply target, balance of international payments target, and exchange rate target.   The money supply target is M_2 nominal growth of 18%, leveling with that in 1997. Since, the price control target is below 3%, the real M_2 growth target is in fact above 15%.   The actual result at the end of June for M_2 nominal growth was 14.6%, the real growth being 17.2%. Between 1995 and 1997, the M_2 nominal growth rates were 29.5%, 25.3%, and 17.3% respectively, the real growth rates being 15.7%, 19.2%, and 16.5%.

Based on these figures, we can say that there has been no noticeable change in the public demand for money supply since 1996 and 1997.   Between 1996 and 1998, the public's real demand for money supply was higher than that in 1995, which showed that the economy was in a trough.   The public remained cautious and continued to save rather than spend. The real demand for money supply by the public showed a rising trend.   As at the end of the year, the M_2 real growth rate is estimated to be about 17%, the M_2 nominal growth rate is 16%–18%, and retail prices will show zero growth.   The M_2 real growth rate will hit the planned target, while the nominal growth will either basically hit the target or be just below it.

In 1998, the external target of monetary policy was a balanced international payment and a stable exchange rate.   In order to meet this target, based on the current condition of the balance of international payments, the State Administration of Foreign Exchange strengthened the management of payments and receipt of capital accounts and achieved the desired result. At the end of June, our foreign exchange reserves increased slightly from that of the previous year.   This showed that China has successfully maintained a balance of international payments.   Because the foreign exchange market in China is only one among the banks, thus, it exhibits the nature of weak speculation.   The realization of the target of the balance of international payments equilibrium guaranteed balanced supply and demand in the foreign exchange market and laid the foundation for a stable exchange rate.   At the same time, China achieved the goal of exchange rate stability.   On June 30, the weighted U.S. dollar/Renminbi exchange rate was RMB8.27987/U.S.$, almost leveling with the RMB8.2796/U.S.$ exchange rate at the end of 1997.   We do not expect any large fluctuation in the RMB exchange rate in 1999.

New Features Emerged in the Transmission Mechanism for the Monetary Policy

The Central Bank's cancellation of the quota system did not result in the expected expansion of bank credits of commercial banks.   The reform did not cause an uncontrolled increase in the money supply.   This showed that the blind expansion of credits by commercial banks was under control under the traditional system.   At the same time, it showed that the Central Bank's change in monetary policy to implement the quantitative model of indirect adjustment was a wise move.

In 1998, the Central Bank released a series of signals that monetary policy was being loosened. Under our current market conditions, the Central Bank's signals should be transformed into the actions of commercial banks. The result of commercial banks' actions was that up to the end of June, there was still a 2–3% gap between the M_2 growth rate and the target rate. The reason was that commercial banks were unwilling to lend and also unwilling to borrow from the Central Bank. The cautious attitude of commercial banks toward bank assets showed that they have tighter risk control and that their priority remains making a profit, not faithfully following the Central Bank's directives. Based on this, we can see that commercial banks' function in the transmission of the monetary policy has undergone obvious changes. From now on, when formulating monetary policy, the Central Bank must fully consider commercial banks' request for profit and requirement for risk avoidance.

The Orientation of Monetary Policy in 1999

Analysis of the 1999 Macroeconomic Situation

In 1999, China's economy will begin a new cycle of surging economic prosperity. First, we observe that the inventory cycle displays the following characteristics:

When there is an overheated economy, increase in inventory as a percentage of capital formation is relatively low. But it is relatively high when the economy cools down. When the economy is in a trough, the percentage of inventory is at its peak. The fall of the percentage of inventory increase in capital formation is the leading indicator for the start of a new economic cycle. Looked at over the long term, the proportion of national inventory increase to capital formation shows a declining trend. The average proportion during the "Seventh Five-year Plan" was 21.6%, and during the "Eighth Five-year Plan," 14.5%. This declining proportion showed an improvement in the utilization rate of China's savings.

At the same time, the ratio indicated the market's strengthening influence over production. Between 1991 and 1997, the proportions of inventory to capital formation were 21%, 13.7%, 13.5%, 12.5%, 15%, 13.1%, and 10%, showing that the task of absorbing inventory was basically complete during the 1996–7 trough period. 1998 should be the turning point for a new economic cycle.

Between January and August 1998, prices maintained a negative growth rate, and the market will further absorb inventory products. The estimated proportion of inventory increase as a portion of capital formation will not exceed 10%. The possibility of continued economic decline in 1999 is not great. The estimated ratio of inventory to capital formation in 1997 was only 10%, which shows that the market restraint in China's economy is now greater than that during the Seventh and Eighth Five-year Plan periods. Considering that in the second half of 1998 the central government's policy to expand fiscal expenditure will be gradually implemented, and there are other factors such as increases in bank loans, it is possible for the economy to climb out of the trough at the end of 1998. The effect of the government's policy to expand domestic demand was primarily apparent in August 1998, when the consumption and production situations were an indicator that the economy would improve.

Furthermore, from the perspective of the long-term cycle, under China's current economic growth model, the room for growth is still very large. However, after twenty years of high economic growth, the problem of the wide disparity in economic development between the East and the Central and the West regions has not yet been solved; nor has the problem of the disparity between rural and urban developments. It is these two disparities which show that our Central and Western cities as well as the enormous rural regions are an enormous potential market.

In terms of regional disparity, taking Guangdong and Henan of the Central-south region as an example, the average personal consumption of the former doubles that of the latter. In terms of urban-rural disparity, since the 1990s, the average level of personal consumption in the rural areas was only 1/3 that in the cities. Even without a large-scale technological upgrade, if only the economic development level of residents of Western and Central cities and the vast rural areas can reach the level in the East, their commodity markets will continue to support a high rate of economic growth for China.   From the angle of the long-term economic cycle, China's potential economic growth rate will not decline in the near future. It is perfectly possible to maintain an economic growth rate of 8–9%.

In 1998, we hoped to achieve the 8% economic growth target. In 1999, considering that the economy will just begin to rise, in terms of macroeconomic policy, we can set the economic growth target at 8% or slightly higher.   However, it is better not to set the target too high because it would not be good to overstimulate the economy.   In 1998, there will be no change or a slight negative growth in prices.   Even if the economy grows in 1999, the chances for sharp price increases are rare.   From our experience, the increase will be kept within 6%, so a feasible target is 3–6%.

The 1999 Monetary Policy Target

In 1999, the macroeconomic policy task is to stimulate a steady economic recovery and a smooth entrance into the beginning stage of a new cycle of economic growth.   Macroeconomic policy should aim mainly at expanding domestic demand.   The monetary policy, as a key component of the macroeconomic policy, should also be centered on expanding domestic demand.   Given a buyer's market, the macroeconomic program should not only concentrate on investment demand, but also on consumption demand.   Therefore, the monetary policy should also be concerned with both investment and consumption demands.

The evaluation of the macroeconomic situation and the target of the macroeconomic program are the basis for establishing intermediate targets for monetary policy.   From our historical experience, the public's currency demand (growth rate in real demand) during a period of economic boom is lower than that during a period of economic decline. From this, we estimate that the public's currency demand will be lower than that in 1998. However, since 1999 is the first year of the rising economic cycle, the decline in the public's currency demand will be moderate. Assuming the real increase in the currency demand to be 16–17%, if the inflation target is 3%, the M_2 target can be set at 19–20%, 1–2% higher than the 1998 planned target as set in the policy of expanding domestic demand. Based on past experience, as long as there is no uncontrolled increase in monetary credit during economic recovery, high inflation is unlikely. M_2 increased by 29.3% in 1986, and 26.5% in 1991. But the result of these large increases was double-digit inflation, which set in two years later. However, if we can control the increase in money supply within 20%, the policy is unlikely to create inflation.

The interest rate policy should maintain the stability of interest rates. The one-year interest rate for 1998 was 4.77%. Assuming that the inflation rate in 1999 is 3%, the real interest rate will be 1.77%. This real interest rate cannot be considered high, and there is no need to adjust the interest rate. If we further lowered the interest rates — after five such adjustments since 1996 — we would create pressure on the stability of the RMB exchange rate.

The external target for the 1999 monetary policy will still be an equilibrium of the balance of international payments. The economic recovery is likely to increase imports. However, in the first year of the economic recovery, the possibility for the current account to go into deficit is slight. Even if there is a slight deficit in the current account, the surplus in capital accounts can make up for it. Consequently, the key point in foreign exchange policy is continued prevention of the illegal outflow of capital.

Under an international payments equilibrium and low domestic inflation, the RMB will enjoy a stable exchange rate. The Central Bank does not have to devalue the RMB. Nevertheless, because devaluation of the RMB is still expected in the international market, the Central Bank has to pay special attention to the supply-demand situation in the foreign exchange market. As long as the RMB does not devalue in the first half of 1999, the expectation for the RMB devaluation in the second half will disappear and the illegal outflow of capital will decrease. This will further ensure the stability of the RMB.

Suggestions for the Central Bank's Monetary Policy

In 1999, the Central Bank should encourage commercial banks to be more active. As the Central Bank can no longer administer commercial banks directly, it can only use the profit lever to influence banks' activities. We suggest that to further increase commercial banks' liquidity, both the reserve rate and the interest rate should be further lowered. We suggest lowering the reserve's interest rate to the level of the interest rate of savings deposits, which is 1.44%, to encourage commercial banks to lend or invest more in assets other than deposits at the Central Bank. The Central Bank can even consider lowering its own interest rates on loans. Further adjustments in interest rate structure will help to consolidate the results of the previous interest rate adjustments.

1999 will be a good time to implement interest rate reform. Under the conditions of a stable macroeconomy and low inflation, the risk of implementing interest rate reform is low, which means the possibility for the interest rate to be out of control is low. We can appropriately expand the range of floating interest rates of loans by commercial financial institutions so as to increase the initiative of commercial financial institutions like banks to expand their loans.

We should set free the discount rate of notes and encourage banks to actively participate in the business of note discounting. The size of the rediscount should be increased, and the ratio of discounted notes in the Central Bank's asset utilization should be enlarged. We can also innovate the Central Bank's rediscounting measures. Besides rediscounting the notes that commercial banks have discounted, the Central Bank can also discount the promissory notes issued by commercial banks. In other words, secure the traditional re-lending measures by notes. The discount rate is set by the Central Bank. We can also use the auction system for discounted note quotas, or the tender system for discount rates.

When foreign exchange's share in deposit increases is rather limited, the Central Bank should employ other measures to issue basic money supply. Other than the above measures to expand the rediscount market, the Central Bank can consider selling basic currency in the inter-bank market.

We have to actively push for the development of the financial market and accelerate the unification of the monetary market. This would create favorable conditions for breaking down the barriers among the inter-bank market, the bond repurchase market, and the discount of notes market.

The window model system should be used to encourage commercial banks to increase the amount of consumer credit. The pace of the reform of the rural financial system should be accelerated. The development of cooperative financial institutions in the rural areas should be regulated. Financial measures should be used to actively develop the rural economy. Financial institutions in the rural areas should be encouraged to actively offer small-size credits and support the development of highly efficient agriculture and non-agricultural development projects in villages.

ANALYSIS AND FORECAST OF THE CHINESE ECONOMY AND TAX COLLECTION IN 1998–1999

ZHANG PEISEN

Research Institute

State Administration of Taxation

Analysis and Review of China's Economic Situation since 1997

Upon analysis and review, China's macroeconomy has displayed the following characteristics since 1997.

First, the country's overall macroeconomic development entered into what might be termed a phase of "growth adjustment" as it changed economic tracks.

With the achievement of the successful soft landing in 1996, both the rate of economic growth and prices declined. The contradiction between aggregate supply and demand has gradually been reduced. A buyer's market subsequently emerged. The problems related to social reproduction were usually structural in nature. The most prominent structural problem was the shortage of high quality products and high-technology generally on the one hand, and the oversupply and huge inventory of low quality and duplicated products on the other. This suggested very strongly that the economy had entered a growth adjustment phase.

The reasons for this assessment are as follows. First, the "track alteration period" does not mean a sweeping change from a planned to a market economy, nor from an extensive model to an intensive model. Rather it signifies a shift of emphasis from traditional industries to modern industries, or from traditional production to modern production. In particular, the industrial transformation now often involves intellectual content, which affords the country the opportunity to transform such traditional industries and production more quickly, while creating other new and/or high-tech industries.

In a sense, the problem is one of perception. We must realize and accept that our economy has entered a new stage. Beginning with the implementation of the First Five-year Plan in 1953 through the current Ninth Five-year Plan, the 50 intervening years amount to a long economic cycle. At present, having entered this so-called track alteration period, we are in the trough of the last economic cycle.

Because of the special rhythm and systemic framework of the Chinese economy, we have achieved not only a soft landing, but also a smooth transition from the trough of the previous economic cycle manifested by relatively low economic growth. It is expected that this low growth period will last until the turn of the century. Also, in the first developmental phase of this new buyer's market, even though the contradiction between aggregate supply and demand is essentially resolved, some structural contradictions remain. Tackling these will be a major priority during the current structural adjustment period.

Economic growth is a major goal of many countries, including China. However, in our particular situation, the overall contribution of the rate of investment is relatively high. This means that our economic growth model is essentially investment driven. During this track-alteration period, during which time we must achieve high quality economic growth — and similarly high profitability — we must also change the growth model. In other words, we must substantially increase our investment in both high-technology and the information industry. In the meantime, we should also systematically upgrade our traditional industries, the faster to realize these crucial changes in terms of the country's industrial *modus operandi*. These are the key issues we will have to grapple with in the coming years.

A second characteristic of the current changes is that inflation has given way to deflation. With the gradual establishment of a buyer's market in 1997, prices have continued to fall.   Retail price inflation was pegged at 6.1% in 1996; it subsequently fell to 0.8% in 1997.   The retail price index continued at low levels in 1998, recording negative growth.   In fact, between March and July 1998, retail prices have experienced five consecutive months of negative growth.   Only in August 1998 was positive price growth restored, when retail prices rose 0.2%.   This is unprecedented in China's economic history.   And it underscores the fact that deflation has appeared in our country.

So what are the features of this deflation? Why has it appeared?

Generally, deflation is characterized by weak markets, poor sales, and a sustained decline in prices. It is not caused by the development of technology or improvements in productivity, but by increased inventory.   As unemployment increases and workers' wages decline, personal disposable incomes decline as well. Deflation emerged in the first half of 1998, reflecting the contradictions and problems already implicit in our economy.   As such, deflation is an inevitable stage in the economic adjustment demanded by the process of track alteration.   Rapid industrialization and technological advances tend to make traditional industries appear backward.   In a buyer's market, the oversupply this creates forces prices into a chronic decline. However, for China, this deflationary stage should be short.

A third characteristic in this scenario of structural change is that China's ownership structure has undergone its own series of rapid changes, especially since the 15th Party Congress in 1997.   A noticeable trend has been that the development of both the non-state sector and the collective sector has been much more rapid than that of the state-sector.   The ratio of these two sectors as a percentage of China's overall economy has increased noticeably.

A fourth element is that the formation of tertiary industry has likewise undergone noticeable changes.   In recent years, the proportion of primary industry in the GDP has declined as the proportion of tertiary industry has increased. The proportion of the secondary industry component has remained steady. We should also note that the proportion of the knowledge economy has increased. This means that tertiary industry's importance to — and effect on — the national economy has grown appreciably.

The fifth factor is that the distribution framework, too, has undergone major change. It was only in 1994 that sweeping reforms of China's fiscal and taxation systems were initiated, along with today's basic distribution system for total products and personal income.

Taxation has become the major source of fiscal revenue. However, in the past two years, a confusing situation has developed. Deficiencies in this system, and abuses of power, have distorted the distribution system, including creating confusing and diffused channels of distribution, and fee collections by various levels of government that exceed the legitimate levels of taxation called for in the official program. These problems of too many fees and too few tax revenues, and of fees abrogating taxes, are very serious. In fact, they threaten to ruin China's legal taxation system and, subsequently, the execution of the government's fiscal expenditure plan.

Under the current fiscal and taxation systems (based on our 1997 estimate), the sum of these arbitrary fees — beyond those called for by legitimate taxation — was equivalent to the total of all taxes collected. Regulatory fee income as collected by various levels of governments constituted about 10% of the country's GDP, while all the illegal fees collected made up another 10%. By contrast, the total taxes collected amounted to only 10% of the GDP. This demonstrates the erosion such practices have inflicted on the government's fiscal capacity. And it points out that we must establish a reasonable system of distribution between the central and local governments and regulate local governments in terms of their revenue collection.

The sixth characteristic is the recent worldwide financial crisis, and its effect on China. Since its beginnings in Southeast Asia in July 1997, it had its first marked effect in Hong Kong, later affecting Mainland exports. Since 1998, this negative impact has broadened considerably to affect many countries worldwide, and as yet there have been no signs that a real recovery has begun. One of the causes was the free flow of short-term capital. This suggests that China should employ effective policy measures to prevent the negative consequences of this phenomenon affecting us. Indeed, this is a challenge most developing countries face during a period of changing economic tracks.

Analysis and Forecast of, and Perspective on, the Taxation Situation in 1998 and 1999

Analysis and Forecast of the Economic and Taxation Situation in 1998

Based on the major targets set for China's economic development in 1998, GDP growth was estimated at 8%, retail price inflation at below 3%, with no devaluation of the RMB. Judging by actual macroeconomic performance in the first nine months of 1998, and the performance statistics covering January to August 1998, the GDP growth rate was 7% in the first half of the year (with constant prices).

Growth turned up in August. And with the rapid growth of fixed asset investment, industrial value-added production in August grew by 7.9%, 0.3% faster than the previous month. Total retail sales also showed a healthy 13% increase, 1.2% higher than in July. But with the price index having declined for five consecutive months, the August price index showed only a 0.6% increase relative to July.

All of these indicators could be said to be a positive result of implementing a series of financial, fiscal, and taxation policies. As the government's major source of fiscal revenue, taxation income from industry and commerce maintained the same growth rate as that seen in industrial added value between January and August 1998. Also between January and August, the growth rate of taxes from industry and commerce stood at 7.9%.

Generally speaking, taxation income is more sensitive to price influences than to economic growth. In other words, the influence of price and economic growth on taxation income is: for a 1% rise in the price level, taxation income increases by 0.56%; for a 1% in GDP growth, taxation income increases by 0.35%. In the first eight months of 1998, the prices basically stayed at negative or zero growth. Consequently, the influence of price on taxation increase was zero. We should also note that among the tax increases in industry and commerce, local taxes increased by 10.9%, while central government taxes increased by only 5.5%. The was mainly due to the fact that local taxes were mostly comprised of asset, transactional, and other specially-designed taxes. In short, local tax increases did not grow with the economy.

In recent years, the development of tertiary industry has provided new resources for taxation purposes. The growth of domestic added value tax and consumption tax was 6.2%, which does not match tax increases on industrial value-added production and total retail sales. The major reason is that with business profitability down, delays in tax payments increased. Many enterprises reported zero added tax value, or even negative added value production. In addition, in order to ensure 8% GDP growth and to stimulate exports, the export tax rebate rate was raised for more than 10 items, such as textile products.

Based on 1998's economic development trend, the achievement of the planned economic growth and taxation income targets is possible; but it will require very hard work. Major factors include weaknesses in the three major engines of economic growth, namely investment, consumption, and net exports. Given the fact that both exports and consumption are trending down, we are only left with investment as a way to increase economic growth.

When the fifth interest rate cut did not have any noticeable effect, fiscal policy was invoked by issuing treasury bonds. The funds raised were used to increase infrastructure investment in the hope of sparking growth. This may well prove effective as a short-term policy. The hope is that this measure will stimulate consumer spending by about 40% and, consequently, drive the development of related industries. Further results will be apparent one or two years hence. But we will also need to find other new areas and ways to increase consumer demand because of the current impossibility of increasing exports. Considering the 1998 economic and taxation situation together, the predicted major economic growth indicators for the year are as follows:

GDP growth will be in the 7.5%–8.1% range (given constant prices); growth of total fixed asset investment will be 16%; composite CPI inflation will be about 1% (retail prices, consumer prices, investment product prices). If the above economic targets are achieved, then the various tax collection targets will be: growth of total taxation by about 9%–9.5%; industry and commerce tax income growth by 10.6%–11.3%; absolute value pegged between RMB835.1–840.1 billion.

Analysis, Forecast, and Prospects for 1999 in Terms of Taxes and the Overall Economic Situation

Based on an analysis of the economic situation and the basic trend in 1998, we predict the country's economic growth in 1999 will remain steady, and perhaps even show a slight increase. The CPI will also increase to a certain extent. Under such conditions, our total taxation income, and industry and commerce taxes, should also be increased.

We should note, however, that since the 1994 tax reform, our collection of taxes has exceeded RMB100 bn for four consecutive years. In 1998, the excess will be RMB80–85 billion. The elasticity coefficient will reach 1.04–1.11 (1.13 for 1996 and 1.6 for

1997). And industry and commerce taxes have exceeded the economic growth rate for three consecutive years.

Because our economy is in the process of track alteration, many industrial enterprises are facing difficulties and are in the process of transforming their operational systems. Therefore, in terms of potential tax increases, the economic base supporting an increase in taxation is very limited. And from this point on, it will be impossible to rely on policy factors as new sources of increased tax revenues. Rather, this result will have to be accomplished through improvements in the quality and efficiency of our economic growth and through tax collecting methods and the reform of the current taxation system. Based on the above analysis, our preliminary forecast of the status of economic and taxation indicators in 1999 is as follows:

(1) If GDP growth is 7.5% (constant prices, same as below), CPI inflation will be 1.5%, and the growth of total fixed asset investment 14%; this means the growth of total taxation revenues will be 9%, with the growth of industry and commerce taxes 11.5%.

(2) If GDP growth is 8%, CPI inflation 2%, and the growth of total fixed asset investment 16%, then the growth of total taxation income will be 10%, and the growth of industry and commerce taxes 11.5%.

(3) If GDP growth is 8.5%, CPI inflation 2.5%, and the growth of total fixed asset investment 18%, then the growth of total taxation revenues will be 11.6%, and the growth of industry and commerce taxes 13.1%.

(4) If GDP growth is 9%, CPI inflation 3%, and the growth of total fixed asset investment 19.5%, then the growth of total taxation income will be 12.5%, and the growth of industry and commerce tax 14.7%.

At present, the improvement of quality is the major task confronting successful structural adjustment. This means that it is desirable that the rate of economic growth should not rise dramatically before the year 2000; 7% is a more useful target.

Achieving this would allow a two or three year period in which to implement an effective structural adjustment plan, and to improve economic development through new technology and technical progress. In our view, this should be the major aim of our national economic policy and the major strategic choice.

Some Policy Suggestions

Make a Determined Effort to Improve the Quality of Our Economic Growth

As regards economic growth, the current policies to expand domestic demand and to prevent further economic decline are correct. However, in a period of changing economic tracks, ensuring an 8% growth is appropriate, if possible; but it is worth remembering that 6% growth is not low. The key issues are the improvement of enterprise management, raising the contribution of technological advances to economic growth, and changing the investment-driven growth model. These should be our priorities before the year 2000.

Consumption-driven Measures Are an Effective Way to Increase Economic Growth

Currently, as domestic demand is weak, so is the market. The profitability of enterprises is generally poor. Under such circumstances, the five interest rate cuts, as a financial stimulant, only showed a diminishing effect. By employing direct investment and the issue of treasury bonds as two key measures, fiscal policy has had some positive impact on the economy. But when exports are under severe constraints, this growth in investment alone will have a very limited stimulating effect because the rate of consumption is too low.

In 1996, when our consumption rate was 60%, the investment multiplier was 2.5. In 1998, the consumption rate is estimated at only 40%, with an investment multiplier similarly reduced to 1.6. Therefore, motivating and stimulating consumption *per se* is likely to be a more effective measure in enhancing longer term economic development. Currently, personal incomes are expected to sink lower against the likelihood of higher expenses in the future. Although personal savings now exceed RMB5,000 billion, except the part of public funds which has been saved as personal savings, it is unlikely to be easy to persuade such depositors to spend or invest. This is because housing reform has increased the necessity for personal savings. Therefore, a more feasible policy is to more actively develop rural markets, and to produce products which satisfy market demand. In a situation of limited spending ability, we should start to provide credit for home purchases so as to stimulate the development of industries related to this sector.

Further Strengthen the Functions of Taxation and Economic Adjustment

With the country's economy in the process of changing economic tracks, taxation-based fiscal revenue and participation in the macroeconomic adjustment should be given equal emphasis. On the one hand, we must complete the national taxation collection plan. On the other hand, we must be aware of the economic changes. Problems that appear in the economy must be addressed case by case and solved in a specific way. For example, for key export products, we must selectively raise the export tax rebate rate further, and exempt taxes for some investments. For investment in high-tech, and in experimental intermediary new technology products, we can exempt the technological transfer tax, and so on.

Reform the Distribution Order and Regulate Government Distribution Conduct

In recent years, the problem of increasing fee collections of various sorts has become extremely serious. The burdens for businesses and farmers alike are heavy, and such practices have sparked widespread social concern and dissatisfaction. We simply cannot wait any longer to discipline the distribution order and regulate the conduct of governments at various levels in the areas of distribution and fee collection.

According to market principles, we must carry out reforms in terms of eliminating fees and establishing legitimate taxes. We must insist on the removal of all kinds of wrongful charges. For fees which are essentially taxes in nature, we should gradually establish a framework to make this officially the case. For fees which amount, essentially, to the recovery of costs, these should be kept subject to regulation. For those fees of a transactional nature, a portion of them should be fixed and incorporated into prices, with the other portion standardized by the relevant institutions.

Government administrative departments must resolutely withdraw from the collection of these fees. For those funds allocated from the central to local governments, we must first resume tax collection. Then based on the nature of the funds, some will be incorporated into the tax base for taxation, some will become taxes, and some will be established as investment funds.

In order to reduce the farmers' burden, we suggest the practice of "three overheads and five unifications" adopted in rural areas be incorporated into the current tax collection system or cited as new taxable items. At the same time, we must resolutely remove all types of wrongfully charged fees. Because of the scope of these reforms, there will be many difficulties and it will take time. Since it involves a power transfer and benefits shift, we suggest that the State Council set up a special team or special organization to organize, guide, and complete this difficult task.

Further Improvement of the Fiscal and Taxation System; Strengthen Management by Rule of Law; and Administer Strictly According to the Law

We must take into consideration the overall situation of the reform when engaged in further deepening reforms of the taxation and fiscal system since those initiated in 1994, when economic growth and inflation were high, the emphasis was on the national income distribution system based mainly on taxation, and the goal was to smooth the distribution system.

By 1998, this original reform had been in operation for five years. On the one hand, it provided important financial support for the country's economic development and further opening up. On the other hand, with the changes in economic development, the previous plan has revealed some problems which are not appropriate for the current market economy and therefore urgently require further amendment.

Specifically, these include the following areas: to combine the reform of fees into taxation; to further reform and refine the local tax system; to regulate the types of local taxes; to further clarify the power divisions between the central and local authorities on administrative, fiscal, and tax matters; and to quickly establish a relatively reasonable transfer payment system appropriately defining the revenue and expenditure relationship between the central and local governments. In addition, we need to strengthen our research on how to effectively carry out much-needed reforms in terms of agricultural and rural economic development. Meanwhile, we must require all governmental institutions to act according to the law. No government institutions should be allowed to abuse their power to intervene in administrative law, for example, to increase or reduce taxes arbitrarily.

Continue to Consolidate the Foundation of Agriculture

During the "Ninth Five-year Plan," the key issue in terms of consolidating the foundation of agriculture is to increase the productivity and the level of commercialization of agricultural products. The technological content of agriculture should be increased; high-tech agriculture should be stressed; the processing of agricultural products and value-added production should be increased; agricultural infrastructural facilities including irrigation and roads should be improved; an orderly and reasonable system of rural labor chaneled to rural enterprises and small towns should be established; and general education in agricultural technology in the villages should be provided.

Employ Coordinated Financial and Taxation Policies

With our economy changing track, we must utilize interest rates, tax rates, and exchange rates as complementary policy tools to regulate the economy. At present, when the interest rate mechanism is not functioning, we should use selective tax adjustments. The emphasis should be on the increase in the rebate rate of exports for some products. We should lower or exempt tax on some aspects of investment projects. In addition, accelerated enterprise depreciation should also be included in policy considerations.

AN ANALYSIS OF THE POTENTIAL GROWTH OF FOREIGN INVESTMENT IN CHINA

PEI CHANGHONG
Foreign Affairs Office
Chinese Academy of Social Sciences

The Efforts and Effects of Expanding Foreign Investments in 1998

In order to ensure the 8% GDP growth target, the central government has decided to expand domestic demand and investment. In addition to increasing domestic investment, the government has also implemented the following new measures to attract foreign investment.

(1) Starting from October 1, 1997, the national tariff rate for imported goods was reduced sharply; 4,874 duty paragraphs (there are a total of 6,633 duty paragraphs presently) would benefit from this measure. The rate of reduction was 26%. The arithmetic mean of the tariff was reduced from 23% to 17%. This cut is advantageous to importing products and also to importing capital goods.

(2) In December 1997, the new *Catalogue of Industrial Projects for Foreign Investment* was published, which expanded the number of encouraged projects, including those export-oriented projects.

(3) Also in December 1997, the State Council altered its taxation policy of importing equipment and machinery. Now, exemption from customs duties and import tariffs will be applied to those projects included in the *Catalogue* belonging to the restricted type B, except those on the "List of No Tax Exemption for Imported Goods by Foreign Investment."

(4)   For licensed foreign-invested enterprises, prior to March 31, 1996, their tax exemption on imports of equipment and machinery and raw materials will hold until the completion of imports.   This policy will continue to be effective in 1998.

Other than the above-detailed measures, there were many similar efforts to expand the utilization of foreign investment. First, the approved foreign areas of investment were expanded and competitive industries were opened to foreign investment.   The amount of foreign participation in petrochemical industry and construction projects was enlarged.   Foreign investment was also selectively introduced into mining.   The service industry was also gradually opened to foreign investment in an orderly fashion.   In the area of tourism and water transportation, foreign investment was actively courted.   Pilot projects were expanded for foreign investment in domestic commerce, foreign trade, and tourist agencies.   More foreign participation was permitted in professional services, such as accounting services, legal advisory services, air transportation, and agency services.   Pilot projects were opened in financial and communication services.   In the meantime, an effective supervisory system was set up to monitor these developments.

Moreover, a variety of new channels and forms was employed to attract foreign investment.   Various types of ownership and enterprise structures were designed to attract foreign investment. Foreign investment was continuously used as an effective tool in the reform of state-owned enterprises.   Private enterprises were permitted to utilize foreign investment for their development.   To attract foreign investment, we continued to use the system of foreign investment joint-stock limited company to develop pilot projects. The number of foreign franchise pilot projects was increased.   Pilot projects for foreign investment were introduced by transferring the operation rights and profit rights in a regulated and orderly manner.

On the one hand, we continued to make steady use of the international stock market to attract indirect foreign investment. On the other hand, we worked hard to increase the efficiency of foreign loans. In 1998, several large state-owned enterprises were selectively listed in international stock markets. The domestic environment for foreign-owned enterprises to be listed in China's stock markets was also improved. We also actively explored the possibility of converting bonds as a means of sourcing capital. Cooperation with international regulatory institutions was expanded.

In addition, we maintained a certain level of foreign debt. With strengthening the management and improving our audit procedures, we also concentrated on improving efficiency of foreign loans. Medium and long-term loans were mainly used for infrastructure and exploration projects. Concessionary loans from international financial institutions and foreign governments were used in projects related to agriculture, irrigation, transportation, energy, environmental protection, and urban infrastructure. The proportion of investment in Central and Western China was increased. Medium and long-term foreign commercial loans were mainly used in the basic industries, pillar industries, new and high technology industries, and projects which could expand China's exports, or for imports of necessary technology, equipment, machinery, and raw materials. Short-term foreign commercial loans were not allowed to fund long-term investment or purchase fixed assets.

Because of the implementation of the above measures and the hard work of local governments, the affect of the Asian financial crisis on our utilization of foreign investment to a certain degree was reduced. Based on a survey, between January and August 1998, the total number of newly approved foreign enterprises was 13,056, down 0.29% compared with the same period of last year. The newly approved foreign contracts amounted to US$31.702 billion, up 6% compared with the same period of last year. The actual use of foreign investment was US$27.417 billion, 1.45% lower compared with 1997. Given the fact that the major capital exporting countries and the regional economies have been in recession, the investment inflow to China in 1998 could be considered to be a satisfactory achievement. Foreign indirect investment also maintained a certain size. Between January and

June 1998, there were 47 approved foreign loan projects. The value of the approved contracts amounted to US$3.041 billion. The actual use of foreign funds was US$1.918 billion. Among these funds, loans from foreign governments and international financial organizations amounted to US$1.1 billion. Export credits were US$487 million. Direct foreign commercial bank loans were only US$321 million. We can see that foreign investment was mainly made up of foreign direct investment in 1998.

The Situation as Reflected from the Location of Foreign Investment

Investment from Asian Countries and Regions Declined, and Investment from the United States and the European Union Rose

Affected by the Asian financial crisis, investment from the 10 Asian countries and regions (Hong Kong, Macau, Taiwan, Japan, Thailand, the Philippines, Malaysia, Singapore, Indonesia, and South Korea) continued to decline, while their relative weight declined even more sharply. Between January and August 1998, the value of newly approved contracts from these countries and regions was US$16.892 billion, making up 53.28% of the total contracts, 10.46% lower than the 63.76% of the same period last year. The actual input of investment from the 10 Asian countries and regions was US$19.338 billion, making up 70.53% of the total actual foreign investment, lower by 5.04% than the 75.57% of the same period last year. Among them, the rates of decline were larger for Hong Kong, Singapore, and South Korea, lower by 4.3%, 3.2%, and 1.37%, respectively. The rates of decline of relative weight of actual investment from Japan, Hong Kong, and South Korea were 3.21%, 1.01%, and 1.22%, respectively.

Investment in China from the 15 European countries and the United States recorded a larger rate of growth. Between January and August 1998, the accumulated total committed foreign investment was US$4.206 billion and US$4.009 billion, respectively. Their relative weight in China's total foreign investment increased

4.98% and 2.97%, respectively. Among them, the relative weight of contracted foreign investment from the United States increased by 2.97% from the same period last year. The relative weight of the actual use of funds rose by 1.67% from last year. The top 10 countries and regions in actual foreign investment during January to August 1998 were Hong Kong, the United States, Taiwan, Singapore, Japan, the Virgin Islands, South Korea, the United Kingdom, Germany, and the Netherlands.

The Position of China in the Global Structure of Exporting Capital

In global foreign direct investment, developed countries are the main sources of funds. In 1996, direct foreign investment from developed countries amounted to US$295 billion, making up 85% of the global outflow of foreign direct investment. In 1997, this amount reached US$374.7 billion, and the percentage increased to 90%. The United States has always been the world's leading country in terms of foreign direct investment. Countries like the United Kingdom, Germany, France, Japan, and the Netherlands are also major capital exporting countries. Since the 1990s, some developing countries also joined the ranks of capital exporting countries. In 1996, the developing countries' foreign direct investment increased to a record US$51 billion. Among them, Hong Kong is the largest foreign direct investor. The total outflow of Hong Kong investment in 1996 was US$27 billion. However, comparing the developed with the developing countries, the amount of investment from Western developed countries is much greater.

There are two major sources for foreign investment in Mainland China: first, from Asian countries, especially the "Four Little Dragons," with the balance coming from Western developed countries. Table 1 shows the proportion of the top 15 countries and regions in foreign investment in China.

From Table 1 we observe that Asian countries and regions were the major source of foreign direct investment in China. The percentage of their investment in Mainland China in their total foreign investment is quite high. Table 2 exhibits the investment in China by the major Asian capital exporting countries and territories.

Table 1
The Proportion of Exporting Capital to Mainland China

Country & Region	Weight (%)	Country & Region	Weight (%)
Hong Kong	53.01	Germany	1.31
Taiwan	8.17	Macau	1.26
Japan	8.13	France	0.95
U.S.	8.01	Malaysia	0.63
Singapore	4.23	Thailand	0.63
South Korea	2.70	Canada	0.63
U.K.	2.49	The Netherlands	0.55
Virgin Islands	1.78		

Table 2
Direct Foreign Investment from Asia to Mainland China

	FDI (US$ billion)	World ranking	% of the total global flow	Investment in China (US$ billion)	% of total FDI amount (%)
Hong Kong	27	4	8	20.7	76.6
Japan	23.44	6	7	3.679	15.7
Taiwan	3.096	17	0.9	3.475	112.2
Singapore	4.8	14	1.4	2.244	46.8
South Korea	4.188	16	1.2	1.358	32.4

Table 2 also indicates that Mainland China was the major investment market for Hong Kong and Taiwan. Half of Singapore's foreign investment was in China, while one-third of South Korea's foreign investment was in China. Under the influence of the Asian financial crisis there cannot be too much growth potential for investments from these countries and regions. Just maintaining last year's level of inflow is difficult. Only one-sixth of Japan's foreign investments came to China. Japan should be a country with big growth potential. However, since Japan has also seriously been affected by the crisis, its overseas investment is weak and the potential for the growth of its investment in China is not great.

Table 3 shows that European and American countries have very large capital outflows, but their percentage of investment in China is low. These countries have the greatest growth potential for investment in China. For the last several years, especially after the Asian financial crisis, China has placed emphasis on attracting investment from these countries. 1998 saw an increase of investment from American and European countries. However, compared with their total value of foreign investment, their investment in China appears to be insignificant. Therefore, we have to find ways to attract investment from these countries. This is an important task for China to attract the inflow of foreign investment.

The Reasons for the Low Percentage of European and American Investment in China and Policy Suggestions

Apart from the different cultural and geographical factors, there are two major economic reasons for the low percentage of European and American investment in China.

Table 3
Direct Foreign Investment from European and
American Countries to Mainland China

	FDI export (US$ billion)	% of total global flow	World ranking	Investment in China (US$ billion)	% of total each country FDI (%)
U.S.	84.9	24	1	3.443	4.1
U.K.	53.5	15	2	1.301	2.4
Germany	28.652	8	3	0.518	1.8
France	25.186	7	4	0.424	1.7
Netherlands	19.984	6	6	0.125	0.6
Switzerland	10.5	3		0.188	1.8

First, it results from the priorities set by the international division of labor. Generally speaking, for direct investment providing countries, the prioritization of investment is set by the number of marginal industries or marginal production processes. However, for investment recipient countries, their ability to attract foreign investment is established by the degree of advantages of the industries and their production processes. Consequently, countries with very close levels of division of industry find it much easier to develop into a provider–recipient relationship in investment. Whereas for countries with a wider disparity of levels of division of industry, it is difficult to develop any mutual investment relationship. When the disparity between the level of division is very wide, an investment providing country usually cannot be supported by the industries of the recipient country and its manpower resources, thus yielding no comparative advantage. This affects the growth in investment.

The variety of levels of European and American countries in their global division of industry, their marginal industries, and their marginal production processes are higher than those of Asian countries and regions. Since Mainland China's level of international division of industry is closer to Asian countries and regions, the advantage can easily match those marginal industries and marginal production processes in Asia, but not those of Europe and America. So, it is easier for China to attract investment from Asian countries and regions rather than from Western countries.

The second factor is disparity in consumption trends. The reason for the large degree of mutual investment in Western countries is the similarity between their level of consumption and the consumption structure. It is easier to secure new markets for investment. Very often, the consumers of a host country are more choosy and more demanding. This helps to improve the quality of products. The level of personal income and consumption structure of developing countries are very different from those of the Western developed countries. In developing countries, not all new investment activities can win over new markets. Although China has a huge population, with great market potential, on the whole the level of spending ability is not very high. Investments from Western developed countries cannot secure unconditional support from market purchasing power.

Based on these factors, we should choose appropriate measures to enhance production and consumption. In terms of production, we propose the following measures.

(1) In regard to high value-added industries and production processes, we should accumulate our comparative advantages to attract direct investment from European and American countries. Currently, our inflow of foreign investment is mainly concentrated on low value-added industries or industrial processes to utilize our labor supply advantage. To attract European and American investment, we should try to accumulate comparative advantage in the higher value-added industries and production processes. For example, in the textiles industry we have a comparative advantage in downstream processing at the present. In the future, we should concentrate our efforts on accumulating advantages in the upstream raw material industry or production processes. Also, in the electronic and electro-machinery industries, we currently have a comparative advantage mainly in the

assembling industry and production processes. In the future, we should concentrate on accumulating advantages in the production of components and parts and semi-manufactured goods. By so doing, we can attract more European and American investment.

(2)   We should further improve the potential attraction of our industrial bases for foreign investment. Some of our industrial bases were developed on heavy and petrochemical industries, which have accumulated rich production experience and techniques. For some industries and processes, they possess certain comparative advantages that could attract European and American investment. The main problem we face now is that our management and the government management structure does not meet the requirement of a market economy, and hence we lack the structural environment to attract large amounts of foreign investment.

In regard to consumption, the following two measures may be considered.

(1)   The income distribution policy must be favorable to increasing the domestic consumption power. An even income distribution level with few differences between consumers' purchasing power is not favorable to the development of initiatives and will yield low efficiency. However, high income disparity with wealth concentrated in a few people is also no good for the expansion of the domestic market and our economic development. Therefore, we need to further adjust and improve China's personal distribution system. An improvement in the income distribution structure will be beneficial to increasing consumer spending, expanding the domestic market, stimulating economic development, and attracting an inflow of foreign investment.

(2)   The consumption structure should be favorable to raising the level of consumption. The level of consumer spending is affected by income restrictions as well as by consumption

structure.   To raise the level of consumer spending, we should raise the level of personal income as well as provide new fashionable products.   In the past, the investments of local governments only concentrated on the formation of material production consumption. The result can only stimulate new investment in production.   However, some investments can directly stimulate personal spending.   The government should expend more efforts in this area.   For example, investment in human resources can lead to direct consumption and help to form new consumer fashions and facilitate long-term economic development.   When the new consumer spending structure is formed, we can increase the consumer spending level of China to a higher rate and turn it into a realistic market so as to attract more foreign investment.

ANALYSIS AND OUTLOOK FOR THE SHANGHAI STOCK MARKET

ZHU PINGFANG, LIU HONG, AND LIU LANJUAN
Shanghai University of Finance and Economics

From 1997 to July 1998, the development of the Shanghai stock market underwent a number of rather important changes. Although the duration of a bull market was not long, and the numbers of listed companies in the Shanghai stock exchange had increased to over 460, A shares prices remained at a reasonable level. On the one hand, this development further strengthened the role of the stock market as a barometer for the economy. On the other hand, it showed the stabilizing effect of investment funds in the stock market. We remain fully confident in the future of the Shanghai stock market.

A Review and Analysis of the Shanghai Stock Market since 1997

The Shanghai B Share Index Fell Sharply, and a Bear Market Prevailed

In the first half of 1997, the market for Shanghai B shares rose steadily and simultaneously in various sectors. This was largely due to the realization of stock value and to multiple explosions of rising trends in A shares. The B share index reached a year-high point of 99.31 on May 6, 1997. Since then the B shares index has declined because the government decided to strengthen protective measures against financial risk, to implement macroeconomic measures to suppress excessive speculative activities, and to increase the capacity of the B share market size. However, trading was still relatively vigorous.

When entering the second half of 1997, because of the financial crisis in Southeast Asia and South Korea, and the crash of the Hong Kong stock market, the B share index declined further. In particular, the bankruptcy of Japan's Yamaichi Securities, which was closely connected with the Shanghai B share market, and the collapse of Hong Kong's Peregrine Securities, caused panic. The lack of investor caution forced a continued decline in the B share index. On December 24, 1997, it fell sharply to the year-low point of 51.93, a decline of 47.6% compared with the highest point of 99.31. It closed at 55.88 for the year. The total market turnover for the entire year was RMB21.294 billion.

Since 1998, with the further deepening of the financial crisis in Southeast Asia, South Korea, and Hong Kong, the Shanghai B share market showed no signs of recovery and the year-end reports were unsatisfactory. This, plus the persistent sharp decline of the Japanese Yen in the world exchange markets, caused further financial chaos and resulted in a bear market in the Shanghai B share market.

Although the unreasonable crash of the Shanghai B share market was caused by the global financial crisis, it also had much to do with the structure of the investor base. This can be demonstrated in the A share market in Shanghai. The Shanghai A share market, with a much greater size, faced the same global financial crisis and very strong expansionary pressure. However, its sharpest decline between January and August 1998 was less than 30%. Hence, it indicates that other than increasing the supervision of the market, the development of the B share market should maintain the balance of supply and demand by employing various corrective measures.

In terms of investment, the urgent task is to expand the sources of investment funds in the B share market. This could be done by setting up a Sino-foreign joint venture investment fund and insurance funds. In addition, in the long term, the merger of the B and A share markets is inevitable. We should consider opening the

B share market gradually to domestic investors. Furthermore, B share companies should strengthen their own operations and financial management to improve their performance in order to attract more investors. With the improvement of the global financial situation, and the targeted 8% GDP growth in China, the recovery of the B share market is only a matter of time.

A Review and Analysis of the Shanghai A Share Market since 1997

Reviewing the development of the Shanghai A share market since 1997, the following features can be summarized.

The Shanghai A Share Market Was Unstable, but the Frequency of Fluctuation Was Reduced

Affected by the Southeast Asian financial crisis and the tremors of the Hong Kong stock market, the Shanghai A share index fell to its lowest point of 1,025, a one-time drop of 500 points. However, from October 1997 to March 1998, the A share index was around 1,100 points. In April 1998, the index started a new ascent, reaching a high of 1,420. The adjustment, which started in June 1998, was quite effective. The constraint of illicit funds and excessive speculative activities were noticeably achieved. The A share index remained basically stable. However, in August 1998, the Japanese Yen declined persistently and the Hong Kong stock market declined sharply. A temporary irrational decline was experienced in the Shanghai A share market as well. The index fell to 1,043, but stayed above its record low. The sharpest decline was less than 400 points. Between the end of August and September 1998, the global financial market and the Hong Kong market had very little influence on the A share market in Shanghai. The Shanghai A share market currently is adjusting itself with a steady fluctuation.

The Increase in the Capacity of the Share Market Was Accelerated but at a Moderate Speed, and the Rate of Increase in Capacity in 1998 Was Not Slow

The increase in the capacity of the stock market showed that the size of the market was greater than before, and its potential ability to raise funds also increased.   This is an inevitable aspect of the development of a stock market.   The increased capacity of China's stock market started in 1996.   However, signs of acceleration were only apparent at the end of 1996.   Based on our survey, in 1997, a total of 85 companies were listed, among which 32 companies were listed between January and May and 34 were listed in June and July.   This demonstrated the management board's determination and efforts in increasing the supply of shares to achieve a balanced supply and demand in the A share market.

Entering into 1998, the pressure on increasing the capacity of the Shanghai A share market was the same, but the strength declined noticeably.   Between January and July 1998, there were 34 new A share companies, only half of the number in 1997.   Differing from previous years, 1998 saw a fund acceleration of the speed of increased capacity in the A share market, which showed the determination of the management board to develop the stock market for the long term.   In the first half of 1998, five new mutual funds were successfully launched in the A share market.   At the same time, the size of the securities firms continued to grow.   Several firms were registered with a capital base of over RMB1 bn; for instance, United Securities, Eastern Securities, and Huabao Securities.   Meanwhile, the number of retail investors expanded continuously.   Between January and June 1998, the number of new accounts opened by investors reached 1.7949 million, constituting a total of 18.928 securities accounts, higher by 18.6% than the same period last year.   The future of the Shanghai A share market is bright.   Currently, in the Shanghai A share market there are more than 460 listed companies with a market capitalization of RMB310 billion, already a sizable market.

The Supervision of the Market Has Been Strengthened to Prevent the Financial Crisis from Affecting the A Share Market since 1997

In China's A share market, the duration of the bear phase was long, while the duration of the bull market was short. The stockmarket's history is rife with incidents of speculative activity. This showed that we needed a stable and well worked out mechanism to regulate the stock market. From 1996 to 1997, the policy orientation of securities regulatory bodies underwent fundamental changes, from ad hoc treatment to a total full-scale market regulation.

From the beginning of 1997, the Chinese Securities Regulatory Commission (CSRC) codified regulatory suggestions for the issue of shares, the auditing of listed companies, and the reporting of annual accounts. In May, the CSRC and related ministries also enforced regulations prohibiting state-owned enterprises and listed companies from speculative share purchases. In June, the People's Bank of China issued a circular prohibiting the use of bank loans in buying shares and carried out thorough checking on sources of funds for share purchases.

Since then, the news that the CSRC would punish those organizations that breached regulations has had some deterrent effect. Securities companies have refrained from carrying out illicit activities. In 1998, the CSRC severely punished some securities firms which had breached regulations in the application of investment funds and maintained private treasure chests. In addition, the CSRC forced through the merger of Guotai Securities and J & A Securities. All these measures fully reflected the government's determination to police the A share market. It was no longer the case that policy measures were only made to regulate stock market behavior. They now took into account the combination of macroeconomic and financial factors in order to prevent financial crisis.

*Great Changes Happened in Terms of the Structure of Investors and
the Mentality of Investment*

The structure of the A share market consists of the securities
firms and retail investors. The bull market between 1996 and 1997
attracted a lot of short-term illicit funds. The structure of investors
underwent great changes within a short period of time. Securities
firms, state-owned enterprises, other enterprises, and futures brokers
became the main body of the market. Along with the measures
against these activities, the flow of illicit funds was stopped. The
structure of investors again reverted to the securities institutions and
retail investors. At the same time, funds from some state-owned
organizations in Hong Kong often flowed into the Shanghai A
market.

Since the second half of 1997, several big securities firms were
forbidden from trading shares on their own account, therefore their
investment in the Shanghai A market was not very much. In
addition, many securities brokers held a pessimistic view of future
stock trading and thus sold more shares and held more cash.
Consequently, retail investors became the mainstream holders of
shares in the market. In the first half of 1998, five investment
funds were introduced to the Shanghai A share market, which led
for a while to an active market. Many retail investors sold out to
cash in. A new investor structure emerged, consisting of three
main bodies, securities firms, retail investors, and investment funds.

Because the strategies of investment funds were basically
medium and long-term, the market was more or less stable. Even
when their short-term purchase of shares created imbalances of
supply and caused sudden price rises, share prices normally fell
again after the purchases. Securities firms usually did not participate
in purchases of investment funds. At the same time, retail
investors would not sell these shares at cut-throat prices. The
inherent value of the shares and the buying support from the
investment funds gave shares the strength to resist downward
pressure. The stabilizing effect of investment funds was obvious.

Currently, supply is plentiful. There has been strong demand in the primary market for new shares, while the secondary market has been relatively quiet. This fully reflects the mixed feelings of the mainstream of investors toward domestic and global financial situations. However, the stock market is by nature always a profit-driven market. As soon as the domestic and global economic and financial situations improve, we are confident that a bull market will return to the Shanghai A share market.

Changes in the Patterns of Market Interpretation

Between 1996 and May 1997, the market level of the Shanghai A share market was determined by shares of enterprises that recorded a good performance, especially those with high growth and high-tech elements. Led by Sichuan Changhong Securities, and driven by huge sums of funds from various sources, the bull market surged.

However, in the second half of 1997, when the CSRC introduced measures and legislation to regulate the market and prevent financial crisis, the inflow of illicit funds in the Shanghai A market was stopped. The mainstream body of the market reverted back to securities firms and retail investors. The inflow of funds was reduced sharply, and the market underwent considerable changes. First, Sichuan Changhong continued to lead the big purchases, but its rising trend was weakened. New shares were still active, but the degree of the rise was much weaker.

New funds in the market did not wish to buy highly priced shares. Old players in the market survived only by actively attracting the entry of new retail investors. Their retreat from the market was obvious. Furthermore, because new funds did not wish to purchase highly priced new shares, a search for new trading shares began.

Consequently, mergers began to become attractive. Shenma Enterprise, Zhongcheng Enterprise (now Cosco Development), Guojia Stock Company, and Steel Transportation Company underwent a process of asset reorganization. Although the reaction of market investors was more rational, these mergers managed to reactivate the secondary market. Thus, it also created an opportunity for those listed companies with poor results. In addition, the trading in new shares noticeably cooled down. Many investors trading in new shares were stuck with their purchases.

Obviously, the second half of 1997 did not see a possibility of a sharp rise. The market was quiet, with some trading activities. But in 1998, the market again underwent changes. The main reasons were the announced strategy by the government to "build the country through technology and education," and the three-year timetable set for reforming state-owned enterprises. Because the size of the investment funds was large, their sense of risk was strong, and their market behavior was rational.

The difficulties of creating a market for new shares increased, and it became even more difficult to purchase good-quality shares. Consequently, market-making activities often targeted poor-quality stocks and the opportunities for market manipulation increased sharply. Against this background and the fourth interest rate cut, in April 1998 a speculative surge in the Shanghai A share market was driven by the actions of asset reorganization and the technology board. Any poor-quality assets were subject to reorganization, and many of their shares doubled and sometimes more.

Any shares related to technology, no matter what their actual performance, would rise spectacularly. But in the first half of last year, the A share market was in the doldrums as it went through further adjustment. The daily turnover was low. Between January and July 1998, the total turnover was RMB780.747 billion. Shares bought by investment funds were relatively stable, however. And shares with high-growth expectations or with flood reconstruction or infrastructure projects associations rebounded quickly. Investors were quite active in trading these shares. Although the market is currently quiet, the future market of Shanghai A shares looks promising.

Prospects for the Shanghai Stock Market from August 1998 to 1999

Our view of the Shanghai stock market from August 1998 to 1999 is one of cautious optimism. This is because the development of the stock market is closely tied to the country's macroeconomic situation, the fiscal and financial policy, supply and demand situation, and the economic and financial environments of our neighboring countries.

The Economic Growth of China in the First Half of 1998 Was Below the Expected Target. Consequently, It Is Very Difficult to Achieve the 8% Growth Target. The Performance in 1999 Is Expected to Be Better

Since 1998, China's economic development has been facing a lot of pressure. As the Asian financial crisis deepened, there were many deep-rooted problems appearing which had accumulated for many years, such as the increasing losses by state-owned enterprises. Economic structural contradictions are prominent. There has been no fundamental solution available for problems like upgrading the consumption and production structures which have restricted economic growth.

The economic growth in the first half of 1998 was 7%, lower than the planned 8% GDP growth. Therefore, in order to achieve the 8% growth for the year, we have to achieve a 9% growth in the second half. We are fully aware of the difficulties ahead. In the meantime, we should also note that the government has tried so hard to help the country reach this target. It has implemented a series of proactive measures for increasing the amount of investment, expanding domestic demand, exploiting domestic and overseas markets, maintaining a stable RMB exchange rate, expanding infrastructure investment, stimulating the steady growth of industry and agriculture, and battling against smuggling. These policy measures hold the key to our economic development. We believe it is possible to achieve the 8% growth target. Furthermore, in 1999 our economic growth will further benefit from these measures. The economic development situation will be more stable.

The Orientation of Future Macroeconomic Policy Is to Expand Domestic Demand by Implementing Fiscal Measures and Appropriately Tight Monetary Policy

When exports accounted for 20% of our country's GDP growth, and foreign investment accounted for 10% of our total investment, the influence of change in the global environment on our economy increased in an unprecedented manner. It now has become increasingly more difficult to stimulate economic growth through the expansion of exports. Thus, the implementation of active fiscal policy has become the major policy lever to expand domestic demand. Affected by the slowdown of growth in personal disposable income, the effectiveness of consumer demand in the stimulation of domestic demand was not very noticeable. Our appropriately tight monetary policy in 1998 became much looser as far as the money supply was concerned. In 1998, the Central Bank lowered its interest rates twice and the rate of reserve requirement dropped by a large degree. The goal was to expand credit lines and to drive the banks to move into the market and find outlets for funds. However, this monetary policy was not effective when China's economic situation was not that good. Consequently, we were forced to adopt more active fiscal policies to expand domestic demand further by increasing government investment in infrastructure.

The Government's Policy to Develop the Stock Market Steadily Will Not Change

Our current implementation of macroeconomic policy cannot be separated from the various complementary functions of the stock market. Therefore, how to utilize the investment funds for the reform of state-owned enterprises through the stock market has become an important and urgent task for policy makers. Under such a condition, the CSRC is even more concerned with the steady development of stock markets. At the same time, the CSRC is also aware of the importance of maintaining policy continuity.

From the second half of 1997 to March 1998, as the Shanghai stock market entered into an adjustment period, the CSRC tried again and again to boost the market. First, the securities investment fund management was passed in principle. Then, CSRC chairman Zhou Zhengqing published his article entitled "Actively and Steadily Develop the Securities Market." Then two investment funds — Jintai and Kaiyuan — were approved to be listed. All these moves reflected the government's concern about maintaining the long-term development of the securities market and the confidence of the investors.

In particular, from June to August 1998, the Shanghai stock market was a bear market. During this period, the government tried frequently to bring good news to the market, for instance the fifth interest rate cut, the reduction of the stock stamp duty, and the announcement that five more investment fund firms would be listed. However, by July 1998, only two companies had come to be listed in the market. The speed of expansion of the market's capacity slowed down noticeably. However, all these developments point to one thing: that is, there will be no change in the government's policy of developing the stock market actively but steadily.

The Increase of the Capacities in Two Ways Will Be Continued

In the development of the stock market, the most important task is to expand the number of stocks and market participants and capital.   To help expand the number of market participants and the amount of capital, the listing of five investment funds, each with funds of RMB2 bn, is only a matter of time.   Funds with different sizes or different investments will be listed in the market in 1999.

In 1998, Huabao with RMB1 bn as a newly registered firm was ready for listing.   Many will follow in 1999. The expansion of the stock market will inevitably give rise to an increase in the number of participants. The continuous expansion of the investors in the Shanghai and Shenzhen stock markets in the past two years is an example.

In terms of the scale of expansion:

(1)   Some difficulties remain in expanding the Shanghai B share market in the second half of 1998 and 1999.   There will be no capacity expansion for Shanghai B shares and neither will there be a relaxation of the foreign investment policy.   We can hardly expect a significant scale of expansion and capacity expansion for Shanghai B shares.

(2)   The pressure on capacity expansion in the Shanghai A share market in the second half of 1998 and 1999 will remain the same, but the market size will continue to expand since the government has concluded that to raise funds through stock markets is one of the major means of solving the problems of state-owned enterprises.   Increasingly, more stocks will be listed in the market in the second half of 1998 and 1999.   The issuing and marketing of stocks will be covered by many regulations and will be subject to the tolerance of the market and the secondary market.

The Local and Periodical Features of the Shanghai Stock Market in the Second Half of 1998 and 1999

Considering our current macroeconomic situation, there will be no room for a further cut of interest rates and the Central Bank will be more cautious in utilizing the interest rate as a tool. There will be no further cut of the stamp tax for the stock exchange in 1998 unless it is absolutely necessary, because the targeted amount of tax is already very demanding. The performance of the Shanghai stock market will be reduced by 13.81% compared with the same period of last year. It is, therefore, predicted that the chances for the Shanghai stock market to rise sharply are slim, but chances for it to display some periodical and local features are many.

The time for the B share market to recover is expected for its very sharp fall. A bull market will not show up in the Shanghai B share market because of the unpredictability of the global stock markets and the limited funds. Some changes may take place in the Shanghai B share market with the fluctuation of the stock markets.

It is expected there will be a downturn in the performance of those listed in the Shanghai B share stock market in 1998 and that this will last till 1999 with no big rise. With more than 10 new investment funds being listed in the market, speculative activities will be inhibited to some extent. The Shanghai A share stock market will see an even development, with some moderate ups and downs. New hot spots for investment will be formed out of poorly performing listed enterprises if their capital can be genuinely reorganized.

A large amount of investment will be drawn by enterprises with genuine high-tech abilities. New hot spots will also be formed out of the enterprises with high development expectations and connected to businesses affected by fiscal policies, such as civil engineering, cement and steel, infrastructure, ecological environment, telecommunications, and environment protection.

Potential investors should be aware that the development at the macroeconomic level is a reflection of the development at the microeconomic level. Therefore, it is an illusion to expect an overall improvement in the performances of the listed enterprises when the growth rate at the macroeconomic level has been lowered.

THE OPERATION OF LISTED COMPANIES AND THE STRATEGY OF REVITALIZING CHINA THROUGH SCIENCE AND EDUCATION

YING DINGWEN

Institute of Quantitative and Technical Economics
Chinese Academy of Social Sciences

Up to the end of August 1998, the total number of listed companies in China was 810 (an increase of 14.73% from the same period in 1997). The total assets were valued at RMB1,063.2 bn and the net assets were valued at RMB529.8 billion. Total net profits were RMB22.9 billion. With this rapid increase in the number of listed enterprises, their importance in the national economy has increased. Under such a situation, it has become a matter of concern for the mainstream of the securities market and for all walks of life to understand the macroeconomy, and the developmental characteristics of some important industries through an overall analysis of the listed enterprises

During the 15th Party Congress convened in 1997, it was decided that building the country through science and education would be one of the major strategies for our country's future development. We have laid emphasis on science and education for more than 10 years in our official propaganda. Since we are putting forward the same policy again, we must come up with concrete complementary measures to make the ideas in the policy a reality. The use of capital markets to facilitate the development of high and new technology enterprises is one of the important measures in realizing the strategic goal of building the country through science and education. This is also an effective way to yield faster economic growth in the age of the knowledge economy, as highlighted by the development of the Chinese listed enterprises.

The Overall Situation of the Listed Enterprises

On the basis of the comparability of statistical data such as financial indicators, we have chosen 684 enterprises that were listed before the middle of 1997 for our research. We compared and analyzed these companies in terms of their businesses, net profits, net profits on assets, and earnings per share.

From what we can see of the listed enterprises in Shenzhen and Shanghai, on the whole, the most prominent feature in the 1998 listed enterprises' interim reports is that in their businesses, enterprise economic efficiency fell further. This phenomenon is in line with the macroeconomy being in the trough of economic cycle. Based on the statistical indicators of the 684 companies, the development of listed enterprises has the following characteristics:

(1) Listed companies, which reported growth in their year-on-year business, made up about 55% of the total. For only 46.4% of the enterprises, year-on-year net profits increased. These figures showed that as listed companies developed, their profits further declined. From the data on year-on-year net profits, we can see that 43% of the enterprises experienced more than a 20% profit decline, and 21% of the enterprises experienced a profit decline of more than 60%.

(2) Among the 684 enterprises, 70 suffered losses (36 in Shenzhen and 34 in Shanghai), making up 10.5% of the total. This figure was higher than the 9.1% in 1997. Among the loss-making enterprises, there were about 20 with ST (special treatment), and as many as 50 enterprises had the potential to receive "special treatment."

(3) On the whole, the effective utilization of funds of listed companies declined further. The average profit rate on net assets was 3.89%, 26% lower than the 5.23% of the same period in the previous year. This figure was far lower than the banks' one-year deposit interest rate (4.77%).

(4) The earnings per share, which directly reflected the investment value of listed enterprises, was RMB0.113, down by 13% from the RMB0.13 of the same period in the previous year.

The Strategy of Building the Country through Science and Education, and the Development of High and New Technology Industry

Currently, there are many problems in our development of science and technology. What is crucial for policy making is to understand and solve these problems.

First, the administrative separation of scientific and technological research from the management of their application has caused serious dislocation. Looking at the history of our scientific and technological development since the founding of the People's Republic of China, we can see that basic research and some basic applied research have been confined to the domain of the Chinese Academy of Sciences and some universities. In the overall Chinese organization and management structure, they are part of the planned economy management, which is suitable for carrying out strategic project research, such as a series of plans for national scientific breakthroughs and pure theoretical research. However, they fail to match the social and economic requirements and rhythm of the market economic development model.

Second, the value of researchers has not been recognized. The question of personnel has always been a major problem in our scientific and technological development. Under the old scientific research system, there have been problems of ranking on the basis of seniority, false reporting, boasting, plagiarism, stealing other people's results, elbowing out people of different schools of thought, and a lack of respect for intellectual property rights. Many young academics, especially those who comprise the backbone of scientific research, fail to be recognized for their professionalism and work. At the same time, overseas scientific research institutions and enterprises offer 10 times the remuneration to attract scientific talent.

This enormous economic disparity causes a serious talent drain, especially backbone research talent in the area of high and new technology. We really need to reflect on the management structure of our scientific research and how to recognize intellectual achievement.

Third, investment in scientific research is insufficient. In 1995, our country's total investment in research and development was only 0.5% of GDP, which was noticeably lower than the 0.8% at the beginning of the 1990s. Government funding for research and development in research institutions and tertiary institutes was made up of about 58% funding by enterprises, while local institutions contributed about 32%. This was in stark contrast to the 70% by enterprises in developed countries like the United States.

Fourth, there is no protection for the results of scientific research, while the value of the practical results fails to receive recognition. A lot of the results of applied scientific research must be put to use and applied in the market. As soon as the results are recognized by the market, the labor of the researchers should be recognized. However, there is no clear definition of the intellectual property rights of many successful new and high technology enterprises. The researchers' contribution has not been recognized. In consequence, the unclear definition of intellectual property rights affects the researchers' motivation.

Reviewing the above problems, we can easily see that the key point is that scientific and technological research fails to develop a close relationship with our economic development. The findings of scientific research fail to develop into commercial products and to have their market value realized. The value of researchers fails to be recognized in their products.

The end result is that, on the one hand, all the scientific research supported by the government stays at a low level (sometimes referred to as theoretical research by themselves). These researchers do not receive support from enterprises. On the other hand, the entire economic development remains focused on low technology industries, resulting in an extensive economic growth model. This "double layer of skin" phenomenon has existed between scientific research and the economy for many years.

The solution to this problem is to build a bridge between the two, so that economic development can be driven by scientific and technological research, and in return can provide resources for research and development.

The development of high and new technology industry is the key to solving the mismatch between scientific and technological research and economic development, and to building a bridge between the two. Through the development of high and new technology industry, the results of scientific research can be effectively turned into commodities and can create brand name products for enterprises.

In addition, this sort of research can stimulate economic development and help to transform the economic growth model. Meanwhile, the development of high and new technology enables enterprises to make more profits in the market, part of which can be reinvested in scientific research, pushing scientific research and technological innovation to a higher level. The result is a beneficial cycle among scientific research, technological innovation, and economic development.

The Development of High and New Technology Industry Requires a Capital Market

At present, there are some problems in the development of high and new technology industry. These problems can be summarized as inadequate investment and unreasonable financing structure. Moreover, the size of enterprises is too small, which affects their ability to compete internationally, and further affects their ability to innovate.

In addition, the risk investment system and the ownership system of enterprises are imperfect. The development of high and new technology industry has the special characteristics of high investment, high risk, and high return. Its development requires much innovation in labor and application of new technology. Consequently, it involves a lot of risk and uncertainty. These risks include: first, the large investment by enterprises in research and development may not produce a return within a defined time limit, and may thus affect the normal operation of enterprises. Second, the unitary operation of enterprises carries operating risks in the macroeconomic environment. Third, competitors in the same field may achieve breakthroughs in research and development which change the market structure, affecting the market share of enterprises. However, high and new technology enterprises, while facing high risks, bring high profits to investors.

It is because of the special characteristics of high risk and reward in the development of new and high technology that hi-tech enterprises' capital requirements are different from other enterprises. The security of capital is of paramount importance under the banking operation system of indirect financing.

Furthermore, stability should be built in for those taking out bank loans. Since high and new technology carries high risks, investment in such enterprises is always something banks would like to avoid. However, in a capital market, the direct investments of investors are reflected in their different preferences over the risks (for example, investments in stock exchange markets). The transfer of the investments of the risk investors into investment in high and new technology enterprises would meet the goals of both the investors and the enterprises.

Facts Show that the Development of the Listed High and New Technology Enterprises Is Accelerated in the Capital Market

In our stock markets, more than 120 listed enterprises have been licensed by the government as high and new technology enterprises. Their importance in the market is continually increasing. The capital obtained by issuing stocks of the high and new technology enterprises has amounted to RMB17 bn in the past five years, which exceeds the total investments for innovation and reconstruction planned in the national budget.

According to the calculations for the total capital and net capital of 17 companies listed before 1993, their average annual growth rates were as high as 44% and 66% respectively — far beyond the growth rates of other enterprises and the entire economy. The stock markets have fostered some listed enterprises with excellent growth of their main business and high net profits. Among them are the Shenzhen Science and Technology, Zhongxing Telecommunication, Little Swan, Changchun Lanbao, Fenghua High-Tech, Xiang Computer, Nanjing Zhongda, Xinjiang Tianye, Environment Stock Company, Jiangsu Chunlan, and so on.

These companies experienced rapid growth in their main business and net profits, so the return on each share reached more than RMB0.30 in mid 1998, thus creating a group of "blue chip stocks." And companies such as Tuopu Software, Guojia Enterprise, and Xinghu Stock Company have become the market's "dark horse" enterprises after their capital was reorganized into high and new technology enterprises, making their main business and profits increase rapidly.

INDUSTRIAL SECTORS

AN ANALYSIS OF THE TARGETS AND CONSTRAINTS OF INDUSTRIAL GROWTH

LÜ ZHENG

Institute of Industrial Economics
Chinese Academy of Social Sciences

Industries make up about 44% of China's total GDP. Under normal conditions, the growth rate of industrial value-added production is about 2–4% higher than GDP growth. Between 1980 and 1996, average GDP growth in China was 10.14%, with industrial growth pegged 2.06% higher at 12.2%.

Nevertheless, in each of the five-year plans, there were large disparities in the relationship between industrial and GDP growth. For example, during the "Sixth Five-year Plan," from 1981–1985, the average annual growth of industry (9.9%) was 0.8% lower than the GDP growth rate of 10.7%. The main reason was that during this period, industries underwent adjustment and consolidation for the first time since the beginning of reform and opening up.

From 1980 to 1981, industrial growth was slow. However, during the "Sixth Five-year Plan," primary industry, with agriculture as its mainstay, experienced an exceptionally high average annual growth rate of 8.2%. Tertiary industry, by contrast, averaged 15.2% growth on an annualized basis. During the "Eighth Five-year Plan" from 1991 to 1995, the average annual GDP growth rate stood at 12%; the average industrial growth rate was 17.6%, or 5.6% higher, which was considered extraordinary.

This was mainly due to the fact that while primary industry during that period grew by only 4.1%, tertiary industry grew by an average of 9.9%. Industrial production capacity expanded rapidly over this time, in large part due to a substantial increase in fixed asset investment.

However, since the mid 1990s, China's economic development has entered a new phase, one exhibiting very different growth characteristics amid major structural changes. These recent changes have developed out of the conditions and environment, as well as the more conventional tasks of industrial development. Looking at the changing trends in terms of the speed of growth as seen now, the period of high industrial growth in China has essentially come to an end. Exceptionally high growth is no longer apparent in the primary and tertiary industries. Yet in order to achieve the overall GDP growth target of 7–8%, the industrial growth rate should reach 9–10%.

From 1981 to 1996, China experienced 16 consecutive years of high industrial growth. The average annual growth of value-added industrial production was as high as 12.2%. Between 1991 and 1996, this edged even higher, to 16.8%.

There were four main reasons this happened. First, there was a change in the economic *modus operandi*, namely from a traditional planned economy to a market economy. Second, long-term economic shortages had created enormous market demand, creating the driving force for industrial growth. Third, the implementation of the opening policy resulted in average annual export growth of 14.1%. Fourth, a large supply of excess manpower had been transferred to non-agricultural industries, enabling the mainstream of rural industries. As a result, rural industries became one of the key factors in industrial growth.

Since the beginning of the "Ninth Five-year Plan," new changes and turns have appeared in the pattern of China's industrial growth. The fundamental theme is that today's industrial growth has changed from reliance mainly on quantitative expansion to a new stage focused on quality improvement. Meanwhile, very high growth has given way to a simply high, or even medium, expansion rate. Average annual industrial value-added production growth is expected to decline from more than 12% to 10% or less. Even without the Southeast Asian financial crisis, the rate of industrial growth could not have sustained a 12% plus growth rate.   Evidence supporting this conclusion is as follows:

First, by the end of the "Eighth Five-year Plan," the quantities of most major industrial products in China had more or less reached parity with the world's major industrial countries.   The task of catching up with and surpassing the developed countries, at least in terms of aggregates, had essentially been accomplished.   However, on an average per capita basis, China's industrial production still lagged far behind large developed countries such as the United States and Japan.

If we set the average per capita industrial product consumption of the developed countries as the benchmark, China's goal in terms of quantitative industrial expansion has not yet been completed. However, we must realize that it is impractical for China to catch up with average per capita consumption in the United States, given our population size, resources, and need for environmental protection in the context of industries that require enormous consumption of natural resources.   Rather, we need to define a development and consumption model that suits China's situation. Features of this model would include addressing the need to consistently raise consumption demand and quality of life in general, while at the same time effectively conserving and protecting the environment. In fact, there is only one approach possible, namely raising the quality of our industries, and thereby the entire economy, by scientific and technological advancement.

Second, there have been some fundamental changes to market supply and demand conditions *vis-à-vis* industrial products; the fundamental shift from long-term shortages to relative oversupply. Currently, major industrial products with a relatively high utilization rate amount to 36.1% of the total; those with a very low utilization of capacity and/or idle capacity of 1/5–1/3 constitute 27.2% of the total; those with one-half idle capacity constitute 18.9%.

Most products are in balance in terms of supply and demand, or in oversupply.   By the end of June 1998, based on a survey of

613 types of consumer products, 67% showed supply and demand in balance, while 33% were in oversupply. This oversupply situation was also evident in production materials, demonstrating that in the future room for achieving reproduction growth simply by establishing new projects is getting smaller. Instead, the future growth will be led by high quality reproduction. In particular, when the production capacity in processing industries is saturated, there will be substantially less scope and fewer opportunities to bring new processing industry projects on stream.

Third, the situation for sustaining high growth in rural industries has changed; or rather, their growth rate has gradually declined. The size and the speed of the transfer of excess rural labor into non-agricultural employees have therefore been constrained. Between 1980 and 1996, rural industries absorbed some 70 million rural laborers. The production value gained by rural industries exceeded that of the country's total industrial production by 1/3. Between 1992 and 1996, the growth rates of rural industries were 33%, 35%, 25%, 15%, and 21% respectively. However, in 1997, the growth rate inevitably dipped to 12%. In the years ahead, it will be difficult for rural industrial development to regain the heated growth rate seen during the "Eighth Five-year Plan." This is because:

(1) with the gradual rise in the prices of agricultural products, the price scissors of industrial and agricultural products is gradually narrowing;

(2) industrial goods are in oversupply, and their market has subsequently been reduced. There are fewer opportunities for rural industries to find a market;

(3) after the level of the organic formation of capital for rural industries was increased, the amount required to invest in a rural enterprise increased from RMB10,000–RMB20,000 in the 1980s to more than RMB50,000 now. Thus, the difficulty for farmers to finance rural enterprises has increased;

(4) legislation aimed at protecting both the environment and resources in general has gradually been refined. Development of rural industries that sacrifice the environment and/or resources is being restrained;

(5) as the markets have gradually restored order, the activities of profiteering from poor quality and counterfeit goods, common practices in the earlier stages, are also being constrained. Consequently, the development of rural industries from now on should not aim at quantitative expansion, but rather, at systemic innovation, asset reorganization, technology innovation, product upgrades and replacement, and change from extensive mode to intensive model.

Fourth, other changes are under way in the consumption demand paradigm as it pertains to urban residents. Insufficient effective rural consumption demand is one of the main causes limiting industrial growth.

Taking a broad view, we can see, on the one hand, that living standards of urban residents have more or less reached relative prosperity. The percentage of consumption on food has fallen from about 70% in the beginning of the 1980s to 48% in 1996. The percentage of households owning home electrical durable appliances has exceeded 85%. The percentage of spending on transportation, communication, education, cultural activity, and entertainment has risen rapidly. Demand for clothing and daily necessities is stable in quantitative terms but rising in quality and class. However, spending on items costing more than RMB100,000, such as housing and cars, is still hampered as a result of the necessary purchasing power being saved. Currently, this sector remains a high potential market yet to be effectively tapped.

On the other hand, with limited income restricting consumption, there is insufficient effective demand. The most prominent contradiction in the current economic structure is the poor coordination between agriculture and other segments of the national economy, in particular, those in industry. Since agricultural production efficiency is low, the growth of farmers' incomes is slow.   This led to a shrinkage of farmers' incomes and consumption levels in the mid 1980s, which only expanded in the 1990s.   In 1978 the ratio of consumption between urban residents and farmers was 2.9:1. This shrank to 2.3:1 in 1984, but rose again to 3.2:1 in 1996.

The widening disparity between urban and rural incomes and spending levels has increased the relative oversupply of industrial products, with the growth of farmers' purchasing power *vis-à-vis* industrial products being very slow.   For example, the current capacity utilization of color television sets is only about 50%. Only 20% of rural families have color television sets.   This means 80% of rural families, or 180 million families, do not own color television sets, amounting to 4.5 times the production capacity of color television sets.   Excess supply and inaffordability coexist in this case.   And a similar situation can be seen in terms of the supply and demand pertaining to other products.   From this we can see that, without raising the efficiency of agriculture and increasing farmers' incomes, it will be difficult for industry to emerge from its current recessionary difficulties.

With respect to the relationship between fixed assets and industrial growth, under normal circumstances, the growth of total fixed assets investment should be double that of industrial growth. In order to guarantee the GDP growth target of 8%, the growth of fixed assets investment should reach as high as 20%.   Fixed asset investment in the first half of 1998 was 16%.   As the government implemented new fiscal and monetary policies to expand infrastructure construction aimed at stimulating domestic demand, the growth of fixed assets investment reached 22% and 26% respectively in July and August 1998, a sign of noticeable recovery. The estimated full year growth of fixed asset investment may reach 20%, basically meeting the requirement of the 8% GDP growth target.

We must point out that in expanding the amount of investment in fixed assets, besides increasing infrastructure construction in areas such as transportation, communications, flood prevention, and urban facilities, we should also increase investment in technology and the innovation of existing enterprises in order to accelerate the pace of technological progress within those enterprises.   Currently, the disparity between China and the advanced countries does not lie in the quantities produced but in the level of production technology, product structures, and labor productivity.   To uplift the technological level of Chinese enterprises, we must continue to increase investment in their research and development capability. At present such R&D spending only amounts to 0.5% of GDP, of which only about 36% goes to the actual research and development efforts of such enterprises.

In market economies, the transition from low growth to prosperity classically involves a large scale upgrading of equipment and machinery, plus significant technological innovation. Sustained economic growth is thus built on a foundation of new technological capability.   Therefore, when considering how to most effectively expand domestic demand, we must give serious consideration to making the appropriate investment in technological innovation.

As for exports and their influence on industrial growth, the value of industrial exports was about RMB120 bn in 1997, of which value-added amounted to RMB45 billion, or about 15% of the growth of total industrial value-added production and about 7.6% of GDP growth.   The negative impact of the decline of exports on economic growth has not been too serious because China is very different from the export-oriented economies of Southeast Asia. The country's large domestic market serves as a greater buffer. Through expanding domestic demand, we can effectively compensate for the shortfall created by the decline in export earnings.

RAILROAD TRANSPORTATION: MANY PASSENGERS, LESS FREIGHT

WENG ZHENSONG AND WANG HUIJUN
Institute of Economic Planning
Ministry of Railways

Between January and August 1998, total passenger rail traffic was 632.5 million, a growth of 1.4% from the same period in 1997. Total freight traffic was 997.9 million tons, a drop of 6.85% relative to the same period in 1997; within this, the quantity of coal transported was off by 10.3%.

The main reasons for the increase in passenger loads were:

(1) management and sales strategies were effective, at least initially;
(2) rail speed was increased, sharpening its competitive edge in passenger transport;
(3) a cyclical recovery based on price comparison between railroads and roads; the price advantage of railroads was very clear.

The main reasons for the decline in freight transport were:

(1) the amount of coal transported continued to fall sharply. In the first eight months of 1998, the decline in coal transport was 10.3%;
(2) the quantity of grain transported also fell sharply. In the first eight months of 1998, it fell by 24.3%;
(3) the negative influence of fare adjustments as regards freight. Starting on April 1 1998, the rate increased by RMB0.01 per ton-kilometer.

The projected railway transport situation in 1998 and 1999 is: first, passenger traffic will continue to increase at a rapid rate. Facing competition from roads and air freight, the railways have accelerated their program of raising speed limits. After successfully opening express train routes such as the "Pioneer" (Shanghai–Nanjing), "Beidaihe" (Beijing–Qinhuangdao), the railways successfully opened a new express service on August 28, 1998 between Guangzhou and Kowloon, with the first electric train reaching the "new speed" of 200 km/hour.

Starting from October 1, 1998, the railways implemented a newly arranged network of passenger service, and the speed of passenger trains rose again.   In 1999, train speed will rise once more, generally to 140–160 km/hour.   At the same time, the authorities will continue to adjust and improve the passenger transport schedule, and increase shuttle trains between cities.

Passenger traffic in 1999 is expected to reach 95 to 96 million, a growth of over 2%.   But it will be difficult to turn around the declining trend in freight transport.   The estimated 1998 total rail freight transport is about 152 million tons, a 10 million ton reduction from 1997.   Estimated rail freight volumes are expected to roughly equal those of 1998, or rise slightly.

THE SITUATION OF THE AGRICULTURAL ECONOMY: A REVIEW OF 1998 AND PROSPECTS FOR 1999

LI ZHOU, DANG GUOYIN AND, TAN QIUCHENG
Institute of Rural Development
Chinese Academy of Social Sciences

The last year of the 20th century will soon be with us. Over the past one hundred years, all of China's developments that have aroused international and domestic interest have stemmed from the rural sector. Since the reform, the rural economy has not only made a unique contribution to the supply and demand balance as it pertains to agricultural products, it has also performed a critical function in the transformation of the country's employment structure and GDP growth. This is underscored by the fact that achieving 8% economic growth in 1998 is, to a very large extent, attributable to the 18% growth contribution made by rural enterprises.

The Effect of the Recent Catastrophic Floods on Agriculture

In the summer of 1998, there were exceptionally severe floods characterized by enormous volumes of water, long duration, and high flood levels occurring in both the north and the south. Taken together, these floods amounted to the most traumatic event of the year.

These floods also exposed many problems related to agriculture. The mere fact they occurred over such a broad expanse of territory showed that China's ecological environment is still beset with serious problems. This puts a severe limit on any irrationally optimistic views we may hold. It does not, however, suggest that we should take an irrationally pessimistic view. At least, our ecological environment has not deteriorated into an implacable series of vicious cycles. Over the last 20 years, the fertility of our farmland has not declined. Fight-against-disaster projects and 10 major forestry projects have been implemented, facilitating the development of forestry, for example. And China, as a result, has entered a growth stage in terms of its forest areas and its accumulation of water, at a point when GDP per capita stands at several hundred U.S. dollars.

On September 1, 1998, the country's natural forest protection project began to be implemented; the number of various types of reservoirs under construction or reconstruction was close to 10,000, with total storage capacity of 500 bn m³. Through the management and control of small tributaries, the amount of sand flowing into the Yellow River was reduced by 300 million tons per year. In 1998, the highest flood crests in different stages of the Yangtze River generally did not reach historic heights. This was directly related to the ecological engineering projects accomplished since the reform.

Even though these ecological engineering projects are of major importance, problems such as a lack of investment, slow progress, low quality, and unsatisfactory results are still evident. The 1998 summer grain harvest was estimated to have been reduced by 19.5 bn kilograms. Stimulated by increased grain prices and the implementation of the policy of a price guarantee for grain purchases, the planted area for autumn grain and the average input of cultivated land units were set to increase. Current estimates of the autumn harvest are pegged at about 20 bn kilograms. This means 1998 grain production will likely be level with that seen in 1997. Based on the three-year cycle and after offsetting the cyclical variations, we can see that since the reform, grain production has been growing, increasing at about 100 bn kilograms per decade, stabilizing at the 500 million ton level of the present time. It is estimated that grain production in 1999 will reach 510 million tons, another record.

In 1998, the total yield of aquatic products and oil cereals grew by about 5.6% and 3% respectively. Affected by the floods, total cotton production fell by about 8%. As a result of the strong macroeconomic adjustment measures, total production of tobacco declined by a wider margin. In 1999, we expect a continued growth in aquatic products and oil cereal production. If cotton textiles' market competitiveness is increased, cotton production may also recover.

In the first half of 1998, the prices of all agricultural products fell. In the second half of the year, these prices recovered, though at a marginal rate. The result was that there was no marked effect on either supply or demand. The variation of grain prices has exhibited both a delaying and magnifying effect.

In 1999, in the disaster-stricken areas where the grain supply-demand situation underwent noticeable changes, grain prices may show an upward trend which could spread nationwide. If so, it will conclusively show that the effects of severe flooding are more severe than those of drought conditions.

China is a country with a water shortage. Generally, the area affected by droughts is larger than the area affected by floods. Droughts, however, tend to reduce the yield, whereas floods wipe out the entire harvest in the affected areas. In addition, droughts will not affect the reserve stock of grain. Floods, by contrast, can destroy reserves accumulated for years in one fell stroke. So floods have far more serious consequences for grain supply and demand in certain areas.

As to price rises in the disaster-stricken areas spreading throughout the country, the principal cause is rooted in modern media and communications. In addition, grain prices can be affected by the policy of price marketization. Since implementation of this policy, grain prices have tended to rise. However, the purchase of grain has been affected by the farmers' psychology of selling when prices fall, but not when prices rise. This means that the present situation may continue until prices start to fall. Before farmers are motivated to actively sell their products, it is unlikely that the government will lower grain prices. These combative conditions may cause grain prices to remain at the present high levels.

There are other factors at work in preventing large-scale fluctuations in domestic grain prices, however: international grain prices for one. Following the increase in China's grain imports and exports, and the shrinking differences between domestic and international grain prices, international price levels can scarcely help but influence domestic prices. Second, productivity in the grain sub-sector of agriculture has become more stable, which will, to a certain extent, suppress price fluctuations. Third, improvements in transportation and the government's ability in macroeconomic regulation and control will tend to have the same effect.

Development of Rural Enterprises

In 1997, rural enterprises achieved added value of RMB1,800 billion, with the value added by industry amounting to RMB1,250 billion, an increase of 18% and 17.9% from the previous year respectively. The growth of rural enterprises, though doubling the economic growth rate of 8.9%, has nevertheless fallen for four consecutive years; the rate posted in 1997 was the lowest seen in the 1990s.

The added value of rural enterprises already comprises 30% of GDP and 50% of industrial value added. It has become an important engine of economic growth and structural transformation for the country as a whole, and the main means of increasing farmers' incomes and absorbing excess rural manpower.

Rural enterprises, however, are now confronting a daunting series of difficulties.

(1)   Short-term credit has for some time been an important means of support for rural enterprises to expand their scale of operations and number of transactions. In 1993, after the government implemented the economic adjustment policy aimed at tightening the money supply, the original extending transactional relationship for rural enterprises ground to a halt because of the absence of transactional means. In short, the

existing credit relationship system fell apart.   The production and distribution flow dependent on this credit system was obstructed.

(2)   The lack of effective demand has triggered increased losses in rural enterprises.   Some losses have even led to plant closures.

(3)   In the aftermath of the Southeast Asian financial crisis, some export-oriented enterprises have lost their markets.

(4)   Competition is becoming more intense between rural enterprises and their state-owned counterparts.   Rural enterprises lack competitiveness in terms of size, technology, and product quality.

(5)   Collective rural enterprises in different places are undergoing reform in the ownership forms.   The bargaining between rural governments, businessmen, and workers has affected the normal production of such enterprises, at least to some extent. According to statistics issued by the relevant departments, there were 252,000 rural enterprises affected by floods in seven provinces and cities.   The direct economic losses amounted to RMB11.8 billion, plus RMB22.2 bn in indirect losses, for a total of RMB34 billion, about 0.2% of the rural enterprise value added in 1997.   Still, this change will not have a significant negative effect on the 18% growth target for rural enterprises.

Because of these restraining factors, rural enterprises cannot possibly achieve a growth rate of over 40% during the "Eighth Five-year Plan."   However, the possibility of continued decline is not great either.   And it should prove possible to maintain the 18% growth rate for 1998.   Moreover, if the government's economic policy succeeds in effectively stimulating market demand, some of the small- and medium- size enterprises that have been closed will be reopened.   In this case, the 1999 growth rate will be several percentage points higher.

Farmers' Income and Expenditures

Up to 1997, the average net income of farmers had already reached RMB2,090, up 4.6%. Based on an estimate by the "Basic Index of Comfortably Well-off Families in Villages," the percentage of rural families that have obtained so-called comfortably well-off status is 81.5%, contrasted with the much smaller 18.5% who have not.

Various factors affect farmers' incomes. In terms of absolute quantities, farmers' incomes are mainly derived from family businesses such as crop planting, animal husbandry, cultured fisheries, as well as basic wage remuneration (or labor income). Income from transfers and assets comes last. In terms of the overall growth trend, the relationship between labor income and farmers' net income growth is the highest. The coefficient of the two is as high as 0.93. In terms of variables in the macroeconomy, price factors, particularly the change in grain prices, have a significant influence on farmers' incomes. However, there is presently very little room for the government to raise the price of grain purchases. The growth of government investment is also a very important factor in the growth of farmers' incomes.

The main reason for the slowing of farmers' income growth in 1998 is that prices of grain, cotton, pigs, and other agricultural products all declined in the first half of the year, with floods in the second half of the year causing a reduction in grain production and the complete cessation of some rural enterprise production. The number of farmers moving to the cities to work has been reduced.

The main reason for the increase in farmers' incomes is that the number of rural enterprises continues to grow at a high rate, while food and agricultural products prices rose throughout the second half of the year. At the same time, it is estimated that in 1998 actual average income growth in rural areas will be lower than was the case in 1997, namely 2.2–2.5%.

In 1999, if the weather conditions improve and there is no recurrence of the scale of flooding seen in 1998, total grain production will be higher than in 1998. Influenced by the national economy, the prices of food and agricultural sideline products may stay at the level of autumn 1998. Thus, the growth of farmers' incomes from primary industry may reach 1%. With other factors included, it is estimated that in 1999 actual average net income growth in rural areas will reach 5.7%.

Given the above conditions, some difficulties still need to be addressed if China's farmers are to reach the comfortably well-off level.

Based on statistical reports, average consumption on a cash basis per farmer in the first half of 1998 was RMB554, a reduction of RMB4 from the same period of the previous year. Even deducting the price factors, this is still slightly lower than that recorded in the same period of the previous year. The average production expense on a cash basis was RMB276, RMB5 less than the previous year with the price factors deducted, showing real growth of 3%. Some of the material loss in the 1998 summer floods will be compensated for by farmers' savings and government subsidies, creating purchasing power. This was one of the factors bearing on consumption growth. This means the real consumption growth rate in rural areas would be about 6% in 1998. This is expected to remain constant in 1999.

Problems and Suggestions

After 20 years of reform and opening up, China's rural economy has undergone a historic change. Most significantly, it has entered a new stage of development. This is mainly manifested in the substantial rise in the comprehensive productivity of agriculture, which has put an end to ages of shortages in terms of major agricultural products. Currently, most of these have completed the fundamental transformation from a seller's market to a buyer's market, albeit that this buyer's market is at a rudimentary, low level and even primitive stage. The entire rural economic structure has made fundamental adjustments, including the emergence of rural and township enterprises and the unprecedented industrialization process at the village level. Moreover, this transformation of the rural economic structure has been mainly market oriented, and is becoming more rational. The trend toward professionalism and unification in agriculture is more pronounced. Some signs of commercialization are even apparent. In addition, farmers' livelihoods have improved noticeably, meaning most are now on the threshold of being not only well-fed but comfortably well-off as well.

In the long run, the major problems confronting rural economic development are as follows:

(1) Although the comprehensive productivity of agriculture has increased substantially, the foundation of agricultural production is still weak, particularly in the area of establishing the conditions for modern agricultural production. The level of farmers' savings and their ability to accumulate capital resources for agricultural enhancement are both inadequate to turn farmers into a competitive mainstay of the market economy. The entire farm stratum remains vulnerable to the impact of natural and human disasters.

(2) The competitiveness of the rural and township enterprises is severely compromised. This means the ability of these enterprises to absorb excess labor is declining.

(3) The structural adjustments under way throughout the entire economy have influenced the growth of both rural economic development in the broad sense and farmers' incomes specifically. Doing work in the cities remains a major source of farmers' incomes. However, the problem of employment for the unemployed and redundant workers in the cities will create pressure on this transfer of excessive rural labor to the cities, affecting the increase in farmers' incomes.

(4)   The question of the farmers' burden is very prominent. In some places, it remains very heavy, sometimes to the point of being coercive. In other places, the local governments have not solved the problems of the equal sharing of taxes on slaughtering animals and on special products of agriculture. This has led to the rebound, in some villages, of activities purely to "hit the target." Moreover, the farmers' hidden burdens increased in 1997. Some places still forcibly levy service charges on farmers without actually providing any services. Borrowing to pay these charges remains an all too prominent feature of the rural economy.

(5)   Regional disparity in the rural areas is increasing. In the vast western region, because of the poverty implicit in the area's natural conditions, agricultural production methods remain backward. The infrastructure of the region's villages and the overall market prevailing there do not encourage systematic stable growth of farmers' incomes.

(6)   There are some changes in the supply and demand situation for some agricultural products. Uncertainty is great in terms of projected market prices, which is unfavorable to farmers' plans for arranging planting based on the requirements imposed by increased production. Because of regional and departmental interests, along with management problems, protectionism is practiced in some places. The food departments and middlemen profit greatly, while the farmers themselves do not derive any actual benefits from their efforts.

(7)   The marginal effect of the reform in the agriculture system in the 1980s, which enabled farmers to earn substantially higher incomes, has been reduced in recent years. The contract system for farmers increased their initiative in their input on the land. However, when contract terms are relatively short and the rights they enshrine unstable, this initiative is likely to be strictly short term.

Our major policy suggestions are:

As short-term measures, to ensure a stable growth of grain production and farmers' income, the main priorities for 1999 should be, first, to insist that the basic policies of the central government for rural economic development are followed in the sense of increasing the thoroughness of their implementation. Moreover, we must work hard to enable the disaster-stricken areas to resume production and rebuild homes, and to ensure the supply of production materials, so that 1999's spring planting can go ahead smoothly. In addition, opportunities exist to make use of increased government investment to create more employment opportunities in non-agricultural sectors for farmers. As well, the effort to reform the grain circulation system should continue so that farmers will receive their fair share of profits from grain sales. Finally, we can expand the exports of rural enterprise products by regulating foreign trade policy.

From a longer-term perspective, rural economic development must be achieved through deepening reforms at the village level, a more rapid adjustment of the rural economic structure, and an accompanying transformation of the growth modes implicit in China's rural economy. The major measures we suggest are:

(1) At the most fundamental level of the market reform of the rural economic system, we believe a rural economic system should be established on the basis of a family contract system, using the agricultural social service system, the agricultural product market system, and the government's support and protection for agriculture as the main support pillars if the requirements of the socialist market economy are to be met.

(2) We must emphasize the development of enterprises in counties and small towns and create conditions conducive to solving the problems of transferring several hundred million excess rural workers.

(3) We must increase the government's support of agriculture as regards financial resources and technical assistance, while raising the level of government service at the village level.

(4) We must reform the rural economic management system and, in particular, the tax collection system in order to reduce the farmers' burden.   This means we must first raise the economic status of farmers through development of the rural economy, so that farmers have a much larger voice heard in social interest groups.   Furthermore, we must develop democratic elections at the village level, while establishing a sound and open system for village committees and village affairs.   Doing this will assist farmers in developing all types of economic and social cooperation organizations as well as increasing their political participation and awareness.

CHINA'S AGRICULTURAL PRODUCTION: NO MAJOR CAUSE FOR CONCERN

GU HAIBING
People's University of China

The areas affected by the catastrophic floods in 1998 reached 320 million *mu*. The flooded areas themselves amounted to 200 million *mu*. The summer harvest, compared with the great harvest of 1997, was reduced by 20,000 million kilograms, and the early harvest by 4,500 million kilograms. In these circumstances, domestic and international observers were very much concerned about China's, and indeed Asia's, agricultural prospects and their social stability.

Considering China's rate of population growth (more than 100/∞), and the country's average grain production growth rate (2.2% average during 1985–1997) as well as the high growth rate of grain production in 1996, although negative growth was recorded in 1997, -3%, we still consider 1998 and 1999 as years of no serious problem.

On the whole, in 1998 the favorable conditions outweighed the unfavorable conditions in grain production. And production conditions in 1999 are expected to be better than those in 1998. Grain production in 1999 will be at least 2% higher than that posted in 1998, and a moderately high growth rate of 4% is at least possible.

Favorable conditions will also outweigh unfavorable conditions in cotton production in 1999, with the annual yield expected to be higher than in 1998. Naturally, because of various factors, including imported alternatives, chemical fibers, and wool, we do not expect further growth in cotton production. Still, production growth could reach about 5%, a moderately high rate. Because of excessive inventory, even though cotton production was reduced by about 10% in 1998, no alarms have been triggered; and 1999 looks even better.

In oil cereal production in 1999, there is a 70% probability of a moderately high growth rate of above 4%, and a 30% probability of zero or 1–4% growth. This means that, whatever the present difficulties, neither 1998 or 1999 are likely to be years fraught with emergencies in this sub-sector.

THE SITUATION OF THE MATERIALS MARKET: AN ANALYSIS OF 1998 AND A FORECAST FOR 1999

CHEN KEXIN

Materials Information Centre of China

Analysis of the Materials Market in 1998

In 1998, market demand for national production materials was weak in two ways. Actual materials supply was severely restricted and market prices were in consistent decline.

Demand for Materials Was Weak in Two Ways

In the first half of 1998, China's economic development was still in decline. In fact, the growth rate declined each quarter. In order to stimulate demand and jump-start the market, the government implemented a series of loose measures with monetary policy at the core, while executing counter-cycle adjustment from the fourth quarter of 1997. These measures included five consecutive downward interest rate adjustments in financial institutions, lowering the deposit reserve ratio, as well as the expansion and increase of export tax rebates.

The implementation of the above measures has had some genuine effect in terms of stimulating demand and fueling economic growth. As a result, China's economy still managed to grow at a higher rate even while the global economy was in recession and, neighboring countries were reeling from financial crisis and the concomitant negative growth.

Based on our preliminary estimate, the total sales of materials in the first half of 1998 was about 2.8% higher than over the same period of 1997. The growth rate was 7% lower than that in 1997, however. And the growth rate for the entire year is expected to be less than 6%, lower than the 1997 equivalent. The main reason for this slow growth in production materials' total sales, which was much lower than 1997 levels, was that demand for materials was weak in both the external and domestic market, and there were more constraints in both markets.

In terms of domestic demand, growth was slow in the first half of 1998. Between January and August, total sales of national heavy industrial products grew by only 2.6%. Based on an authoritative estimate, in the first half of the year, the consumption growth rate of 19 major materials nationwide was about 0.9%. The effective demand was obviously insufficient. The consumption of some major materials declined from 1997 levels, thus inventory accumulation increased. Total consumption of the 19 major materials was expected to increase by 2% over the previous year, with a growth rate in the second half exceeding 3%.

In terms of export demand since 1998, the financial markets in some Asian countries have continued to be in turmoil. Those countries already in recession did not recover; instead they deteriorated. Countries such as Japan, South Korea, Indonesia, and Thailand have implemented adjustment programs and have increased their exports. This has seriously affected China's exports. We estimate that exports of the 19 major materials will decrease by 17.8% relative to the same period in 1997. And in the second half of 1998, this export decline rate will increase. As a result, a very serious negative effect on consumption growth is likely.

Materials Supply Increased at a Low Rate

The weakness in both external and domestic demand has seriously affected enterprise production growth. The growth rate of total production of these 19 major materials did not even reach 1% in the first half of 1998 and the growth rate in the third quarter was also low.

Among these major materials, coal production nationwide fell by 8% from January to August relative to the same period the previous year; crude oil production fell by 0.9%; and timber production was off by 1.7%. The production of electro-mechanical machinery, such as generators, alternating-current motors, tractors, and industrial boilers, fell by more than 10%. And production of other items, such as automobiles, synthetic rubber, copper, and cement, all grew slowly.

On the materials supply side, imports of 19 major items in the first half of 1998 fell by 1.7% compared to the same period in 1997. And the rate of decline seen in steel, diesel, and automobiles was even greater.

Even though resource supplies are declining due to insufficient demand and excess inventory, materials markets in 1998 will remain in an oversupply situation and consequently will be weak for some time.

Market Prices Continued to Fall

This oversupply in the materials market has forced prices down on an ongoing basis. Based on statistics from the Materials Information Centre of China, the overall market price level of these materials from January to August 1998 fell by 4.5% compared with that at the beginning of 1998, and by 5.5% compared to the same period in 1997. Moreover, the rate of decrease was gaining momentum. Of the ten large categories of products, nine declined from the beginning of the year. Improvement is expected after the fourth quarter of 1998. But on an annualized basis, decline is inevitable.

Future Materials Market Forecast

On the Government's Implementation of a More Active Fiscal Policy Aimed at Stimulating the Economy

Against the continuing decline in economic growth and the weak market which preceded it, the government has increased the strength of its stimulus measures, while continuing to implement counter-cycle regulatory measures. The recent adjustment policies are mainly designed to correct the means employed to stimulate growth in the previous period and to compensate for "loopholes" in that policy. In other words, while continuing to implement an ever more finely-tuned monetary policy and loosening the money supply to an appropriate degree, a more active fiscal policy has been invoked to once again stimulate the economy.

These measures include reducing the burden on businesses, increasing government investment, expanding export tax reimbursements, and building a purchasing system for the government for its large purchases of commodities. They also entail issuing a prudent number of treasury bonds, specifically a major government issue aimed at solving the problems of lacking major investors body as well as raising more capital for investment. Not long ago, the government issued an additional RMB100 bn worth of treasury bonds on the basis of the original plan. The national commercial banks have augmented this with a loan of RMB100 billion. This means there will be a total of RMB200 bn new capital for investment in various infrastructure projects and public facility construction. This will lead to an increase in demand for various construction materials. It is estimated that this measure will boost economic growth by about 2%, and that a large amount of treasury bonds will still be issued in 1999.

We predict that financial institutions will continue to lower their deposit and loan interest rates at appropriate times, albeit slightly, to reduce financing costs and increase the stimulating effect of this fiscal policy, assuming future price levels do not rebound sharply and there is no large-scale outflow of savings deposits.

The capital raised from these treasury bond issues will be used, as noted above, mainly for various infrastructure and public facility constructions. Over the next three years, China will invest US$750 bn in infrastructure construction in order to stimulate domestic demand and to make up for the shortfall occasioned by the decline in exports. Based on the figures provided for the next three years, China will spend RMB250 bn on railroad construction; RMB220 bn on large-scale renovation of urban and rural electricity grids, resulting in 80–100 million more kilowatts of new electricity generating capacity; telephone owners will be increased from the planned 10% to 13%; the total number of telephone exchanges will increase to 190 million; and the rates of treatment of urban sewage and garbage into harmless materials will be increased from the present 7% and 6% respectively to about 20% for both treatments. The major portion of these investments will be made in 1998 and 1999. Meanwhile, in 1998, RMB180 bn will be invested solely in road projects creating another 33,000 kilometers of motorways. As for flood reconstruction, government investment in irrigation construction will reach RMB35 billion, more than four times greater than the previous year. It is estimated that large-scale fixed asset investment will be maintained in 1999.

The Total Materials Market Will Develop a Supply and Demand Equilibrium

Stimulated by a more active national fiscal policy, the materials market will gradually develop into a balanced supply and demand equilibrium with four major characteristics:

Increasing Consumption Demand for Materials

A large amount of investment will stimulate materials consumption, particularly in terms of those materials required by these investments. Based on an analysis of relevant data, an 18% plus growth rate will result from the full year's fixed asset investment, a significant increase over the original target set at the beginning of the year. Investment growth in 1999 will be no less than 15%. Based on a benchmark calculation of RMB200 bn invested in 1998, the amount of investment according to the budget at the beginning of the year, along with additional investments from various enterprises and the private sector for reconstruction in disaster areas, the consumption of construction materials could be even greater. As it stands, the projected annual demand growth for major materials in 1998 will be about 3%, and growth in the second half of the year will far exceed that in the first half. In 1999, this consumption of major materials will continue to increase by an estimated rate of about 5%. Thus, in 1998 total materials sales growth will be about 5%, with 1999 growth expected to be even higher.

With the financial crisis still affecting some regions of the world, global economic growth will slow. Moreover, many of China's neighbors' economies will be in recession. This is fueling trade protectionism over a range of countries and even regions. The result will be weak export demand in terms of materials, meaning export growth is expected to continue declining.

Obvious Structural Characteristics of the Growth of Consumption Demand

Although consumption demand for materials will be subject to stimulation from now on, with market conditions clearly improving, particularly from the perspective of market access, not all businesses will benefit; in fact, many enterprises will be eliminated as demand increases.

The first problem pertains to product structure. As regards the direction of its economic stimulation, the measures invoked by the government are mainly aimed at increasing infrastructure construction plus increasing the number of public facilities and private housing. Accelerating technological renovation in industry and business is another goal.

Taken together, the investment needed to realize these goals is enormous. The demand for purchases will be strong for production frontline materials, construction materials like steel, cement, construction machinery, construction materials, and in other areas of investment like electro-mechanical equipment and machinery. Of course, not all of the products produced by current investment will be equally prosperous. On the contrary, because of the deepening enterprise reforms, the number of redundant and unemployed workers will increase and the growth of consumption capital will be slow. Furthermore, because of the anticipated reforms in housing, medical care, retirement, and education, the tendency for people to worry about the future and "save for a rainy day" will get stronger. Consequently, the purchase demand for general consumer products will decline. Therefore, in this round of domestic demand expansion, the materials related consumer goods are not expected to benefit a lot.

The second problem is in the current enterprise structure. Under the government's more active fiscal stimulus policy, in addition to the different share of profits and losses among different industries producing different products, enterprises in the same industry will naturally encounter different situations. Quality enterprises with a low cost structure can capitalize on these circumstances as an opportunity to expand further. Backward enterprises with a high cost structure will find it difficult to do likewise. This type of competition will not only be intense among different domestic enterprises but also among domestic and foreign enterprises.

These important demand-stimulating measures have attracted the attention of the major industrial countries. It has been said that in the last three years of the 20th century, the most fiercely competitive market will be that in China. Certainly this time will be a period featuring prosperous development of private enterprises. And if the state-owned enterprises do not take this opportunity to accelerate their reform programs, change their systems, improve their technology, product quality, and market research, they will be squeezed out by foreign, private, or other high quality enterprises. In short, the net beneficiaries of this new economic stimulus will be organizations other than enterprises.

Excessive Resource Supply Has Been under Control to a Degree

The Asian financial crisis has alarmed China. From now on, financial institutions will further strengthen their risk management by reducing or actually halting loans to enterprises with already large inventories. After a reasonable readjustment of industrial and business structures, many poor quality enterprises classically go bankrupt and shut down. The production of many products already in great supply will be seriously affected. When supply greatly exceeds demand, some enterprises will jointly reduce their output, particularly in areas such as coal and copper production, triggering production reductions downstream of many other materials. In 1998, limiting production and inventory was one of the major tasks for the non-ferrous metal industry. Copper production was reduced by several tens of thousands tons and the glass industry by 10%. Coal production too was reduced to the local supply level, with production limitation targets set at more than 100 million tons.

At the same time, government customs departments and others have strengthened their efforts to combat smuggling, especially smuggling by legal entities, greatly restraining the entry of tax-evading goods. In July 1998, an anti-smuggling conference was convened in Beijing.

Because of the crackdown on smuggling, the domestic refined oil market recovered from the doldrums. Sales increased, prices rose, and the market gradually became more active. With the continued strengthening of anti-smuggling measures, smugglers — and their effect on markets — are becoming marginalized. Proof can be seen in the fact that, even now, the amount of smuggled goods has declined sharply and prices have risen.

In addition, the government will increase ecological and environmental oriented construction. Logging in the forests of upstream river regions will be strictly forbidden. This will cause the supply, in terms of domestic resources, to fall. Based on forecasts by the Materials Information Centre of China, the supply growth rate of major materials in the first half of 1998 did not even reach 1%. Nevertheless, the growth rate increased in the second half of the year, following a demand upswing. The full year growth rate is expected to be around 2%. In 1999, driven by a further increase in demand, the growth rate of material resources will accelerate; the growth rates of the major ones may reach 3%.

It Will Be Difficult for Market Prices to Rise Sharply

As the materials market moves toward an equilibrium between supply and demand, the prices for many material products will cease to decline and become stable. In fact, the prices of many products will rise again. But so long as overheating does not occur, the margin of these rises will be limited. Some product prices will decline further, however. The reasons are as follows:

The overall market will still be a buyer's market. No fundamental change will occur, despite the government's demand stimulus measures. In recent years, many projects begun earlier have been completed. And China's materials productivity has increased substantially. A full-scale buyer's market has emerged for the first time. The operating rate of many industries is below 70%. So even though market demand will show a certain degree of growth from now on, as the previously idle capacity is utilized there is still enough supply to meet the demand.

In the future, the situation of a seriously weak market will definitely disappear. However, the present buyer's market will continue for some time. Even if the government implements a stronger stimulation policy, it must still emphasize the structural adjustment and the transformation of the model of economic growth. In order to protect this hard-won buyer's market, we cannot overstimulate demand, because it may cause materials shortages, and inflation. Therefore, we must fundamentally suppress excessive price increases.

Under the pressure of competition, enterprises will lower their costs in order to survive. From now on, market competition will intensify. This will force enterprises to scrutinize their costs, strengthen their management, raise their technological capability, and approach the material consumption level of advanced international standards. From now on, enterprises will likewise be forced to reduce their staff and increase their profits. A large number of workers will become redundant. This will obviously reduce salary expenses. The government urges the achievement of the two transformations. High-cost and backward enterprises will be eliminated. Low cost, low waste enterprises will prosper, making the entire country more competitive. This means that considerable room will be generated for business profits to grow, even at lower price levels, while preventing a sharp rebound in market prices. This provides enormous room for the enterprises profits to grow under a lower price level, while preventing a sharp rebound in market prices.

Analysis of Market Trends of Major Material Products

Based on the above analysis, the forecast of the market trend for major material products is as follows:

Coal: It was estimated that the national consumption of coal in the first half of 1998 would decrease, falling by about 0.5%. Over the entire year, the estimated demand for coal can possibly recover from the decline. Growth will be realized in coal consumption at about 1–2% in 1999.

Steel: Influenced by government stimulation policies and large-scale reconstruction after the summer floods, the total demand for steel will increase to a certain extent. However, the structural feature is very clear. While the demand for construction materials such as steel spiral rods and wires will experience stronger growth, demand growth for steel products used in light industries will not be noticeable. Based on the increased RMB200 bn investment in 1998, the increased consumption demand for steel is estimated at 6–8 million tons from now on. The major increase will be mainly in construction steel. Annual steel consumption in 1998 is expected to grow by about 3.5% (lower than estimated at the beginning of the year). Consumption is expected to be about 110 million tons. The increase in steel demand in 1999 will not exceed 5%, and export demand will continue to decline. The growth rate of new resource supplies will also be below 5%.

Cement: On the whole, the cement market will become more active, with corresponding price rises, particularly during and after the spring of 1999. But of China's total cement production, only 15% can match advanced international standards. The estimated growth rate of demand in 1999 for cement stands at about 3%. Increase in new supply and demand will exceed 500 million tons.

Non-ferrous metals: Currently most non-ferrous metal products are in oversupply. Prices are falling sharply. Domestic production is being restricted. The major causes are the lack of effective demand in the country and the decline of international prices which was caused by the Asian financial crisis. The projected 1999 copper consumption demand is about 1.3 million tons, an increase of about 4%. But at the same time, the increase in new supply is more than 1.3 million tons. The consumption of aluminum is about 2.75 million tons, an increase of about 5%; estimates of new supply are pegged at about 2.75 million tons, an increase of about 7%.

Automobiles: In recent years, productivity in domestically manufactured automobiles, especially cars, has increased substantially. The result is a currently serious oversupply situation. The market in 1999 will still be weak. At present, domestic automobile prices are on the high side. Even though the relevant departments are implementing measures to prevent destructive competition, price wars cannot altogether be eliminated when the market is so seriously oversupplied.

Rubber: In the past two or three years, China imported too much rubber, particularly synthetic rubber. Thus the domestic rubber market is seriously oversupplied. Prices continue to fall sharply. In 1999, the domestic car market will continue to be weak. This means the demand for tires and rubber products will be limited. It is projected that rubber consumption in 1999 will not exceed 1.8 million tons, a growth of about 4%. Both international and domestic rubber markets are in oversupply. Supply is plentiful, so it is unlikely prices will rise sharply. However, because current prices are too low, enterprises are experiencing huge losses. But prices have bottomed out and will start to rise again.

Refined Oil Products: The anti-smuggling crackdown started in the second half of 1998 has achieved some gratifying results. As quantities of smuggled refined oil products fell sharply, the domestic petrochemical enterprises made an effort to cut production and stimulate price stability in the domestic oil markets. The result is that petrochemical businesses have rebounded from loss to profit. At present, petroleum prices are recovering noticeably. The anti-smuggling crackdown is expected to continue in 1999. The organizations concerned will adjust their production according to the market demand, and actively implement measures to regulate the refined oil market and set price targets. In addition, with the large-scale infrastructure project construction and reconstruction being launched after the flood disaster, the demand for refined oil will increase, meaning market demand will further improve.

CHINA'S CONSUMER MARKET: AN ANALYSIS OF 1998 AND A TREND FORECAST FOR 1999

GUO SHOUZHONG
Commercial Information Centre
Ministry of Internal Trade

In 1998, China's economic development continued to face a rather severe and complicated domestic and global environment. The Southeast Asian financial crisis that started in the second half of 1997 showed no sign of ending in the new year, but instead was intensified and caused a widespread economic recession. Domestically, the country was undergoing a wide-ranging economic structural adjustment. The new Cabinet has started to implement the structural reform of the state sector.

Many enterprises ran into difficulties and their profitability declined. The number of unemployed and laid-off workers has increased and caused insufficient effective demand. Meanwhile, the framework of a buyer's market has been primarily established. Thus, the market has more control in the development of our economy. Under the situation of low inflation or even deflation, the market is weak. There are no official figures of the economic loss caused by the floods. However, the extent of the damage, the size of the flooded areas, and the number of victims are all unprecedented in recent years.

The Situation of the Consumer Market

Under the influence of oversupply, insufficient effective demand, and deflation, the 1998 consumer market has showed the following characteristics.

The Price Levels in 1998 Have Remained Low

With the establishment of a buyer's market, the 1998 consumer market was stable but quiet.   After the third quarter of 1998, it started to recover.   In the first half of 1998, the nominal growth rate of total retail sales was 7.6%, compared to the same period last year, which was a 6.5 percentage points drop.   The total retail sales for August 1998 were RMB231.5 billion, a nominal growth of 9.3% from the same month last year.   Between January and August 1998, the total retail sales were RMB1,858 bn with a nominal growth rate of 7.3%, a real growth of 9.9% with the price factors deduced, which was still 5.6 percentage points lower than the same period last year.   However, the gap was narrower than the figures from January to June 1998.

Many Enterprises Suffered from Heavy Losses with Undercapacity Production.   The Sales Rate of Products Was also Poor

There was no fundamental improvement in the serious overstocking of manufactured goods.   In the first half of 1998, the personal income of urban and rural residents increased slightly. (In the first half of 1998, the personal disposal income of urban residents was RMB2,799, with a real growth of 6.2%, or 3.6 percentage points higher than that in the last year.   The average income of farmers in cash was RMB977, with the real growth rate level the same as last year or slightly lower).

However, because people had higher expectations of future uncertainty, the personal marginal propensity to save or to invest increased.   Current consumer spending was thus affected.   Non-commercial consumption was apparent.   Up to July 1998, the total amount of savings of both urban and rural residents has exceeded RMB5,000 billion.   Based on a special survey done by the China Economic Situation Monitor Centre on the saving propensity of the residents in Beijing, Tianjin, and Shanghai, their willingness to spend was suppressed by the uncertainties about their future income due to the possibility of unemployment and the expected increase in future expenses on education and medical care. Among them, 20% of the residents saved for emergency needs, 10% for their children's education, 7% for the sake of security, and 10% for purchase of property. The total percentage of the population that saved for the above purposes was 64%.

More Intensified Competition in the Market

Disparity exists between different ownership structures, between urban and rural sectors, and between different regions. The total retail sales of state-owned enterprises and collective enterprises recorded a 5.4% decline and a 1.4% rise respectively between January and July 1998. Private, self-employed, and foreign-owned enterprises grew by 29.9%, 14.8%, and 23.9%, respectively. In terms of industries, the food and beverage industry grew by 16%, much higher than the growth of other industries. The sales growth rates of urban and rural markets were the same. Among the 31 provinces and cities, the nominal growth rate of 15 provinces was higher than the national average. The growth rates of Jiangsu province, Zhejiang province, and Xinjiang province were relatively low.

Because of the rapid and uncontrolled development of the retail industry, retail competition intensified in the consumer market. The market was in oversupply and consumption was weak. Because of unregulated, improper, and excessive competition, price wars were waged. This has caused consumers to be more likely "to buy when prices are up and not to buy when prices are low." This situation in turn forced enterprises to fall into the trap of further price wars. Undoubtedly, this kind of condition delayed the market recovery and was unfavorable to the healthy development of the consumer market.

Structural Contradiction of Products Was Obvious

There was a large disparity among the sales growth of different products. Based on the monitoring report of the Commercial Information Centre of the Ministry of Internal Trade on 100 large national markets, among the 20 large categories of consumer products between January and August 1998, the categories with higher sales growth were food, clothing, electrical appliances, audiovisual products, medicine, newspapers and magazines, and automobiles. They grew by 22.5%, 11.4%, 13.5%, 23.2%, 78%, 24.2%, and 52.3%, respectively, compared with the same period of last year.

Based on a survey done by the Commercial Information Centre on the supply-demand situation of 610 major products, the supply-demand situation in our commercial products markets after several years of structural adjustment was seen to be developing toward a reasonable one. However, the supply-demand imbalance was still obvious. Of 600 products, one-third of them were in oversupply, showing an increasing trend compared with the first half of 1998. In particular, the products of some industries had poor sales and had been in serious oversupply for a long time. Some goods have been stuck in the oversupply situation for several years.

The total summer harvest was 226.2 bn *jin* (= ½ kilogram), a reduction of 29.2 bn *jin* compared with 1997 due to serious droughts in the north and floods in the south. However, the full year grain production will hopefully reach the planned target of 985 bn *jin*. Based on a survey done by the Ministry of Agriculture, the growth of animal husbandry in the first half of 1998 was stable. The supply of animal products was abundant. Quantities of hogs increased by 2.5% over the same period last year. The quantities of pork, beef, and lamb grew by 4.8%, 7.6%, and 7.8%, respectively. The production of poultry and eggs increased by 5.9% from the same period in 1997. The total production of aquatic products was 16.73 million tons, 11% higher than that in the same period last year.

The supply of main and sideline food products which are closely connected to people's daily lives was abundant. The fluctuation of prices of some food products, vegetables, meat, and eggs was normal. Because the central government was very firm on the crackdown on smuggling, the price of edible oil recovered moderately, which was helpful in reducing the domestic stock of edible oil.

Since 1998, the retail sales of industrial products were both fast and slow. In the urban markets, electrical appliances with domestic and international brandname recognition maintained strong sales. Durable consumer goods, which began to fill Chinese households in the 1980s, such as color TVs, refrigerators, and washing machines, were being upgraded by consumers. Sales in the 1990s have mainly concentrated on goods such as air-conditioners, audiovisual products (hi-fi systems, VCD, CVD), and PCs. Among the high-price consumer goods, the sales of automobiles still managed to maintain a high level of growth

Trend of Market Development in the Third Quarter of 1998 and the Full Year

A stable and gradually recovered macroeconomic environment was one of the key factors for the stable economic growth in the fourth quarter of 1998. And as the government adjustment measures continue to be implemented, the economy should recover gradually and steadily. With the increase in fixed asset investment, the newly issued RMB100 bn worth of treasury bonds should exert a positive influence on increasing demand, employment, and the personal income of urban and rural residents. It should also help expand consumption demand.

The floods and the battle against them provided a pulling factor to stimulate the growth of the economy (mainly in construction materials and daily needs). At the same time, the construction after the floods may also boost consumer confidence.

The supply of major commercial and industrial products was sufficient. This will provide a reliable foundation for the consumer market for the last few months of 1998.

Personal income is expected to grow slowly. The disposable income of urban residents should reach RMB5,400 in 1998, with a nominal growth of 4.65% from 1997. The average rural personal net income is expected to reach RMB2,190, with a slow nominal growth of 4.7%.

The personal income of urban residents is expected to be higher than that of rural residents. Consequently, the growth of urban consumer spending will be faster than that of rural consumers.

Because of sufficient supply and inadequate demand, the possibility of a rebound in price levels is low. The expected total retail price index in 1998 will decline by about 2.5%. The consumer price index could be 0.5 percentage points lower than that in 1997.

In summary, it is estimated that total retail sales in 1998 will reach RMB2,930 billion, a nominal growth of 9% compared with 1997. The real growth will be slightly higher than 1997 or about the same. Among them, urban retail sales will be about RMB1,800 bn, with a nominal growth of about 9.8% compared with that in 1997. Total retail sales of counties and villages will be RMB1,130 billion, with a nominal growth of about 8.1%. The consumer market still exerted a certain degree of pulling force for GDP growth.

Trend and Development of the Consumer Market in 1999

In 1999, China will again face a complex, uncertain domestic and global economic environment.

In terms of the global environment, there was no obvious improvement in the Southeast Asia financial crisis in 1998. The global deflation seemed to be highly contagious. Under these circumstances, China shouldered an extremely heavy burden to stabilize its economy, such as the 8% GDP growth target for 1998, the promise not to devalue the RMB, and the important reform measures announced in 1998. The global economic recession will continue to affect China directly, in particular by even more severely limiting export demand.

The issue of the 8% GDP growth target for 1998 is not so much about a quantitative target, but is actually a question of whether or not the expected results can be obtained or used as a measure for building up confidence. It is hoped that the realization of the target will raise the confidence of domestic and international investors in China's ability to achieve her economic growth. This will invite a positive response from domestic enterprises to the government's efforts to increase public investment, to stimulate economic growth, and thus to jump-start the economy.

We expect more constricting factors in national economic development in 1999. Thus our estimate of GDP growth in 1999 is lower than the 8% target, at about 7%.

In 1999, the reform of the government structure will enter into a new stage. Various local governments will follow through on their structural retrenchment. The growth of the expected income of urban and rural residents will not be higher than the growth rate of 1998. The estimated nominal growth rate of urban disposal income will be about 4.5%. The average net income of farmers will grow at a nominal rate of about 4% compared with that of 1998.

In regard to supply, the consumer market of 1999 will show that the supply of food will grow slowly. Because of the large inventory, supply should not be a problem. There will be no supply gaps for meat, eggs, sugar, and edible vegetable oils. Because of the oversupply of basic products and insufficient demand, the contradictions in the industrial product structure will remain as prominent as they used to be. There will not be big fluctuations in the prices of industrial products in 1999 because of the expected economic recovery, the price level fixed by supply and demand will rise to a certain degree. The actual rise could be 3.5% higher in real terms than that in 1998, which is still low.

Based on the above analysis, it is estimated that total retail sales in 1999 will grow at about 9% nominally from 1998, for a total of RMB3,200 billion. Because so much actual work has been done in developing rural markets by the government in 1998 (for example, the increase in the construction of electricity grids in villages and adjustment of electricity charges in rural areas) and because of farmers' income increases, the relative weight of the rural market as a percentage of total retail sales in 1999 will be increased 1–2 percentage points from 1998.

In 1999, the consumption structure is still in the process of gradual transformation. The Engels coefficient will fall to 50.5%, 1% lower than that in 1998. The retail sales of food products will grow at about the nominal rate of 7.1%. Spending on clothing will make up 13.15% of total retail sales, growing at a nominal rate of about 5.6%. Spending on other items, including non-commercial products, will grow at a nominal rate of about 19.6%.

Suggestions

During an economic recession, stimulating and maintaining high social expectations is an important issue that deserves special attention. The government, other than insisting on economic development, should introduce some operationable measures for social security. Stabilizing people's psychological expectations is beneficial to social stability and to China's long-term economic development.

The slow growth in personal income of urban and rural residents is the chief constricting factor. Thus, in the coming years, we should place more emphasis on solving the unemployment problem and on raising personal income levels.

During a period of deflation, we should make timely and appropriate adjustments to taxation and price policies to stimulate the growth of effective demand.

Adopting the premise of protecting consumer rights, we should regulate the prices of important industrial products and prevent destructive competition, thus maintaining market order. The crackdown on smuggling and counterfeit goods should be strengthened to protect the legal rights of commerce and industry and to create a fair and equal competitive environment for China's economic development.

The key to the rural market lies in developing the rural economy and raising the income of farmers. The facilities in small towns should be improved and the process of urbanization should be accelerated. The consumption environment of the rural areas should be improved to change the spending preferences of farmers so that the potential market in the rural areas will become an actual one. However, we should be aware of the complexity and difficulties in solving this problem.

AN ANALYSIS AND FORECAST OF CHINA'S STEEL MARKET

WANG JIXIANG
Metallurgy Economic Development Research Centre

Currently, there are 46 steel mills whose annual production is more than 500,000 tons and 28 steel mills producing more than 1 million tons annually. The top 10 steel mills are Baoding Steel, Anshan Steel, Capitol Steel, Wuhan Steel, Baotou Steel, Ma'anshan Steel, Panzhihua Steel, Benxi Steel, Handan Steel, and Taiyuan Steel. The production of these leading steel mills make up about 50% of China's total production.

In 1995, steel consumption in China reached 100 million tons, but after 1995 the growth in demand started to slow down to an average annual growth rate of 2%. Due to the fact that domestic steel production capacity has increased sharply and due to large-scale steel imports, the market is in a state of oversupply. The current production capacity of steel has reached 190 million tons, while the production capacity of steel products exceeds 175 million tons.

Meanwhile, China has scrapped around 30 million tons of backward steel production capacity over the past two years. Based on our estimate, the next peak of steel demand will appear in 2000–2001, when demand for steel will increase at a faster rate. The consumption of steel products is then expected to reach 127.6–139.8 million tons. However, this demand quantity is still less than the production capacity. The accumulated steel production between January and August 1998 was 74.14 million tons, which is 6.1% higher than that last year. The accumulated steel products were 66.4713 million tons, 6.9% higher than that in last year. Based on the statistics provided by the customs, accumulated imported steel between January and August 1998 was 7.64 million tons, down by 11.6% from the same period last year. The accumulated steel between January and August 1998 was 2.24 million tons, down by 20.4% from last year. The estimated steel production in 1998 will reach 104.8 million tons.

The demand for steel products in 1999 will grow more noticeably than that in 1998 because of the stimulus to the economy. As a result of market demand, actual steel product consumption in 1999 will reach 107.5 million tons. The price drop in 1998 will remain significant. But in 1999 we expect to see an increase of total demand and production. Some improvement is also expected in the supply-demand balance. The price of steel products will remain stable, although a small rise of 3%–5% is possible.

REGIONAL DEVELOPMENT

AN ECONOMIC ANALYSIS AND FORECAST FOR TIANJIN CITY

FENG LING, FAN XIAOMIN, ET AL.[1]
Tianjin Information Centre

Tianjin is the largest coastal city in the north of China, and the economic center of the Bohai Bay region. The city has continued to increase its overall economic strength by providing a multitude of diverse services to the surrounding area. Its economic development and prosperity are of vital importance to accelerate the economic development of the Bohai Bay area and North and Northeastern Asia generally.

Analysis of the Current Economic Situation

Stable Quantitative Economic Growth, with Continuous Improvement in the Economic Structure

Between January and August 1998, the GDP of metro Tianjin was RMB83.366 billion, 8.7% higher than that recorded over the same period of the previous year. This growth rate was 0.11% higher than the rate between January and July. Growth in the three industrial tiers stood at 4.99%, 7.22%, and 12.49% respectively. The proportion of tertiary industry within GDP rose to 43.3% from 41.63%, providing the main engine of economic growth.

Within this sector, real estate and transportation and telecommunications grew at the fastest rate, showing 16.53% and 12.22% expansion respectively. These sub-sectors also demonstrated the best development potential.

---

[1] Other writers are ZHANG Junping, LIU Shuhua, and LIANG Na.

Favorable Conditions for Agricultural Production and Stable Conditions for Industrial Production

In the second quarter, Tianjin's drought eased. The summer harvest was excellent, producing 1.52 bn catties, just short of the historic record. Last autumn 4.4 million acres were planted. Production of major farm products ranging from meat, eggs, and vegetables to aquatic items remained stable. Taken together these provided a firm material foundation to anchor the city's growth stability at a prudent level.

Between January and August 1998, the city's total industrial production was pegged at RMB148.318 billion, up 7%, which was 0.3% higher than the rate recorded between January and July. Shareholding enterprises and joint-venture enterprises showed a remarkable recovery, surging 21.4% and 13.9% compared to the same period a year earlier. By contrast, state-owned enterprise production fell by 2.7% during this time. Nevertheless, this decline was tending to level off with each passing month. Sales between January and August stood at 95.96%, or 0.23% higher than was the case the previous year.

Stable Growth of Fixed Asset Investment

Between January and August 1998, fixed asset investment for the city as a whole totaled RMB22.075 billion, growing by 18.3%, 6.2% higher than the rate of expansion over the same period in 1997, but 3.3% lower than that seen between January and July. Many large projects were initiated before August, with some new ones percolating in the preparation stage. On the whole, since 1998, Tianjin's growth rate in terms of fixed asset investment was high. This investment demand stimulus became the main spur for economic growth in 1998.

Growth in Exports, but Decline in the Utilization of Foreign Investment

Between January and August 1998, total external trade (in terms of import/export value) for the entire city amounted to US$6.176 billion, with exports pegged at US$3.536 billion, 15.5% up on a comparable basis. At the same time, growth was off 4.6% compared to the same period in 1997. The total value of exports from joint-venture enterprises was US$2.41 billion, up 29.6%. These comprised 68.2% of Tianjin's total exports for the year, up from 60.7% in 1997. They were also the dominant factor empowering the city's export growth. Tianjin's diversification strategy in exporting had clearly delivered noticeable results.

Between January and August, total committed foreign direct investment in the city was US$2.43 billion, down 7%. Within this amount, committed investment from the United States increased by 25%. By contrast, foreign direct investment from Asian regions and countries such as Hong Kong, Taiwan, and South Korea continued to decline, a by-product of the Asian financial crisis.

Stable Growth in Fiscal Income; Positive Changes in Financial Deposits and Loans

Between January and August 1998, Tianjin's fiscal revenues stood at RMB12.61 billion, up 12.5% and achieving growth targets. Local fiscal income was RMB6.695 billion, up 11.8% on a comparable basis. Since August, positive changes have become apparent in the deposits and loans of financial institutions in Tianjin. Compared with the previous month, at the end of August, various types of deposits in all the city's financial institutions increased by RMB3.479 billion, up RMB2.568 bn on a comparable basis. Business deposits increased sharply, by RMB2.113 bn at the end of August. Growth in personal deposits declined while expenditures on housing, education, and medical care increased.

Increasing Market Demand as Prices Continued to Fall

During the first eight months of 1998, total retail sales in the city were pegged at RMB3.763 billion, up 9.3% on a comparable basis, amounting to a real growth rate of 13.3% after adjustments for price increases. The building of various types of markets continued in a smooth fashion. The sales of food, clothing, and daily goods increased full scale. In short, markets were booming and stable. Nevertheless, overall price levels in Tianjin remained low, with the monthly trend continuing down.

The retail price index between January and August was 96.5, with the consumer price index pegged at 98.9, down 0.4% and 0.6% respectively from the first half of 1998.

Major Problems Continue in Current Economy

Industrial Development Quality Remains Poor, with Unsatisfactory Business Profitability

A survey of 200 enterprises in the city of Tianjin in the second quarter of 1998 showed that the general running of industrial enterprises declined relative to the first quarter. The leading index was off at -0.2, with the key indicator as regards enterprise production conditions pegged at 0.52. Product sales stood at -0.06%, and enterprise profitability at 0.05. Together, these showed slow growth in Tianjin's production output. The connection between sales and production was erratic, and enterprise efficiency low.

Defense Capability in Terms of the Asian Financial Crisis Was Not Strong Enough

Tianjin's exports to major Asian markets all declined by various degrees. Based on a customs survey in the first half of

1998, exports to Korea were down by 32.2%, to Japan by 5.5%, to Hong Kong by 17.7%, and to Singapore by 38.8%. Between January and August, committed foreign direct investment declined by 7%. Not only were Tianjin's exports to Asian countries affected, so was the utilization of foreign direct investment. In essence, this confirmed that Tianjin's capability to fend off the negative fallout triggered by the Asian financial crisis was insufficient.

1998 Economic Forecast

In 1998, the city of Tianjin aimed at maintaining a healthy pace of economic development. In a broad context, China's GDP growth is expected to reach at least 9%. Looking forward to 1998–1999, we can see several favorable factors:

First, China's national macroeconomic policy is favorable to Tianjin's economic growth. Since 1998, the central government has introduced a series of measures to increase fixed asset investment and stimulate the market and economic development in general. These measures will be instrumental in expanding exports, accelerating structural adjustment, and stimulating economic growth. The practical result of this increased investment is expected to spark an upswing in late 1998 and 1999, providing Tianjin with a looser macroeconomic environment.

Second, the city of Tianjin has implemented a development strategy aimed at consolidating a diversified multidimensional economy. A feature of this is to continuously expand the scope of our cooperation with foreign countries. Beyond actively developing markets in Africa, Europe, and America, the city is also concerned with domestic cooperation — in particular extending cooperative arrangements and activities with different provinces and cities — and attracting domestic investment. This domestic connection is seen as a key to stimulating regional economic development, thereby sustaining the functional improvements in the modernized coastal cities.

In line with this, the guiding principle for Tianjin's development is to build the city through science and education. The thrust will be toward nourishing new focal points for economic growth and developing new and high technology industries in general. The Tianjin Binhai New Area, which has become the window of Tianjin's economic development and Tianjin's pillar industries, and which is dependent on advances in science and technology, has become the core of the program for Tianjin's economic development.

Based on model analysis and actual development conditions, Tianjin's economy was expected to grow by 9% in 1998. The major economic indicators used in this analysis are shown in Table 1.

Forecast of Tianjin's Economic Development in 1999

The influence of the following unfavorable factors must be considered when attempting to forecast Tianjin's economic development in 1999:

The international economy and world trade have been adversely affected by the Asian financial crisis. Global economic growth in 1998 stood at approximately 2%, down 1.2%. Tianjin's exports and utilized foreign direct investment have also been affected to a certain degree. Asian countries and regions make up more than 50% of Tianjin's export trade. The negative effect of the Asian financial crisis has thus had a decided impact on Tianjin's effort to expand exports.

Table 1
Forecast of 1998–1999 Tianjin Macroeconomic Indicators

Indicators	1997 actual	1998 forecast	1999 forecast
GDP* (RMB bn)	124.04	138.027	155.415
Growth rate (%)	12.1	9	9.6
Primary industry* (RMB bn)	7.455	7.875	8.282
Growth rate (%)	7.7	11.7	
Secondary industry* (RMB bn)	64.388	70.218	78.045
Tertiary industry (RMB bn)	52.197	59.934	69.088
Growth rate (%)	13.4		
Food production (million tons)	2.0616	1.965	2.03
Growth rate (%)	-0.4	-4.7	3.3
Added value of industrial production* (RMB bn)	58.021	63.46	71.028
Growth rate (%)	11.8		
Total fixed asset investment (RMB bn)	49.866	60	66.6
Growth rate (%)	14.4	20	11
Total retail value of goods consumed (RMB bn)	53.502	59.651	66.279
Growth rate (%)	13.0	11.5	11.1
Retail price index (previous year = 100)	100.7	97.3	99
Cost of living index (previous year = 100)	103.1	99.5	101
Fiscal income (RMB bn)	16.912	18.725	21.33
Growth rate (%)	13.5	10.7	13.9
Fiscal expenditure (RMB bn)	12.28	13.888	15.981
Growth rate (%)	8.5	13.1	15.1
Balance of deposits of financial institutions at end of year (RMB bn)	163.495	185.667	210.124
Growth rate (%)	16.6	13.6	13.2
Balance of loans of financial institutions at end of year (RMB bn)	150.291	171.12	197.164
Growth rate (%)	10.5	13.9	15.2
Total imports (US$ bn)	5.005	5.789	6.569
Growth rate (%)	17.8	15.7	13.5
Total exports (US$ bn)	5.018	5.536	6.228
Growth rate (%)	23.9	10.3	12.5
Utilized foreign investment (US$ bn)	3.423	3.689	4.206
Growth rate (%)	14.7	7.8	14
Average personal income of urban residents (RMB)	6,608.56	7,269.73	8,186.44
Growth rate (%)	10.7	10	12.6
Average net income of rural residents (RMB)	3,548	3,950.49	4,339.68
Growth rate (%)	12.9	11.3	9.9

Note: The absolute figures with * are current prices. Growth rates are calculated on a
comparable basis. Fiscal expenditure is calculated according to the local standard.
Imports and exports are calculated according to foreign trade standards.

Tianjin is a city with a strong industrial base. The tasks of merging, reforming, and reorganizing the city's key enterprises are arduous. Most enterprises, especially those in the state-owned sub-sector, carry even heavier burdens. On the one hand, facing fierce competition in the market, these enterprises must find their own ways to develop, reform, and renew themselves while increasing investment. At the same time, these enterprises carry with them the implicit heavy burden of overcoming the difficulties of re-employing substantial numbers of unemployed workers while taking care of some retired workers' livelihood. As a result, the deepening of the reforms and enterprise development plans now face serious challenges.

Domestically, businesses in general must address the situation created by the emerging buyer's market. Any changes in the production and management of some of these large enterprises cannot help but affect the economy of the whole city. Since 1998, price wars have been rampant over a range of products such as microwave ovens, air conditioners, VCDs, and mobile phones, affecting sales — and profit — growth. Meanwhile, low economic efficiency has forced many of these enterprises to limit production, thus adding to the drag on the local economy.

In 1999, although many of these unfavorable factors still prevail, a counterbalancing effect that will once again be favorable to growth can be seen given the direction of China's national macroeconomic policy. Current macroeconomic regulation and control will tend to stimulate demand and help to facilitate healthy economic growth. The supply environment needed for economic development is relatively loose; this environment is now becoming a reality in Tianjin, meaning the city's macroeconomy is becoming a more ideal environment in terms of maintaining sustainable, healthy, and steady economic growth. In fact, this environment may amount to a rare, and even historic, opportunity for Tianjin's development to enter the next century. As the reform of state-owned enterprises and adjustment of other key structures continue to deepen, Tianjin will achieve new thresholds of success in its effort to reform its economic system and structure.

On the basis of the real economic situation in Tianjin in relation to macroeconomic analyses of domestic and international conditions, Tianjin will maintain an appropriate economic growth at an estimated rate of 9.6% in 1999. The percentage of the three tiers of the city's industries relative to GDP will increase to 44.5%. Moreover, the development of tertiary industry will contribute to a qualitative improvement in the kind of economic growth that results (see Table 1).

Industry: In recent years, as the industrial structure has improved, automobiles and machinery, electronics, chemicals, and metallurgy have become the four pillar industries of Tianjin. Indeed, some of the city's leading industrial products have earned an enviable reputation both domestically and internationally. So as domestic and international markets change, Tianjin aims to accelerate the pace of its development of new and, in particular, high technology industries, while continuously improving production technologies. 1999 is likely to be fraught with both opportunities and challenges for Tianjin industries. Major tasks — and challenges — will include strengthening both the management and operation of the city's enterprises, and addressing the need to nourish new points of economic growth.

Agriculture: The guiding development principles in this sector will be to stabilize the rural economy, increase investment in agricultural technology, and to maintain the stable growth of production of grain and other major agricultural products.

Investment and consumption: In 1999, a looser national macroeconomic environment should provide a substantial boost in terms of demand and overall market activity. The consumer mindset is maturing, and evidence of this can be seen in changes in consumption styles, namely the trend toward diversification. Housing, for example, will become a hot point for investment.

Fiscal and financial sectors: The year-end balance of deposits in financial institutions in 1999 is estimated at RMB210.124 billion, a growth of 13.2%. The balance of loans on the books of financial institutions is expected to be RMB197.164 billion, a growth of 15.2%. With an estimated growth rate of 15.1%, the growth of fiscal expenditures will be higher after investment demand is stimulated. This will make a real contribution to Tianjin's ability to withstand future financial crises.

Foreign trade: With the ongoing negative fallout resulting from the Asian financial crisis, Tianjin implemented timely diversification measures to explore multi-dimensional export markets. As exports to countries like Japan, Korea, and Singapore declined, Tianjin has actively developed new markets in other Asian regions, as well as in countries in Africa, Latin America, and Europe, to offset this negative aspect.

Tianjin's economy in 1999 will maintain an appropriately vigorous and prudent development. With the stimulation of investment and consumer demand, more markets have been opened. This means a 9.6% GDP growth rate for the city can be realized if the effort necessary to achieve this goal is sustained, difficulties notwithstanding. In keeping with this, we must work hard to acquire new knowledge, and innovate within our existing systems, both in terms of our thinking and our actual day-to-day work. In the face of the historic changes we face at the turn of this century, all of the city's citizens must unite to seize the opportunity to develop Tianjin into an important modern port and economic center in northern China. This is the basis for the city's brimming hope and energy as it enters a new millennium.

AN ECONOMIC ANALYSIS AND FORECAST FOR HEBEI PROVINCE

NIE CHENXI, ET AL.[1]

*Research Department of the Hebei Provincial People's Government;
and Hebei Economic Information Centre*

Analysis of the Current Situation in Hebei

Following the implementation of the central government and Hebei Provincial Government economic policy measures, the province's economic growth rate has increased gradually. In the first quarter of 1998, provincial GDP grew by 9.2%, by 9.6% in the first half, and by 10.2% for January to September, which was consistent with expectations.

Industrial production recovered quickly. Between January and August 1998, the total value of industrial production stood at RMB167.55 billion, an increase of 10.4% compared with the same period in 1997; in short demonstrating a slowly developing rising trend.

The growth of fixed asset investment accelerated. Between January and August 1998, the completed value of such investment was RMB45.13 billion, a growth of 21.6% relative to the same period last year, and 3.6% higher than that recorded in the previous seven months. The value of actual investment in August was RMB8.4 billion, an increase of 37.2% compared to August 1997. Investment in infrastructure projects grew rapidly. These investments were made in line with the requirements of national infrastructure industry policy, specifically in the areas of agriculture, electricity, transportation, telecommunications, and urban infrastructure construction. In the first eight months of 1998, they stood at RMB27.95 billion, an increase of 52.2% compared with the

---

[1] Other authors of this chapter are CHEN Wanqin, MA Zhankui, and LIU Yuqi.

same period last year. In fact, they have become the major feature of increased investment in Hebei.

The consumer market, meanwhile, remained steady. Between January and August 1998, total retail sales in Hebei reached RMB80.97 billion, a growth of 10.5% over the same period the previous year. And in August 1998, the growth rate was pegged at 11.7%, suggesting a slow recovery was under way.

Prices generally continued low, while the prices of some major commodities began to rise once again. Between January and August 1998, the total retail price index in Hebei was down by 2.2% compared with the same period of last year, while the consumer price index was down by 1.5%. In August 1998, these figures fell by 3.8% and 3.4% respectively. Up to August 1998, retail price inflation in Hebei had fallen for forty-four consecutive months.

Other problems, however, are apparent in Hebei's economic development, the most noticeable being:

The rate of fund realization for project construction was low. In the first eight months of 1998, there were a total of 120 either continuing or new projects in the whole province, with the actual investment rate being only 49.9%, a drop of 3.1% compared with the same period last year. The failure of investment to materialize became one of the major causes of construction delays.

Enterprise profitability also declined. Between January and August 1998, the total provincial budget for actual industrial production was RMB40.154 billion, up by 1.4% compared with the same period last year. Realized profits and taxes fell by 36.1%. As a result, business losses were up by 68.9%.

Also, exports and the effective utilization of foreign investment were off. Between January and August 1998, total exports from Hebei province were US$2.05 billion, down by 0.6% compared with the same period in 1997, and within this exports to Asia were down by 14.3%. The actual utilization of foreign investment was US$950 million, down by 18.7% on an equivalent basis, of which foreign direct investment was pegged at US$790 million, down by 18.1% compared with the same period in 1997.

Growth of farmers' personal income was likewise slow.   And loans to industries were down, meaning sources of production capital were uncertain. Thus pressure increased in terms of ensuring the basic living standard of those workers laid off by state-owned enterprises along with plans for their redeployment.

Estimate of Hebei Province's Economic Performance in 1998

In general, most of the economic targets were expected to be achieved as planned.   Gross GDP was estimated to reach RMB445.07 billion, up by 11%.   Within this, primary industry was expected to turn over RMB82.05 billion, an expansion of 6.3%; secondary industry RMB221.45 billion, up 12.4%; tertiary industry RMB141.57 billion, up 11.1%.   Total fixed asset investment will amount to about RMB169.2 billion, a 16.2% growth over the year. The investment rate is pegged at 38%, while average urban personal income will reach RMB4758, a growth of 5.2% in real terms. Average rural personal net income, by comparison, will reach RMB2,510, a growth of 5.9% in real terms.   Total retail sales have been fixed at RMB133.1 billion, up 11.5%.   Fiscal revenue will be RMB34.16 billion, up 13.6%.   The fiscal expenditure will be RMB31.18 billion, up 14.2%.   Total export sales have been estimated at US$4 billion, a growth of 2.8%.   The retail price index for 1998 will be 99 (100 for 1997); the consumer price index will be 100.

Economic Forecast for Hebei Province in 1999

Analysis of the General Macroeconomic Environment Influencing Economic Growth

1999 is an extremely important year as well as being the last year of the 20th century. The outlook for Hebei's economy in 1999 is full of challenges, and yet is also replete with opportunities.

In light of the global environment: the financial crisis, which started in the emerging market countries of Asia in 1997, soon spread to Japan, Russia, and South America, resulting in an economic recession in one-third of the world's countries. And there are signs that the crisis may well get worse. Even the United States is beginning to feel the impact. Based on authoritative estimates, global economic growth in 1999 will be 2%, down 1.2% from 1998. Although there will not be a great depression in 1999, the present situation remains extremely severe.

Domestically, Macau will return to China in 1999; The People's Republic of China will celebrate its 50th anniversary, while the macroeconomic situation is expected to move in a favorable direction.

First, the implementation of various policy measures in 1998, such as the increase in investment, the expansion of domestic demand, and the encouragement of exports, will act as a strong stimulus in promoting economic growth. In addition, the fiscal, financial, investment, consumption, and export policies of 1999 will be positive and proactive.

Second, because the RMB is not internationally convertible in its capital accounts, and because of the limited openness of our stock markets, expectations for the inflow of short-term international funds remain limited. Thus, the chance of chaos triggered by foreign speculators is very slim. In fact, it is most unlikely China will encounter a financial crisis in 1999.

Third, although the pressure for creating employment opportunities has gone up, our society's ability to endure the pains of unemployment has also increased.   As a result, the possibility of social instability has been reduced.

Fourth, strong government leadership and appropriate counter-measures will provide important backups for the province's and country's economic development in 1999.

Analysis of Hebei's Economic Situation in 1999

Analysis of investment demand: investment in infrastructure projects for 1998 increased, as did the number of new and ongoing projects.   In 1999, still more projects will come onstream. Investment demand will be maintained at a high level.

At the same time, in 1998 both the nation and Hebei province undertook extraordinary measures to ensure the expansion of infrastructure construction and the realization of investment funds. It will be difficult to match the same intensity of effort in 1999. There are fewer valuable projects and the selection of good projects is becoming more difficult.   Not surprisingly, then, investment demand in 1999 is expected to be weaker than that in 1998.

Analysis of consumer demand: The expenses expected for housing, medical care, social security, and education will increase. The propensity to save will also increase as current spending capability decreases.   In other words, at least a portion of current spending will be suspended and held over for long-term spending. Savings will increase and the propensity to spend will decrease. Although there are no hot items available in the consumer market, infrastructure construction will stimulate the production materials market in urban areas. Sales of production materials, like steel and cement, will increase sharply.   In particular, flooded areas along the Yangtze River and the Songhua River will spark strong demand. These two regions are prime markets for Hebei products, so demand from them will affect the provincial market and invigorate the production of consumer products.

Analysis of export demand: In the aftermath of the Asian financial crisis, the global economic environment will deteriorate in 1999. Export growth is expected to show a continued decline. In 1998, Hebei's exports benefited from large increases in exports to Latin America, Europe, and North America at rates of 64.9%, 33.2%, and 23.8%, respectively. However, as the economies of Latin America and the United States slow down, this market vitality will wane. Nevertheless, as the government implements a new export tax rebate policy, "export fever" on the part of the province's businesses may yet make up for the shortfall caused by these global factors.

Analysis of capital supply: In terms of funding sources, funds made available from the national budget and treasury bonds have been in decline. This reflects the fact that funds raised by the central government, provinces, and counties are also showing varying degrees of decline. As a result, the actual supply of funds is understandably inadequate. Although the government has tried to increase the credit lines of the banks, the banks themselves have strengthened their control over risk management and are now tending to refrain from lending. Moreover, as a result of the financial crisis, Hebei's and China's advantage in attracting foreign investment is gradually diminishing. A buyer's market has been formed. Industrial production capacity of enterprises is in surplus. The average rate of production utilization has fallen. And, in our view, the whole utilization of foreign investment in 1999 will not show any substantial increase.

Analysis of prices: By the end of 1998, the price index will bottom out. In 1999, prices will remain stable or show a gradual rise. The major support for this argument is as follows:

First, 1998 saw the second biggest harvest in Hebei's history, and this, in turn, provided a strong foundation for stable market prices. However, due to the implementation of the reforms in grain distribution and the effect of the 1998 floods, food prices still increased slightly, helping to push up the prices of products related to animal husbandry and fishery. Second, the government's implementation of its expansionary policy aimed at boosting domestic demand will inevitably begin to have an effect, albeit after a delay. And with the recovery of demand, market prices will rise to a certain extent.

Forecast of Key Economic Indicators — and Their Impact — in Hebei in 1999

By applying mathematical models on the basis of three grades of high, middle, and low, we arrive at the following three projections (see table 1).

Table 1
Forecast of the Increase Rate of Major Economic Indicators in Hebei Province in 1999

Unit %

Indicators	Projection 1	Projection 2	Projection 3
GDP (Current price)	10.5	11	11.5
Primary industry	5.4	5.8	6.1
Secondary industry	11.7	12.2	12.8
Tertiary industry	10.8	11.3	11.8
Total fixed asset investment	15.8	16.5	17.2
Urban resident average annual personal income (RMB)	5.7	5.9	6.1
Rural resident net annual personal income (RMB)	5.4	5.7	6
Total retail sales	12.1	12.6	13.1
Fiscal revenue	13.5	14.1	14.8
Fiscal expenditure	14	14.7	15.2
Total exports	10	10.6	11
Retail price inflation rate	2	2	2
Consumer price inflation rate	3	3	3

Seven Key Measures of the Recent Macroeconomic Adjustment Program

In Terms of Investment, We Must Concentrate on the Development of Real Estate

At the end of 1998, welfare housing will come to an end. Housing distribution will be monetarized. We must seize this favorable opportunity to expand investment in real estate to about the RMB20 bn level. Doing so will help to increase Hebei's GDP by 3%.

In Terms of Agriculture, We Must Concentrate on the Construction of Agricultural Facilities and, in Particular, Increase Winter Production Capacity

Combining a high-tech and high-yield farm showcase, we need to build a series of new model greenhouses to develop factory breeding, horticulture, fruit farming, and no-soil cultivation. In addition, we must mechanize the planting and sprinkling in greenhouses.

In Terms of Industries, We Should Concentrate on Helping Small- and Medium-sized Enterprises to Improve Their Level of Technology

Currently, small- and medium-sized enterprises suffer from the lack of capital, lack of channels for loans, and lack of funds for technological renovation. We place technology improvement in small- and medium-sized enterprises at the top of the priority list in terms of expanding domestic demand.

As Regards Distribution, We Should Concentrate on the Construction of Commercial Facilities in Small Towns

During the urbanization process, we should emphasize establishing commercial facilities in small towns. Industry and commerce should cooperate to extend new brand products and their sales networks to rural areas. Specifically, a wide range of products should be offered to farmers.

In the Area of Taxation and Fiscal Finances, Tax Management Should Be Strengthened, and the Distribution and Management of Fiscal Resources Should Be Made More Reasonable

On the one hand, we must improve the collection and management of non-mainstream taxation and non-tax fiscal income. In particular, we must continue to exploit the potential tax resources of enterprise profits, personal income, and deed tax so that we will be able to collect all that is due. On the other hand, we must adjust the expenditure structure to increase investment in technology, education, and agriculture. Priority should be given to funding social security and deployment and textile production. Expenses based on management fees should be reduced. The scope of the government's purchase of goods should be expanded.

In Terms of Foreign Trade, Exports to Developed Countries Should Be Strengthened; Technology Imports Should also Be Stressed

Based on the export performance of Hebei in 1998, there is still great potential for growth in exports to North America, Europe, and Latin America. On the basis of market diversification, we should concentrate our emphasis on expanding export markets in the developed countries.

In Regard to Prices, We Should Increase and Improve Our Control over the Prices in Real Estate and Various Services

In supporting the reform of the housing system, we should establish an appropriate pricing framework for a new housing system, and gradually improve the way prices are set. We must also carry out a full-scale eradication of fees and charges connected with real estate transactions. Unreasonable fees should be scrapped; excessively high charges should be lowered; and the overall housing price structure synchronized. Management should be strengthened to control the prices of services like medical care and education and various agencies should be empowered to prevent chaotic increases in charges.

Six Relationships Must Be Handled with Care

Handling the Relationship between Development Enthusiasm and Financial Reform Properly

Aiming at achieving the 11% growth target, Hebei province has demonstrated its enthusiasm and has set targets for financial institutions throughout the province. The key at the present time is to maintain enthusiasm for development while preventing any irresponsible investment or possible financial crisis. We must be very cautious about achieving development at the cost of sacrificing economic control. We should not coerce banks into making loans to unprofitable enterprises and projects merely for the sake of development. As importantly, we should not drive the next round of economic development in the wrong direction. Therefore, we should, on the one hand, maintain economic growth, and on the other, balance the following relationships:

* between economic and financially prudent development
* between macro and micro economic benefits
* between an increase in lending and proper guarantees of credit worthiness

Only by doing these things will we effectively meet the capital requirement of enterprises and the quality requirement demanded by new credit suppliers.

We Must Handle the Relationship between Direct Fiscal Investment and the Leveraging Effect of Fiscal Policy Properly

Under the current situation, we can increase — to a certain extent — the funds needed for infrastructure investment through payment adjustments, and by increasing income and reducing expenditures.   However, a large-scale increase is not feasible. This means that in infrastructure investment, we must utilize more broad fiscal means; measures such as interest subsidies or tax exemptions may prove effective in solving this problem.   We should fully utilize the leverage potential of fiscal policy in guiding and stimulating domestic demand, and in increasing the proportion of private and foreign investments.

We Must Properly Handle the Relationship between Stimulating Investment and Consumer Demand

The stimulation of investment demand, especially *vis-à-vis* infrastructure, is a relatively simple task, because the government will play an essential role. Comparatively speaking, the government has fewer measures available to stimulate consumer demand. Its guiding effect is, therefore, weaker, and the stimulation effect takes longer.

There is a risk of a runaway increase in investment when direct stimulation is employed. By comparison, in stimulating consumer demand, we can spark the recovery of investment demand, which can in turn increase total demand and realize the ultimate aim of economic structural adjustment.   We must fully understand the policy of the central government in expanding domestic demand, and effective consumer demand in particular.

We Must Handle the Relationship between the Economic Growth Rate and Economic Benefits Properly

For Hebei province, the low rate of growth seen in industrial production was the major cause for the decline in enterprise profitability in 1998.   Because of insufficient effective demand, the supply-demand relationship deteriorated further, resulting in falling prices.   Without a high growth rate, there is no economic benefit. Therefore, we must implement all of the central government's measures to expand effective demand while stimulating economic growth in order to maintain a high rate of growth.

At the same time, a high growth rate alone cannot guarantee substantial economic benefits.   Currently, the more important issue in the decline of enterprise profitability is a structural one.   Thus, while aiming at a high rate of growth, we must make an even greater effort in solving the mismatch between supply and demand structures and overcoming other serious problems such as the high rate of debt among the province's enterprises, the slow turnaround of capital, the low level of enterprise management, and so on.   In short, we must work hard to shift the decline in enterprise profitability and to raise the quality of economic growth.

We Must Handle the Relationship between Economic Stimulation and Structural Adjustment Properly

In 1998, with both global and domestic challenges, the government's policy of increasing investment in infrastructure as the starting point for economic stimulation was indispensible. However, we should also concern ourselves with the adjustment and improvement of our economic structure.   In particular, as the economic situation in 1999 improves, economic stimulation should not be the major issue; structural adjustment should be the main theme.

In the current relaxed investment environment, the most effective means for adjusting the economic structure is to alter the investment structure. For Hebei province, recent investment in high-tech has been comparatively low. In 1997, total investment in equipment and machinery made up 33% of the total, whereas construction made up 66%. Our national ratio between equipment and machinery on the one hand and construction on the other is 38:62, while the ratio in developed countries is 45:55. Therefore, for medium and long-term development, we must adjust our investment structure to raise investment in high-tech. First, in terms of infrastructure, we need to upgrade our technology and enlarge the investment proportion allotted to education. Second, we must select promising projects with high-tech, high profitability, and which give a strong impetus to economic growth. Third, to catch up with the world's technology leaders, we must increase the proportion of fixed asset investment in high-tech equipment and machinery.

We Must Handle the Relationship between Short-term Economic Growth Targets and Long-term Social Development Goals Properly

Because of the changes in the global and domestic external environments, our economy has entered a period of sub-par growth. It is now impossible, and indeed improper, to aim at a higher growth rate. In addition, facing the reality of oversupply, expanding production will only create overstocking and wastage. We must establish a new development vista by changing from the simple pursuit of economic growth to a pursuit of human development, and from an emphasis on material resources to human resources. We must aim, in other words, at improvements in the quality of life, and the expansion of opportunities for human development and capability.

AN ECONOMIC ANALYSIS AND FORECAST FOR JILIN PROVINCE

QU XIAOMIN , GAO YOUFU AND FU CHENG[1]

Jilin Academy of Social Sciences

Estimate and Forecast of the Rate of Economic Growth of Jilin Province in 1998

Since the beginning of 1998, Jilin province has faithfully followed the spirit of the central government's policies in order to stimulate economic growth. We have organized three major assaults involving the reform of state-owned enterprises, structural adjustment while reducing losses and increasing profits, and the reemployment project. In order to raise the quality and efficiency of economic operations, we placed emphasis on the adjustment and improvement of the economic structure. Even in the difficult macroeconomic environment, we managed to maintain reasonably stable operating conditions through expanding domestic demand and working hard to stimulate both the investment and consumer demand. Based on the forecasting model, and an empirical analysis of actual production, investment, and consumption figures, we predict that the total fixed asset investment of Jilin province in 1998 will grow by 10%, total retail sales by 7.2%, and the GDP growth of the province by 8.3%, slightly higher than the national average.

Analysis of the Total Supply

(1) The fundamental position of agriculture in the national economy was strengthened. The bumper harvest and the development of cattle ranching provided strong support for

---

[1] This article is based on research conducted by the "Analysis & Forecast of the Economic Situation" project team of the Jilin Academy of Social Sciences and was written up by Qu Xiaoming, Gao Youfu, and Fu Cheng.

economic growth.   Since the beginning of 1998, Jilin province has followed through with the implementation of various agricultural policies.   Investment in agriculture also increased. After a disastrous year in 1997, food grain production recovered.   Total production will reach 45.5 bn jin, which is close to the historic record in 1996.   It is estimated that agricultural production over the entire year will increase by 10.4%. Primary production will increase by 9.4%, contributing 2.47% to GDP growth.

(2)   Industrial production maintained a slow rate of growth. Between January and August 1998, acetylene, cement, plate glass, steel, and steel products increased by 23.2%, 2.2%, 31.6%, 18.4%, and 9.3% respectively, as compared to the same period in the previous year.   However, the production of automobiles, railroad passenger carriages, and other industrial products all fell in absolute terms.   The growth rates of total industrial   production and   industrial value-added production, after falling to -16.2% and -20.6% at the beginning of the year, gradually   recovered   to   6.9%   and   5.8%   in   August.   The industrial   value-added   production   of   the   entire   year   is estimated   to   grow   by   7.0%,   contributing   3.38%   to   GDP growth.

(3)   The construction industry gradually recovered.   The growth rates of value-added production in construction in the first and second quarters were -29.9% and -5.1%.   Following increased government investment, the estimated full year growth in construction is 3.9%, contributing 0.48% to economic growth.

(4)   Growth   in   transportation,   post   and   telecommunications industry was slow, and internal structural change occurred. The amount of freight transportation by rail and road in the transportation industry and freight turnaround showed a monthly decline.   The total business volume of the post and telecommunications industry grew amid fluctuations, and between January–August was up 41.8% as compared to the same   period   in   1997.   The   transportation,   posts   and

telecommunications industry is estimated to grow by about 7.8%, contributing 0.48% to economic growth.

(5)   In commerce, stable growth was maintained but the rate declined slightly.   Affected by insufficient demand, the wholesale industry, retail industry, restaurants, and catering industry all declined monthly.   By August, the growth rate had declined by about 50%.   The first quarter growth rate was 11.9%, and the overall rate for the first half of the year was 8.4%.   The estimated full-year growth is about 10.9%, contributing 0.73% to economic growth.

The five major industries as mentioned above will collectively contribute 7.27% to GDP growth, and about 88.1% of the total GDP value-added.   These are similar to the figures in recent years.

Analysis of Total Demand

(1)   Fixed asset investment increased monthly and this provided effective support for economic growth.   For reasons similar to elsewhere in the country, the decline in exports and insufficient consumer demand in Jilin in 1998 reduced these factors' role in economic growth.   Therefore, the role of investment demand will have to be greater than the average historical level in order to make up for the shortfall in export demand and consumer demand.   Only thus will it be possible to achieve the economic growth target.   Between January and August, the growth of fixed asset investment by the state-owned enterprises in the province was 18% higher than that in the same period last year.   Taking into consideration the active adjustments in the national investment plans and the fiscal capability of Jilin province, the estimated full year fixed asset investment in the province will reach about RMB40 bn, about RMB3.54 bn up on the figure in 1997.   Based on these estimates, this will result in general GDP growth being about 8.3%.   If fixed asset investment does not reach RMB40 bn, the provincial GDP growth may well be below 8%.   If RMB42 bn in investment is

reached and the consumer demand increases appropriately, economic growth of 9% may be achieved.

(2) The decline in the growth rate of consumer demand reduced its role in stimulating the economy.

From the beginning of 1998, the growth of consumer demand in Jilin province declined monthly. A direct effect of this was a decline in the growth of retail sales from 13% at the beginning of the year to 5.6% in August, which was lower than the GDP growth rate. This was the second occurrence of such a serious situation since 1978. The reasons for this were: First, industrial production declined. The number of enterprises which stopped or half-stopped their production increased. The number of workers who did not get paid or were made redundant increased. The size of the urban low-income group increased, which changed the income expectations of the urban residents. Based on the model analysis, the average cost of living for urban residents in 1998 was RMB3,784.2, down by 0.6% from last year. Second, since the beginning of 1998, the Government has introduced reform measures for housing, social security, medical care, and education, which increased the expected expenditure of residents. This forced an increase in personal propensity to save and affected current consumer spending. Thus, the insufficient consumer demand will not change for the better in a noticeable way in 1998. However, as some of the investment was transformed into consumer demand in the second half, the full year's consumer demand can still maintain a certain rate of growth. The estimated full year growth rate of retail sales will be about 7.2%.

(3) The interprovincial trade and export situation are serious. Since the beginning of 1998, there has been no change in the net import situation in interprovincial trade either in consumer products or investment products. In addition, because of the tighter total economic situation, as well as product structure and product quality factors, the net import situation has become even worse. In external trade, Jilin's main export markets are

Japan, North and South Korea, and Russia. As a result of the effects of the Southeast Asian financial crisis, there was a rather large decline in exports. The figures indicate that the total export/import trade completed by the province between January and August 1998 was US$1.029 bn, down by 1.7% on an equivalent basis. The total exports were valued at US$795 million, down by 8.5% on an equivalent basis.

The effects on the province's economic growth of the increase in interprovincial trade imports and reduction in exports were obvious. In addition, the growth of consumer demand was slow, which certainly affected the effects of investment demand on economic growth to a certain extent. Even if the total fixed asset investment can reach RMB40 bn, up by 10% from last year, the economic growth rate will only reach about 8.3%.

We must point out that even though 8.3% economic growth is 1% lower than that in 1997, it is already quite high, compared with both the historic records in the past 20 years and with the figures of other countries. We must also recognize that when the international environment for economic development is unfavorable, when domestic demand is shrinking, and in a situation where the pressures on employment are increasing and new growth points have not yet been formed, achieving a rate of growth like this is already quite a success.

Characteristics and Major Problems in the Economy in Jilin in 1998

The Environment for Economic Growth – Great Difficulties in Jump-starting Economic Growth

Since the beginning of 1998, in order to stop the declining rate of economic growth, the Chinese government has implemented measures to jump-start economic recovery, in order to ensure the realization of the 8% goal for economic development. In the international environment, the effects of the financial crisis, which affected some Southeast Asian countries, have become apparent in China. The role of exports in promoting China's economic growth has weakened, and the national economy has become a buyer's market. The market for general processing industries has seen serious oversupply. To jump-start economic growth in such an environment, the government cannot increase investment by simply providing large amounts of loans, but needs to expand investment in basic industries in order to stimulate the total investment demand. When the investment situation is unclear as at present, we have to make great efforts both in Jilin and in the country as a whole if we are to achieve the jump-starting of the economy.

The Structure of Economic Growth – Some Improvement in the Structure of Industrial Growth

The economic structure of growth in Jilin province has been fragile, and the ability to withstand a market crisis has been weak. Since the beginning of 1998, this situation has started to change. On the one hand, the support areas of the pillar industries for economic growth have increased. The scale of the automobile and petrochemical industries, which were developed as pillar industries for Jilin province, is rather large, and their development is comparatively mature. However, hampered by weak market sales, their role in promoting economic growth of the province has been relatively weak. Three other industries — pharmaceuticals, food, and electronics — which are being cultivated as future pillar industries, developed at a faster rate. Their contribution to economic growth was more noticeable. In the first half of 1998, the total production of these three industries constituted 43.9% of the total industrial value-added production in the province. Between January and June, the growth rate of the total production of medium-sized to large industrial enterprises was only 2.7%, while the growth rate of production by small to medium-sized enterprises was 29.5%. The latter constituted 71.3% of the total industrial added value. These changes in the two areas showed that although the contribution of Jilin's industry to the total economic growth of the province has declined in the last few years, the structure of growth within industry has started to improve and the area of support for economic growth has expanded.   This is beneficial to increasing the contribution of industry to economic growth and will thus be beneficial to improving the overall structure of economic growth.

The Mechanism of Growth – the Guiding Role of the Market Has Been Further Strengthened

Since the beginning of 1998, the capacity of the light industries and non–state–owned enterprises to adapt to market changes has increased.   The light industries have reversed the former situation whereby they grew at a rate slower than the heavy industries. Between January and August, the growth rate of value-added production was 7.7% higher than that of heavy industries, and 6.1% higher than industry overall.   Between January and June, the production of the non-state sectors grew by 21.2%, which was 16.5% higher than the figures for state-owned and state-controlled economic production.   This shows that the guiding role of the market has become more powerful.

The Quality of Growth – the Unsubstantiated Element of Economic Growth Has Been Reduced

Because the jump-starting gave rise to an increase in investment in basic industries and strengthened investment in renovation, the investment structure has become more reasonable. As a result, the unsubstantiated element of economic achievement has been reduced.   Between January and August 1998, fixed asset investment in the state sector of Jilin province grew at a rate 18% higher than that last year, and the investment in renovation increased by almost 50%.   Of 188 key projects, 115 came under the category of renovation.   This will have a positive effect on the upgrading and development of current products and new products, which will in turn facilitate the upgrading of industry.   Although the rate of economic growth declined, the quality has been raised.

Given the above conditions, the overall economic situation of Jilin province is good.   However, the situation of a sustained reduction in the economic benefits of industry has not yet been turned around.   The problem is quite prominent.   There are three main reasons for this: First, there have been changes in demand, the industrial structure, product structure, and enterprise structure, in order to adapt to the conditions of a buyer's market.   A great number of assets are also now awaiting reorganization and cannot yield their potential benefits.   Second, the pilot projects for reform of state-owned enterprises have just now ended, and the experiences are now only starting to be spread more widely.   The innovation of a modern enterprise system is now only in its initial stage, and it cannot yet generate any positive contribution to economic growth.   Third, some of the reformative measures, the introduction of many fee-charging projects, and the increase of fund-raising projects have resulted in a transfer of economic benefits, an increase of the cost of business for enterprises, and a redistribution of some of the enterprises' profits.   In addition, the historic burden of the state-owned enterprises is heavy and has lowered the ability of some enterprises to stand up by themselves, lacking the strength to follow through on development.   This adds to the difficulties in production and operation.   Some enterprises are in difficulties in maintaining even simple reproduction.

Outlook for Economic Development in 1999

In 1999, the economy of Jilin will see a steady situation, and the growth rate will be slow.   However, there will be marked progress in the fostering and building up of economic growth potential.   The major reasons for this are:

First, the policy measures implemented by the government in contra-cyclical adjustment will create positive effects on economic growth in 1999.   The emphasis on increasing investment in infrastructure since the beginning of 1998 will stimulate investment demand.   The estimated multiplier effect of investment will be realized in 1999, thus providing new development opportunities for infrastructure and related industries.   The improvement in the fixed asset investment structure will have positive effects on future economic growth.

Second, the construction of agricultural field infrastructure facilities and irrigation facilities have been identified as key supporting spheres in the policy of expanding domestic demand. The substantial increase in investment by the government will further strengthen the protection systems for agricultural production in Jilin.   The bumper harvest in 1998 will raise the potential for productivity increases by farmers in 1999.   The effective progress in the industrialization of agriculture and the increase in the size of operations have created favorable conditions for the steady growth of the ranching industry in agricultural regions.   All these will provide strong support for growth in the agricultural economy in 1999.

Third, the further deepening of the structural adjustment and enterprise reform will encourage the integration of the supply system and market demand.   In the current buyer's market, the major contradiction between total supply and demand is due to the failure of the supply structure to adapt itself to the market.   The problem with the system and structure of supply is a fundamental one.   In the new year, the government will further accelerate the strategic reorganization of the state sector economy and increase funds to support the reform and development of state-owned enterprises. Thereby, some of the state-owned enterprises which are able to adapt themselves to market development will see enhanced vitality.   The non-state sector will also, after receiving "state-owned enterprise treatment," see faster development.   The degree of concordance between the supply system in the national economy and market demand will increase to provide a new structural foundation for future economic growth.

Fourth, new and high technologies will be developed at a faster rate, following the implementation of many encouragement measures by Jilin province.   Projects in bio-engineering, electronic information, new materials, and advanced production technology will be gradually completed, and thus will create a certain promotional effect on economic growth.

Certainly, there are still many factors that will limit economic growth in 1999. The major ones are: first, the Southeast Asian financial crisis and slow growth in the international economic environment will exert a negative effect on China's exports and ability to attract foreign investment. Second, the long-term accumulated contradictions and difficulties of the state-owned enterprises are difficult to resolve. The mismatch between the supply structure and demand structure is difficult to resolve in a fundamental way within a short period of time. Furthermore, consumer demand will not see swift growth soon, as it is constrained by the slow growth in personal income and consumption expectations. This will also affect economic growth.

Based on the above analysis, the results of our forecast for 1999 are: the economy of Jilin province will maintain steady progress and GDP growth may reach 7.7%. See Table 1 for the major indicators.

Directions of Work and Policy Suggestions for 1999

Based on our knowledge of the current economic situation in Jilin province and recent development trends, we suggest the following directions for work in Jilin in 1999: Economic results should be seen as the core objective; we must insist on taking market demand as the guide; the expansion of domestic demand should go hand in hand with the upgrading of production; the structure of growth should be transformed; and technological innovation should be stressed, so as to achieve economic growth of high quality. We should concentrate our efforts on solving the following problems.

Table 1
Jilin Province Economic Forecast for 1998 and 1999

	1998	1999
1. Total volumes and industry indicators		
GDP growth rate	8.3%	7.7%
Total investment (RMB billion)	56.49	60.08
Total consumption (RMB billion)	97.71	102.95
Primary industry value-added growth rate	10.8%	5.9%
Agricultural production growth rate	10.3%	6.1%
Grain production (billion catties)	45.5	46.5
Secondary industry value-added growth rate	6.8%	8.3%
Manufacturing industry value-added growth rate	8.2%	8.7%
Construction value-added growth rate	6.1%	5.3%
Tertiary industry value-added growth rate	8.5%	8.1%
Transportation, posts and telecommunications growth rate	7.8%	7.5%
Commerce value-added growth rate	10.9%	10.0%
2. Total fixed asset investment (RMB billion)	40	44.1
Growth rate	10%	10.2%
3. Total retail sales (RMB billion)	66.43	70.75
Growth rate	7.2%	6.5%
4. Prices		
Retail price index	2.0%	2.5%
Consumer price index	2.3%	2.2%
5. Personal income		
Average urban cost of living (RMB)	3,780	3,983
Growth rate	-0.6%	5.4%
Average net rural income (RMB)	2,469.8	2,678.4
Growth rate	12.8%	8.4%
6. Fiscal data		
Fiscal income (overall) (RMB billion)	17.35	19.25
Growth rate	10.0%	11.0%
Fiscal expenditure (RMB billion)	18.04	19.71
Growth rate	7.5%	9.3%
7. Financial data		
Balance of various deposits (RMB billion)	124.7	135.5
Growth rate	3.3%	8.7%
Outstanding balance of bank loans (RMB billion)	197.7	212.5
Growth rate	3.3%	7.5%

We Should Reinforce the Concept of Market Constraints as the Guideline and Economic Benefits as the Core Objective in our Economic Work

We should adapt our way of thinking to suit this period of economic readjustment and understand that in the expansion of domestic demand, emphasis should be laid on expanding the effective supply.   Market-embedded growth is the only manifestation of an effective rate of development.   In the present situation, when conditions for the market economy have been initially established, if we blindly pursue economic growth without regard to the market, we will achieve neither economic benefit nor speed.

We Should Further Expand Domestic Demand in Order to Ensure a Steady Growth in Demand

As domestic demand has not yet been fully jump-started, we should continue to expand government expenditure on public affairs and raise the proportion of fiscal investment in the total investment, in order to lead and stimulate an increase in enterprise investment. Currently, when the enterprises lack confidence to invest, we should work out some corresponding concessionary policies and further loosen the government's controls on new projects.   The non-state sector should be allowed to enter the competitive markets dominated by the state-owned enterprises, and should be given support in financing and project applications.   The capital market policy should be adjusted to provide diverse avenues to help enterprises to overcome their difficulties in obtaining financial support.

Consumption policies should be actively adjusted to quickly jump-start consumer spending.   We should promote the full-scale implementation of the wage system, and make sure that every reform having to do with the people's welfare should be reflected in wages, so that the wages of urban residents will not drop in absolute terms due to the implementation of the reform and inhibit their desire to spend.

We Should Accelerate the Pace of Industrial Structural Adjustment, and Increase the Promotional Effects of Manufacturing Industry

Jilin province should carry out a reform of the grain distribution system and ensure that the government, by guaranteeing the supply and the strategic storage of grain, takes care of the farmers when their income decreases but their financial burden increases at harvest time. At the same time we should optimize the crop mix and develop production of high-yield and high-quality strains, in coordination with the industrialization of agriculture. An export-oriented agricultural industry which can earn foreign exchange should be established and efforts should be made in various projects to raise farmers' incomes.

In order to deal with the decreasing contribution of manufacturing industry to economic growth, Jilin province must make more efforts in adjusting the industrial structure. The important work at present is to actively develop new points for economic growth on the basis of the integration of industrial strategies. In particular, we must do well in the work of restructuring assets and utilizing capital in pillar industries which are being fostered, and further bring into play their role in promoting economic growth. The investment in technological renovation should be skewed toward these pillar industries rather than the traditional enterprises which are on the edge of bankruptcy.

We Must Cultivate and Institute New Systems, and Upgrade Production Through Technological Innovation

We should introduce new foreign technologies, encourage cooperative production and joint venture production, and continue to renovate enterprises in an orderly and comprehensive fashion. At the same time, we should increase efforts in breaking new technological ground, and selectively establish new plans to absorb, digest, redevelop, and innovate technologies to create new enterprises. In encouraging technological innovation, we should ensure that the medium-sized and large enterprises set up research and development institutions, and simultaneously establish profit encouragement systems and protection systems.   We also need to establish a system of tax concessions and interest discounting to support and assist complex and costly technological innovation, particularly during its initial stages, so that it can quickly be turned into productive capacity.

We Must Continue to Deepen the Reform of State-owned Enterprises with Emphasis on a Market System which Brings about Asset Reorganization and Produces Entrepreneurs

Currently, the managers and executives of the state-owned enterprises in Jilin are not professionals.   Their selection and appointment is mainly a matter for the governments and are not subject to optional deployment through the market.   Thus, we should concentrate on creating a mechanism which produces entrepreneurs through the market in order to solve the problem of low quality management of the enterprises and in order to deepen the reform of state-owned enterprises.   Respecting the principle of market competition, we should establish a system for the selection of entrepreneurs and provide training for them.   A system of encouragement and supervision should be instituted to make the entrepreneurs more professional and market-oriented.

We Must Properly Resolve the Prominent Problems That Have Emerged in the Process of Reform Which Affect the Personal Interests of Workers in Order to Promote Stable Development

Currently, the effects of the reform measures are borne by three sides — the government, enterprises, and the people.   The ability of enterprises and the people to bear the burden of the reforms has fallen, and there are serious problems with social order and security. Therefore, we need to adjust the redistribution system of the national economy, reasonably balance the costs of reform between the central government and the local governments, and build up people's confidence and support for the reforms.   At the same time, we need to create a sound social security system, to implement a reemployment project, and to properly solve the prominent problems which have emerged during the reforms and which affect the personal interests of the workers.   We can thereby create a more relaxed environment for enterprises to bear the burden of redundant workers and to be able to maintain social stability.

AN ECONOMIC ANALYSIS AND FORECAST FOR ZHEJIANG PROVINCE

YU ZHENG, WANG NINGJIANG, AND YANG JIANCHENG

Economic Information Centre of Zhejiang Province

The Zhejiang Economy in 1998 and an Analysis of the Economy over the Full Year

The Basic Condition of the Economy since the Beginning of 1998

Affected by conditions of deflation, economic growth in Zhejiang in 1998 saw contraction. However, the rate of decline is now slowing down. The basic characteristics of the economy are:

There has been a continued decline in economic growth, but we have seen initial apparent signs of stability. Based on preliminary statistics, the GDP of Zhejiang in the first half of 1998 was RMB209 billion, up by 9.4%. In the second half, the decline in the industrial growth rate started to slow and began to stabilize.

The growth of investment recovered sharply while consumer demand remained stable. The expansion of exports was hindered. Propelled by the strenuous efforts of the government to expand domestic demand, the fixed asset investment completed by Zhejiang in the first half of the year was RMB60.3 billion, up by 6% from the full-year figure in 1997. The rate of growth of the state sector was even stronger, increasing from 11.2% in the first half to 25.9% between January and August, in which the increase in infrastructure investment was 31.3%, 20% faster than that in the first quarter. Investment in renovation and reconstruction reversed the trend of decline and grew by 54.4%, but from a rather low base figure. Investment in real estate also turned from decline to growth. While investment demand saw a remarkable rise, the total consumer demand of Zhejiang remained stable and the urban and rural residents' propensity to consume dropped instead of increasing. Between January and August 1998, total retail sales were RMB121 billion, showing a real growth of 10.5% with the price factors deducted. Compared with the same period in 1997 and the first quarter of 1998, the increase was less than 1%. As the influence of the Asian financial crisis intensified, the growth of exports fell sharply in the second half of 1998. Between January and August, the growth of total exports of Zhejiang was 10.7%, down by 5% from the first half. In July, the growth rate was only 0.3%, and in August the growth rate was -2%, which was the first negative growth since 1997.

The overall economic efficiency declined greatly before it started to improve recently. Directly affected by weak effective demand, more market constraints, and a sustained decline in the production growth rate, the efficiency of enterprises could not maintain the improved condition seen since 1997 and started to decline again. Between January and July, the total audited taxes of industrial enterprises under the new measurement declined by 0.4% from the same period in 1997. The total profits declined by 9.3%, and the proportion of loss-making enterprises increased from 24.9% in January to July 1997 to 30.2% in the same period in 1998. Losses increased sharply by 39.3%. Overall economic efficiency was clearly worse than that in 1997. However, as the decline in economic growth slowed down, the deteriorating trend in the economic efficiency of the enterprises also basically stopped, as shown in the increased ability of enterprises to make profits and reduce losses. At the end of July, the decline in profits tax and gross profits was 1.9% and 3.1% lower than those in June, and the size of losses was also reduced by 0.1%. The rate of growth in losses has gradually declined, and economic efficiency is turning slowly in the direction of improvement.

At the same time, there are some problems worthy of attention in the current economic operating conditions. First, grain production is unstable, and the contradiction between the production and sale of agricultural and sideline products has become prominent. Second, the investment in industrial technological renovation has been inadequate and the effective demand has been weak.   Third, the circulation of capital is not smooth and the reproduction cycle has been obstructed.

Estimate of Economic Development in 1998

In the last few months of 1998, the economic growth of Zhejiang province will shake off the declining trend, as the policies by various levels of governments to expand domestic demand gradually begin to take effect.   In particular, the government has implemented more aggressive and flexible fiscal measures to stimulate growth.   There are already some aspects showing strong positive trends:

(1)   the demand for funds is rising noticeably, and lending by financial institutions has maintained quite swift growth;

(2)   the rate of growth in heavy industry has accelerated since April, for the first time breaking away from the pattern over the last 23 months in which light industries took the lead;

(3)   the accumulated stocks of finished products in enterprises have been reduced with each passing month.

(4)   the leading indicators of cement and steel have seen an increase, signifying that investment increases are showing results in the relevant industries and are having an effect in the downstream industries.

Based on the changes in the trend of short-term demand, the estimated full-year fixed asset investment of Zhejiang in 1998 will be RMB191 billion, up by 12.7%.   The estimated full-year total retail sales will be RMB192.5 billion, up by 9.5%.   The estimated full-year export trade will be US$12.2 billion, up by 9.7%.

Putting all these analyses and estimates together, we can state that the economic growth of Zhejiang will show a slow rising trend in the final months of 1998.   The estimated full-year GDP will be RMB502 billion, reaching the planned growth target of 10%.   Since the negative effect of 1997 on prices in 1998 is about 1.5%, the estimated new price increase factor is about 1%.   The estimated full-year retail price index of Zhejiang will be 99.5%, a slight decline from 1997.

Forecast of the Trend of Economic Development in Zhejiang in 1999

An Estimate of the Environment for Economic Development

With an increasingly open market economy, the trend in regional economic development is mainly dependent on the external environment and the competitiveness of the regional industries. In terms of the external environment, there is no reason for us to be optimistic about the world economy and trade in 1999.   The main objective in maintaining economic growth in China will be to expand domestic demand.   We can say that the policy of relying on the expansion of demand is not only an expedient policy for the present, but is also a policy which needs to be further implemented and improved in order to deal with the problem of inadequate final demand.   However, the fundamental conditions for economic growth in recent years have seen various development stages, and this has meant that the role of the government in leading and jump-starting the current economy in economic growth has been reduced. In particular, there are many obstacles in the transformation of the enormous potential domestic demand into current demand. Therefore, market constraints will be a prominent factor in economic growth in 1999.

Analysis of the Conditions of Industrial Support

Under the current market environment and policy background, the key to Zhejiang's economic growth lies in the competitiveness of our own industries. This is because, for a regional economy, the only way to achieve the expansion of market demand through policy is to create effective supply through competition. In particular, as a typical processing trade zone, the base of demand for economic growth in Zhejiang needs to be the entire country and even international markets. Based on a tentative estimate, more than 60% of Zhejiang's growth is contributed by the effects of demand in other provinces and overseas. Consequently, industrial competitiveness is a determining factor for Zhejiang's economic growth. The current support for Zhejiang's economic growth comes mainly from the labor intensive industries which are suited to the initial stages of industrial development. The foundation for new leading industries is rather weak. Besides machinery, the proportion of key industries like electronics, petrochemicals, and pharmaceuticals is even lower than the national average. The proportion of industries with new and high technologies, which have strategic significance to sustainable economic development, is even lower. The proportion of value-added production of high technology industries like communications equipment, biomedicine, and computer equipment is less than 13%. The proportion of traditional industries and products in the process of adjustment is relatively large, while the number of newly-emerging industries and products is relatively low. Industries which respond to market demand and are able to gear to market trends are not seeing obvious progress and the market share of the products in domestic markets faces critical challenges. In 1997, the industrial sales of Zhejiang constituted only 6.13% of the national total. Between January and August 1998, the sale rate of industrial products was 94.8%, lower than the national average of 95.39%. In the increasingly competitive market, the existing industrial structure cannot support a fast rate of economic growth in Zhejiang.

Forecast of Major Economic Indicators

Seen from the perspective of the demand variables which will have direct impact on economic growth, investment will still be a very active factor in 1999. This is because: First, the substantial increases in investment in the previous period will lead to further expansion in the scale of succeeding investment.   Second, the more than RMB2 bn allocated to Zhejiang from the RMB100 bn in state treasury bonds recently issued has now been delivered.   Third, the proportion of government investment in infrastructure construction has increased sharply, which means that the estimated total fixed assets investment in Zhejiang in 1999 will reach RMB214 billion, up by 12%, slightly lower than the level of 1998.

Consumer spending will maintain stable growth.   In a buyer's market environment, the level of consumer spending is generally affected by income level and constrained by consumer psychology and habits.   Current consumer spending by high-income careers is mainly satisfied by imported products or domestic substitutes of high quality.   Although the demand elasticity is large, the growth in demand will be small.   At the same time, the growth in demand for consumer goods by customers of middle incomes will not expand much.   The tapping of the potential demand by low-income level consumer spending will have to wait for an increase in real purchasing power and an improvement in the consumer environment. Consequently, the consumer market of Zhejiang will maintain stable growth.   The estimated full-year total retail sales will reach RMB212 billion, up by 10.1%.

Export growth may well see a great decline.   In 1999, the international economic condition will be complex and chaotic.   The environment for export trade is rather severe, with many limiting factors on exports and many uncertainties.   First, the Asian countries and regions, which have been seriously harmed by the financial crisis, will not be able to shake off the difficulties of their economic depression within a short period of time.   This situation constitutes a direct threat to the quantity of Zhejiang's exports as well as the economic benefit to be derived from them.   Second, the damage caused by the Asian financial crisis and economic depression are hindering the strategic diversification of Zhejiang's exports.   Third, in 1999, China will likely maintain the stability of the value of the RMB.   This will objectively weaken our export competitiveness.   Therefore, in 1999, the difficulties in maintaining stable export growth for Zhejiang will be many.   The estimated full-year export trade value will be US$12.9 billion, up by 5.7%, but the rate of increase will decline sharply.

With the active stimulation provided by the government's increase in investment, Zhejiang can hope to achieve a small rise in growth in the latter part of 1998, and subsequently will meet the planned growth target.   However, based on an analysis of the development environment and support conditions, and the changing trends in demand factors, there will be many difficulties in maintaining the 10% growth rate for Zhejiang in 1999.   Investment will maintain a relatively fast rate of growth, while consumer spending will fluctuate mildly while also maintaining steady growth. Our tentative forecast for Zhejiang's GDP in 1999 is RMB554 billion, up by 9.3% on an equivalent basis, slightly lower than the 1998 growth level.   In this, the growth rates of primary, secondary, and tertiary industry will be 2%, 10%, and 9.5% respectively. According to initial estimates, price levels in Zhejiang in 1998 will affect price levels in 1999 by a figure of -0.5%.   If there are no unforeseen factors, the price increase in 1999 will thus be about 2%. The estimated retail price index for the year will rise by about 1.5%.

AN ECONOMIC ANALYSIS AND FORECAST OF THE ECONOMIC SITUATION IN HUBEI PROVINCE

HU SHIJIAN AND WU RANGSONG
Development Research Centre
Hubei Provincial People's Government

Basic Characteristics of the Hubei Economy in 1998

In 1998, the most serious flood since 1954 ravaged the Yangtze River region and caused enormous damage to people's lives and property. The floods consumed enormous amounts of manpower and resources, and seriously affected the industrial and agricultural production in this region. Based on an incomplete survey, the total agricultural disaster area covered 28 million acres; 8.8 million acres of crops were totally wiped out, and 13,000 enterprises stopped or partially stopped production. The direct economic loss was as high as RMB50 billion, and about 4.78 million flood victims needed relief and resettlement. In the face of the serious difficulties produced by such a severe situation, the entire province showed unparalleled spirit in fighting against the flood, and protected the infrastructure and economic development. Yet, even in a year of disaster, the Hubei economy still managed to maintain a good development trend.

In the first half of 1998, the GDP growth rate of Hubei province was 9.5%, 2.5% higher than the national average. The estimated full-year growth is 10.5%.

Between January and August 1998, total retail sales in the province grew by 9.3%, 11.4% lower than that in the same period in the previous year. The estimated full-year growth rate is 12%.

Between January and August 1998, the investment demand grew by 12.7%. The estimated full-year growth is 18%, 7% higher than 1997.

The growth in exports and imports declined monthly. The estimated full-year growth rate is 5%, 8% lower than that of 1997.

Since April 1998, the growth rate of industrial production has been the lowest since 1992. The estimated full-year growth rate of light industrial value-added production is 12%, down by 2% from 1997. Between January and August 1998, the total amount of profits and taxes declined by more than 50%, while the amount of enterprise losses increased by 41%.

The estimated growth rate of fiscal income in 1998 is 15%, and the financial situation is stable. The outstanding loans as of the end of August 1998 were up by 15.6%.

The Hubei Economy Is Expected to Grow at a Fast and Steady Rate in 1999

Based on an analysis of the national environment, the government implemented more active fiscal, and financial policies to stimulate the economic recovery. In the third quarter, a noticeable recovery was evident in the national economy. Hubei is an old industrial base and a production base for industrial raw materials. The government's increased investment in infrastructure projects and fixed asset investment had a direct influence and remarkable promotional effect on Hubei's economy. Toward the end of the third quarter, the rate of growth of Hubei accelerated, total demand recovered, and the microeconomic situation improved gradually. This was because:

(1) The huge flood did not hurt the spirit of Hubei, and the economic foundation was preserved. The growth rate of total industrial production was higher than the national average.

The estimated fiscal income in 1998 will increase by 15%. The financial situation is stable.

(2)   The central fiscal and finance departments gave their firm support to Hubei.   Banks promised to make loans to enterprises with market availability and repayment ability. Large amounts of money and materials poured in from all over the country to support Hubei's fight against the floods and guaranteed Hubei's success in fighting the natural disaster.

(3)   The central government supported Hubei's reconstruction work after the flood strongly.   The central government arranged many projects in the spheres of flood protection construction and reconstruction of disaster areas.   The large amounts of money which poured in helped the flood victims to recover and also aided the economic recovery of the province. The work in resettling flood victims, rebuilding towns, and reconstruction and repair of damaged houses have started in full swing.   This was a huge investment in the "housing project" for the flood victims.   This will stimulate the growth of ten or more related industries like construction, construction materials, and metallurgy, and will form a new growth point for the economy.   As the relief funds turn into material goods, the development of industries like food, textiles, clothing, and daily appliances will be stimulated.   In turn, the economy and the market will be stimulated and create conditions for large-scale flood relief, large-scale adjustment, large-scale demand, and large-scale development.

(4)   Following the huge disaster, the entire province was mobilized and high spirits were displayed in the fight against the floods. We can now concentrate on production and on rebuilding our homes.

It follows from an analysis of various factors that Hubei's economy will maintain a fast rate of economic growth and improve its economic structure and competitiveness in 1999.   The estimated GDP growth rate will be 11% over the previous year, while investment will grow by 20%. The total retail sales growth rate will be 14%. The export growth rate will be 8%; fiscal income will grow by 15%; the savings of urban and rural residents will increase by 20%; outstanding bank loans will increase by 18%; average urban personal income will increase by 6%; and average personal rural net income will increase by RMB180.

The year 1999 is the most strategic year for the "Ninth Five-year Plan." The floods in 1998 affected Hubei seriously. The disaster areas, especially the serious disaster areas, suffered enormous losses. The tasks for flood victim resettlement, reconstruction of homes, and restarting production are extremely difficult. After the floods, all the problems concerning the payment of wages and basic livelihood protection of redundant workers will be more acute. Therefore, in 1999, we must maintain an appropriately fast rate of growth for Hubei, take the initiative in implementing the national macroeconomic adjustment policy, and seize the opportune time to expand domestic demand. We must seize the development opportunities of rebuilding Hubei after the serious floods in order to accelerate economic development.

Increasing the Scale of Investment to Stimulate Economic Growth

We must identify several projects as key breakthrough areas in order to stimulate the full-scale rapid increase in investment of the entire province. A total of 29 key projects were approved by the provincial government in 1998, which constituted 55% of the state infrastructure investment. These 29 projects have had 9 pivotal effects on the acceleration of investment growth. We should increase our supervision and monitoring on these investment projects, and concentrate our financial and material resources to ensure the smooth progress of these projects. In 1998, Hubei was affected by enormous flood damage, and Hubei needs large-scale investment in manpower and resources to fight against floods annually. The burden and damages for Hubei province are heavy and enormous. The central government must substantially improve the flood protection facilities in the middle stretches of the

Yangtze River.   The repair and reconstruction work of the
damaged roads, electricity supply, telecommunication facilities, and
irrigation facilities must be completed.   We have to request the
central government to find a fundamental solution to the flooding in
the middle stretches of the Yangtze River as a top priority and a
major national project.   Using the breadline of vision employed in
the Three Gorges Dam, we can widen the river channels in the
middle stretches of the Yangtze River and build levees for flood
protection.   Funds should be raised from all available sources to
guarantee the completion of the investment goal.   Since the central
government will place development emphasis in the middle and
western part of China through the issue of additional treasury bonds,
we must submit well-documented project applications in order to
win projects beneficial to Hubei in infrastructure, basic industries,
and industries which employ new and high technologies.   The local
governments must show their organizational abilities in the
development of these projects.   We can utilize means such as
government organization, fiscal participation, fiscal interest
subsidies, and fiscal guarantees to raise and absorb society's funds
to utilize in the construction of infrastructure projects and basic
industrial construction.   For projects with good returns, we can use
a joint-stock system to raise funds and allow personal and collective
shareholders.

Expanding the Market, Stimulating Consumer Spending, and Raising the Market Share for Hubei Products

The reconstruction of disaster areas creates enormous
consumer demand.   The industries in the province should seize the
opportunity to organize the delivery of daily items and production
materials to the villages, to guarantee the supply of important goods
such as blankets, food, medicine, fertilizers, agricultural chemicals,
seeds, agricultural equipment, cement, and steel products.   They
should also promote sales of the products of pillar industries
including vehicle, iron and steel, construction materials, electrical
and mechanical equipment, tobacco, wine, and clothing industries.
Policies should be put in place to increase sales of local products.

Industry and commerce should cooperate in various forms of promotion to expand sales of local products and support the development of the pillar industries. To meet the demand for product upgrading in the structural transformation of urban and rural consumption, we should make great efforts to search for new avenues of consumer credit, and to gradually expand the coverage of consumer credit. Through this, we can open up new hot points for consumer spending. The business of the banks should be concentrated on switching from production credit to a combination of production credit and consumer credit. The banks should undertake research on the operating methods of personal credit systems, and establish operating systems for installment payments, bank mortgages, secured lending, supplier credit, and other types of consumer credit as early as possible. Right now, we can extend credit for housing purchases. At an appropriate time, we can extend credit for large consumer items, family equipment, and cars.

Widening the Scope of Our Ideas in Order to Expand Export Trade and Overcome the Negative Effects of the Asian Financial Crisis

A number of things can be done in this respect. First, we can continue the adjustment of the export product structure in order to diversify the export markets. Alongside the development of the pillar industries of Hubei, we can place emphasis on the development of the traditional large backbone products and competitive products. We can also develop light industrial and handicraft products, farm by-products, and electro-mechanical products with competitive advantages. We can support strong enterprises with their overseas investment and establish overseas factories to stimulate the export of Hubei products. Second, we must speed up our research of the international market and collect information from all channels. We should establish a research organization for the international market to investigate international economic trends, demand for major products, and to offer timely market information. Third, we should accelerate the strategic reorganization of the export trade enterprises. Large holding companies should be established with exports as their key element or with production as their core, so that trade and industry can be combined, in order to expand the exports capability of Hubei. We can accelerate the systemic innovations in the state-owned foreign trade enterprises through the establishment of internal encouragement and restraint mechanisms so as to raise the competitiveness of enterprises. We must improve the capital structure and financial condition of foreign trade enterprises, improve their strength, and raise the quality of their information. Fourth, we should implement various policies which encourage exports. These include export credit and closed credit policies, drawback policies which "exempt, offset, or rebate" export taxes, and fiscal subsidies for products which are exported in large quantities.

Taking the Market as the Guide and Adjusting the Product Structure to Increase Competitiveness

We must establish a structural readjustment ideology which supports "famous and quality products" and structure the industrial production chain in Hubei to apply the name brand strategy, and cultivate Hubei's competitive edge in name brands. We should concentrate our resources on cultivating a series of name brand products, and on maintaining the current name brands, so that a series of products with good potential can be developed. While cultivating brand names, we should upgrade the quality of broad line products. We should seize the current opportunity to raise the market share of Hubei products through suitable and strategic adjustment of broad line products when the housing market and the rural market are starting to recover. Through the development of an outward-oriented economy and joint venture and cooperation channels, we can establish a series of new, high-quality products. We can make use of foreign investment, technology, and management to develop our new key products, so that the product structure of Hubei can move to a higher plane.

Actively Developing New Economic Growth Points

Seen from the trends of market competition and the patterns of economic development, the potential for sustainable high growth in traditional industries is declining. We must look to the long term and recognize the new economic vista for the next century. The new growth points for Hubei in the next century will be in four areas: housing and construction, tourism, information technology, and culture and sports. Currently, there are still limiting factors in these four industries, like dispersed locations, serious duplicated construction, small scale of economy, and poor production capacities. Because of these problems, we have an enormous task on hand to foster these growth points. We should establish a development plan for building new industries, provide policy support, and guide consumer spending, to stimulate effective demand and provide support for these industries. In this way, the new industries will be able to expand and become new pillars supporting fast economic growth in the future.

ANALYSIS AND FORECAST OF THE ECONOMIC SITUATION IN WUHAN CITY

WU YONGBAO, TANG SHIMING, AND DA JUN

*Wuhan Academy of Social Sciences; and
Institute of Economics, Wuhan City*

The year 1998 witnessed the flood of the century ravaging the entire Yangtze River region. Between July 20 and 23, a historic deluge drowned our city. The inner city area was seriously inundated. During July and August, the most important task in the city was to prevent disaster, fight against the flood, and drain the water. Based on an initial survey, by the end of August, the total flooded farmland was 2.3342 million acres. The areas with total loss of harvest amounted to 922,400 acres. Fish ponds affected by the flood covered 283,000 acres, of which 90.4% were in the city and suburbs. In industries, 1,692 enterprises were flooded, constituting 50% of all enterprises. A total of 1,183 enterprises stopped production, and 509 enterprises partly stopped production. The endangered housing floor areas totaled 110,000 square meters. Because navigation in the Wuhan section of the Yangtze River and the Han River was stopped for over forty days, the production and sales of large enterprises like steel and petrochemicals were seriously affected. The flood disaster caused financial and economic losses throughout the city of close to RMB4.4 billion. Despite the serious flood damage, Wuhan's economy still managed to grow strongly. In 1998, the city is hoping for an economic rebound after achieving 11.3% growth between January and August. The GDP growth rate is expected to reach 13.5%. Total industrial production will also grow by 13.5%. Agriculture production will grow by 4%. Total foreign trade will grow by 2%. The actual utilization of foreign investment will be US$1.05 billion, 12.9% higher on an equivalent basis. Fiscal income will grow by 16.83%.

Based on our estimate, the nominal growth rate of the total fixed asset investment in Wuhan in 1999 will be above 14%. The investment rate will be 41.11%, while the GDP growth rate will be 14%.

With the maintenance of steady economic growth, the estimated fiscal income of the city in 1999 will grow by 16.6%, reaching RMB11.637 billion.   The local fiscal income will reach RMB5.69 billion, higher by 17%.   Overall, local fiscal expenditure will be RMB7.13 billion, up by 18%.

The price level will continue to show a rising trend in 1999, but the growth will be small.   The estimated retail price index will be 105%, and the consumer price index 102%.   For urban residents, it is not clear whether personal incomes will rise.   On the other hand, substantial increases in the net per capita income of suburban farmers are most likely.

HONG KONG ECONOMY

HONG KONG SPECIAL ADMINISTRATIVE REGION: RECENT ECONOMIC SITUATION AND PROSPECTS

TANG KWONG YIU

Economic Analysis Department, Financial Services Branch
Hong Kong Special Administrative Region

The Recent Economic Situation

The Economy Is in a Situation of Adjustment and Consolidation

The economy of the Hong Kong Special Administrative Region (HKSAR) was strong in the first half of 1997. In the several months following the reversion to the motherland on July 1, 1997, the economy still maintained a high rate of growth. Hong Kong people were fully confident in the implementation of the "one country, two systems." However, in the second half of 1997, the Asian financial crisis started to affect Hong Kong. The economy began to decline in a noticeable way, and it saw a reversal of the trends of economic growth and rising capital asset prices of the previous two years. All economic activities in the SAR, particularly those in investment and consumption, were seriously affected by the sharp decline in securities and real estate prices, high interest rates, and the worsening unemployment rate.

The GDP real growth rate of the SAR in 1997 was 5.3%. However, in the first quarter of 1998, the economy shrank by 2.8%, and the decline was even greater in the second quarter, estimated at 5%. This mainly reflected a further decline in exports and domestic consumption from the first quarter. In addition, the second quarter of 1997 was the peak of the economic growth cycle in that year, creating a high base figure for comparison.

The Slowdown in External Trade

In the first seven months of 1998, the external trade of the SAR, both visible trade and invisible trade, fell sharply from the same period in 1997.

In exports, due to the effects of the Asian financial crisis, exports to East Asia declined noticeably. At the same time, the weak Japanese economy caused a sharp fall in the Yen exchange rate, which produced a marked decline in exports to these markets. Although the exports to Mainland China continued to grow, the rate of growth slowed sharply, mainly because of the slowdown in import demand from the Mainland.

However, the SAR's exports to Europe and America still recorded reasonable growth. From this we can see that the devaluation of Asian currencies did not weaken the export competitiveness of SAR exports to these traditional overseas markets. Despite this, total SAR exports in the first seven months in real terms still declined slightly from 1997 because of the generally poor performance of exports to Asia.

Imports, in the first seven months of 1998, declined by 4% in real terms from 1997. Within this figure, retained imports, as compared with 1997, declined at a greater rate of about 9%. This mainly reflected the slowdown in both domestic demand in the SAR and exports, which caused a decline in demand for imports of raw materials, machinery, and consumer goods.

In the first seven months of 1998, the SAR recorded a visible trade deficit of HK$71.2 billion, about 8.4% of the SAR's imports, showing a reduction of the HK$110.8 bn trade deficit (12.1% of imports) from the same period in 1997. The reduction in the visible trade deficit was mainly due to the fact that as the economy changed direction, demand for imports shrank noticeably. The continuing rise in the trade price ratio was also one of the major reasons for this.

In terms of invisible trade, because of weakness in tourism and the slowdown in visible trade, service exports in 1998 declined further.   Recent figures have shown that in the first eight months of 1998, the number of visitors declined by 13% from the same period in 1997, a rate greater than the 11% decline for the year of 1997. As for service imports, only small growth is expected.   On the whole, a large-scale invisible trade surplus will likely be maintained during this period and thus will compensate for the majority of the shortfall in visible trade.

Consumption Continued to Be Weak.   Investment Performance Varied

Consumer spending in the first seven months of 1998 showed no sign of recovery.   The rise of unemployment and decline in capital asset prices seriously affected consumer confidence and desire to spend.   The high level of interest rates, apart from increasing the burden of families who have to pay for mortgages, also dampened their spending on high price items.   In addition, spending by tourists fell sharply, further depressing the local retail trade.   Consequently, retail sales between January and July fell by 16% from the 1997 equivalent figure.   Sharper falls were recorded in goods sold at emporiums, clothing, durable goods, and goods easily affected by interest rates like cars, jewelry, and watches. However, there was almost no change in the sales of daily necessities such as food and supermarket products.

In terms of fixed asset investment, overall growth was registered.   However, the performances varied from category to category.   In terms of purchases of equipment and machinery, retained imports in the second quarter of 1998 rose by 11% from last year in real terms.   This was a noticeable improvement from the 12% decline in the first quarter.   In housing and construction, although developers had become cautious in starting new housing construction, construction continued on projects in progress. Private sector construction in the first quarter of 1998 rose by 15% from the 1997 equivalent figure.   An increase was expected to continue in the second quarter. As for the public sector, construction of public estate housing was still very active, but civil engineering work slowed down to a certain extent mainly due to the completion of the core airport project. In the first quarter of 1998, public sector construction was down by 8% from the previous year, and no improvement was visible in the second quarter. In addition, because of the sluggish real estate market, expenditures on interior decoration also declined.

Real Estate Prices Were Soft and Transactions Were Slow

With interest rates staying high, unemployment deteriorating, and banks tightening their lending policy, the real estate market was weak in the first nine months of the year. The number of transactions shrank sharply.

The real estate market remained stable for a short period at the beginning of the year. However, following further turmoil in the financial market and tightness in the local capital market, the real estate market weakened noticeably in April and this has lasted to the present. Because the desire to purchase was weak, developers successively followed suit and cut prices of new flat pre-sales and offered flexible mortgage arrangements. This created some downward pressure on the second-hand market, while their sale techniques increased the sales of new flats. Cases where second-hand flats were sold at losses increased.

In terms of residential property prices, in September 1998, prices were down sharply by 40% compared with the 1997 year-end figure, and by 50% compared with the peak in October 1997. Also, because of the abundant supply of residential flats to lease, the rental market also suffered from large downward adjustment. In the second quarter of 1998, rents on newly-signed residential leases fell by an average of 3% from the first quarter and were down by 14% from the peak in the third quarter of 1997.

In commercial properties, because of the high interest rates and uncertain business prospects, users and investors in the office market took a wait-and-see attitude. On the other hand, the weak retail market and the continued slump in tourism depressed the retail shop market. The retail shop prices and the number of transactions fell noticeably. The industrial property market was quiet. In addition to the relocation of the manufacturing industry to Mainland China, the poor export performance and quiet real estate market all contributed to weakening the demand for industrial properties.

In terms of supply, the completion of residential flats and office buildings increased noticeably from last year. The construction of warehouses rose sharply because of the completion of the airport airfreight terminal. However, the construction of other types of commercial building like commercial, commercial/industrial, and industrial buildings was down substantially. In addition, as the local real estate market declined, and the working capital shortage became acute, plans submitted for the development of all types of properties declined sharply from last year.

Oversupply in the Labor Market

The labor market of the SAR changed from the tight market during the first three quarters of 1997 to a situation with increased labor supply. Because of the increase in returning emigrants and new immigrants from the Mainland, the increase in the number of fresh graduates from schools, and the increased rate of labor participation, the supply of labor increased sharply. On the other hand, as economic development slowed, total labor demand slowed down noticeably. Job vacancies in various businesses also declined noticeably.

The unemployment situation has also continued to deteriorate. After the seasonal adjustment, the unemployment rate in the third quarter of 1997 was 2.2%, but rose to 5.0% during June to August in 1998, which was the highest in fifteen years. The underemployment rate also increased from 1% to 2.5%. Between June and August 1998, the total number of unemployed was estimated at 175,000 and the number of underemployed at 85,000.

The industries with a noticeable rise in unemployment are those more seriously hurt by the Asian financial crisis, especially retailers, real estate businesses, restaurants, and hotels. At the same time, the unemployment rate for the construction industry also rose noticeably. This was mainly due to the completion of the airport core projects and the weak real estate market. Relatively speaking, the unemployment rate in financial services, insurance, social services, and personal service industry was lower. In underemployment, the rise was concentrated in construction, transportation, manufacturing, restaurants, and hotels. Other industries remained stable.

The oversupply in the labor market, in addition to bringing higher unemployment and underemployment rates, depressed the growth in salaries and wages of employees. In the first quarter, total labor income, in monetary terms, increased by 5% from last year. However, the growth was zero after deducting inflation factors. This was a substantial decline from the respective 9% and 4% figures in 1997. Recent indications suggest that this trend will last for a while.

Inflationary Pressure Continued to Decline

Because of the slowdown in salary increases and substantial declines in real estate prices and rent, inflationary pressure from domestic sources declined noticeably. In addition, as competition is intensive, enterprises have undertaken cost-saving measures to streamline their structures and raise their productivity. Many discounts have been offered, which has helped to ease the inflationary pressure. At the same time, import prices have softened because of the strong exchange rate of the Hong Kong dollar.

All these factors have caused price inflation to moderate. The inflation rate measured by the comprehensive consumer price index fell to 2.7% in August, the lowest figure in 17 years. The average inflation between January and August was only 4.3%, much lower than the 5.8% in 1997.

The Financial Industry Faced a Difficult Situation but the Foundation Was Solid

In the first nine months of 1998, the Hong Kong dollar–U.S. dollar current exchange rate was stable, within the range of 7.735–7.75 for most of the time, standing firmly on the strong side of the pegged exchange rate of HK$7.8. At the end of September, the current exchange rate was 7.745. In the same period, wild fluctuations were seen in regional currencies on several occasions, which caused larger fluctuation with respect to long-term U.S. dollar contracts. In particular, in August, the Hong Kong dollar weakened for a short period of time. In September, the Hong Kong Monetary Authority introduced a series of measures to strengthen the monetary issue system. After the introduction of these measures, the long-term U.S. dollar exchange rate strengthened and stabilized.

Relatively speaking, the fluctuations were more serious in the Hong Kong interest rate market and the stock market. This reflected serious instability in overseas markets on the one hand, and influenced by speculative interests, speculative activities were very prominent in August on the other. Some market makers took advantage of the lack of confidence and spread rumors and negative information on the instability of the linked exchange rate. At the same time, they sold a substantial amount of Hong Kong dollars, and short sold Hong Kong stocks and Hang Seng index futures. The interest rate of the Hong Kong dollar came under pressure and rose sharply, which in turn caused sharp losses in Hong Kong stocks and Hang Seng index futures. Market makers exploited and controlled the two markets to gain profits.

In the face of such a critical situation, after some careful consideration, the SAR government acted decisively to stop these speculative activities.   In addition to utilizing its reserves to participate in the stock and futures markets to directly attack the speculators' activities, the SAR Government also introduced a series of measures to strengthen the operation of the pegged exchange rate mechanism, to stabilize the stock and futures markets, and to restore market order.   As a result, these measures achieved their expected results, and the pressures forcing Hong Kong dollar interest rates up gradually disappeared.   The Hang Seng index also slowly recovered.   At the end of September, the Hong Kong dollar interest rates for overnight and three months were 6% and 8% respectively, compared with 4.5% and 9.125% at the end of 1997.   The Hang Seng index at the end of September recovered to 7,883, still 26% lower than the figure at the end of 1997.

It should be noted that the SAR banking system did not suffer from the fluctuation in the financial markets.   The banks' financial positions are still strong.   The capital adequacy ratio remains at a high level, while bad and non-performing loans stayed at the low level of 0.3%.   There were however some reductions in profits. The public's confidence in the banking system did not vacillate. Total deposits at banks in August rose by 1.4% from July, while the percentage of Hong Kong dollar deposits rose from 56.3% at the beginning of the year to 57.3% in August.

However, demand for loans was still weak.   On the one hand, this was due to the economic slowdown and rising interest costs. On the other hand, it showed that the banks were adopting a cautious attitude in granting loans.   In the second quarter, loans to financial institutions, stockbrokers, wholesale and retail industries, export/import trade, and manufacturing all declined.   Only loans connected with properties, including mortgage, construction, real estate development, and investment loans, rose slightly.   Loans to transportation also increased.

Recent Economic and Financial Measures

Since the beginning of 1998, the SAR Government has introduced a series of measures to stabilize the entire economy. The main measures have enabled some important segments of the economy like real estate and finance to operate within a stable environment, and smooth and effective adjustments have been carried out. This also enabled the SAR to recover quickly, and eased the difficulties faced by enterprises and individuals. We must stress that the implementation of these measures is not an indication that the SAR has changed its economic and financial policy making. The formulation and implementation of these policies met the following criteria:

(1) Considering the market supply and demand situation, and ensuring the leading position of the market;

(2) Respecting the principle of cautious fiscal management;

(3) Maintaining the confidence of investors;

(4) Not affecting the pegged exchange rate.

Economic Assistance Measures

At the beginning of 1998, the SAR announced in its budget many tax cuts and exemption policies, including reducing the personal income tax, profit tax, and stamp duty on stocks. At the same time, funds were allotted to implement the Chief Executive's policy directives to expand public investment. These measures further improved the business environment, increased the SAR's competitiveness, stimulated the economy, and helped various industries and businesses to develop steadily.

On May 27, the SAR Government announced seven measures to ease the difficulties of tight working capital faced by businesses, to stabilize property prices, and to assist in the development of tourism.   On June 22, nine more measures were introduced by the SAR Government to further ease the lack of credit support and the lack of working capital faced by businesses, to stabilize property prices, to assist citizens in buying properties, and to reduce family expenses and costs of operating businesses.   The SAR Government announced at the same time the freezing of the salaries of top civil servants at grade 3 and above, so that they shared the burden of difficulties with ordinary citizens.

In addition, in June the SAR Government established a special working group on employment with the financial secretary as the chairperson.   The team included both employer and employee members, scholars, and government officials.   Its goal was to explore ways and means to solve unemployment problems and increase employment opportunities against the current unemployment situation.   At the same time, services were expanded in employment counseling, and employment-matching services, professional training and retraining programs, continuing education, youth social services, and prohibition of hiring illegal workers.

Financial Stability Measures

In order to further stabilize the financial market system and to avoid further speculative attacks, the SAR Government introduced a series of measures at the beginning of September, including seven measures to strengthen the operation of the pegged exchange rate, and thirty measures to strengthen the operation and increase the transparency of the stock market and the futures market.   The former was to guarantee that banks could change U.S. dollars to Hong Kong dollars at the fixed exchange rate of 7.75 to meet the settlement requirement.   The discount window function was changed so that banks could obtain overnight funds more easily, to avoid excessive rises in local short-term interest rates.   The latter was aimed at increasing supervision over the short selling of stock and over risk management, and reducing opportunities to manipulate stock and futures markets to artificially low levels.   The stock transaction settlement rules were tightened and brokers who failed to settle on time were liable to punishment. In addition, in order to strengthen the cooperation and communication between different financial markets, the SAR Government authorized the establishment of a super committee in charge of all financial markets. This committee was chaired by the financial services secretary and its members included senior executives of the Monetary Authority, the Securities and Futures Commission, the Stock Exchange of Hong Kong, and the Central Clearing House, in order to exercise recurrent supervision.

Short-Term Economic Prospects

Because of the lack of improvement in the international environment and the internal economic conditions of the SAR were still weak, the SAR Government has revised its forecast for economic performance in 1998, according to which the economy in 1998 is estimated to shrink by about 4%. Other than a likely moderate increase in government spending, all other major links of the economy, like personal spending, fixed asset investment, and external trade, will show varying degrees of decline.

In visible trade, total exports are estimated to fall at a real rate of about 2%. Because of the decline of import demand in Japan and the Southeast Asian countries, exports to these regions will continue to weaken. Exports to Europe and the United States will continue to perform well, but will make up for only part of the shortfall. At the same time, imports will decline further. The real rate of decline in imports in 1998 is expected to be 3.5%, of which the real decline in retained imports will be 7%.

In the area of invisible trade, since the SAR introduced various new measures in 1998, tourists from Mainland China and Taiwan will increase. The estimated service exports will decline by 4% in real terms. In addition, imports of services in 1998 will rise slightly, by 1%. As the number of the unemployed increases and income decreases, the number of outgoing tourists will get smaller in the next few months.   Service imports connected to other trades, and professional and commercial service imports, will continue to be weak in an environment of weak domestic and regional demand.

In the sphere of domestic demand, because there has been no improvement in the unemployment situation, income growth is slowing down, and the capital market is languishing, it will be difficult for consumer confidence to recover.   At the same time, high interest rates will suppress consumer spending.   In addition, since economic growth in the second and third quarters of 1997 was strong, a higher base of comparison has been formed.   On the whole, personal consumer spending is expected to decline by 4.5% in real terms.   Government spending, calculated on the base of personal income accounting, will register a moderate increase of 2%.

Calculated on the basis of local fixed capital formation, investment for the entire SAR is estimated to decline by about 4.5% in real terms.   As many civil engineering projects are completed, and some new projects are delayed, the construction expenditure on private housing will noticeably slow down in the short term.   In addition, because the number of real estate transactions will fall sharply, the interior decoration work and the transfer fees for land and properties will also decrease sharply.   In the public sectors, as the airport core projects are wound up, the amount of civil engineering work will show a short-term contraction.   Some major projects like railway construction will get started near the end of 1998.   There will not be many early stage works projects.   The budget for public housing is still very tight and can offset only part of the shortfall.   The expenditure on equipment and machinery is estimated to decrease because of the weak economy and unclear future industrial prospects.

In the first eight months of 1998, the consumer price index inflation, calculated by the comprehensive consumer price index, will continue to fall.   This is an inevitable process while the SAR is suffering from the turmoil of the Asian financial crisis.   It is predicted that in the short term, both locally-pushed inflation and import-pushed inflation will continue to be kept under overall control.   Up till now, food prices have been little affected by the serious flooding in China.   The estimated comprehensive consumer price index for the entire year will only rise by 3.5%.   By the year-end, consumer inflation will fall to a very low level.

In 1999, we still do not expect a full recovery in the economy and financial markets of Asia.   Currently, many economies in the region are in recession.   Some are experiencing social instability, which creates more uncertainties for their economic recovery.   The weak Japanese economy, with its unstable financial system and weak currency, is worth our special attention.   In addition, the chain reaction from the Asian financial crisis has already spread to the advanced economic systems outside the region and some emerging markets.   The SAR, as a free and open economic system, and an international financial, trade, and service center, cannot be immune from the fluctuations caused by the continuing financial crisis in Asia and other regions.

In terms of domestic demand of the SAR, whether or not personal investment and spending will strengthen depends on whether local interest rates will drop and achieve stability, whether there is improvement in the tight supply of capital, and whether the business environment can maintain its attractiveness and competitiveness.   Within the scope of fixed asset investment, the start of some public projects, like the Cheung Kwan O Mass Transit Railway Line, the Western Rail System, and the building and reconstruction of some large public estates, can make up for some of the shortfalls in the reduction in private investment.

Because the SAR has high flexibility in costs and prices, its economy is already in rapid transformation, and its competitiveness is being enhanced.   Wage increases have slowed down, and real estate prices and rent have fallen sharply from the peak in 1997. The inflation rate has fallen to the lowest level since 1981. Therefore, the cost of living and cost of doing business in the SAR have moderated substantially.   At the same time, workers have already adapted themselves to the difficult employment situation, while enterprises are streamlining their scales and structures so as to increase their productivity and efficiency.   As soon as the internal environment in Asia stabilizes and domestic confidence recovers, these adjustments will lay the foundation for the SAR to recover and to grow at a normal rate again.

INTERNATIONAL BACKGROUND

REVIEW AND PROSPECTS OF THE WORLD ECONOMY IN 1998–1999

Yu Yongding

Institute of World Economic and Politics
Chinese Academy of Social Sciences

The Asian Financial Crisis and the Overall World Economic Situation in 1998–1999

In 1998, the worldwide financial crisis, which started with the currency crisis in Thailand, intensified and the world economy deteriorated. When the Thai Baht was devalued on July 2, 1997, the currency crisis in Thailand quickly began to spread to the neighboring countries of Malaysia, Singapore, Indonesia, and the Philippines. In October of the same year, Taiwan and Hong Kong currencies successively came under attack from international speculators. In November, South Korea fell into serious financial crisis. After devaluing their currencies by 40–90%, most East Asian countries and regions have achieved initial improvement in trade and stability in currency. Hong Kong has successfully maintained the pegged exchange rate, while Taiwan province and Singapore saw their currencies devalue by about 20%. In 1998, the stock markets of the East Asian countries and regions fell sharply from their historic highs in 1997 (generally falling by more than 80%). A short recovery was followed by another sharp fall. The situation now seems to have stabilized. However, the price paid for financial stability is that the East Asian countries and regions have sunk into serious economic recession with a sharp rise in inflation (see Table 1). As the financial situation in the East Asian countries and regions was stabilized, the financial crisis swiftly spread to other countries and regions of the world. Like dominoes, an increasing number of countries and regions came under attack by international speculators and sank into financial and economic crisis.

Suffering from both the Asian financial crisis and the banking crisis caused by bad debts, the Japanese economy, which had started to recover in 1996, has sunk into serious deflation since the fourth quarter of 1997; in 1998, the Japanese economic recession is becoming more serious.   As a result, large amounts of Japanese capital have flowed out of Asian countries and regions.   This huge capital outflow has seriously affected the recovery of Asian countries and regions and jeopardized their efforts in restoring their international balance of payments and economic growth.   At the same time, because of the lack of confidence in Japan's future, large amounts of international capital have left Japan for the United States. The Japanese Yen has thus depreciated substantially against the U.S. dollar.   In June and July 1998, the Yen–U.S. dollar exchange approached the crucial rate of 150:1.   Japan's recession and the depreciation of the Yen have further affected Asia's economic recovery and exerted strong pressure on the RMB.

Because of the fall in the prices of oil and primary products as a result of the Asian financial crisis, and the deterioration in domestic fiscal conditions in August 1998, the Russian Government stopped repaying its short-term debt.   Large amounts of capital thus flowed out of Russia.   The Ruble fell sharply in value, and Russia fell into a serious financial crisis, while the Russian economy was on the brink of collapse.   One more domino had fallen.

The Russian economic crisis caused serious losses for international speculators.   Panic started to spread in western financial markets.   In September, the hedge fund Long Term Capital Management lost billions of dollars through failed speculation and was about to collapse.   The American Federal Reserve Bank stepped in and organized a rescue effort.   However, the financial health of the American system itself was under question, and the U.S. Dow Jones index fell sharply.   In October, the U.S. dollar–Yen exchange rate saw a historic turnaround, and the U.S. dollar dropped sharply in value.   The prospects for the American economy suddenly looked dim.

Table 1
The Macroeconomic Condition of Various Countries and Regions in East Asia
(compared with the same period in the previous year)

(Unit: %)

	3rd quarter 1997	4th quarter 1997	1st quarter 1998	2nd quarter 1998
China Hong Kong				
GDP growth	6.0	2.7	-2.8	-5.0
Inflation rate	6.1	5.5	5.0	4.4
Trade balance	-4.0	-4.1	-4.2	-4.5
Indonesia				
GDP growth	2.5	1.4	-7.9	-16.5
Inflation rate	6.0	10.1	29.9	52.1
Trade balance	3.6	4.0	3.4	4.3
South Korea				
GDP growth	6.1	3.9	-3.9	-6.6
Inflation rate	4.0	5.1	8.9	8.2
Trade balance	-1.5	2.2	8.4	11.7
Malaysia				
GDP growth	7.4	6.9	-2.8	-6.8
Inflation rate	2.3	2.7	4.3	5.7
Trade balance	0.5	0.4	2.2	3.4
Philippines				
GDP growth	4.9	5.6	1.7	-1.2
Inflation rate	5.9	7.5	7.9	9.9
Trade balance	-3.1	-2.4	-1.1	-0.3
Singapore				
GDP growth	10.6	7.7	6.1	1.6
Inflation rate	2.3	2.3	1.1	0.3
Trade balance	-2.5	-1.4	0.9	2.4
China Taiwan				
GDP growth	6.9	7.1	5.9	5.2
Inflation rate	1.1	-0.2	1.5	1.7
Trade balance	1.6	2.5	-0.1	1.3
Thailand				
GDP growth	-4.2	-11.5	-16.8	-15.8
Inflation rate	6.1	7.5	9.0	10.3
Trade balance	-0.9	2.5	3.1	2.6

Source: IMF, *World Economic Outlook*, October 1998.

At the same time, the economic situation in Latin America deteriorated further, and countries like Brazil were in danger of financial collapse.

In 1998, the European economy has seen slow but stable growth. The Euro would soon be introduced, and Europe is the only place of some hope. However, due to the disparities between the various countries in the Euro region, the success of the Euro still needs to be proven in practice. The international financial crisis will continue to exert an adverse influence on the economic stability of Europe.

On the whole, the Asian financial crisis, which started in July 1997, has developed into the most severe global financial crisis since the breakdown of the Bretton Woods agreement. In 1998, the various new trends and developments in world economic development since the breakup of the Soviet Union in the early 1990s saw varying degrees of reversal. Because of the deepening and expansion of the financial crisis, the world economy is facing the danger of global recession. Compared with that in 1997, the growth rate of the world economy in 1998 will slow down noticeably. In the *World Economic Outlook* published in October 1998, the International Monetary Fund further lowered its forecast for world economic growth in 1999 and 2000 (see Table 2). Taking into consideration the panic in the American financial markets and the report of the discussions held by the Open Market Committee of the American Federal Reserve on the lowering of interest rates, we can predict that the world economic growth rate will be actually lower than the IMF estimate. In particular, the possibility of a worldwide recession cannot be excluded. Furthermore, reviewing world economic development in recent months, the possibility of a global deflation has increased rather than decreased. The rate of growth of world trade in 1997 was 9.7%. Based on the IMF estimate, the 1998 world economic growth rate will fall dramatically to 3.7% and will recover to 4% in 1999. Considering the deterioration of the economic prospects of the major countries and regions in the world, the IMF estimate of world trade growth in 1999 may be too optimistic.

Table 2
IMF Estimates for World Economic Growth

(Unit : %)

	1997	1998	1999
World production	4.1	2.0	2.5
Developed countries	3.1	2.0	1.9
European Union	2.7	2.9	2.5
U.S.	3.9	3.5	2.0
Japan	0.8	-2.5	0.5
Developing countries	5.8	2.3	3.6
Asia	6.6	1.8	3.9
Latin America	5.1	2.8	2.7
Transitional economies	2.0	-0.2	-0.2
Central and Eastern Europe	2.8	3.4	3.6
Russia	0.9	-0.6	-0.6

Source: IMF, *World Economic Outlook*, October 1998.

The prospects for world economic growth will mainly be decided by the prospects for economic development in the developed countries.   In turn, these are decided by the prospects of the United States, Europe, and Japan.   In order to better understand the basic development of world economic growth in 1999, below we will review and forecast in more detail economic development in these three economic entities.

The U.S. Economy in 1998–1999

The record for the longest period of American economic expansion was created in the 1960s.   That period of expansion lasted more than eight years, or more than 100 consecutive months. The current economic expansion has lasted more than seven years, near the historic record.   Since 1991, the U.S. economy has maintained a high rate of growth, extremely low inflation, and comparatively low unemployment.   Productivity recovered to increase again, and product competitiveness rose markedly. In the 21st century, strong leadership in the high technology field will be maintained. In the first quarter of 1998, the U.S. GDP growth rate reached 5%, while it fell to 1% in the second quarter. The GDP growth rate in the second half of 1998 is estimated to be 2% (the potential growth rate). This continuous economic growth in the United States with low inflation has been achieved by raising productivity and lowering production costs.

In 1998, the main driving force of U.S. economic growth is the increase in consumer spending, as a result of increases in personal income. However, at the same time, the U.S. personal savings rate is extremely low, at only about 1%. This shows that the foundation for U.S. consumer spending growth is extremely fragile. If consumer confidence deteriorates, and consumers increase their savings for the future, the growth in consumer spending will slow down rapidly. Since 1992, U.S. fixed asset investment has maintained a continuous rising trend, and reached the highest level in 1998 (over 3.5%). Due to the effects of the Asian financial crisis, the export and import growth rates of the United States in 1997 were 12.4% and 14.3% respectively. The trade deficit was US$113.6 billion. In 1998, the growth of U.S. exports fell sharply (possibly to below 5.6%), but the decline in imports was slower. Consequently, the American trade deficit will rise noticeably, and is estimated to exceed US$170 billion. The recurrent account deficit will reach US$227.8 billion.[1] In 1998, the U.S. Government succeeded in reducing the federal budget deficit, which is now almost close to zero, and the budget (including social security) will show a surplus over the full year. Fiscal expenditure played a neutral role in economic growth.

Since the beginning of 1998, the U.S. utilization rate of production capacity has been maintained at a high level of above 82%. (Since 1967, the highest utilization rate has been 85.4%, the

---

[1] IMF, *World Economic Outlook*, May 1998.   The forecast in October by the IMF was US$236 billion.

lowest has been 71.1%, and the average was 82.1%.) However, in 1998, America was not affected greatly by inflation. Even though the employment cost index increased rapidly by 4%, the growth in productivity and the reduction in the prices of primary products as a result of the Asian financial crisis, as well as the price reductions in intermediary products and petroleum products, all helped to keep inflation in check. The inflation rate was only about 1%.

Within the six years between 1991 and 1998, the U.S. stock market has maintained a rather strong rising trend. There is no doubt that a serious bubble economy exists in the United States. On August 31, 1998, the Dow Jones Industrial Average crashed 512 points. We cannot preclude the possibility of even greater fluctuations in the U.S. stock market.

Even more worrying than the stock market is the question of the stability of the U.S. financial system. In October 1998, one of the largest hedge funds in America — Long Term Capital Management — was on the verge of collapse because of failed investments. The sudden exposure of serious losses at Long Term Capital Management revealed the fact that the U.S. financial system was not as sound as the American Government propagated or as the American people believed. Panicky investors scrambled to unload American assets, which caused the U.S. dollar to fall one-fifth in value against the Japanese Yen within a few days. This kind of drastic plunge has rarely been seen since the breakdown of the Bretton Woods agreement. The hedge funds played an inglorious part in this Asian financial crisis. Many hedge funds had lifted rocks only to drop them on their own feet. Because of the leveraged trading in derivatives by the hedge funds' wide-ranging speculative activities, they can earn spectacular profits and at the same time suffer serious losses much greater than under normal circumstances. The failure of the hedge funds caused serious losses to their own investors, and their borrowings from banks and other financial institutions caused even more widespread losses. In order to avoid and prevent losses, hedge funds are reducing their investments, and banks are reducing lending to them. Safety has become the chief goal of financial institutions now. When everyone is after cash, it can easily lead to a "credit crunch" which can affect the entire economy. As the Asian economy is already mired in deflation, if a credit crunch appears in America, the U.S. economy could easily fall into a vicious cycle of deflation.

The American Federal Reserve has rearranged its policy priority from fighting inflation to fighting deflation, because deflation appeared in the world as a result of the Asian financial crisis, because of the automatic crash of the American stock market, and because the losses suffered from lending to hedge funds affected the stability of the American financial system. In September 1998, the Federal Reserve cut the base rate from 5.5% to 5.25%. On October 15, the Federal Reserve announced another surprise cut of the base rate to 5%. The discount rate was cut to 4.75%. The two rounds of rate cuts within half a month showed the Federal Reserve's concern over deflation. We should note that, because the American budget has achieved a balance, the inflation rate is only 1%, and there are no serious problems in the financial system; the American Government has a lot of room to maneuver in terms of cutting interest rates or taxes to stimulate the economy.

There are still great uncertainties concerning the American economy in 1999. The IMF in its *World Economic Outlook* published in October 1998 predicted American economic growth rates in 1998 and 1999 to be 3.5% and 2.0% respectively. There is a consensus among economists that economic growth in America in 1999 shall noticeably decline from 1998. At the same time, the possibility cannot be excluded that the American economy will see greater difficulties.

The Japanese Economy in 1998 and 1999

After the bursting of its economic bubble, the Japanese economy has fallen into a prolonged period of decline. The economy, which was once proclaimed to be the foremost in the world, is now achieving some of the worst results among the western developed countries.

Because of the fiscal austerity policies implemented in 1997, and the influence of the worsening financial crisis caused by the non-performing debts and the Asian financial crisis, the Japanese economy has fallen sharply since the fourth quarter of 1997, and has recorded three consecutive quarters of negative growth.   Based on the estimate of the Japanese Ministry of the Economy, in 1998 the Japanese economy will decline by about 1.6%, to 1.8% from last year.

The Japanese economy in 1998 is in the worst condition since the war.   This economic crisis, with deflation as its main characteristic, started in the fourth quarter of 1997.   There were two reasons for the serious worsening of deflation: the increase of non-performing loans and the implementation of the ill-timed fiscal austerity policy.   The Asian financial crisis just made the situation even worse.

The increase in non-performing loans created serious adverse effects on the Japanese economy:

(1) The non-performing loans caused a series of financial institutions to fail.   As a result, the financial system could not operate properly and the normal operation of the overall economy was affected.

(2) Because of the large amounts of outstanding non-performing loans, the credit ratings of Japanese banks were downgraded by international credit agencies.   The cost of funds paid by Japanese financial institutions in the international markets rose, and the so-called "Japanese discount" appeared (that is, the payment of higher interest rates).

(3) In order to avoid the increase in non-performing loans, and as a way to satisfy the capital adequacy ratio of the Bank for International Settlements, the banks reduced their lending to enterprises, especially to small and medium-sized enterprises. A serious credit crunch thus appeared in the Japanese economy.

In 1996, the Japanese Parliament passed the legislation needed to implement a new fiscal policy in 1997. However, the fiscal austerity policy, which started in 1997 and extended into 1998, and in particular the introduction of the sales tax, seriously affected the recovery of the Japanese economy.

Because of the deterioration in non-performing loans, and the negative influence of the fiscal reorganization policy in 1997, the problem of insufficient demand in the economy has worsened since the fourth quarter of 1997. Because of insufficient demand, prices fell and the real interest rate rose. The rise in risk further increased the cost of doing business for enterprises. When the personal debt level was high, bankruptcies of enterprises rose sharply because of shortages of capital and the rising cost of funds. For enterprises that struggled for survival, the fall in prices forced down the profit margin, which in turn caused deterioration in enterprises' expectation of GDP growth. The expected fall in GDP growth caused a decline in enterprise investment. Banks' reluctance to lend forced even enterprises with good future prospects to reduce investment. According to the latest figures published in September by the Ministry of Finance, in the second quarter of 1998, corporate profits in Japan fell by 34%. The fixed asset expenditure fell by 11% from the same period last year. Business confidence for the future of medium-sized and large enterprises fell to a historic low.[2]

The reduction in consumer spending in 1998 was caused by a fall in consumer confidence. The closure of large enterprises created job anxiety for consumers, and the employment environment deteriorated. In 1998, the demand for manpower was weak. There were only 61 job openings for every 100 job seekers (January 1998). Because of the deterioration in the job market, and the slow rate of growth in personal income, consumer confidence has deteriorated noticeably since the fourth quarter of 1997. As a result, personal propensity to save has increased. The growth in consumer spending in 1998 will only reach 0.6%. Furthermore, because of the deterioration in consumer confidence and the slow rate of growth

---

[2]   *Asian Wall Street Journal,* September 10, 1998.

in personal income, in order to maintain the balance of income and expenditure, personal investment in housing declined noticeably. The number of house construction commencements started to fall monthly after the second quarter. At the beginning of 1998, the decline was 16.3%.[3]

Since 1997, Japan's trade surplus has continued to increase. The cause for the large increase in the trade surplus was that while exports were increasing, import growth was slowing down (a decline was recorded in several months in 1998). The major cause for the decline in imports was the weak domestic demand in Japan. The sharp fall in crude oil prices was also one of the major causes for the slowdown in the value of imports. The devaluation of the Yen and the relative prosperity of the American and European economies increased Japan's exports to these regions. At present, export growth has become the only effective way to maintain Japanese economic growth.

The Bank of Japan started to lower the discount rate way back in July 1991, and implemented an expansionary monetary policy in order to shake off the recession caused by the collapse of the bubble economy and to maintain a wider interest margin to strengthen the commercial banks' ability to tackle the problem of non-performing loans. However, the stimulation effect on the economy of the expansionary monetary policy has become less and less effective. Therefore, some economists believed that the Japanese economy fell into a "liquidity trap," where monetary policy lost its effectiveness.

Because of the sustained deterioration in the economy, the Japanese Government abandoned the fiscal reconstruction policy which had just begun. On April 20, 1998, the Hashimoto Cabinet announced the largest "Comprehensive Economic Package" in history with a Japanese Yen 16,650 bn economic stimulus plan

---

[3] Consumer confidence is measured by the consumer sentiment index. See *NRI: Quarterly Economic Review,* May 1998, Vol. 28, No. 2, p. 6.

(US$128.1 billion).   There were three themes in this economic policy:

(1)   The stimulation of domestic demand through increases in government expenditure and temporary tax reductions,

(2)   Improvement in the economic structure to increase the country's potential for long-term economic growth,

(3)   Facilitating the handling of non-performing loans.   The Ministry of Finance personnel estimated that the new comprehensive economic policy would increase Japan's nominal GDP growth by 2%.[4]   After the announcement of the Comprehensive Economic Package, the Japanese Government shifted the emphasis of the fiscal policy to permanent tax cuts. In his first policy speech, the new Premier Obuchi declared that the highest personal tax rate was to be cut from 65% to 50%, while the corporate tax rate was also to be cut from 46% to 40%.   The government would issue national bonds to fund tax cuts and spending increases.   The Japanese Government hoped to stimulate consumer spending through tax cuts and also to assist enterprises to increase sales and profit levels.[5]

However, skeptics of Japan's fiscal policy pointed out that in 1998, the outstanding national debt would exceed 100% of GDP. Japanese consumers knew that the current so-called "permanent tax cuts" and public works with low return on investment would cause increases in future taxes.   Consequently, consumers did not increase their spending.

For a long time, the Japanese Government vacillated in its handling of the non-performing loans.   It hesitated to use public funds and instead wanted to rely on the improvement of the

---

[4]   *Summary of the Comprehensive Economic Package*, supplied by the Japanese Embassy, April 24, 1998.

[5]   *BBC Internet News*, August 7, 1998.

economy and the recovery of the real estate market. Since the end of 1997, the Japanese economy has declined noticeably. The government and the opposition started to realize that the financial instability caused by non-performing loans was seriously affecting confidence in the economy. They saw that the economy could not be improved before the problem of non-performing loans was resolved.

On the whole, the outlook for the Japanese economy is not optimistic. The policies and measures undertaken by the Japanese Government up till now have not shown any noticeable results. Facing a deteriorating economy, the Japanese Government has been unable to come up with better measures. Perhaps, as the Japanese economy continues to sink, people will come to the conclusion that the economy just cannot sink any further. Then, as expectations change, in the not too distant future, the Japanese economy will start to recover. Or perhaps, in the new future, some expected changes will occur in the international economic environment which will create favorable conditions for Japan to recover. Recently, the Japanese Government presented a second Japanese Yen 10,000 bn supplementary budget, and established a permanent tax cut of Japanese Yen 7,000 billion. The Japanese government has now spent Japanese Yen 30,000 bn to stimulate the economy. With respect to the handling of non-performing loans, the ruling party on October 7 announced "emergency measures to reform the financial institutions as soon as possible." The government is to inject public funds into the financial institutions before they go bankrupt. Furthermore, a new "reconstruction financial system fund" of Japanese Yen10,000 bn has been established in addition to the Japanese Yen1.7 bn deposit insurance fund. The investing public warmly responded to these measures by the Japanese Government. The Japanese Yen and the Nikkei Index started to recover. In particular, because of the weakness of the American economy in the American stock market, and increased risk in American financial assets, the Japanese Yen strengthened from its formerly weak position. However, we still need time to observe whether all these measures undertaken by the Japanese Government will have any positive effects. Currently, both in Japan and outside Japan, people still hold pessimistic views on the immediate outlook for the Japanese economy. The general estimate is that it will take two years for the Japanese economy to recover. In 1999, even under the most favorable conditions, the Japanese economy will only just begin to recover.

The Economy of the European Union in 1998–1999

The countries of the European Union are still in a stage of economic recovery. In 1998, the economic recovery of the EU countries was further strengthened and consolidated within the latest economic cycle (economic growth was only 1.7% in 1996). Compared with other countries and regions, the economies of Europe were relatively stable in 1998. In 1997, in order to meet the requirements of the Union, the EU countries all maintained rather tight fiscal and monetary policies. In 1998, in order to withstand the negative effects of the Asian financial crisis, the EU countries loosened the fiscal and monetary policies slightly. The general fiscal deficit was about 2.5% within the Euro region. In 1998–1999, the percentage of fiscal expenditure as a percentage of GDP will decline from about 48% to about 47%. At the same time, fiscal income as a percentage of GDP will decline from about 46% to about 44%. Between 1997 and 1998, the growth of the money supply M_3 was about 4%. Currently, the rate of growth of the money supply is showing signs of rising. In 1998, the real short-term interest rate in EU countries is about 2–3%, and the real long-term interest is 4-5%, showing a decline. Just like in the United States, the European stock markets had risen sharply since 1993, but started to decline after August 1998. In 1997, the main driving forces for economic growth in Europe were the growth in consumption and investment. Because Asia is both a major market and a competitor for Europe, the Asian economic recession and currency devaluation caused by the Asian financial crisis seriously affected Europe's exports to Asia. (Asia and Russia make up 11% of the EU's export markets.) However, the effects were effectively canceled out by gains in the improvement in trade conditions, the low interest rate, and the expansion of non-Asian markets.   In 1998, the EU countries will maintain an overall trade balance (or possibly a small trade deficit).   The prediction of most economists of the European Union economies is that the rate of economic growth will be around 3% or higher.   There will be no strong economic growth or economic recession (see Table 3).   In a certain sense, the European Union is the only bright spot in the world economy.

Table 3
Economic Growth of the European Union and Major Countries

(Unit %)

	1997	1998	1999
European Union	2.7	2.9	2.5
France	2.3	3.1	2.8
Germany	2.2	2.6	2.5
Italy	1.5	2.1	2.5
Britain	3.4	2.3	1.2

Source: IMF, *World Economic Outlook*, October 1998.

Because of the inflexibility of the labor market and other structural causes, high unemployment has always been a major problem plaguing the European economies.   In 1998, the unemployment rates of major European Union countries all dropped, but were still much higher than those in America and Japan in recession.   In 1999, no obvious changes are expected in the unemployment rates of these countries.   (See Table 4.)

In 1998 and 1999, inflation in the European Union countries will continue to stay at a low level.   (See Table 5.)   Because of the slow growth in wages, and the fall in the prices of oil and primary and semi-manufactured goods as a result of the Asian financial crisis, serious inflationary pressure does not exist in the European Union. In the future unified monetary policy under the control of the European Central Bank, differences in the inflation rate will mean differences in real interest rates.   This will create problems for Euro countries.

Table 4
Unemployment Rates of Major European Union Countries

(Unit %)

	1996	1997	1998	1999
Germany	10.4	11.3	10.9	10.6
France	12.4	12.5	11.8	11.2
Britain	7.3	5.5	4.8	4.9
Italy	12.1	12.3	12.1	11.8
Spain	22.2	20.8	19.2	18.3

Source: IMF, *World Economic Outlook*, October 1998.

Table 5
Consumer Price Index for Major European Union Countries

(Unit %)

	1996	1997	1998	1999
Germany	1.5	1.8	1.0	1.4
France	2.0	1.2	1.1	1.3
England	2.9	2.8	2.8	2.8
Italy	3.9	1.7	1.8	1.7
Spain	3.5	2.0	2.1	2.4

Source: IMF, *World Economic Outlook*, October 1998.

The most important event in 1999 in the European Union will no doubt be the official launch of the Euro.   Most economists are optimistic about the Euro.   They believe that the launch of the Euro will further enhance the unification of the European economies, which will increase the competitiveness of Europe.   The Euro is based on the strength of the strong European economies, and will become a serious challenge to the dominance of the U.S. dollar.

Some economists even predict that after the launch of the Euro, international capital from the United States and other countries will flow toward Europe. The effects of the Euro's official launch on the world economy and world capital flow and changes in international currencies are worthy of special attention.

The year 1998 has been a year full of uncertainties in the world economy. For many countries, it was a year of disasters. The world economic outlook for 1999 is still not optimistic. If the governments of various countries, especially of the developed countries, cannot implement proper economic policies to turn around the deflationary phenomenon which has affected many countries, then in 1999 a serious global recession may occur. In 1997, the growth in world trade was 9.7%. Based on the IMF forecast, in 1998 and 1999, the growth in world trade will decline to 3.7% and 4.6% respectively. Based on current conditions, because of further deterioration in the world economic condition, and the efforts by developing countries to improve their international balance of payments, the export situation of China will be even more severe in 1999. In 1999, because of the deterioration in the international financial crisis, international investors will be even more concerned about the liquidity and safety of capital funds. There is no reason for us to be optimistic about China's efforts to attract international capital. However, when China formulates its external and domestic economic policies, it should take into consideration that the world economic situation will deteriorate further in 1999. While continuing to increase exports and attract foreign investment, the Chinese Government should place more efforts on deepening the reforms, improving the production structure, and expanding the domestic market, so that we can accomplish swift and stable economic growth.

PROSPECTS OF THE GLOBAL ECONOMIC SITUATION IN 1999

ZHENG JINGPING AND LÜ QINGZHE
International Statistics Information Centre
State Statistical Bureau

Badly affected by the financial crisis, Asia's economies declined sharply in 1998. The national economies of North America, the European Union, and Latin America were also affected by the crisis to varying degrees. Therefore, world economic growth in 1998 was expected to be at least 2% lower than the previous year. Meanwhile, the growth rate in world trade was expected to be only 3.7%, much lower than the 9.7% in 1997. The prospects for the world economic situation in 1999 will be basically the same as, or a bit better than those for 1998.

The World Economic Situation in 1998

Economic Growth in the United States Slowed Down

Having recorded an economic growth rate of 3.9% in 1997, the U.S. recorded a strong economic growth of 5.5% in the first quarter of 1998. However, in the second quarter, the growth rate declined sharply to 1.6%, the lowest level in three years. Overall, the growth rate for the first half was 3.5%. The decline in the economic growth in the second quarter was mainly due to the decrease in business orders. The inventory continued to grow rapidly for two consecutive quarters. The strike at General Motors also caused a slowdown in production activities. In addition, the Asian financial crisis caused the trade deficit to continue to expand. The pace of corporate development slowed down; the manufacturing sector declined, and enterprise earnings fell. But although the pace of expansion of American prosperity began to slow down, the economy is still on the right track. We expect that the 1998 American economic growth rate will fall from last year's 3.9% to 3.5%, the inflation rate will be 1.6%, and the unemployment rate 4.5%.

The Japanese Economy Remained Weak

In the first quarter of 1998, Japan's economic growth declined by 1.3% from the fourth quarter of last year, which is equivalent to an annual rate of 5.3%. This margin of decline has rarely been seen in recent years. The economy in the second quarter declined by 0.8% from the first quarter, or 3.3% on an annual basis. This was the first time since World War II that the economy had declined for three consecutive quarters.

Under the influence of the Japanese Government's austerity measures, the economy has fallen into the twofold difficulties of insufficient domestic demand and oversupply. The insufficient demand caused prices to drop which in turn caused a fall in enterprise profits and a slower increase in salaries, adding to the problems of insufficient demand. This vicious cycle created a recession in the Japanese economy, and cast a pall over investment and production. The more serious problem was that the interwoven problems of insufficient domestic demand, deflation, and non-performing loans in the financial system increased the difficulties for economic recovery. Affected by non-performing loans, banks could not make any loans. "The reluctance to lend" blocked the lifeblood of the economy. The number of enterprises that went bankrupt or were on the brink of bankruptcy because of the lack of capital increased sharply. In 1998, although there have not been frequent closures of financial institutions, many financial institutions including large banks have sunk into financial difficulties because of non-performing loans.

Since the beginning of 1998, the Japanese Government has changed the austerity policy adopted last year into an expansionary one. Public investment has been increased substantially; and corporate and personal taxes have been reduced to help stimulate growth in domestic demand. At the same time, public funds have been used to stablize the financial situation. Various legislative and other means have been used to help financial institutions clean up bad loans. However, because implementation of the policy needs time, and because of changes in the political scene, it will be difficult to see any effect of the stimulus package in the short term. The new Liberal Democratic Party government has not taken any new measures since it came to office. The economic recovery is expected to occur no earlier than the spring of 1999. The estimated growth rate of the Japanese economy in 1998 is -2.5%, the inflation rate 0.4%, and the unemployment rate 4.1%.

Good Economic Prospects for the European Union

In 1998, the countries of the European Union have been experiencing a growth in industrial investment, a recovery in domestic market demand, an expansion in export trade, and improvement in employment, despite the negative effects of the Southeast Asian financial crisis and the three consecutive quarters of negative growth in Japan. Except for Britain, which experienced a slowdown in economic growth, the economies of most European Union member countries were all expected to see steady growth.

External trade is still the main pillar of support for the economic growth of the European Union, mainly because of the expansion of markets in Latin America and Central and Eastern Europe, as well as the increased flow of goods among member countries. The major reason for the improvement in the economy of the European Union is that it has appropriately resolved the problems of monetary union and unemployment. With the beginning of 1998, the EU entered into the final preparatory stages for the monetary union. All the countries implemented active measures to adjust their economic policies, keeping the average inflation rates of member countries below 2.2%, lowering the long-term interest rate by 0.4%, and the fiscal deficit to below 3%. The average tax rate and major economic indicators have all been improved.

At the special meeting of heads of state convened in early May in Brussels, 11 member countries became the founding members of the single Euro currency. The European Union also pushed its member countries to solve the problem of unemployment and internal cooperation and encouraged interaction among the member countries, the local governments, and the economic organizations in their development of tertiary production by small and medium-sized enterprises. Financial assistance for technological training, professional training, and tax concessions have all showed positive results. The estimated economic growth rate of the European Union in 1998 is 2.7%, the inflation rate is 1.7%, and the unemployment rate is 10.3%.

The German economy continues to see recovery. In the first quarter of 1998, Germany's GDP grew by 3.8% from the same period last year, signaling the strongest beginning in years. Commodity exports increased by 15.9% from last year. GDP growth in the second quarter was 1.7% higher than that in the same period the previous year. This does not mean that German economic growth is slowing down, but rather that it is steadily rising. A 2.9% growth figure for the first half is a very credible figure, faithfully reflecting Germany's economic strength. The estimated economic growth rate in Germany in 1998 is 2.7%, with the inflation rate being 1% and the unemployment rate 10.9%.

The French economy also performed well. In the first quarter of 1998, the French economic growth rate reached 3.4%. Industrial production, consumer spending, consumer confidence, and investment all rose steadily. The unemployment rate fell monthly, while enterprise orders increased sharply. The operating rate of manufacturers generally rose. Economic growth in the second quarter maintained a rate of 3%. The French economy is seeking the most powerful revival in recent years. As exports continue to grow, domestic demand steadily increases; enterprise inventory is reduced, and the speed of money flow also accelerates. It is estimated that the growth rate of the French economy in 1998 will reach the target of 3%, the inflation rate will be 1.1%, and the unemployment rate 11.8%.

After several years of consecutive high growth, the British economy started to slow down in 1998. In the first and second quarters, the GDP growth rate was 3% and 2.6% respectively, lower than the 3.1% and 3.5% last year. The major problem encountered by the British economy was that rising labor costs reduced the competitiveness of their products. The ability of enterprises to reinvest and produce was therefore cut back. Meanwhile, the strong British pound affected exports. Economic development was also restricted by the rise in inflation and the Bank of England's interest rate increases. Because there were many domestic problems with the British economy, the confidence of investors was seriously impaired, and the inflow of international capital was noticeably reduced. The estimated growth of the British economy in 1998 will decline from 3.4% last year to 2.3%, the inflation rate will be 2.8%, and the unemployment rate 4.8%.

Southeast Asia: The Economic Situation Is Still Serious

At the beginning of 1998, even though the financial storm was raging, both the Southeast Asian countries themselves and the international community generally thought that the regional economies could withstand the pummeling of the financial crisis, and after two or three years would recover fully through active adjustment of the economic foundations built in past years.

However, after three-quarters of 1998 had passed, there had been no sign of the financial crisis easing. Within this period, the Thai cabinet has changed, and President Suharto, who ruled Indonesia for 32 years, was forced to resign after national violence caused by the financial crisis. Looking at economic developments since the beginning of 1998, the ASEAN economies have not shaken off the shackles of serious economic decline. As indicated in the economic development indices recently announced by various countries, there is no sign for optimism.

With negative growth of 0.4% in 1997, the Thai economy is expected to record negative growth of 4–5.5% by the end of the fiscal year in September 1998. Given no unforeseen occurrences, the Thai economy is expected to stabilize in the final quarter of 1998. The estimated Thai economic growth rate throughout 1998 will be -7.8%.

Because of the sharp decline in domestic market demand, the Malaysian economy carries heavy burdens. In the first quarter of 1998, the economic growth rate was -1.8%, which was only the second negative quarterly growth in Malaysia's economic history since 1985. The negative growth in the second quarter was even more serious at -6.8%. Throughout 1998, Malaysia's economy will see a contraction of more than 2%.

The GNP growth rate for the Philippines in the first quarter of 1998 was 2.5%. Because the financial situation in the Philippines was relatively stable and the government introduced a series of measures to attract foreign investment, the inflow of foreign investment in the first half of 1998 rose sharply by 42%, reaching US$670 million, showing that foreign investors regained their confidence in the Philippine economy. The estimated 1998 economic growth rate of the Philippines will be 1.5%. The current high level of foreign debt at US$45.5 billion constitutes the biggest threat to the sustained development of the Philippines.

The economic situation of Indonesia was the most serious of all. The growth rate in the first quarter was -7.9%; the inflation rate reached 40.6%; and the number of unemployed reached 15 million. The total number of people whose living standard had fallen below the poverty line was 80 million. Economic growth in the second quarter was even more critical, falling by 16.5% from the same period last year. It is estimated that throughout 1998 the Indonesian economy will contract by 16.8%.

The economic performance of Singapore in the first quarter was excellent, recording 5.6% growth from the same period in 1997. However, because of the serious economic recession in the neighboring countries, Singapore's exports, especially of electronic products, declined. In addition, the devaluation of the Japanese Yen and the Korean Won added to the competitive difficulties of enterprises whose profits were already declining. The GDP growth rate in the second quarter was 1.6% lower than that in the same period of last year. The estimated economic growth rate in 1998 will be 1%.

In the first quarter of 1998, the economic growth rate in South Korea was down by 3.8%, which was the lowest figure since 1960 when South Korea started to document economic data.   Figures for the second quarter were no cause for optimism, with a 6.6% decline from the same period last year. South Korea is in the process of implementing drastic economic restructuring, and domestic demand will fall dramatically; enterprises will reduce their investment in equipment and machinery and shift their business focus to the sale of stocked items.   Consequently, the economic situation will deteriorate further, and South Korea will likely see a negative growth rate of -6.2%.

In the Hong Kong Special Administrative Region, GDP growth fell by 2.8% in the first quarter. The decline was even more serious in the second quarter, with an estimated figure of -5%. Hong Kong's exports in the first half declined by 2.1% from the same period last year, but the export growth rate in 1997 was 4.2%. In terms of domestic demand, consumer spending has noticeably declined because of the weak stock and real estate markets and the decline in tourism.   Total retail sales in the first half declined sharply by 15% from the same period last year.   In unemployment, the rate rose from 3.5% in the first quarter to 4.4% in the second quarter.   The economic outlook is not optimistic, and the estimated economic growth rate over the entire year is -3.1%.

The economic performance of Taiwan province in the first quarter was quite good, with an increase of 5.9% from last year.

The economic growth rate in the second quarter was 5.2%. However, affected by the Asian financial crisis, exports between January and July declined by 8.6% from last year. Imports have declined by 6.4% and this situation will become more serious. This will create unfavorable effects on Taiwan's economic development. The economic growth rate for Taiwan in 1998 may reach 4.8%.

Economic Growth in Latin America Has Been Slowing Down

Because of the Southeast Asian financial crisis, and the decline in raw material prices in international markets, the economic growth of Latin America has been slowing down in 1998. The estimated growth rate will decline from last year's 5.1% to 2.8%. The developmental levels of the three major Latin American countries vary. The estimated growth rates of Brazil and Argentina are 1.1% and 5%, respectively. Although Mexico is less affected by the Southeast Asian financial crisis, the estimated economic growth rate will decline from 7% to 4.5% because of the decline in petroleum prices. The inflation rate may fall to 13% and unemployment will increase to 4%. Because of the weakness in raw materials prices in international markets, poor weather conditions, and the unstable political environment, the economic prospects for countries like Colombia, Ecuador, and Venezuela are dim. For Chile, the continuous decline in copper prices has given rise to an increase in the trade deficit. The Central Bank has had to devalue the Peso and reduce its fiscal spending. The estimated growth rate has been revised down from 7.1% to 5%.

The Recovery in Eastern Europe and the Former Soviet Union Countries Has Slowed Down

Affected by the Asian financial crisis and the slowdown in world economic growth, the economic growth of Eastern Europe and the former Soviet Union has been slower than expected. The estimated economic growth rate for Central and Eastern European countries in 1998 will be 3.4%. In the first half of the year, the economies of Poland, Hungary, Slovakia, and Slovenia grew at about 5%. Affected by a monetary crisis and withdrawal of foreign investment, the economy in the Czech Republic shrank. The estimated Czech economic growth rate in 1998 will be 1.5%. In countries like Bulgaria, Romania, and Albania, political stability and progress have been achieved and the economic decline has been stopped. In 1998, the Romanian economy will grow by 2%, while the Bulgarian economy will grow by 1%. In 1998, Hungary's recurrent account deficit will decline, foreign direct investment will increase, and inflation will be effectively controlled. The estimated economic growth rate in Hungary in 1998 will reach 4.3%. The economic growth rate in Poland will be about 5.7%, a rate lower than that in 1997.

In 1997, the Russian economy stopped declining for the first time since the breakup of the Soviet Union. The GDP growth rate was 0.9% higher than in 1996. However, between January and August 1998, the Russian GDP declined by 2.1% from the same period last year. Industrial production also fell by 2.6% from the same period in 1997. The major cause for the decline in industrial production was the reduction in operating hours of industries and the decline in the automobile manufacturing industry. A further decline in agriculture in 1998 will be inevitable. In the latest round of financial crisis and political instability, the Russian economy is again facing collapse. The full year's record was expected to reflect serious problems in the economy. The estimated economic growth rate in Russia in 1998 will be -3.7%, and the inflation rate will rise from last year's 14.7% to 48.4%.

Prospects for the World Economy in 1999

In 1999, although there will be various uncertain factors such as the political and economic crisis in Russia and the effects of the financial crisis on Latin America, based on an analysis of the current situation, we believe the world economic environment will be similar to that in 1998 or slightly better. The economic growth rate will reach about 2.5%, and the growth in world trade will recover to

4.6%. The situations of individual regions and countries will be as follows:

Asian Economies Will Show Recovery in Growth

On the one hand, the two years of economic decline have impaired the economic growth base for many Asian countries. On the other, the economy in many countries is moving toward stability following the uncertainty of 1998. Consequently, the economic growth rate of the Asian region in 1999 will be higher than in 1998. For example, the growth rate of South Korea will rise from -6.2% in 1998 to 1.4%; Singapore will rise from 1% in 1998 to 3%; Malaysia will rise from -2% in 1998 to 0.5%; Thailand will rise from -7.8% in 1998 to -0.7%; the Philippines will rise from 1.5% to 4%. Both India and Vietnam will maintain a growth rate above 5%. China's economic growth will also be better than that in 1998. It will be difficult for the Japanese economy to show a strong recovery in 1999. However, it will still do better than in 1998. The main reason for this lies in the series of measures implemented by the Japanese Government, like the Yen16,000 billion of public investment, the increased supply of short-term funds by the Bank of Japan, and the further lowering of savings deposit rates, to name a few. The effects of these measures will gradually become manifest. The estimated growth rate for Japan in 1999 will be about 0.5%.

U.S. Economic Growth Will Decline Slightly, But Will Still Be Reasonable

Since the second quarter of 1998, U.S. economic growth has started to slow down, but it remains on the right track. Inflation is mild and is showing a declining trend, while the consumer confidence index is also stable. Other economic indicators, like construction investment, car sales, and wage growth, all reflect positive trends. This is the result of the inflow of capital which resulted from efforts to avoid the uncertainties before the launch of the Euro and of the Asian financial crisis, and the readjustment and upgrading of the economic structure driven by high- and new technology industries. On September 29, the Federal Reserve lowered the overnight interbank rate by 0.25%, showing its determination to stimulate domestic economic growth and even up the world's economic growth.   Meanwhile, some signs of a bubble economy have emerged.   The U.S. dollar is too strong, and the stock and debt markets are too high.   Many economists point out that the American economy just cannot do any better. The estimated American economic growth rate in 1999 will be lower, at 3.0%. The U.S. dollar will also depreciate.

The European Union Will Be the New Bright Spot in World Economic Growth

The estimated economic growth rate of the European Union in 1999 will be 2.8%, slightly higher than the 2.7% of 1998. The reasons for the economic recovery in the European Union are: First, the Euro's launch into general circulation.   On January 1, 1999, the Euro will be officially launched.   The exchange risk that various Euro countries now have to bear will be reduced or will disappear, and the ability to defend the Common Market will be greatly increased. The "Euro region" has become the most powerful weapon within the European Union to defend against outside attacks.

Since the stock markets in Western Europe have not risen as much as the American markets, the potential for development is greater.   International funds, including those from the United States, have started to flow into Western Europe, which will no doubt bring vitality to the region's economy.   In addition, the Euro will make trade within two-thirds of the European Union countries freer and more economical, which will stimulate economic growth.

Second, the European Union's employment rate is rather low. Manpower resources are plentiful, and quality is high.   As large sums of capital flow in, economic growth will be further facilitated.

Third, the extent to which the United Stated has been affected by the Asian financial crisis is greater than that of the European Union, and signs of a slowdown are becoming apparent in the American economy.   On the other hand, Asia, which has gone through a long period of high growth, will need a long time to recover from the latest crisis.   Consequently, the European Union will hold an important position in the world's economic growth in the next few years.

The Economic Growth Rate in Latin America Will Decline Slightly in 1999

The estimated growth rate in Latin America will decline from 2.9% in 1998 to about 2.8%.   The major reasons are the influence from the Asian and Russian financial crises, and the fall in the prices of commodities, such as copper and oil.

Economic Growth Will Be Maintained in Countries Which Are Changing Their Development Tracks, Except for Russia

The estimated growth rate in these countries in 1999 will still be negative (-2.9%).   If the Russian economic situation does not deteriorate further, economic growth in Central and Eastern Europe will continue to rise, at a rate of 3.6% which will be higher than that in 1998.

To summarize, the economies of Europe, America, and Japan, which combine to make up two-thirds of the world economy, will continue to grow or stay at their current level.   For countries changing development tracks, and developing countries like China, economic growth will be maintained, except in the case of Russia. Southeast Asian countries will recover to grow again.   Therefore, on the whole, world economic growth and growth in world trade in 1999 will see a slight improvement from 1998 or will remain the same as in 1998 (see Table 1), though uncertainties and negative influences will continue to hang over Russia and Latin America.

Table 1
Forecast of Major World Economic Indicators

	1996	1997	1998 forecast	1999 forecast
I. Economic growth rate (%)				
World	4.2	4.1	2.0	2.5
Developed countries	2.8	2.9	2.3	2.3
U.S.	3.4	3.9	3.5	3.0
Japan	3.9	0.8	-2.5	0.5
Germany	1.3	2.2	2.7	2.9
France	1.6	2.3	3.0	2.8
Britain	2.2	3.4	2.3	1.6
Developing countries	6.6	5.8	2.3	3.6
African region	5.8	3.2	3.7	4.7
Asian region	8.2	6.6	1.8	3.9
Hong Kong, China	4.9	5.3	-3.1	0.8
Taiwan, China	5.7	6.8	4.8	5.6
India	7.5	5.6	5.0	5.1
Vietnam	9.3	8.7	5.2	5.0
South Korea	7.1	5.5	-6.2	1.4
Malaysia	8.6	7.8	-2.0	0.5
Singapore	6.9	7.8	1.0	3.0
Thailand	5.5	-0.4	-7.8	-0.7
Indonesia	8.0	5.0	-16.8	-2.7
Philippines	5.7	5.1	1.5	4.0
Latin America	3.5	5.1	2.8	2.7
Countries changing track	-1.0	2.0	-0.2	0.8
Central and Eastern Europe	1.6	2.8	3.4	3.6
Russia	-5.0	0.9	-3.7	-2.9
II. Consumer price index (%)				
Developed countries	2.3	2.0	1.5	1.7
U.S.	2.9	2.3	1.6	2.3
Japan	0.1	1.7	0.4	-0.5
Germany	1.5	1.8	1.0	1.4
France	2.0	1.2	1.1	1.3
Britain	2.9	2.8	2.8	2.8
Developing countries	14.1	9.1	10.3	8.3
African region	26.7	11.0	7.7	7.1
Asian region	7.9	4.7	8.3	7.0
Latin America	20.8	13.9	10.8	9.4
Countries changing track	41.4	27.9	29.5	34.6
III. Unemployment rate (%)				
Developed countries	7.7	7.5	7.1	7.1
U.S.	5.4	4.9	4.5	4.8
Japan	3.3	3.4	4.1	4.3
European Union	11.3	11.0	10.3	10.0
Germany	10.4	11.5	10.9	10.6
France	12.4	12.5	11.8	11.2
Britain	7.3	5.5	4.8	4.9
IV. World trade growth rate (%)	6.8	9.7	3.7	4.6

APPENDIX

Statistics

Year	GDP growth rate (%)	Primary industry value added growth rate (%)	Secondary industry value added growth rate (%)	Heavy industry value added growth rate (%)	Light industry value added growth rate (%)
1978	11.7	4.1	15.0	19.9	13.9
1979	7.6	6.1	8.2	9.0	8.9
1980	7.8	-1.4	13.6	8.3	21.9
1981	5.3	7.0	1.9	-5.2	12.3
1982	9.0	11.5	5.5	7.4	3.8
1983	10.9	8.3	10.4	11.4	7.5
1984	15.2	13.0	14.5	15.9	13.3
1985	13.5	1.8	18.6	15.7	21.7
1986	8.9	3.3	10.3	7.5	12.5
1987	11.6	4.7	13.7	12.5	14.1
1988	11.3	2.5	14.5	13.0	18.2
1989	4.1	3.1	3.8	4.8	5.3
1990	3.8	7.4	3.2	2.9	4.0
1991	9.2	2.4	13.9	13.0	14.6
1992	14.2	4.7	21.1	23.9	19.5
1993	13.5	4.7	19.9	22.0	19.8
1994	12.7	4.0	18.4	16.6	19.7
1995	10.5	5.0	13.9	12.0	16.7
1996	9.6	5.1	12.0	12.4	13.1
1997	9.5	3.5	10.8	10.5	11.7
1998	9.7	3.2	9.2	9.7	9.3
1999	9.7	3.5	10.2	11.0	10.3

Year	Tertiary industry value added growth rate (%)	Transportation, postal service, and telecommunications industry value added growth rate (%)	Commercial service industry value added growth rate (%)	Total value of fixed assets investment (current prices RMB billion)	Nominal growth rate of total fixed assets investment (current price, %)
1978	13.7	8.9	23.1	89.90	19.9
1979	7.8	7.7	8.8	97.70	8.7
1980	5.9	5.7	-1.3	91.08	-6.8
1981	10.5	1.9	30.0	96.10	5.5
1982	13.0	11.6	3.9	123.04	28.0
1983	15.2	10.0	21.8	143.01	16.2
1984	19.4	14.9	21.5	183.29	28.2
1985	18.3	13.5	28.9	254.32	38.8
1986	12.1	12.8	10.6	312.07	22.7
1987	14.4	10.0	13.5	379.12	21.5
1988	13.2	13.4	14.3	474.68	25.2
1989	5.4	4.7	-8.3	441.03	-7.1
1990	2.3	8.5	-4.8	451.76	2.4
1991	8.8	11.2	4.5	559.46	23.8
1992	12.4	10.5	13.1	808.04	44.4
1993	10.7	12.4	6.6	1,307.23	61.8
1994	9.6	9.5	7.7	1,704.29	30.4
1995	8.4	12.0	5.9	2,001.93	17.5
1996	7.8	11.4	5.4	2,291.37	14.5
1997	8.2	10.7	8.5	2,494.10	8.8
1998	8.3	10.8	8.5	2,880.01	15.5
1999	8.5	11.0	8.5	3,330.01	15.6

Year	Real growth rate total fixed assets investment (constant price, %)	Investment rate (%)	Retail price index inflation rate (%)	Investment product price index inflation rate (%)	Consumer price index inflation rate (%)
1978	19.5	24.8	0.7	0.3	1.5
1979	4.7	24.2	2.0	3.8	2.1
1980	-8.5	20.2	6.0	1.9	7.0
1981	2.9	19.8	2.4	2.5	2.6
1982	25.1	23.2	1.9	2.4	1.9
1983	13.3	24.1	1.5	2.6	1.2
1984	23.9	25.6	2.8	3.4	1.7
1985	30.1	28.4	8.8	6.7	7.6
1986	15.8	30.6	6.0	6.0	6.5
1987	14.1	31.7	7.3	6.4	7.3
1988	10.0	31.8	18.5	13.9	18.8
1989	-12.9	26.1	17.8	6.7	18.0
1990	-3.0	24.4	2.1	5.6	3.1
1991	15.0	25.9	2.9	7.6	3.4
1992	25.3	30.3	5.4	15.3	6.4
1993	27.8	37.7	13.2	26.6	14.7
1994	18.1	36.4	21.7	10.4	24.1
1995	10.9	34.2	14.8	5.9	17.1
1996	10.1	33.4	6.1	4.0	8.3
1997	7.2	33.4	0.7	1.6	2.7
1998	16.3	35.8	-1.5	-0.7	1.0
1999	14.6	37.9	1.7	0.9	2.5

Year	Real growth rate of urban household average income (%)	Real growth rate of rural household average income (%)	Urban household consumption real growth rate (%)	Rural household consumption real growth rate (%)	Total consumption real growth rate (%)
1978	-2.4	6.7	-	-	-
1979	19.6	17.6	10.4	6.8	25.2
1980	6.2	17.4	11.7	9.4	0.3
1981	1.6	11.4	16.0	8.9	4.2
1982	5.8	21.1	4.8	10.0	7.2
1983	4.3	14.7	5.2	11.7	7.5
1984	12.5	12.7	12.1	13.6	19.6
1985	0.9	8.5	15.8	14.3	7.9
1986	12.9	2.6	10.1	3.6	8.4
1987	1.7	3.9	9.1	6.5	1.6
1988	1.2	4.0	12.4	7.3	-2.4
1989	-3.3	-1.3	2.4	0.2	-0.2
1990	8.9	5.2	10.5	1.5	7.4
1991	5.9	5.7	12.4	7.8	21.5
1992	9.0	3.2	18.7	10.7	16.0
1993	10.2	3.2	12.5	6.7	12.3
1994	8.8	5.0	8.8	6.7	7.2
1995	4.9	5.6	10.0	9.8	-4.6
1996	3.9	9.0	6.3	10.2	4.7
1997	3.4	4.6	6.8	5.8	11.3
1998	4.9	2.2	6.8	5.7	16.3
1999	4.8	3.1	7.6	5.6	15.0

Year	Total value of retail sales (RMB billion)	Total retail sales nominal growth rate (current price, %)	Total retail sales real growth rate (constant price, %)	Fiscal revenue (RMB billion)	Growth rate of fiscal revenue (%)
1978	126.49	7.7	7.0	113.23	29.5
1979	147.60	16.7	14.4	114.64	1.2
1980	179.40	21.5	14.7	115.99	1.2
1981	200.25	11.6	9.0	117.58	1.4
1982	218.15	8.9	6.9	121.23	3.1
1983	242.61	11.2	9.6	136.69	12.8
1984	289.92	19.5	16.2	164.29	20.2
1985	380.14	31.1	20.5	200.48	22.0
1986	437.40	15.1	8.6	212.20	5.8
1987	511.50	16.9	9.0	219.94	3.6
1988	653.46	27.8	7.8	235.72	7.2
1989	707.42	8.3	-8.1	266.49	13.1
1990	725.03	2.5	0.4	293.71	10.2
1991	824.57	13.7	10.5	314.95	7.2
1992	970.48	17.7	11.7	348.34	10.6
1993	1,246.21	28.4	13.4	434.90	24.8
1994	1,626.47	30.5	7.2	521.81	20.0
1995	2,062.00	26.8	10.4	624.22	19.6
1996	2,477.41	20.1	13.3	740.75	18.7
1997	2,729.87	10.2	9.4	865.10	16.8
1998	2,930.05	7.3	9.0	1,005.03	16.2
1999	3,240.03	10.6	8.7	1,168.00	16.2

Year	Fiscal expenditure (RMB billion)	Fiscal expenditure growth rate (%)	Fiscal deficit (RMB billion)	Outstanding of urban and rural savings deposits (RMB billion)	Growth rate of outstanding of urban and rural savings deposits (%)
1978	112.21	33.0	1.02	21.06	15.7
1979	128.18	14.2	-13.54	28.10	33.4
1980	122.88	-4.1	-6.89	39.95	42.2
1981	113.84	-7.4	3.74	52.40	31.2
1982	123.00	8.0	-1.77	67.54	28.9
1983	140.95	14.6	-4.26	89.25	32.1
1984	170.10	20.7	-5.82	121.47	36.1
1985	200.43	17.8	0.06	162.26	33.6
1986	220.49	10.0	-8.29	223.76	37.9
1987	226.22	2.6	-6.28	307.33	37.3
1988	249.12	10.1	-13.40	380.15	23.7
1989	282.38	13.3	-15.89	514.69	35.4
1990	308.36	9.2	-14.65	703.42	36.7
1991	338.66	9.8	-23.71	911.03	29.5
1992	374.22	10.5	-25.88	1,154.54	26.7
1993	464.23	24.1	-29.33	1,520.35	31.7
1994	579.26	24.8	-57.45	2,151.88	41.5
1995	682.37	17.8	-58.15	2,966.23	37.8
1996	793.72	16.3	-52.97	3,854.82	30.0
1997	923.40	16.3	-58.30	4,631.41	20.1
1998	1,102.00	19.3	-96.97	5,577.02	20.4
1999	1,268.01	15.1	-100.01	6,721.98	20.5

Year	Newly-issued credit (RMB billion)	Total value of imports (US$ billion)	Growth rate of total value of imports (%)	Total value of exports (US$ billion)	Growth rate of total value of exports (%)
1978	18.67	10.89	51.0	10.20	34.4
1979	18.96	15.68	44.0	13.58	33.1
1980	37.47	20.02	27.7	18.12	33.4
1981	35.03	22.01	10.0	22.01	21.5
1982	28.77	19.29	-12.4	22.32	1.4
1983	37.88	21.39	10.9	22.23	-0.4
1984	98.85	27.41	28.1	26.14	17.6
1985	148.59	42.25	54.1	27.35	4.6
1986	168.49	42.90	1.5	30.94	13.1
1987	144.20	43.22	0.7	39.44	27.5
1988	151.89	55.28	27.9	47.52	20.5
1989	380.88	59.14	7.0	52.54	10.6
1990	332.06	53.55	-9.5	62.09	18.2
1991	365.71	63.79	19.1	71.84	15.7
1992	498.51	80.58	26.3	84.94	18.2
1993	662.02	103.96	29.0	91.74	8.0
1994	703.29	115.61	11.2	121.01	31.9
1995	1,056.81	132.08	14.2	148.78	22.9
1996	1,068.02	138.82	5.1	151.07	1.5
1997	1,373.47	142.36	2.5	182.68	20.9
1998	1,445.88	152.47	7.1	192.50	5.4
1999	1,498.61	170.01	11.5	205.96	7.0

Note: Figures for newly-issued credit after 1989 include those for all financial institutions. The 1998 and 1999 figures are estimates.

(Compiled by SHEN Lishen)

INDEX

Printed in the United States
by Baker & Taylor Publisher Services